The Homeowner's Guide to Foreclosure

The Homeowner's Guide to Foreclosure

2nd Edition

How to Protect Your Home and Your Rights

James I. Wiedemer

PUBLISHING

New York

This publication is designed to provide accurate and authoritative information in regard to the subject matter covered. It is sold with the understanding that the publisher is not engaged in rendering legal, accounting, or other professional service. If legal advice or other expert assistance is required, the services of a competent professional should be sought.

© 2008 by James I. Wiedemer

Published by Kaplan Publishing, a division of Kaplan, Inc.
1 Liberty Plaza, 24th Floor
New York, NY 10006

Printed in the United States of America

June 2008
10 9 8 7 6 5 4 3 2 1

ISBN-13: 978-1-4277-9768-1

Kaplan Publishing books are available at special quantity discounts to use for sales promotions, employee premiums, or educational purposes. Please email our Special Sales Department to order or for more information at kaplanpublishing@kaplan.com, or write to Kaplan Publishing, 1 Liberty Plaza, 24th Floor, New York, NY 10006.

19

Contents

Introduction

The years 2007 and 2008 have seen the onslaught of what has come to be known as the "mortgage meltdown" in the U.S. It all started in the summer of 2007 with mortgage backed securities buyers becoming increasingly skittish about default rates on mortgage pools. (CMOS's) As a result, buyers stopped purchasing new and old CMO's and other mortgage backed securities. Eventually heavy pressure forced the down rating of certain "subprime mortgage" backed securities by certain bond rating agencies. **The problem:** Too many bad loans were found in certain mortgage pools, and many mortgage bonds were moved to AA and A status from their former AAA (triple A) status. Some bond rating agencies finally felt forced to down rate a few of them to "junk bond" status, causing investors in such bonds to lose millions in bond values. This triggered a subsequent wave of trouble. Many mutual funds are not even allowed to own anything but AAA rated bonds. Fewer investors wanted to buy into mortgage pools that held subprime mortgages., and in early 2008 the situation is fairly serious in that relatively few securities issues (with not just the old style hard core subprime, but even relatively stronger mortgages) are not selling all that well. Subprime lending, as a result, has crashed, and in the fall of 2007 subprime mortgage originations (creations of new loans) dropped as much as 90% or more for major mortgage companies. Alt-A loans (nicknamed liar loans) and non-sub prime loans with teaser or low introductory rats were hard hit as well. In Washington, D.C. or California, for example, perhaps half the new mortgages have had affordability features such as teaser rates, no principal payments or negative amortization schedules. It is all on a downward spiral. As Alan Greenspan has predicted on the nationally televised show "60 Minutes,", the situation is likely to get worse before it gets better, and the loss of subprime mortgages could pull upwards of 15% or more of the buyers out of the home market. This in turn is fueling a general downturn in real estate prices; and there is something of a spiral here that is extremely tricky to stop. With prices falling, investors may begin to back off from home purchases, persons who can wait to buy may do so until they perceive the market is settling, and people who need to sell their homes cannot sell quickly or at good prices. It is that last situation that tends to trigger most of the foreclosures. In high price times, borrowers who lose jobs or divorce, or die, simply trigger home sales at the high prices, whereas in low price times, the same circumstances often trigger foreclosures. The situation is not constant throughout the whole U.S. Previously high flying areas in Florida, Las Vegas, Phoenix, Northeast cities, and California seem to be hit the hardest, and they will be among the first to experience stepped up foreclosure rates, which in turn helps to further depress the market. Eventually, I predict a national financing problem will affect every area of the country though in varying degrees. Many homeowners do not know what to do when faced with such circumstances, and this book is specifically dedicated to try to give them some insight and help. It is not meant as a substitute for lawyers, brokers, and lender workout specialists, or other competent professionals , but the more the homeowner knows, the better you can meet the challenge, and hopefully, survive, if not thrive.

The original edition of this book was written in 1992, but it has been extensively revised with up to date material. It is remarkable how much the introduction written in the down market of 1992 is still very true for the down market today. I invite you to read on.

Throughout the United States, many cities are experiencing down markets, at least for a short period of time. Once a city's economy slows down, homes can't be sold, prices fall, and foreclosures increase.

The foreclosure phenomenon feeds on itself. When a lender forecloses on a house, the lender usually takes title and tries to resell it. The lender cuts the home's price to move it quickly, and the market becomes glutted with homes for sale at low prices. Many homeowners who need to sell for the usual reasons—job loss, job transfer, divorce, death, or moving within the city—suddenly have trouble selling at prices that are high enough to pay off their existing loans.

The desperate homeowners don't know what to do. Some put off dealing with the problem and hope that it will go away. Some discouraged homeowners just give up, move out, and abandon their houses to foreclosure. That puts more houses on the market, competing for the ever-shrinking pool of buyers.

When home prices fall in a city, investor-buyers refrain from buying. Existing homeowners who would have sold older, smaller homes to buy newer, larger homes now postpone their plans. No one wants to buy a house when the prices are falling, so potential buyers wait until the market bottoms out. Then they buy and get a really low price. But as the market continues to fall, the foreclosure problem compounds itself.

During the 1980s in Texas, the oil bust generated some of the worst market conditions in the country, and people were unprepared to deal with foreclosures. Lenders had inexperienced personnel; borrowers didn't know their rights. However, as time passed, it became apparent that workout measures such as lender forbearance, private mortgage insurance (PMI) assisted presales, or even assumptions could have prevented many foreclosures. Even if a foreclosure took place, homeowners did not know their rights to minimize damage to their long-term credit.

This book is intended to share as many tricks and tips and as much hard-earned advice as possible with a homeowner who may be faced with foreclosure in a down market. Homeowners in this situation should never give up until they have explored every possible avenue of relief. The earlier the homeowner learns about such measures, the better the chances of success.

The Homeowner's Guide to Foreclosure is organized to provide a reader with the information needed to deal with foreclosures. The chapters are arranged to follow the order of events in a foreclosure, beginning with a discussion of initial loan arrangements, then proceeding to the legal rights and actions for foreclosure. The possible workout scenarios for Federal Housing Administration (FHA), Department of Veterans Affairs (VA), and conventional loans follow. Last-ditch measures, such as foreclosure presales or deeds in lieu, are next, followed by legal steps to fight an impending foreclosure, including bankruptcy. Consequences after the foreclosure are considered, including credit problems, adverse tax consequences, and deficiency judgments. The final chapter covers picking up the pieces after a foreclosure.

One of the key features of this book is a guide to foreclosure laws in all 50 states. These laws vary considerably from state to state with no real standardization. Large companies, such as FNMA, have tried to develop uniform legal instruments for loans and foreclosures in all 50 states, but unfortunately, the nonstandard laws require that the actual foreclosure documents, mortgages, and deeds of trust be drafted separately for each state. Therefore, the only way to explain these laws is through a state-by-state analysis. Even such an analysis can give a reader only an overview. Anyone faced with foreclosure in a given state should consult an attorney who is licensed in that state.

If I may cast a ray of hope on those caught in a down market, just remember: this too must pass. Over the long term, down-market conditions cannot last, although they often persist until prices drop substantially. In Houston, prices fell below replacement cost, and they remain there for some types of real estate. But it can't go on forever. Eventually prices will recover. Many would-be buyers who postponed purchases will jump in once prices recover, renewing the upward march of prices. To worried homeowners, my message is: don't give up hope! Just be sure to do all that you can—and no less.

Trapped!? What Are Your Choices When Faced With Foreclosure?

Although this book discusses foreclosure laws, it is not intended to replace individual advice and counsel from an attorney or another professional. However, this book does outline some of the options open to a person who is faced with the difficult situation of foreclosure.

The first principle is this: don't give up. Many people become so negative about the possibilities in such circumstances that they do nothing more vigorous than move out of their homes when the situation looks bad enough. Most people who do nothing live to regret it. Often they could have taken actions to forestall, reduce, or even eliminate the harmful consequences of foreclosure.

But you must act! Do not wait! Settle down, give the matter some hard thought, and decide on a concrete, positive course of action. Inaction makes it much more likely that the worst will happen.

Also, remember that life goes on after a tough period. Taking action before the foreclosure may be a big help to restore your long-term credit, reduce tax problems, and make the best of a bad situation. Rest assured, you can and should act when you are faced with foreclosure.

THE SITUATION

You've lost a job or become involved in a divorce or have too many debt obligations. You can't make the payments on your home loan. Foreclosure is usually inevitable if you miss two to six months' worth of payments, although sometimes it may take as much as a year.

Once foreclosure looms, two questions determine what approach to take: (1) Will things get better, and if so, when? (2) How close is foreclosure? The answers to these questions tell you the most effective approach to take.

WILL THINGS GET BETTER?

Of course, you could just wait and hope things get better. This sometimes works out if a new job appears, divorcing partners reconcile or settle easily, or new opportunities arise. However, you can't count on such luck.

Things Won't Get Better

Some problems are insoluble. Following are some examples:

- A divorce may eliminate one income with which to make payments while generating enormous expenses.

- A lost job cannot easily be replaced. A high-level management position or a specialized job in a strained industry may be impossible to replace at the same level of income.

- Medical bills, business problems, or poor investments may generate unsustainable expenses and losses. Cancer or heart disease may be financially ruinous.

- A personal business may fail. Most small businesses fail in the first two years of operation, and many more fail within five years.

- Poor investments, such as the purchase of rental properties that can no longer be leased for enough to pay the mortgage, can be catastrophic.

If things aren't likely to get any better, it puts the missed payment situation in a very different light than when improvement is likely.

Things Will Get Better

Things may get better for someone who has lost a job, such as computer programming, that involves skills that may be valuable to many companies. This person can find a new job with some searching. A divorce may generate problems, but a new spouse with an income could solve them. A medical condition, such as an injury, may heal. A business can be sold or reorganized and put on a paying basis. If things can get better, you see matters in a different light.

HOW CLOSE IS FORECLOSURE?

Generally, two to six months of missed payments will trigger a foreclosure, but a year may sometimes go by before it happens. Wise borrowers take action as soon as they foresee missing payments. Foolish borrowers wait until the last minute.

Delay puts homeowners further and further into the hole, decreasing available options. A week or two before foreclosure, the situation is very difficult. The earlier you choose to take concrete, positive action, the better. Your choices will vary depending on your financial situation and where you are in the foreclosure process, as figure 1.1 illustrates.

The strategies listed in figure 1.1 may or may not work for a particular loan in a particular situation. Each procedure is described in greater detail later in the book. The reader should take a close look at the appropriate sections.

Figure 1.1 Strategy Chart—Avoiding or Stopping Foreclosure

	Time to Foreclosure	Strategies
The Situation Won't Improve	2 to 6 months	Straight Sale
		Sale by Assumption
		Private Mortgage Insurance Company Presale
		Sale with short payoff
		DVA compromise sale
		Deed in lieu
	1 month or so	Bankruptcy
The Situation Will Improve	2 to 6 months	Forbearance
		Refinancing
		Modification
		Recasting
		FHA mortgage assignment
	1 month or so	Temporary restraining order
		Temporary Injunction
		Hard Bargaining

STRATEGIES FOR AVOIDING FORECLOSURE

Figure 1.1 summarizes strategies for fighting foreclosure in several categories. First, suppose foreclosure is far away and things won't get any better. Here are six strategies to consider under these circumstances:

1. Straight sale of the house
2. Sale by means of an assumption
3. Foreclosure presale
4. VA compromise sale
5. Sale with short payoff
6. Deed in lieu of foreclosure

Straight Sale

One of the easiest ways to avoid foreclosure is simply to put the house on the market. I once received a call from a couple who thought they needed legal services to deal with a foreclosure. I had several initial questions.

Q. Have you received a foreclosure notice?

A. No.

Q. How many payments have you missed?

A. None.

Q. Do you have any equity in the house—is it worth more than what you owe?

A. They had a lot of equity in the house.

Q. Do you know of any big problems with the house, such as a bad foundation?

A. The house was in fine condition.

Q. Have you tried to sell the house?

A. They had.

These people had tried for over a year to sell the house, but their broker could not find a buyer. They were running out of money and would soon begin missing payments, so they expected foreclosure to follow. This problem certainly did not require legal work to stop the foreclosure. All it required was a new broker.

Many people have the mistaken impression that houses do not sell or that all sales are slow. I can assure you that you can sell a house that is in good condition, has positive equity, and is not deep in foreclosure. A mansion in the best part of town priced at $1 will sell tomorrow. Somewhere above $1, there is a price at which it will sell. I gave the couple who phoned me the name of an excellent broker in their area, and a few weeks later, I learned that the house had been sold.

Selling a house may involve problems, such as a need for substantial repairs, negative equity, or a short length of time before foreclosure. Such a situation is much more difficult but still not hopeless.

A house that needs substantial repairs may be sold by means of special financing. FHA 203(k) loans include money for repairs along with funds to purchase the house. However, these loans are tricky. The repairs must increase the value of the property in an amount at least equal to their cost. An experienced loan officer knows 203(k) loans are the key to success. Some lenders will make a loan with some of the money held in a repair escrow, with those funds to pay for repairs to the property.

A house has negative equity when it is worth less than what is owed on the loan used to buy it. (As a nickname, some call this an "upside-down house.") In this situation, consider private mortgage insurance (PMI) assisted presales, Department of Veterans Affairs (VA) compromise sales, or short payoffs, which are described later in this chapter.

If the house is close to foreclosure, negotiate hard for a delay to work things out. If not, consider selling the house at a steep discount just to get it sold.

Sale by Means of Assumption

An owner who purchased a house with an Federal Housing Authority (FHA), VA, or old loan may be able to sell the house on an assumption basis. (Before 1973, loans did not have due-on-sale clauses to block assumptions.) The seller would turn the house over to the buyer, who would get a deed and continue to make the payments on the old loan. In essence, the buyer would take over the seller's old loan.

This is not possible with most loans. It is legal with FHA or VA loans, but lender approval is required for VA loans since March 1, 1988, and FHA loans created since December 15, 1989. Loans made before those dates are generally assumable without lenders' permission or approval.

Usually, the lender will approve an assumption only when the buyer is creditworthy and has income sufficient to meet standard loan qualification ratios. Even then, the lender may withhold approval. However, the lender can approve a loan assumption to avoid foreclosure. Unless the lender has a program in place to do this, it is unlikely to prevent an impending foreclosure.

Assumption sales can be done when few other types of sales could work. They are possible even where a house has low, or even negative, equity. Assumptions may also be possible, as explained above, with a buyer who has bad credit. A buyer may want to buy a house in a rising market, but bad credit may prevent that. Assumption sales without lender approval are much easier to make than other types of sales in such a situation. However, assumptions have many problems, as described later in this book.

Foreclosure Presales

A foreclosure presale can be a regular sale made in anticipation of foreclosure, even close to the time of foreclosure. In a particularly important type of presale, a private mortgage insurance company may subsidize the sale, even when the house has negative equity. The PMI company simply pays off part of the loan.

As long as the amount to be paid stays within the policy limits, the PMI company will provide funds to keep the amount needed to pay off the loan at about the same amount as the market price of the house. As part of the deal, the house will be sold to pay off the rest of the loan. Usually, the seller has to put enough cash or other assets into the sale to make the deal attractive to the PMI company, which would otherwise have to cover the entire loss up to the limits of the policy. The seller's contributions would reduce that loss payout. However, the seller gains a release from further liability.

VA Compromise Sales Agreements

Presales are not restricted to private mortgage insurers. The VA's equivalent of a presale is a compromise sale agreement. The VA guarantees loans, much as PMI companies insure loans, except that the U.S. government picks up part of the lender's loss when a VA mortgage is foreclosed. To the extent that the VA has liability to the lender, it may be willing to absorb all or part of a loss to avoid a foreclosure. The arrangement should be worked out when a buyer is found and the sale is made.

The compromise sale agreement will spell out the terms of the deal. The FHA, unfortunately, has no presale program.

FHA Presale

Although FHA lacked an effective presale program years ago, it now has one. It will, effectively, subsidize part of the loss on sale, up to certain limits, should circumstances require it.

Short Payoff

All the major lenders and insurers now provide for short payoffs. In a short payoff, a house that is about to be taken in foreclosure is sold at a loss through a broker. The lender, the loan owner, and/or the loan insurer agree to share some or all of the loss as part of the deal for the seller.

Deed in Lieu of Foreclosure

In a deed in lieu procedure, the borrower simply sends the lender the deed. Some used to mail the keys to the house along with it. One lender even suggested a drive-through key-toss receptacle for both!

The chances for the deed in lieu procedure vary depending on the state. Generally, lenders in states with quick, out-of-court foreclosure procedures avoid the deed in lieu of foreclosure. In contrast, in states where foreclosure is a long, drawn-out process, the deed in lieu may be quite acceptable to the lender. Lenders generally do not favor the deed in lieu because they sacrifice their right to sue the borrower for any remaining balance on the loan after they recover what they can by reselling the house. The borrower should carefully consider the deed in lieu of foreclosure, since it generally won't work unless the lender voluntarily accepts it.

WORKOUTS

The term *workout* refers to strategies that are appropriate when things will probably get better and foreclosure is far away. Workouts consist of forbearance, loan modification or refinancing, and assignment of the mortgage.

Forbearance

In forbearance, the lender temporarily permits the borrower to make no payments or smaller payments. To do this for a short time may require little formality. To do so for a longer time may require a more involved approval. The lender may want verification and documentation of the source of the borrower's problems and the reason they will get better. The parties agree on an appropriate schedule of reduced or suspended payments. Forbearance is strictly up to the lender. The borrower cannot force the lender to accept the deal.

Loan Modification or Refinancing

In loan modification, or refinancing, the interest rate or term may be changed. If the same lender substitutes a new loan for an old loan, the arrangement could be called either "loan modification" or "refinancing." The FHA may call it "recasting." If a new loan with better terms from one lender is used to pay off the old lender, this is refinancing. A written agreement will be required, and the change is permanent, resulting in smaller payments due to either a longer payout term or a lower interest rate. Obviously, the latter strategy tends to work better if interest rates have fallen since the loan was initiated. Generally, positive equity in the property is required for these strategies, but not always.

ELEVENTH-HOUR TACTICS

It is best to address the problem of foreclosure as early as possible. However, when time is short, there are still a few legal means of stopping foreclosure: hard bargaining, temporary injunction, and bankruptcy.

Hard Bargaining

Borrowers may try to bargain their way out of foreclosure. This is probably best done through an attorney, but a borrower's own efforts may be enough. The best way to do this is to make up the missed payments. If the borrower can come up with the money, the lender can often be induced to stop the foreclosure, unless the same thing has happened before.

As another alternative, the borrower can threaten a lawsuit. This is seldom a believable threat, however, if the borrower can't even afford to make payments on the loan. Few, if any, attorneys will take cases to stop foreclosures on a contingency-fee basis (in which the attorney is paid only if the suit is won). Commercial foreclosures generate most lender liability suits. Although threatening a lawsuit to stop a residential foreclosure for failure to make payments is a poor strategy, at best, some very unusual circumstances may give this approach a chance. Threatening bankruptcy almost never works. Lenders simply ignore the threat and proceed to foreclose.

Partial payments may delay foreclosure, but not necessarily. Most lenders have well-defined policies on how much must be paid to stop foreclosure. It's usually more than the borrower wants to pay, often nothing less than the full amount of all the missed payments. Still, you can try! The FHA and the VA may allow delays in foreclosure through partial payments.

Temporary Injunction

An injunction is a court order commanding the lender and the lender's trustee to stop foreclosure. This approach should be considered if things will get better. (If not, why spend money and time merely to delay a foreclosure temporarily?) If things will get better, however, or if the lender has moved unreasonably quickly to foreclose (after one missed payment, for example), then this approach should be seriously considered. It may cost quite a bit of money to get an attorney to file and litigate the injunction. A borrower who is hard pressed to make payments is in no position to pay an attorney. Also, there may be no legitimate basis for the injunction if the borrower has truly defaulted on the loan. However, for a borrower who has the money and a good reason to stop the foreclosure, this is a good approach.

Bankruptcy

Bankruptcy costs much less than a temporary restraining order (TRO) or a temporary injunction, and it will always stop a foreclosure, whether things will get better or not. An automatic stay, or freeze order, issued at the outset will stop a foreclosure. Later on, however, the stay or freeze order may be lifted unless the borrower can keep up the loan payments. Payments on the homeowner's principal residence cannot be reduced by a Chapter 13 "wage earner" bankruptcy plan, although other loan payments can be, which may allow the borrower to keep up with the home. (Congress is debating changing this particular bankruptcy provision.)

Bankruptcy seriously damages a person's credit rating. Although some people may be able to get credit shortly after a bankruptcy, large loans are usually out of the question for years to come—two to three years, at least, for home loans.

CONCLUSION

Choose the best option for your circumstances and put some effort into making your choice work. Remember: don't give up! Don't abandon your home without doing everything you can. Take action to keep a bad situation from being worse than it has to be. You never know—you might even be able to save everything! Certainly your odds are better if you fight against your troubles instead of giving up.

The Basics of Real Estate Financing

2

Central to the problem of foreclosure is the manner in which a home is financed. It is hard to understand foreclosure processes or the subsequent resale of a foreclosed home without first understanding how home mortgages and loans work. This chapter presents a basic overview, broken down into three parts: the types of lenders, the investors and institutions that buy loans, and the role of loan insurers.

THE LENDER AND THE MORTGAGE LOAN

Borrowers usually seek out one of two types of lenders—savings and loans (S&Ls) and mortgage companies. The personnel at these two institutions deal directly with the borrowers and make loans to them. In some parts of the country, borrowers may use mortgage brokers, but the lending institution makes the loan and deals with the borrower afterward. Regular banks make about 11 percent of all U.S. residential mortgage loans, though they may play a larger role in some local markets. S&Ls and mortgage companies account for much of the rest.

Savings and Loans

Depository institutions were once the major source of home loans, particularly S&Ls. Today, that is certainly not true. Depository institutions are, at best, a small part of the mortgage market.

S&Ls are the oldest and have been, until recently, the largest source of money for the residential mortgage market. Savings and loans were originally chartered to make home loans. Even today, most states require that S&Ls make "first and prior" mortgages on homes. The federal government also regulates S&Ls through the Office of Thrift Supervision. (The Federal Home Loan Bank Board [FHLBB], which used to do this, has been abolished.) S&Ls are backed by deposit insurance issued by another federal agency, the Federal Deposit Insurance Corporation (FDIC), which took over this function from the defunct Federal Savings and Loan Insurance Corporation. If an S&L fails financially, the government will take it over.

S&Ls take in deposits and lend the money to borrowers. Years ago, this was a relatively simple business. Legal limits defined the interest the S&L could pay depositors. (Remember the advertising disclaimer, "We pay the maximum interest rates allowed by law"?) Generally, the S&L could lend at a higher rate than what it paid depositors. The old saying was, "Take the money in at 7; loan it out at 12; hit the golf course by 3." It was a wonderful life.

Operating an S&L is no longer so simple, though. When interest rates jumped through the ceiling in the late '70s and early '80s, S&Ls faced stiff competition for deposits from money market mutual

9

funds, which paid rates that were double or even triple what S&Ls were paying. The outflow of deposits forced the S&Ls to accept deregulation; in the end, they actually lobbied for it. However, as part of the package, the S&Ls demanded, and got, the right to make commercial as well as residential loans. They reduced their traditional emphasis on home loans and charged headlong into the commercial loan business. The executives who led this charge took large risks, led fast lives, and ran many an S&L into the red. S&Ls went through a huge shakeout as a result of such operations. The government, which insured S&L deposits, stepped in and cleaned up the mess, but S&Ls have never regained their former share of the market.

Today, S&Ls may simply operate much the same way as private mortgage companies: they package and sell mortgage loans onto the secondary market. The Federal Home Loan Mortgage Corporation (FHLMC), for example, is a company that was established by the U.S. government to buy S&L-originated mortgages. In this role, they are still a source of mortgages.

Mortgage Companies

Mortgage companies are privately owned and operated corporations. Some are as simple as three-room offices; others have offices in all 50 states. Mortgage companies face relatively little regulation, needing no special government charter. They just make loans (called "origination" in the lending business), after which they sell the loans to buyers in the secondary market, such as the Federal National Mortgage Association (FNMA).

Origination of Loans

Origination is the process of creating a new loan. To originate loans, most mortgage lenders employ three types of people: loan officers, loan processors, and loan underwriters. Loan officers deal directly with borrowers. Working for commissions, their job is to find borrowers and drag them into the lender's office. Usually they find borrowers by means of referrals from real estate salespeople and brokers. Loan processors pull together appraisals, inspections, credit reports, income verifications, and supporting calculations to submit to the underwriter. The underwriter decides whether or not to give a loan.

The lending institution then gives the money to the seller at closing. Paying out the money, called "funding," often occurs the day after the closing. In return, the mortgage lender receives signed paperwork from the borrower, including a note and a mortgage or a deed of trust.

Once the lender originates the loan, it is sold on the secondary market to companies that buy loans, such as the FNMA, the FHLMC, or the Government National Mortgage Association (GNMA). Normally, the lender charges the borrower at least 1 percent of the loan amount as an origination fee.

Servicing Loans

After a loan is sold on the secondary market, the mortgage lender still plays an active role. In fact, the borrower may never even know that the loan has been sold. The mortgage company gives the borrower payment coupons to mail in with a check for each month's mortgage payment (or sets up automatic withdrawals from the borrower's bank account). The payments go to the mortgage company, which sends the money on to the company that bought the loan. This process is called "servicing the loan."

Servicing loans is a principal money-making activity for a mortgage company. If the loan goes into default, then the servicer must handle the problems this causes. The FNMA has developed a tier-ranking system for servicers. If a servicing company succeeds in its foreclosure workout efforts with borrowers, it gains a higher tier ranking. A higher tier ranking entitles a servicer to larger fees than lower-tier servicers. This gives servicers a large incentive to work effectively with borrowers.

The servicer will try diligently to work out a deal with the borrower, but if this fails, will foreclose on the house. It will ultimately turn the house over to the secondary market loan buyer or arrange to sell it on behalf of the loan owner.

Secondary-Market Influence

The secondary market ownership of a loan can have a great impact on the foreclosure process. Usually, the secondary market company that buys the loan exercises a certain amount of control over foreclosure, generally approving the foreclosure directly or at least setting guidelines and rules that tell the loan servicer what to do and when to do it. The lender may have little choice but to follow the loan owner's instructions. The disposition and resale of the foreclosed property are also subject to the loan owner's direction.

SECONDARY MARKET COMPANIES THAT BUY LOANS

There are at least two broad groups of loan buyers: government-chartered corporations or agencies and purely private buyers. The government has chartered two major corporations to buy loans from mortgage companies, the Federal National Mortgage Association (FNMA or Fannie Mae) and the Federal Home Loan Mortgage Corporation (FHLMC or Freddie Mac). A third agency, Government National Mortgage Association (GNMA or Ginnie Mae), is actually part of the government.

Fannie Mae and Freddie Mac

These corporations were created for the purpose of buying loans from mortgage lenders. FNMA normally buys loans from mortgage companies. FHLMC normally buys loans from savings and loans. FNMA will buy loans only from Fannie Mae–approved mortgage companies called seller/servicers.

To become an FNMA-approved seller/servicer, the mortgage company must employ suitable personnel, such as FNMA-approved underwriters, among other requirements. Once approved, FNMA will buy loans from the mortgage company for up to $25 million at a time. A seller/servicer contract signed by the mortgage company will specify the terms and conditions under which FNMA will buy loans, including the types of loans, the forms and procedures that must be used, and the standards by which they must be serviced. FNMA's contract fills a four-volume set of loose-leaf binders, and it spells out in great detail what FNMA wants in a loan and in a loan originator. Loans that meet these standards are called "conforming loans." Mortgage companies that fail to meet these standards are out of business, since other loan buyers have similar policies and procedures. FNMA is the largest single buyer of loans, holding about 10 percent of the total, but the rest of the secondary market is quite substantial.

Ginnie Mae

GNMA, the principal buyer of VA and FHA loans, operates in a very similar manner as FNMA. GNMA is actually a part of the federal government, as distinguished from FNMA and FHLMC, which are corporations chartered by the government. Unlike GNMA, FNMA and FHLMC sell stock on the New York Stock Exchange and otherwise operate relatively independently.

Private Loan Buyers

Many private firms buy loans. One such firm, General Motors Acceptance Corporation (GMAC), is more famous for buying automobile loans but is also the largest private buyer of home mortgage loans in the country. General Electric Credit Corporation (GECC) is also a major loan buyer.

The hundreds of companies that buy loans can be divided into many types. Life insurance companies buy loans, as do pension plans, large mortgage companies, and S&Ls. Stock brokerage firms have become enthusiastic buyers of loans, often organizing giant real estate mortgage investment conduits (REMICs). These tax-advantaged mortgage pools hold mortgages worth half a billion dollars or more, shares of which they sell to investors as collateralized mortgage obligations (CMOs).

LOAN INSURERS

When a buyer fails to make house payments, the loan on the home goes into default. The lender may wait but will ultimately foreclose on a loan that remains in default. After the foreclosure, if not before, the lender will file a claim with its loan insurance company. Just as a car can be smashed up in an accident, a home loan can be smashed by a default. Good insurance policies cover both kinds of loss.

A closely related concept is a loan guarantee, like those issued by the VA. A loan guarantee differs from loan insurance in that the borrower does not have to pay the full cost of the loan protection. The main types of loan insurance and guarantees include FHA loan insurance, VA loan guarantees, and private mortgage insurance (PMI).

FHA Insurance

The FHA, or Federal Housing Administration, is a part of the Department of Housing and Urban Development (HUD). The FHA insures loans made by private lenders, but it does not lend the borrower money to buy a home, as a private mortgage insurance company does. The FHA insures the repayment of the loan to the lender. If the borrower fails to repay the loan to the private mortgage company, the FHA will do so. Please note that the borrower is still fully liable and responsible for the repayment of the loan, even though the FHA covered the lender's losses in full.

FHA's insurance is strong. It repays the lender for 20 percent of any loss on the loan resulting from the borrower's default. If there is sufficient value in the property, the FHA will pay off the lender's full unpaid loan balance, and the lender in return would deed the home to the FHA, which would then market the property to the public through its foreclosure resale program.

Veterans Administration

The Department of Veterans Affairs (often called the "Veterans Administration" or VA) does not insure loans; instead it guarantees them. Although the VA charges a funding fee, it makes no explicit charge to guarantee a loan. This is something the country does for vets after they did something for the United States. Since Uncle Sam picks up the tab for a loan default, the VA constantly works to cut its costs, which are not offset by any insurance premiums coming in from vets. The vet is not relieved of liability upon defaulting on a loan. Until recently, the FHA paid off lenders and left good-faith defaulters alone; the VA, however, may come after the vet for unpaid loan amounts it had to make good to a lender.

The VA guarantees only partial repayment to a lender. It will cover a loss only up to a set figure. For small loans, it will cover a large percentage, upwards of 50 percent of the loan; but for larger loans, it will cover only about 25 percent. The VA sets a maximum repayment figure for its loans (the guarantee). The guarantee has been much lower in times past. The loan guarantee for a particular loan is set at its origination.

When a VA loan goes into default and the lender forecloses, the title will normally be conveyed to the VA, which will pay the fair market value of the property, plus any portion of the amount still owed on the original loan up to its guarantee limit for the loan. If the lender's loss is greater than the VA's limit, the VA will not take the property. Lenders dread this no-bid situation. Instead, the VA will cut a check to the lender in the amount of the VA guarantee for the particular loan. If the VA takes title to the property, it will sell it as a foreclosure resale much as the FHA does.

Private Mortgage Insurance

The third type of insurance on loans is made by private mortgage insurance (PMI) companies. A private mortgage insurance company will normally insure only a portion of a loan, just as the VA guarantees only a portion of the loan. Normally a PMI company will insure the balance in excess of 80, 85, 90, or 95 percent of a loan at the lender's option. If the buyer makes more than a 20 percent down payment, PMI is not needed. This makes the loan easier to obtain, because PMI companies impose strict standards for borrowers' credit in any area that has suffered numerous foreclosures. Normally, a PMI company will insure the loan only during the early years, when risk is greatest. Most defaults occur early in loans' terms. PMI charges continue while the loan is insured.

KEY MORTGAGE CONCEPTS

Mortgage

A mortgage is an arrangement in which a borrower pledges a house as security or collateral for a loan. Normally the borrower signs a real estate lien note and a deed of trust or mortgage. The deed of trust or mortgage gives the lender the right to foreclose if the note is not paid according to its terms.

Equity

If the value of a home exceeds what the owner owes on any valid mortgages, then the owner has equity in the house. It is a net asset for the owner. If a house has no equity, foreclosure is much more likely when the borrower can't make the payments, because it is difficult to sell a home that has no equity. However, please note that a PMI-assisted presale or a VA compromise sale agreement may do the trick.

Assumptions

An assumption is an arrangement in which the buyer takes title to the property and agrees to pay an existing loan. The buyer can either take responsibility to make the loan payments, which is a true assumption, or refuse to accept liability for the payments although promising to make them, which is called a "subject to" arrangement. The lender's sole remedy in such an arrangement is foreclosure.

In either case, the original borrower remains liable for the loan, regardless of what the buyer agrees to do, until and unless the lender releases the old borrower from the loan obligation. Many lenders ban assumptions, although they are permitted on certain conventional loans and on all FHA and VA loans. Assumptions in which buyers are not approved by the lenders are now restricted by the FHA and the VA.

FINANCING AND FORECLOSURE

The differences in financing arrangements have a tremendous impact on the borrower's situation at foreclosure. In general, the government-insured or purchased loans involve extensive relief programs and procedures for borrowers who are in default. Private lenders may not be so helpful, but they often make decisions much more quickly and are not as rigidly bound up in regulations and bureaucracy. Private lenders can often provide help when it is truly needed.

The borrower faced with foreclosure should recognize that a lender focuses on its loan owner and loan insurer, so trickier foreclosure workouts must involve these parties. Because the loan owners and insurers absorb much of the loss in a foreclosure, they are often more willing to extend assistance or forbearance to a borrower than the loan servicer, such as the mortgage company or S&L, would be. The borrower should try to look at a loan the way the lender does to plan the next move and save the house from foreclosure.

The Foreclosure Process

3

Many people have mistaken notions about foreclosure. Some are convinced that if they don't pay their loans, then one day, with no real warning, a sheriff or some similar officer of the law will appear at the door and order them out of the house. Real foreclosures are bad enough, but every state in the United States requires that the borrower receive plenty of warning before they occur. Individual states' laws specify many other borrowers' rights and vary from state to state. Other rights are determined by the papers the borrower signs when purchasing the house.

State laws can be grouped in several ways. Different states have different theories about who owns a house while it is mortgaged, what types of instruments can be used to mortgage the property, and how foreclosure will proceed.

In title theory states, the lender owns the property until the borrower repays the debt the mortgage secures. Once that happens, the lender's claim to title is defeated (returned) to the borrower automatically, without the need for any other instrument. In lien theory states, however, the borrower owns the house until the lender acquires title through a proper foreclosure.

Most U.S. states follow the lien theory. South Carolina became the first lien theory state in 1791. Since then, 33 states have opted for the lien theory, while 9 still use the title theory and nine are intermediate theory states.

WHO OWNS YOUR HOUSE PRIOR TO FORECLOSURE?

Laws that state who owns the house while the loan is being paid fall into three categories: title theory, lien theory, and intermediate theory states. Figure 3.1 groups the states by these categories. The fundamental differences between title theory, lien theory, and intermediate theory states revolve around the following question: When you borrow money from a bank to buy a house, who owns the house, you or the bank?

In title theory states, the bank does. In lien theory states, the borrower does. In intermediate theory states, the borrower owns the property, but it shifts to the lender by the terms of the mortgage when the borrower defaults on the loan. Title theory states may impose somewhat different requirements on foreclosure than lien theory states. In lien theory states and most title theory states, the foreclosure is usually a sale. However, in some title theory states, the lender's title becomes complete once the lender's right to foreclosure is established in court. Both the nature of the mortgage instrument and the procedures for foreclosure are influenced by the nature of the ownership theory behind the mortgage. It might not make sense for a lender to hold a foreclosure sale in which it acquires title if it already owns the property, while holding a foreclosure sale makes perfect sense in a lien theory state.

Fortunately for borrowers, no state allows a lender to take away a house without going through formal procedures, which are always more complicated than simple evictions. Degrees of complexity vary depending in part on whether the state permits out-of-court nonjudicial foreclosure or requires judicial foreclosure, which involves going to court.

Figure 3.1 Ownership Theory

Lien Theory			Title Theory	Intermediate Theory
Alaska	Louisiana	Ohio	Alabama	Arkansas
Arizona	Michigan	Oklahoma	Georgia	Connecticut
California	Minnesota	Oregon	Maine	Delaware
Colorado	Missouri	South Carolina	Maryland	District of Columbia
Florida	Montana	South Dakota	Mississippi	Illinois
Hawaii	Nebraska	Texas	Pennsylvania	Massachusetts
Idaho	Nevada	Utah	Rhode Island	New Jersey
Indiana	New Hampshire	Washington	Tennessee	North Carolina
Iowa	New Mexico	West Virginia	Vermont	Virginia
Kansas	New York	Wisconsin		
Kentucky	North Dakota	Wyoming		

HOW THE LENDER FORECLOSES

Two major theories govern foreclosure methods: judicial and nonjudicial foreclosure. In nonjudicial foreclosure states, various out-of-court procedures are used. On the whole, these are quicker and less involved than judicial foreclosure. Nonjudicial foreclosure is often done through a power of sale clause in some form of trust deed. In effect, the borrower preauthorizes the sale of the house. In contrast, judicial foreclosure states require that the lender file a lawsuit against a borrower, win the lawsuit, and then obtain a court order commanding the sale of the house.

Judicial Foreclosure

Judicial foreclosure can vex any lender. Imagine the scene in the courtroom. The jury, when buyers are entitled to one, sees the borrowers' adorable children, the young boys scrubbed and on their best behavior, the girls wearing ribbons in their hair and holding pictures of the family pets. The brave young parents are doing their best to save the family's home. The lender's attorney must level a finger at the borrowers, face the jury, and argue: "Do you see those defaulters? Kick them out of their house! Take the swing set away from those kids!" The jury includes grandmothers and grandfathers and people who've been out of work themselves. The young parents argue that they are doing everything they possibly can to find work and pay the mortgage, but times are tough. They had a spotless payment record until they were laid off through no fault of their own.

If the lender's attorney is not careful, the borrowers may wind up winning! The wise lender is in the back of the court room with a long face buried in shaky hands, muttering, "This is awful." That's judicial foreclosure. States where it is used are listed in figure 3.2.

Even in judicial foreclosure states, most lenders will try every form of pretrial motion to avoid full-blown trials. Most states authorize judicial foreclosure by summary legal processes that do not ordinarily require full-blown trials. These include summary judgments, scire facias ("show cause") hearings, and other specialized foreclosure hearings.

A summary judgment proceeding is a quick hearing in which a judge can decide a case in favor of one side or the other, provided that none of the material facts in the case are disputed. A summary judgment can be granted without a trial.

In a scire facias proceeding, the lender files a sworn pleading with a court, which issues a summons to the borrower. If the borrower fails to appear, the foreclosure will be granted. If the borrower shows up to fight the foreclosure, the borrower usually bears the burden of proof to show why the foreclosure should not be granted. Unless the borrower has a strong case, the foreclosure is likely to be ordered.

Figure 3.2 Judicial Foreclosure States

Arkansas	Nebraska
Delaware	New Jersey
Florida	New Mexico
Hawaii	New York
Idaho	North Dakota
Illinois	Ohio
Indiana	Oklahoma
Iowa	Pennsylvania
Kansas	South Carolina
Kentucky	South Dakota
Louisiana	

Even at its simplest level, judicial foreclosure involves the following:

- Title research to establish the current owners and the interests owned
- Filing a lawsuit, in the form of a plaintiff's original petition, a foreclosure bill of complaint, or a request for the issuance of a writ of scire facias (a summons to show cause why there should not be a foreclosure), along with service of process
- Recording a lis pendens notice, warning any interested person that a lawsuit is in progress that could affect the title to the land
- Attending and winning a hearing before a judge, a court master, or even a jury
- Obtaining a decree or judgment
- Publicly posting or otherwise publishing a notice of sale
- Conducting the sale, issuing a certificate for the sale, and reporting the sale back to the court

The sale itself is normally conducted in the same manner as an execution sale for any judgment. It is done by a sheriff or constable at a public place, such as a courthouse, in accordance with the previously issued order of the court. This is a complex and daunting procedure for any lender.

Lenders don't favor judicial foreclosure, and there is a case to be made for the lender's position. Without some power to foreclose, few loans would be made, and young families would be hard-pressed to buy houses without loans. Banks obtain the money they loan from much the same people as borrowers do. One lender explained that he needed a foreclosure to protect the assets in a mortgage investment pool because he had his children's college education funds tied up in it.

The harder it is to foreclose on a loan, the harder lenders are on potential borrowers who want loans. They tighten up loan qualification requirements. Considering that, nationwide, just a bit more than 1 percent of all mortgages go into actual foreclosure, it may not make sense to increase the burden on all potential borrowers to provide defaulting borrowers a little extra time in their houses.

Some states require judicial foreclosure even if the borrower signs a mortgage or deed of trust with a power of sale clause to preauthorize a foreclosure sale. Such states require filing of lawsuits but provide for quick hearings rather than full-blown trials. However, if facts are in dispute or the borrower has a good case against the foreclosure, the lender may have to go to trial to obtain the court orders needed to foreclose.

Nonjudicial Foreclosure

In nonjudicial foreclosure states, borrowers preauthorize sales of their homes in their loan documents, usually in trust deeds. Power of sale clauses authorize such foreclosures. A loan document with this clause acts much like a power of attorney, granting a person, typically called a "trustee," the right to sell the borrower's house if the lender notifies the trustee that the loan is in default. Many states do not require the lender to file a lawsuit if there is a power of sale clause.

Though the trustee may be authorized to sell the house, however, most states require the trustee to comply with detailed regulations concerning the time, place, and manner of the sale. They specify the advance notice the trustee must give to the borrower and to the interested public. States with nonjudicial foreclosure provisions are listed in figure 3.3.

States' power of sale laws differ. Moreover, as a privately created document, the deed of trust or mortgage with a power of sale clause could easily alter the state's arrangement. The document itself could require extra notices or special sale conditions, although such a privately created document is not allowed to reduce the borrower's rights to advance notice and a fair sale below certain statutory minimums. Many states specify the length of time lenders must wait between default and beginning foreclosure.

Once this time is up, the lender or trustee must give formal notice of the impending foreclosure sale, usually no less than 21 days in advance and sometimes more. The lender or the trustee must almost always mail the notice to the borrower's last known address, possibly the house itself, and to any coborrowers. In addition, the notice may be filed, posted publicly, and possibly published in a newspaper with an appropriate circulation. (Not all states require this.) The notice must give the date, time, and place of sale. At that date, time, and place, the sale must be openly and fairly conducted according to well-defined rules. This usually means a public place (usually a courthouse) during business hours on a business day. Anyone can bid, and the lender usually has no special status, except it may be able to bid by cancelling the debt it is owed. Overall, the procedures are relatively quick, simple, and efficient.

Figure 3.3 States With Nonjudicial Foreclosure

Alabama	Maryland	Nevada	Utah
Alaska	Massachusetts	New Hampshire	Virginia
Arizona	Michigan	North Carolina	Washington
California	Minnesota	Oregon	West Virginia
Colorado	Mississippi	Rhode Island	Wisconsin
District of Columbia	Missouri	Tennessee	Wyoming
Georgia	Montanaa	Texas	

Some states use a hybrid system in which the house may be foreclosed out of court but the lender must go to court to get certain rights. For example, in some states, the lender loses the right to sue for a loss owing to the foreclosure, called deficiency, if the foreclosure is done out of court. California's one-action rule effectively requires this.

Occasionally, the constitutionality of the power of sale clause has been challenged on the premise that the borrower is being deprived of a valuable piece of property without due process of law. The main argument supporting the constitutionality of the power of sale clause holds that the foreclosure is, in essence, a privately authorized and privately conducted sale. Anyone can sell his own home. A competent person can authorize someone else to sell her home. Making this part of a loan must be legal and constitutional. In addition, most states regulate the time, place, and manner of power of sale foreclosures. Most also require advance notice. These procedures further counteract the argument that a person is being deprived of property without due process. In general, the power of sale foreclosure is constitutional.

Strict Foreclosure

While strict foreclosure is used little today, describing it offers an excellent opportunity to discuss how current mortgage law and the concept of foreclosure developed. Strict foreclosure is a holdover from an earlier time. Centuries ago, real estate was mortgaged quite differently than it is today. In medieval Europe, Christian lenders were not allowed to charge interest on loans, although Jewish lenders could. Naturally, inventive, business-oriented individuals always tried to circumvent such restrictions. Lenders set up loans so they received full title, subject to the condition that as soon as the loan was repaid, the title would revert back to the borrower. This is called a "conditional" fee. In the meantime, the lender could take both possession of the property and the rent from it in lieu of being able to charge interest. Even worse, the lender could sell the land, will it to heirs, and even let it be seized by creditors.

More severe still was the consequence of nonpayment. A payment date, called "law day," was set on which the payment was due or else the borrower forfeited every right to the property. If a payment was even one day late, the hapless borrower lost all, even if he could not find the lender on law day! The traditional courts at law saw no problem with such a severe result. However, the British chancellor's courts (also called "courts in equity"), as the "keepers of the king's conscience," did not like such severe punishment for late payments. By the 17th century, the courts in equity routinely forced lenders to return land titles when borrowers came up with late payments by a principle called "tardy redemption" and, later, the "equity of redemption."

Once redemption rights developed, lenders demanded protection. They argued that it was unfair to give borrowers a right to redeem property by coming up with loan payments at some indefinite later date. Title to land became uncertain for prolonged periods of time under such circumstances. This problem cried out for more equity, but this time in favor of the lender. The courts eventually helped lenders by awarding foreclosure, in which the borrower was ordered by the equity court to come up with the loan payments by a certain time or else forever lose the right to redeem the property.

To complicate matters even more, in the 18th and 19th centuries, Americans made further changes to the traditional mortgage system. Many (but not all) states passed laws giving borrowers extra time to come up with unpaid loan sums. This so-called statutory right of redemption would last for a set period of time past the equity foreclosure time limit. The prerequisite to any statutory right to redeem was a valid foreclosure, which cut off the equity right to redeem. Then the statutory right started, ending by a time set in the statute. The extra time presumably helped borrowers come up with the money. It also made it more difficult for lenders to obtain title to land worth more than the loan balance.

Under strict foreclosure, a throwback to an earlier period, the lender must go to court and obtain an order showing the borrower to be in default under the terms of the mortgage. At that point, title shifts to the lender. However, during a set period of time, the borrower can redeem the property. If the borrower fails to come up with the money during that time, she loses everything absolutely.

The drawback to strict foreclosure is that the lender obtains title to land that might be worth much more than the balance remaining on the original loan. This is a windfall profit for the lender. Strict foreclosure involves no sale at all—not even at the courthouse steps. The lender is certainly not required to resell the property in any way to benefit the borrower. Any resale proceeds go to the lender. (This is also true in most other states.) Fortunately this procedure is not used much anymore, but two states, Connecticut and Vermont, allow it.

Entry and Possession States

The only other foreclosure method, entry and possession, also hearkens back to the old days. When Christians could not charge interest and lenders took possession and title in the land to collect rents instead of interest, lenders commonly retained possession. As time passed, the lender let the borrower retain possession, subject to the lender's right to kick the defaulting borrower off the property. Today this procedure, once called "ejectment," would be called a suit for a writ of entry or possession. It is currently practiced in only one state: Maine.

TYPES OF MORTGAGE INSTRUMENTS

The paperwork for most loans involves two types of documents: a note, which defines the borrower's obligations to make payments every month, and a security instrument. Virtually all loans use a note as one of the main loan instruments. The note is basically a glorified IOU for the money borrowed. A second instrument, a security instrument, is needed to make sure the note is paid and that the lender can foreclose if it isn't paid. In turn, there are two basic types of security instruments to assure the repayment of residential mortgage loans: the mortgage and the deed of trust.

Among the most common mortgage instruments are the FNMA/FHLMC uniform instruments. In any state using these documents, the first 18 clauses are exactly the same. Any differences in state law are accommodated after clause 18.

The functions of the deed of trust or mortgage are to make sure the borrower pays back the loan and to protect the lender's rights to the house as collateral. The mortgage or deed of trust also defines the lender's foreclosure powers, although this area is often heavily regulated by state statutes. The lender's right to a monthly loan payment will normally be defined in the note.

The Note

The note defines the borrower's obligation to repay a house loan. It may set forth exact payments, or in the case of an adjustable rate or graduated payment mortgage, it may specify the manner in which payments are to be calculated. It also specifies how payments must be made and some of what happens if payments aren't made. Most home loan notes are one or two pages long and comparatively simple.

A note falls into the class of legal papers called "negotiable instruments." Such a document confers highly defined rights, stated for the most part on the face of the document itself, so that it may be easily bought and sold. A note specifies the monthly principal and interest payments the borrower must make. (The deed of trust or mortgage describes tax and insurance obligations.) The note sets out the interest rate, the years over which the loan will be repaid, and rights to prepay with or without penalty. The note also requires the borrower to pay attorneys' fees and foreclosure costs in the event of default.

Note Forms

The FHA, VA, FNMA, and FHLMC all specify relatively standardized notes for use in most states. Security documents (mortgages or deeds of trust) are almost completely nonstandard, and FNMA/ FHLMC had to develop a special document for each state since foreclosure laws differ in every state. (This book features a 50-state summary of these laws in the appendix.)

Notes can be standardized in part because all 50 states have passed some form of the Uniform Commercial Code (UCC), which governs the law of notes. Nonstandard notes do exist, however, and they require very careful reading by an attorney. Often, notes overstate the lender's rights under a given state's laws, so a borrower should never trust the language of a nonstandard note until a lawyer confirms that it is consistent with state law. In contrast, uniform documents, such as FHA, VA, and FNMA/FHLMC notes, almost always conform to state law. Actually, they provide the borrower with extra rights beyond those granted under state law.

Acceleration

If the borrower stops making payments, the lender does not have to sue for each payment one by one. Instead, the lender may accelerate the note and make all future principal (but not interest) payments due at once. Payments that were missed prior to acceleration and attorneys' fees may also be counted in the sum due under an accelerated note, but future interest payments may not be counted. The note may ask the borrower to waive rights to prior notice, demand, grace, presentment, or cure, but any state statutes that give the borrower such rights remain in force regardless of what the note says.

A wise borrower should look for a note that requires the lender to give the borrower notice of default and an opportunity to cure it by paying missed payments. Some state laws require the lender to accept missed payments and stop a foreclosure, even after acceleration. In other states, once the note is accelerated, the lender need not accept missed payments but may demand the full—often enormous—unpaid principal balance before stopping foreclosure.

Cross-Default

Once a note is in default through nonpayment and the lender has given proper notices as required by the terms of the note or state law, almost every state allows the lender to declare the deed of trust or mortgage in default in such a way as to authorize foreclosure. Generally, a default on the note is a default on the mortgage or deed of trust. Conversely, some defaults on the deed of trust or mortgage, such as failure to maintain insurance, pay taxes, or make repairs, are also usually defined as defaults on the note. Almost every mortgage, deed of trust, and note in every state contains such a cross-default clause.

Mortgage States

True mortgages involve two parties, the lender and the borrower. The mortgage provides that the lender (or another party that buys the mortgage) can take title to the property, either by judicial foreclosure or by a power of sale clause, in the event the borrower doesn't pay. The term mortgage is derived from the Old French words mort, which means "dead," and gage, which means "pledge." A mortgage is a "dead pledge," which means that the lender holds property (in a title theory state) or a lien on it (in a lien theory state) as security for a loan, until the pledge is dead—that is, until the loan is repaid in full. The borrower then owns the property free and clear of the mortgage.

Mortgages are still in widespread use in the United States. Figure 3.4 shows the states where true two-party mortgages are used.

The mortgage document should state the conditions that constitute default. It should have a remedy, which may be a power of sale clause, if state law allows, or judicial foreclosure.

Mortgage documents are created in three basic ways: major loan buyers, insurers, or guarantors draw up uniform mortgage instruments; state bar associations write uniform instruments; or specific parties create home-grown or custom-drafted instruments. Uniform mortgage instruments are part of an ongoing revolution in the field. The need for a standardized mortgage form is apparent to those who deal with the resale of loans in the secondary market. (In the primary market, lenders deal directly with borrowers; in the secondary market, third parties buy loans originated by primary lenders.) Secondary market loan buyers need to know what they are buying, and a uniform document drawn up by a major national corporation or government agency is clearly a known quantity. This makes it easier to compare mortgages' essential financial characteristics, such as interest rates, loan terms, and principal amounts.

Many types of secondary market documents exist. FNMA and FHLMC have their own forms. Although drafted separately for each state (see figure 3.5), the documents employ as many common provisions as different state laws allow. The VA and the FHA each have their own forms. Further discussion of some borrowers' and lenders' rights under these documents are covered later in this book.

State bar association forms have the advantage of being drawn up by experts. They cover many different problems, as skilled members of the bar soon identify defects in such forms and fix them through addenda or small modifications to suit specific circumstances. Usually a variety of such forms with a variety of provisions exists in almost every state.

Nonuniform or custom-drafted instruments usually do not benefit borrowers. They are typically drafted by the lender to favor its position. Some are not true mortgages at all but rather contracts for deeds, rent-to-own arrangements, or lease option schemes. Many such schemes are no more than efficient vehicles for parting fools from their money. Custom-drafted, lender-oriented documents are frequently offered to tempt a reluctant and naive tenant into paying a premium rent for property that doesn't deserve it by offering bait in the form of a chance for future ownership. Often, the purchase just doesn't happen.

On the other hand, some custom-drafted forms may be the best in the business. Such documents must be reviewed with great care to determine their true effects.

Figure 3.4 Mortgage States

Alabama	Minnesota
Arkansas	New Hampshire
Connecticut	New Jersey
Delaware	New Mexico
Florida	New York
Hawaii	North Dakota
Illinois	Ohio
Indiana	Oklahoma
Iowa	Pennsylvania
Kansas	Rhode Island
Kentucky	South Carolina
Louisiana	South Dakota
Maine	Vermont
Massachusetts	Wisconsin
Michigan	Wyoming

Deed of Trust or Trust Deed States

Probably the most common mortgage instrument in the United States is the deed of trust. Figure 3.5 lists states that use this method.

When an American in a deed of trust state borrows money to buy a house, she signs two documents: a real estate lien note and a deed of trust. The note is basically a glorified IOU for the money the buyer borrows to pay for a house, as explained previously. The deed of trust is the foreclosure document. It gives the lender the power to force the sale of the home to pay off some or all of the loan. The deed of trust is neither much of a deed nor much of a trust. Although it is called a deed, it moves title only in the event of foreclosure. The reason for using two documents rather than one will be explained later.

The Initial Loan Arrangements

To understand foreclosure, we must analyze the underlying loan transaction. The seller transfers ownership of the home to the buyer by means of a deed, usually a general warranty deed and never a deed of trust. (A seller who finances part of the purchase price will receive a deed of trust, but he will still give a deed, such as a general warranty deed, to transfer ownership to the buyer.) Now the buyer owns the house. This fact is very important to savvy foreclosure buyers.

To get the money to pay for the house, the buyer will take out a loan from the lender. Before handing over that big check, the lender will require the buyer/borrower to sign two documents: the note and the deed of trust. Only one original of the note should be made, and it will be held by the lender. However, everyone who signed the note, including any guarantors, should get copies. The same is true of the deed of trust, except that multiple originals as well as copies can be made. The signed deed of trust should be recorded.

The deed of trust appoints a trustee as a third party to the deal with the lender and the borrower. (The note has only two parties, the lender and the borrower, who are identified as the payee and the maker, respectively.) The trustee, usually the lender's attorney or a bank officer, is important only in the event of foreclosure. The lender may appoint a new trustee, called a "substitute trustee," to handle foreclosure, although this process varies in different states.

DEFAULT

Whether a state uses a mortgage or a deed of trust, the conditions that constitute default are fairly similar. Most states allow two kinds of deed of trust forms: the state bar's standard form or the FNMA/FHLMC form for that state. The nature of the assurance for the loan, such as a VA guarantee, FHA insurance, or private mortgage insurance, will also have an important effect on the exact conditions of default. In general, the conditions of default fall into three broad categories:

1. Nonpayment of the note
2. Violation of a due-on-sale clause
3. Failure to keep up taxes or insurance, or to make repairs

Nonpayment of the Note

When the borrower persistently fails to make the loan payment, sooner or later, a foreclosure is inevitable. It may take time and involve trouble, but the lender will eventually win and foreclose. One big question is how quickly a lender can foreclose for missed payments.

Q. Can the lender really foreclose if I make one payment one day late?

A. Sometimes it can, but not on FHA, VA, or most privately insured mortgages.

The note usually calls for a certain schedule of payments. If the borrower fails to make payments on time in the correct amounts, this is a default under the deed of trust. Depending on how the deed of trust is written, missing only one payment or paying late can be cause for foreclosure. Legally, the lender may have that much power, because it usually picks or drafts the documents the borrower signs. However, the lender does not have such powers in every deed of trust state, and those that do will almost never foreclose under such circumstances. Generally, the lender is not eager to foreclose for a host of practical and legal reasons.

Timeliness of Payments

The question of timing is such a large issue that a later section of this chapter explores late payments in great detail. For now, we will examine the implications of simple failure to pay loan payments.

Default provisions in the deed of trust are often triggered if the borrower sells the house without paying off an existing loan or obtaining the lender's consent. Such provisions are called due-on-sale clauses. A closely related concept, the due-on-encumbrance clause, triggers default if a new lien or mortgage is placed on the property without paying off the old loan or obtaining the old lender's consent. A due-on-encumbrance clause will have a negative impact on assumptions by preventing second-lien loans, which are often needed in assumption situations. It will stop second or later liens in any other situation, as well. The due-on-sale clause is designed to prevent the assumption of an existing loan.

Figure 3.5 Deed of Trust States

Alaska	Nebraska
Arizona	Nevada
California	North Carolina
Colorado	Oregon
District of Columbia	Tennessee
Idaho	Texas
Maryland	Utah
Mississippi	Virginia
Missouri	Washington
Montana	West Virginia

The due-on-sale clause is legal in most states, since a federal law legalized it in any state that did not opt out of the federal law. Any loan with no due-on-sale clause in the deed of trust or mortgage is automatically assumable. However, if a due-on-sale clause is written into the loan papers and if it is legal in a given state, then the property may not be sold or transferred without the lender's consent.

Under federal law, a contract for deed arrangement (also called a land contract, installment sales contract, or installment land contract) is specifically barred if there is a due-on-sale clause in the mortgage. Even though a contract for deed does not pass title to the property to the buyer until the end of the contract after all payments have been made, it violates the due-on-sale clause as soon as it is signed and the buyer takes possession.

Leases can also violate a due-on-sale clause, particularly a lease with an option to purchase or a lease of over three years' duration. A short-term lease, defined as one for less than three years without an option to purchase, is permitted under the regulations associated with the federal St. Germain Act (Garn).

Rent-to-own arrangements, which operate much like contracts for deed, may also violate due-on-sale clauses. The owner can rent the property every three years. If the renter has enough money to buy, then the owner can sell and pay off the loan. The legality of a right of first refusal, in which the tenant must be offered the property before other buyers get a chance to buy, raises some questions, but this may be legal. Always consult an attorney.

In a silent wrap, the seller moves out and the buyer moves in and picks up the payments on the seller's old loan without notifying the lender. This is a dangerous legal situation, especially if the buyer makes checks out directly to the seller, since the seller may cash the checks and fail to pay the mortgage. If the lender's late notices or on-site visits trigger contact between the lender and buyer in the house, then a foreclosure is very likely. The lender may not consent to the arrangement at such a late date. In fact, many secondary market loan owners prohibit lenders from consenting to such a sale, even years after the fact. The lender may go forward with the foreclosure and sue for fraud, as well. The naive buyer will lose the house and all the payments he has made.

Federal law exempts a few kinds of transfers from due-on-sale clauses, so these do not constitute default. These are: (1) transfer of title incident to a divorce; (2) transfer of title due to death; (3) second lien loans; (4) certain home appliance loans; (5) certain transfers of title into trusts; and (6) leases for less than three years. The borrower can always ask for permission to assume the loan. If the market rate is high enough, the lender may consent. Without consent, a default and subsequent foreclosure will occur if there's a due-on-sale clause in the mortgage or deed of trust.

Failure to Pay for Taxes, Insurance, or Repairs

Most deeds of trust have covenants, or contractual agreements, in which the borrower agrees to keep the property taxes paid, maintain adequate insurance, and maintain the property in good repair. Although foreclosure for the breach of one or more of these covenants is not common, it is possible. A court may view foreclosure for anything other than nonpayment of the note with considerable caution.

Failure to Pay Taxes

Property taxes usually have the highest priority of any real estate lien. If they are not paid, the land may be sold to a new owner. The obligation to pay property taxes stays with the property as a lien regardless of who paid or failed to pay them. Due to their high priority, unpaid property taxes could cause a foreclosure regardless of the existence of a loan lien against the property. Because the lender's lien is destroyed by a property tax foreclosure sale, most lenders require the borrower to pay property taxes.

Although property tax authorities are often slow to foreclose, failure to pay property taxes could cause foreclosure by the lender. Usually when the borrower makes less than a 20 percent down payment, the lender administers an escrow account that holds part of the borrower's monthly payment until property taxes fall due and then pays the taxes itself. However, some lenders allow borrowers to pay taxes on their own rather than collecting them with each mortgage payment. If the borrower fails to pay property taxes, particularly if the lender doesn't require payments into an escrow account, the tax authorities may notify the lender, who will usually notify the borrower that the taxes must be paid. If the borrower fails to do this, the lender will pay them and bill the borrower. If the borrower fails to repay the lender, it will foreclose, even though every principal and interest payment has been made.

In a most reprehensible practice, a lender can take one-twelfth of the borrower's taxes with each monthly payment and then abscond with the money or fall into bankruptcy without paying the taxes. In such an event, the hapless homeowner could wind up paying the taxes twice for the year, once to the lender as part of the monthly payment and again to the taxing authority when the lender goes bankrupt. State taxing authorities can be lenient in such a situation, but many are not. Many states treat homeowners' association dues just like taxes, allowing foreclosure if they are not paid.

Failure To Maintain Adequate Insurance

If the borrower fails to keep adequate insurance on the property in force, the lender may declare a default and foreclose. Lenders can require either mortgage insurance or hazard insurance, or both, but usually they focus on hazard insurance. Without hazard insurance, the lender would be stuck foreclosing on ashes if the house burned down. Few borrowers will keep up the payments on a burned-down house unless they have hazard insurance to rebuild it.

Some states even permit the lender to pocket the insurance proceeds after a fire to pay off the loan, leaving the borrower with no money to rebuild the house but mortgage-free ownership of the ashes. This problem occurs all too often when financing is not arranged through regular lenders or experienced attorneys. Most buyers may overlook this possibility.

In a closely related problem, the borrower can cause the hazard insurance to lapse. One of the most common triggers for this situation arises when an area experiences a declining real estate market and the borrower moves out. Frequently, houses sell very slowly in a down market unless owners severely slash prices, which most hate to do. In the meantime, some borrowers must move out due to job pressures but may mistakenly believe that if they keep up the house payments, the hazard insurance will remain in force. Often, this is not true.

Hazard insurance policies to insure vacant properties against fire and other hazards cost more because the risks of a destructive fire or other damage are greater in a vacant house than in an occupied one. Most regular policies require the borrower to occupy the house, and the companies will cancel the policies after a certain period of vacancy, such as 30 to 60 days.

If the borrower does anything else that causes the insurance carrier to drop coverage, the lender may have a default that justifies foreclosure. For example, if the ground in an area subsides or is subject to erosion, hazard insurance may be unobtainable or obtainable only at exorbitant rates the borrower can't afford. If so, the lender may be able to declare a default and foreclose. Most lenders have the right to pass on insurance rate increases to a borrower who is paying monthly payments. If insurance rates rise to a level that a borrower on a fixed income can't afford, default on the loan may become likely.

Failure to Keep the Property in Good Repair

The lender normally requires the borrower to keep the property subject to the deed of trust in good repair. Otherwise, if it foreclosed, the lender would lose money repairing the property or accepting a reduced price for resale. Many properties suffer from lack of repairs as they near default when borrowers lack funds to maintain them or interest in doing so.

The borrower's obligation to keep the property in good repair is easy to understand but hard to define in a written document. A good example is the following hypothetical case. A Nevada resident, Smith, sold 160 rental homes to a Texan, Slim, for $1.2 million. The seller financed the purchase, taking a note from Slim with payment secured by a deed of trust. The deed of trust defined one condition of default as the failure of the borrower, Slim, to keep the properties in good repair "to the personal satisfaction" of the seller, Smith.

Smith tried to foreclose under this provision. Although the Midland, Texas, trial court found that the properties in question were more than 25 years old, "undoubtedly" needed constant repair, and suffered somewhat from tenant abuse, it did not agree that Slim had violated the "good repair" obligation. Slim had spent thousands for repairs, including $2,000 for supplies and more than $4,000 for outside labor. Slim also spent $200 a week to pay a maintenance worker. Despite the alleged poor condition of the property, there were no vacancies.

The court also found that the foreclosure was not undertaken in good faith by the lender, Smith. It appears that Smith demanded that Slim spend $35,000 in "repairs" to avoid foreclosure while seeking a $250,000 deficiency judgment. Slim contended that Smith sought not just repairs but capital improvements that would have put the properties in a better condition than when Slim bought them. The appeals court determined that a personal satisfaction standard for good repairs is not absolute and must be exercised in good faith. Smith was not permitted to foreclose. A similar result could probably be obtained in almost any state. It is truly difficult to define exactly what constitutes a suitable standard of good repair.

Lenders have tried to abuse provisions requiring borrowers to keep properties in good repair, especially when the borrowers have built up a lot of equity in their houses. This means the outstanding loan balance is much less than the value of the home, such as in the twenty-ninth year of a 30-year mortgage or after years of rising property values. Lenders, particularly sellers who financed purchases or other noncorporate lenders, have tried to foreclose for such ridiculous conditions as peeling paint, warped or cracked wood, or a bad roof. The borrower faced with such a situation should read the chapter in this book on fighting foreclosures in court and be sure to consult with an attorney.

Unusual Default Triggers

A creative lender can specify some unusual default triggers. If the deed of trust requires the borrower to keep a property leased, the lender could foreclose if the borrower were to fail to keep a paying tenant in the property at a certain monthly rent. In another unusual default trigger, a deed of trust might specify that a drop in the fair market value of the property below a certain level would constitute default permitting a foreclosure. Such provisions are common on loans for stocks and bonds.

One unusual default trigger is not a good idea: to specify that the filing of a bankruptcy petition by the borrower constitutes a default. Any attempt to foreclose will be stopped by the bankruptcy court until it gives its permission. Second or later liens should be carefully examined for such clauses. Nonstandard, noncorporate paperwork drafted by a lender's attorney may contain such clauses.

FAILURE TO PAY ON TIME

Obviously, few lenders will foreclose for one payment made one day late. As a quick rule with many, many exceptions, about four months of missed payments will draw a response of some kind from the lender, such as one of the preliminary notices in the foreclosure process. More optimistically, the lender might offer to accept lower payments. Some lenders have waited as much as a year. We'll explore some common restrictions on the power of lenders to foreclose in a minute, but first let's consider some general factors that influence a lender to foreclose.

If the borrower has substantial equity in the property, the lender will probably foreclose more quickly. When the lender knows the borrower will pay off the loan in full if it forecloses, the lender has every incentive to hurry and little incentive to wait.

The state of the borrower's finances influence the decision. If the lender knows the borrower has found a new job and will be able to pay in the future, it may be more lenient.

The willingness of the borrower to communicate with the lender and try to work toward a resolution of the problem may slow the process. A borrower who refuses to talk to the lender is asking for trouble faster. This is not to say that trying to talk to the lender will always resolve a problem. In many cases, lenders just demand their money and are not very helpful.

The existence of private mortgage insurance may have an effect. Some PMI companies have been very hard-nosed about insisting on prompt foreclosure. Also, the owner of the loan may have rules or policies about when to foreclose.

Lender Policies in Down Markets

When a wave of foreclosures hits a particular area, many lenders tend to select foreclosure too quickly as the solution for default problems. In fact, lenders almost encourage foreclosure by refusing to respond to problems until it is too late, and borrowers' potential loan difficulties mushroom to cause a number of missed payments. I had one friend who lost a job and tried to tell the lender immediately that some flexibility was needed. The lender refused to do anything. An officer at the bank told my friend to quit making payments for a while. That triggered a response but only after several months.

Increasingly, this approach is recognized as shortsighted. Wise lenders react quickly to determine the reason for any nonpayment. See the loan workout section of this book for more information.

How Long Before the Ax Falls?

Once the borrower begins missing payments, most lenders will take immediate collections steps, such as letters, phone calls, and personal visits. If these steps fail to bring results, the lender may begin some of the preliminary steps for foreclosure. The number of months the borrower can miss before the lender actually forecloses depends on the lender, the state, and the type of loan.

Out-of-state lenders or poorly managed lenders tend to foreclose the most quickly. Generally, local lenders are more understanding of the borrower's situation in a down market. State laws are examined elsewhere in the book. Generally, FHA loans allow borrowers two to three months before foreclosure steps begin. The VA will wait at least three months. Privately insured mortgages usually give borrowers about four months; however, their timetables may be advanced if there is no hope that the borrower can come up with the missed payments. Later chapters give more detail on each of these types of loans.

LATE PAYMENTS

Late payments do not always result in foreclosures. There are at least three ways in which a debtor may be late in making payments without causing a foreclosure.

1. If the lender has a past pattern of accepting late payments, it should not attempt foreclosure until it warns the borrower against being late on further payments. Continued acceptance of late payments or simply charging late fees may even create an implied contract to accept late payments.

2. If the foreclosure is undertaken by mistake or accident or the lender's own conduct has helped make the payment late, then foreclosure may not be allowed.

3. If the lender has a motive other than collecting its money as it comes due, then a foreclosure may not succeed. Generally, a lender should at least make a demand for payment and give the borrower an opportunity to make good on past-due payments. Otherwise the foreclosure may be stopped. Summaries follow of some specific cases in which lenders were not permitted to undertake nonjudicial foreclosure even though the borrowers made late payments.

Late Payments as Part of a Pattern

Although there is some variation among states, a lender that has a past pattern of accepting late payments may have to continue to accept late payments until it notifies the borrower of a new policy not to accept late payments. Even if a borrower is chronically delinquent in making payments, the lender's acceptance of late payments without objection may constitute a waiver of its right to accelerate the note and foreclose. The lender must give some notice to the borrower that it objects to short delays and that future installments should be made timely.

In one actual case in a deed of trust state that followed the lien theory, the lenders claimed the borrower's check was returned for insufficient funds by the bank. The borrowers maintained that they were not told that the check bounced. Their first news of the problem was the acceleration notice. The lender did not send the usual warning that the note might be accelerated but simply informed them that it had already been accelerated. Even worse, they were notified that the house had been "posted" for foreclosure in 21 days. The borrowers responded by sending a cashier's check to cover the late payment, but the lender's agent returned the check. One day before the foreclosure sale was to take place, the borrowers paid off the entire note to the tune of more than $240,000! Then they sued for wrongful acceleration and won.

As one possible defense, the lender could put clauses in the note and the deed of trust indicating that if it accepts late payments, it does not waive the right to accelerate or take steps toward acceleration if another payment is made late. One must carefully examine the note and the deed of trust (or mortgage) for such a clause.

Lender Conduct Causes Late Payments

If a lender's conduct contributed to the making of late payments, then the lender may be barred from foreclosing in many states. For example, one borrower repeatedly called the savings and loan to find out the balance in the escrow account. This account was discovered to hold more money than was needed to pay taxes and insurance, and these funds could have been used to help make payments on the loan, but the lender refused to give out the information by phone. The court stated that it is clear that this refusal delayed the borrower's efforts to remit. As a result, the court prevented the lender from completing nonjudicial foreclosure.

Lender Forecloses for Reasons Other than Late Payments

In another case, a note transferred to a new creditor on October 7 was discovered to be in default because one payment due on October 1 hadn't been made. The new creditor took the note to an attorney who immediately issued a foreclosure notice. When the borrower received the letter on October 10, he immediately offered to pay the late installment of $100 in full plus late fees, but the offer was refused. The trial court found that the note holder was not concerned about the lateness of the payment but merely used it as an excuse for foreclosing on a valuable property and eliminating a loan that paid a low interest rate. The foreclosure was judged to be harsh, oppressive, and inequitable, and it was not permitted to occur.

TIME BETWEEN MISSED PAYMENTS AND THE COMPLETED FORECLOSURE

The answer to the question "How long does a foreclosure take?" varies from state to state. Generally the process takes longer in states with judicial foreclosure procedures than in states with nonjudicial foreclosure procedures. Generally, states that allow power of sale clauses in mortgages or deeds of trust will see faster foreclosures than states that do not. The amount of preliminary notice required varies tremendously from state to state. Figure 3.6 shows how many months it typically takes to complete a foreclosure from start to finish in each state.

THREE PROBLEM AREAS

No general discussion of the laws of foreclosure would be complete without a discussion of three important topic areas: rights of redemption, second and later liens, and leases. Another subject, deficiency judgments, is discussed under the chapter on consequences of foreclosure and in the summaries of the 50 states' laws on foreclosure.

Redemption

The right of redemption is the right of the borrower to recover a house after a foreclosure. The historical origins of the right of redemption were discussed earlier along with strict foreclosure. However, the right of redemption today is largely a matter of statutory law rather than common law. Common law rights of redemption are largely nonexistent at present, but many states confer statutory rights of redemption.

If the borrower pays the past-due payments over a period from several months to a year, depending on the state, then the borrower can recover title to the house. Practices vary from state to state; the appendix at the back of this book states whether a right of redemption exists in each state and, if so, gives further details.

In many states, only homeowners can redeem property. In other states, second lien holders may also exercise a right of redemption. They may be entitled to receive notice of impending prior lien foreclosure by recording a request for notice. Unfortunately, not all states require the lender to send such a notice.

Figure 3.6 Countdown to Foreclosure

State	Months	State	Months	State	Months
Alabama	4	Kentucky	7	Ohio	10
Alaska	7	Louisiana	6	Oklahoma	7
Arizona	3	Maine	10	Oregon	7
Arkansas	5	Maryland	6	Pennsylvania	9
California	7	Massachusetts	8	Puerto Rico	12
Colorado	5	Michigan	3	Rhode Island	3
Connecticut	9	Minnesota	6	South Carolina	7
Delaware	8	Mississippi	4	South Dakota	4
District of Columbia	6	Missouri	3	Tennessee	4
Florida	7	Montana	9	Texas	3
Georgia	4	Nebraska	4	Utah	5
Guam	11	Nevada	7	Vermont	11
Hawaii	7	New Hampshire	4	Virgin Islands	10
Idaho	9	New Jersey	12	Virginia	5
Illinois	11	New Mexico	5	Washington	5
Indiana	12	New York	13	West Virginia	5
Iowa	11	North Carolina	5	Wisconsin	12
Kansas	4	North Dakota	4	Wyoming	3

Most states that offer a right of redemption give the defaulting borrower the right to redeem from both the lender and any outside purchaser, although some states restrict the right of redemption to sales in which the lender bought the house at foreclosure. This will not help if an outside purchaser got the house at foreclosure.

A very important question for most borrowers is whether they can redeem the house only by paying off the entire loan or whether paying missed payments will redeem the property. Usually, states require the former. Some states offer redemption rights only if the lender forecloses out of court. A fair number of states offer no rights of redemption at all.

Second and Later Lien Foreclosures

Most states permit a borrower to pledge a property to obtain a second loan on top of the original mortgage. Actually, the second loan may even be part of the original purchase, such as when a buyer assumes an FHA or VA loan, borrowing the difference between the purchase price and the loan balance from the seller. Alternatively, the borrower may take out a second loan for cash. Some states allow $30,000 or $40,000 lines of credit on charge cards, but if the charge card payments are not made, the creditor can foreclose on the borrower's house.

A few states, such as Texas, prohibit such loans against a homestead. Other states restrict the purposes of second or later cash loans against the principal residence, allowing loans for medical expenses or educational expenses only. Finally, almost all states, even Texas, permit mechanic's liens against homes, in which a contractor who is not paid for work on the house can obtain a lien and foreclose.

In every state, second or later lien loans share a common problem: if the first or prior lien is foreclosed, the second or later lienholder's right to foreclose is destroyed. Practices vary from state to state, but the second or later lienholder may be unaware of an impending first lien foreclosure in some states. In others, the later lienholder must be notified of an impending prior lien foreclosure if he records a notice requesting advance warning of a foreclosure. Once notified, the later lienholder may either try to pay off the loan prior to foreclosure, bid at the foreclosure sale, or, in some states, redeem the property after a foreclosure. None of these things are possible without notice, however, and some states, such as Texas, don't have a procedure to give later lienholders notice of impending earlier lien foreclosures.

If the second or later lien is foreclosed, then prior liens must ordinarily be paid off in order of their priority from the foreclosure sales proceeds, or else the buyer at the foreclosure sale must take title subject to the existing liens. To summarize: The foreclosure of a later lien cannot destroy an earlier lien, but the foreclosure of an earlier lien will destroy a later lien.

Once in a while, this priority can generate a fraud suit. For example, suppose someone sold a house to a buyer with questionable credit on condition that the buyer put on a new roof. The buyer finds a contractor who will put the roof on in exchange for a mechanic's lien to secure monthly payments; this is a second lien. If the seller retains a mortgage and forecloses when the questionable buyer fails to make payments, this seller gets a house back with a new roof but without a second lien for the roof. This creates a terrible potential for a fraud suit. A similar situation occurs when a friendly foreclosure is arranged with the objective of wiping out an undesirable lien. Once property is purchased at such a foreclosure, it may be difficult to obtain title insurance for a subsequent resale.

If the value of a house with many loans against it drops, there is a potential for massive foreclosure problems with second liens. Many of these second or later liens may have short loan periods and must be paid off or refinanced when they come due. If the later lien comes due, it cannot be refinanced, and the borrower lacks the cash to pay it off, foreclosure is likely. Legally, the existence of a prior mortgage loan won't stop the foreclosure of a second lien loan.

Since many borrowers may have severe difficulty refinancing second or later lien loans in down real estate markets, a lender who is third or fourth lienholder is exposed to serious risks. If the borrower goes into default, the house may not sell for enough to pay off the prior liens and still pay off the second or later lien. A lender who fears this situation may refuse to refinance the second or later lien and may call it due when its term expires. That would be a serious problem for a borrower who lacked enough cash to pay off a substantial second lien in full. A foreclosure could easily result.

The existence of second liens will hamper the use of many foreclosure avoidance techniques, such as PMI-assisted presales, assignment of mortgages, or workout or forbearance plans. However, the borrower can hope to induce second or later lienholders to cooperate under the threat that a prior lien will foreclose and wipe out the later lien unless the parties can agree on a mutually acceptable workout plan.

Leases

Tenants are exposed to particular risks when a loan is foreclosed. Like second liens, leases are wiped out when an earlier lien is foreclosed, unless the lender has consented to a nondisturbance clause in the lease. In this case, the lease survives the foreclosure. Such clauses are common in commercial leases but not in residential leases. Clauses in some leases give the lender the choice of continuing or rejecting the lease after a foreclosure. If it rejects the lease, the foreclosing lender, as the new landlord, can raise the rent or continue it at its existing level. (Whoever buys at foreclosure would have such rights, not just the lender.)

Unless a clause provides for the survival of the lease after foreclosure, the tenant has the right to walk away if the lender forecloses. This may discourage a lender from foreclosing, or it may help the borrower force the lender to accept a deed in lieu of foreclosure, since otherwise the tenant could walk out on the lease. The tenant's agreement to accept a new landlord, which may be found in the original lease or as a separate agreement, is called an attornment.

In the event of default, the lender may also have a right to an assignment of rentals from the tenant. This can be complicated. Some lenders grab for the rental proceeds as soon as a borrower misses payments. Most states have complex legal rules as to when and under what circumstances a lender can obtain rentals after default in making loan payments.

Tenants often suffer from foreclosure. They may receive little advance warning of a foreclosure, since some states require tenants to be notified of an impending foreclosure against the property owner and some don't. Once the foreclosure takes place, the tenant may be evicted, again with limited notice. Some tenants actually check titles before renting to see who really owns the property and what lenders have rights against it. After a foreclosure, many lenders will negotiate to keep a tenant in the property, provided the rent is adequate. Lenders seldom want to let the defaulting borrower stay in the property, but sometimes it can be done.

WHO HOLDS THE CHIPS?

A familiar offbeat version of the Golden Rule holds that "Them that have the gold, make the rules." Although this is not entirely so throughout the United States, lenders have long had a major influence on our foreclosure laws. In spite of their many options, the truth remains that borrowers who persistently fail to make house payments for long periods of time will lose their houses to foreclosure. It may take time and cost the lender some money, but it will happen. Nevertheless, it is quite worthwhile to understand the legal framework for the lender's right to foreclose.

A working knowledge of the laws of foreclosure is critical to understanding the next few chapters. They describe how a borrower may work with, rather than against, the lender to forestall, prevent, or mitigate a foreclosure. The appendix contains a synopsis of foreclosure laws by state. Readers should familiarize themselves with local regulations and procedures.

FHA Workouts

4

FHA loans are a small part of some markets such as California. They are significant in other markets. In down markets, FHA loans often skyrocket. They are there when there are few other lenders or mortgage insurers.

The FHA does not make loans; it merely insures loans that are made by private lenders. A borrower who can't make the payments on an FHA loan must contact the private lender that services the loan. A servicer is a company that deals with borrowers; it collects payments, sends out late notices, and will arrange for a foreclosure, if necessary. The FHA loan has probably been sold to some investment company on the secondary market. Servicers seldom own the FHA loans they service.

THE SERVICER'S PERSPECTIVE

Many borrowers mistakenly assume that servicers care a great deal about the FHA loans they service. All too often, they don't, as many borrowers learn to their cost. Here is a common misconception.

Misconception

The loan servicer will suffer a loss from the foreclosure.

> Borrower: Please help me. I've lost my job, and I'm probably going to have some difficulty making my payments. I've always been good about paying in the past, and I need you to work with me now. With all the foreclosures in my community, surely you don't want another one on your hands. Another foreclosed home would only add to your loss.

Harsh Reality

As long as the loan servicer follows official guidelines, it is unlikely to suffer harm from the foreclosure.

> Servicer: We don't own this loan; somebody else does. Any loss won't be ours. More importantly, the FHA insures this loan. If you default and we foreclose, FHA insurance will cover every penny of loss from the foreclosure. As long as we've followed proper procedures, we don't care. We need to worry only if we haven't followed procedures. We couldn't care less whether we'll get another foreclosure house.

A borrower who tries to buck the system by talking reason to the loan servicer may be sorely disappointed. Instead, borrowers must learn to play the game. They must recognize that the FHA loan servicer must comply with guidelines to avoid trouble with the FHA. A given loan servicer probably isn't that worried about a threat from the FHA, but the threat is a better bargaining tool than the threat of a loss on the house once it's foreclosed. A borrower would probably have better luck trying to nail the loan servicer on a clear breech of FHA guidelines than trying a down-to-earth, commonsense, businesslike approach to the situation.

In fact, the borrower who learns how the guidelines work can use them, or even abuse them, to his own advantage. A borrower can coolly tie up the loan servicer with a string of delaying tactics while salting away enough money to make the down payment on another home. A skillful and lucky borrower may be able to hold off the loan servicer a year or more by requesting the appropriate relief measures at the right time, through the right means, and in the right manner.

On the other hand, while facing down the mortgage servicer, the worst thing the borrower can do is to lose control and heckle the servicer's representative. This person will simply add a note about the uncooperative borrower in the files and use it as further justification for foreclosure. Threats to sue the servicer are seldom effective. One servicer's response to such threats is this: "Go ahead! Have your attorney call ours."

As a more effective approach, a borrower living in the house might request an assignment of the mortgage to HUD. It may be best to communicate with servicers in writing as much as possible. Send letters certified mail, return receipt requested; address them to a specific person; and send a copy, the same way, to the closest FHA field office. To determine what to write and when to write it, review the following guidelines the FHA has set forth for loan servicers.

FHA SERVICING GUIDELINES

The FHA classes loans with missing payments as being delinquent or in default. The FHA regards a loan as delinquent any time a payment is due and not paid. The FHA regards a loan as being in default when the borrower fails to make any payment or to perform any other obligation under the mortgage, for a period of 30 days. Every month, lenders must report to the FHA on all FHA-insured mortgages that are more than 90 days delinquent. They must also make continuing monthly reports to the FHA on the status of all FHA-insured loans that are over 90 days delinquent.

The FHA gives borrowers the right to cure loan defaults prior to the completion of foreclosure proceedings. However, the borrower must repay to the lender the costs it incurs in any foreclosure proceedings. When written notice of the reinstatement is then given to the FHA, its mortgage insurance and the loan will continue as they were before the default.

To avoid or deal with default, HUD has a variety of collection techniques. HUD also has procedures for foreclosure avoidance, along with specialized relief measures and informal workouts that can be used whenever a loan is in default.

WHAT HAPPENS WHEN A BORROWER MISSES PAYMENTS

Before an FHA lender uses any of HUD's many special relief measures, the borrower normally misses payments for a time. Ironically, as long as payments are current, it is often difficult to get the lender to bother with any specialized relief measures, even though the borrower knows she will have difficulty making payments. Some lenders actually tell borrowers to miss payments, then seek relief. The borrower who anticipates missing payments may have to be really persistent to get an FHA lender to take action to avoid a foreclosure while the payments are still current. The borrower should try to get the lender's attention as early as possible, because even a missed payment reduces the chance that a workout plan will succeed.

Once the borrower begins missing payments, however, the lender will normally go through a variety of collection procedures to get its money. Borrowers should recognize that the FHA lender that persistently calls and writes about the missed payments is doing only what the rules require. Actually, the lender's failure to write or call would be even worse for the borrower than a pattern of calls or letters. The lender wouldn't help the borrower by simply waiting until a set number of payments were missed and then springing a foreclosure on him.

The borrower should keep a careful record of every call the FHA lender makes, noting when it was made, who called, and what was discussed. If the lender fails to follow proper loan servicing procedures, it gives the borrower an argument for more time. The borrower might have grounds to remove the lender and replace it by HUD loan administrators in a procedure called "assignment to the secretary."

HUD'S COLLECTION TECHNIQUES

HUD's collection efforts will begin almost as soon as the borrower misses payments. The borrower should expect HUD to pursue the following steps:

1. Letters and automatic notices
2. Telephone calls
3. Personal interviews
4. Threats and warnings from attorneys
5. Delinquency counseling

It is to the borrower's advantage to become familiar with these procedures.

The borrower should not become aggravated by these preliminary collection efforts. Instead, he should take every advantage of the opportunities they present. The borrower should keep records well enough to tell not only when phone calls were made but also when threats were made or any personal interviews occurred. The sample log in figure 4.1 shows the type of information that should be maintained for all of the lender's communications.

Figure 4.1 Foreclosure Notice Log

Letters	Date on Letter	Date Received	Who Sent Letter	Subject of Letter	Problems with Letter*
	————	————	————	————	————
	————	————	————	————	————
Phone Calls	Date of Call	Time of Call	Caller's Name	Person Who Took Call	Matters Discussed During Call
	————	————	————	————	————
	————	————	————	————	————
Personal Interviews	Date of Meeting	Place of Meeting	Persons Present	Matters Discussed During Meeting	
	————	————	————	————	
	————	————	————	————	

* Computer form notice, ignores your past communications, is based on incorrect information, comes from a lawyer without giving Fair Debt Collection Practices Act notices, etc. Be sure to carefully preserve each letter and the envelope it came in.

HUD Counseling: Demand It!

In particular, a borrower should demand delinquency counseling—and lots of it. The borrower should watch for a letter from the lender that lists counseling agencies in the area. Once again, a borrower should demand counseling if any chance at all remains for avoiding foreclosure. The checklist in figure 4.2 reviews some of the things a borrower can expect from a good HUD loan counselor. Shop for a good one.

Loan counseling gives borrowers important help to deal with troubled loans. When the borrower either has or anticipates problems keeping up with payments on an FHA loan, an FHA loan counselor should be located. Usually the FHA lender or the nearest FHA field office can provide a list of counselors.

The procedures the counselor recommends take time. Some borrowers have abused time lags in HUD counseling, forbearance, and assignment procedures by stretching the time they do not make house payments. They save the money they would have applied toward house payments for a down payment on a new house or a cash deposit on a rental unit. In a down market, some desperate sellers will extend seller financing or permit simple assumptions of loans. This can allow even a delinquent borrower to buy a new, cheaper house. A better option is to use the FHA's workout procedures to fashion a plan to save the house. Above all, the FHA's goals, however, are not quite so ambitious at first.

FHA OBJECTIVE: BRING THE LOAN CURRENT

When a borrower begins missing payments, the FHA's key objective in any of its collection and servicing activities is to bring the loan current, either immediately or within a short time. If the FHA's collection procedures cannot coax or coerce the missing cash from the borrower, it may consider a repayment plan. Above all, the FHA wants to prevent foreclosures.

A repayment plan may be negotiated through correspondence, by telephone calls, or by personal interviews. The plan need not be stated in writing, but it must be thoroughly documented. The repayment plan will serve to bring the loan current. The FHA's collection methods to achieve this goal include letters, calls, interviews, attorney action, and counseling.

Letters and Automatic Notices

The FHA guidelines call for sending both letters and automatic notices. In the FHA's view, computer-printed cards and preprinted form letters may be effective, particularly with the occasional delinquent. However, if form letters are used, the FHA recommends that lenders or servicers institute controls to avoid mailing duplicate notices. Personal letters are also recommended.

Telephone Calls

The FHA recommends phone calls for collections. The borrower should be ready to answer questions about her situation when the lender's operator asks about the causes of nonpayment and default and a likely specific reinstatement date. The caller should also describe what could happen if the loan is not reinstated.

Normally, the lender will use telephone calls before face-to-face interviews. A good set of phone calls may even eliminate the need for face-to-face interviews. The borrower should be prepared to discuss the situation, especially why she can't make payments. The borrower should be careful never to make a promise she can't keep, so the lender will trust her in future efforts to avoid foreclosure. The borrower should keep a careful record of all phone calls from the lender.

If you are sure, as a borrower, that you need more than just a short time to bring the loan current, you should explain the type of relief you think you need. Emphasize the need for both financial counseling and a face-to-face interview with the lender. These requests show the lender that you are serious about making up the missed payments but need some help to do so. This way you can buy time while avoiding foreclosure.

Figure 4.2 Loan Counseling Checklist

_____ Did the counselor explain the FHA's policies on delinquent loans?
_____ Did the counselor explain the mortgage situation from HUD's viewpoint? Explanation should include:
_____ Lien status
_____ Hazard insurance requirements
_____ Property taxes
_____ Escrow account procedures
_____ Did the counselor explain the possibilities for creating a payment plan based on the borrower's potential income?
_____ Did the counselor explain the FHA's loan assignment program (which moves the borrower's loan from the private lender to HUD itself)?
* Did the explanation of the loan assignment program include the following topics?
_____ Purpose of the assignment program
_____ Processing stages for an assignment
_____ Timetable and deadlines for an assignment
_____ Actions for each stage of an assignment
_____ Did the counselor assist you in completing any necessary HUD forms, including the following?
_____ HUD 92068F (Financial Information)
_____ Did the counselor assist you in identifying the cause of default, as defined by the FHA?
_____ Did the counselor assist you in developing reasonable payment plans, if that alternative was selected?
_____ Did the counselor assist you in requesting various conferences with HUD and help in presenting your case?
_____ Did the counselor work with you in the following actions to sell the property, if that alternative is chosen?
_____ Locating a suitable broker
_____ Developing a plan to deal with HUD while selling
_____ Did the counselor assist you in locating auxiliary sources of income or assistance, including the following?
_____ New job (second or primary job)
_____ Lower cost medical services
_____ Disability insurance claims
_____ Food stamps

Personal Interviews

The Code of Federal Regulations governing HUD requires the lender or the servicer to have a face-to-face interview with the borrower or make a reasonable effort to arrange such a meeting before three full monthly installments on the loan are missed. A reasonable effort to arrange a meeting includes at least one letter, sent by certified mail or an acceptable alternative, such as direct delivery. Even if the borrower refuses to accept or respond to the letter, the lender's job is done. That's why the borrower should be very careful to accept any certified letters from the lender. Generally, refusing to accept such letters does not help the borrower, and one such letter will offer a face-to-face interview, which is an opportunity the alert borrower should seize. If the borrower never bothers to respond to the lender, then the lender need not make any further effort to arrange a face-to-face interview.

If you want time, put off the interview but at least keep up communications with the lender. If you have already waited, then call and demand financial counseling.

HUD/FHA regulations state that interviews are not necessary if the borrower is uncooperative, has left the property, is located more than 200 miles from the lender or servicer, or a repayment plan is worked out without a personal interview. To protect this right, an alert borrower will try to cooperate with the lender at all times. The borrower should not permanently abandon the property, which could lead to a quick foreclosure. Also, the property may be vandalized. Reasonable security precautions should be taken if the borrower has moved out of the property. As long as he avoids any overt appearance of abandonment, the borrower can get more help out of the lender. Nothing, of course, prevents a borrower from spending some time away from the house, perhaps even a lot of time, if that's necessary. Once the lender can confirm that the borrower has relocated over 200 miles away, however, it is much more likely to foreclose.

Although a repayment plan can be worked out over the phone, the borrower should make some effort to confirm the deal with the lender. At the very least, write a letter and send it to the lender via certified mail, return receipt requested, or via overnight air express. These services give a receipt confirming that the lender has received the letter from the borrower. In these days of bank buyouts, closeouts, and shutdowns, lenders can lose records. The borrower should never, ever depend on the lender's records for assistance. The borrower should always maintain a good set of records detailing what was communicated to the lender and when. If a repayment plan is agreed upon, the borrower should write down its provisions and, if possible, get the lender to send a letter, a fax, or some other tangible evidence that the plan has been received and accepted. The problem of keeping suitable records gives another reason to insist on a personal interview.

Repayment Plan Interviews

If the parties agree to a repayment plan over the phone or by mail, but the borrower fails to meet its terms, then a face-to-face interview must be arranged within 30 days after the default on the plan and 30 days before any foreclosure is started. However, the face-to-face interview is not necessary if the repayment plan was created by a personal interview in the first place.

The interviewer representing the lender in a face-to-face interview should be empowered to propose reasonable repayment plans. The interviewer should know the limits on plan acceptability. This way, the lender cannot back out of a plan by arguing that the interviewer exceeded her authority.

The lender may hire an attorney to try to collect past due payments, but it may not pass on the attorney's charges to the borrower until and unless a foreclosure is contemplated. The lender may charge the borrower attorney's fees only for the actual foreclosure.

HUD-approved counseling agencies may be used to try to cure a borrower's default. The lender normally withholds foreclosure for 60 days once a counseling agency enters the picture. Further, the lender is supposed to send the counseling agency copies of the borrower's original credit report, verification of employment (VOE) forms, verification of deposit (VOD) forms, and the loan application. The counseling agency will then try to restructure the homeowner's financial habits to assist in restoring timely loan payments.

HOW A BORROWER SHOULD EXPECT TO BE TREATED

An FHA-approved lender is supposed to have a program to discourage borrower delinquency. However, not all features of this program work against the borrower. Part of the lender's job is to determine whether the borrower has a solid reason for nonpayment and to take appropriate action. FHA insists that lenders avoid mechanistic servicing of a loan. FHA procedures require that lenders try to deal with borrowers on a human basis.

Lenders are supposed to make human decisions about whether to return late payments, as opposed to allowing lockbox check collectors to program computers to return payments automatically. A borrower should save anything that appears to be a computer-generated rejection notice along with a record of when it was received. Call the lender and ask who made the decision to return the payment.

Try to establish whether the lender really made a human decision or not. Keep a careful record of what happens when you call the lender, even if all you get is an automated answering system.

Borrowers should realize that FHA regulations call upon lenders to enforce the late-payment provisions of mortgages. A borrower who pays late should expect to pay a late fee. However, the borrower should keep a record of the fees. A careless lender may assess a late charge that violates state usury laws.

A borrower should not expect a lender to accept partial payments under all circumstances. A lender is permitted to return partial payments judiciously, unless the borrower makes arrangements to repay amounts that are past due. (See the later section in this chapter on partial payments.)

An FHA lender must mail the borrower the HUD booklet on delinquency no later than the second month of any delinquency, so the borrower will understand steps to avoid foreclosure. The lender is only required to mail the booklet once in a six-month period. For subsequent delinquencies, it must be sent again.

Borrowers should be aware that lenders keep track of loan defaults and enter them on HUD's nationwide computer system. Even late payments that do not appear on the borrower's credit report will be duly noted in HUD's computer records. This system also allows the lender to see how its loans compare with loans made by other lenders in the area.

AVOIDING FORECLOSURE

HUD's official policy seeks to avoid foreclosure. However, because HUD insures the repayment of a loan to a private lender, HUD will force a foreclosure to cover at least some, if not all of the loss. Though a lender may feel inclined to foreclose just to get rid of the problem loan, the borrower should not hesitate to call HUD directly and ask for help if it appears that the lender isn't seriously cooperating to avoid a foreclosure. The borrower should document each contact with the lender so that he can respond in detail if HUD asks about what the lender did or did not do.

To avoid foreclosure, HUD wants lenders to open direct contact with borrowers to ensure compliance with all HUD procedures and regulations. If the lender omits action that HUD guidelines require, the case should go back to the lender's servicing personnel for more work. Therefore, the borrower should watch for instances of the lender's failure to work with him. Be prepared to discuss it with HUD. Although HUD won't give many direct assurances to the borrower, HUD will often talk to the lender "behind the scenes." A lender that has violated HUD's guidelines in servicing a loan will find itself in a difficult position. It may be forced to delay foreclosure or may become more receptive to actions that it should have allowed all along, such as forbearance, modification, or assignment of the loan to HUD.

Partial Payments

Sometimes borrowers can't pay the full payment on a mortgage loan. Such a borrower may try to make partial payments just to show willingness to make payments. Perhaps the borrower has found a job and can resume partial payments on the way to resuming full payments. FHA has specific rules for how lenders must deal with partial payments.

- *Definition:* A *partial payment* is any payment less than the full amount due under the terms of the mortgage when the payment is tendered (offered), including late charges.

- *Return of partial payments when in default:* If any missed payments have caused the loan to be in default, the lender may return partial payments to the borrower with letters of explanation under several specific circumstances.

■ *Payment is less than 50 percent of the amount due:* The lender can return a partial payment that is less than 50 percent of the amount due. The amount due for this purpose does not include late fees in the FHA's view, though the lender may insist that it does. The borrower can probably win on this point if he argues. The late charges will have to be made up at some point, however.

■ *Payment is less than agreed upon in a workout plan:* The borrower should realize that failure to pay under a workout plan draws harsh treatment from both the FHA and the laws of many states. The lender may simply return a check for less than an agreed-upon sum under an oral or written forbearance plan.

■ *Landlord absconds with rent:* The lender may return partial payments when the property is occupied by a rent-paying tenant and the payments are not being applied to the loan. If the lender suspects the borrower of pocketing the rent money rather than paying the payments, the lender may legally refuse to accept partial payments.

■ *Foreclosure has commenced:* The borrower should try to make payments in sufficient amounts soon enough to keep the loan from going into actual foreclosure. Once the lender has taken the first action required for foreclosure under a particular state's law, then the lender may refuse further partial payments.

■ *Mortgage is in serious default:* If the borrower goes into serious default, foreclosure becomes a very real possibility. Serious default occurs when four payments have been missed or the delinquency has continued for six months. Once four payments have been missed, the FHA rules allow the lender to mail any partial payment back to the borrower, provided it sent the borrower a letter at least 14 days earlier stating the amount due, plus late charges, and a statement that anything less than the full amount due will be returned. Some borrowers deliberately take advantage of HUD's requirements. In such cases, the lender may document the matter and turn it over to the FBI for appropriate handling under the criminal laws.

■ *Mortgage is not in default:* A borrower who sends a partial payment on a current mortgage should recognize that the lender may first assume that the partial payment was simply a clerical mistake by the borrower, not a deliberate effort to withhold payments. Under such circumstances, the lender may simply return a partial payment with a letter of explanation indicating that the payment amount was too low. Recall that if the lender continually accepts partial payments, this could set a precedent that would require the lender to continue to accept them. Of course, if the borrower has made an honest mistake but is able and willing to make the payment, then the lender can properly reject a partial payment. If there's no mistake, the lender should try to work with the borrower and vice versa.

FHA's policy states that a lender should accept partial payments in circumstances other than those listed above. Upon receiving a partial payment, the lender should either apply it to the loan or hold the money in a trust account for the borrower. When the partial payments held in trust total a full month's payment, the money should be used to make the oldest payment first. This does not change the date on which HUD regards the delinquency as first occurring.

THREE MISSED PAYMENTS BEFORE FORECLOSURE

Borrowers have some protection against instant foreclosure upon violation of the slightest provision of the mortgage. Lenders should not begin foreclosure until the due date on the third unpaid monthly installment passes. Any partial payments must be credited, so foreclosure cannot begin until three full monthly payments have been missed. There are, however, three exceptions to the rule:

1. *Abandonment and vacancy.* When the lender determines the property has been abandoned or vacant for over 60 days, it can begin foreclosing.

2. *Willful dishonor.* If after being advised of the options available for relief, the borrower has stated clearly, in writing, that she will not honor the loan obligation, the lender can begin foreclosure.

3. *Absconding with rent.* If the borrower owns two or more properties occupied by tenants who are paying rent, but the rent is not being applied to the mortgage on the property, the lender can foreclose. Foreclosure may not be started if the only portion of the payment that has been missed is the late charge.

Last-Minute Reinstatement

Even after foreclosure has begun, but before its completion, the FHA requires lenders to permit reinstatement of the loan (that is, call off the foreclosure) if the borrower tenders a lump sum that is large enough to pay all past-due payments, late charges, interest on the past-due amounts, reasonable collections costs, and attorneys' fees. If, however, the borrower has accepted reinstatement after the institution of foreclosure proceedings within the two years immediately preceding the current foreclosure, FHA will not permit a second reinstatement.

HUD-APPROVED SPECIAL RELIEF MEASURES

To save a house from foreclosure, HUD has some special relief programs. These programs often help when they are available. HUD's four special relief measures are the following:

1. Informal and formal forbearance

2. Special forbearance, Type I and Type II

3. Loan modification, sometimes called recasting

4. Partial claims (no-interest loan from HUD)

(Note: Assumption sales, deed in lieu of foreclosure procedures, and foreclosure presales are covered in later chapters.)

A lender should consider these special relief measures when it can reasonably believe that the borrower can and will resume loan payments. The lender can choose whether or not to employ these methods, but it should not foreclose if special relief measures will save the loan. Regular refusal to use these measures to prevent foreclosure may lead HUD to suspend or terminate the lender's FHA-approved status, which would remove its authority to make future FHA loans.

Informal Forbearance

In informal forbearance, the borrower asks the lender to hold off foreclosure. If the lender agrees, it simply permits the borrower to continue in default or to make smaller payments for a limited time without beginning foreclosure. However, the borrower should recognize that the lender will want to comply with the FHA deadlines on the various types of informal forbearance. If the arrangement is set down in writing, it is termed "formal" forbearance.

HUD guidelines permit the lender to wait for as long as one year from the initial default before initiating foreclosure. Recall that default consists of nonperformance on the loan for more than 30 days. The time needed to apply for and obtain this extra year might stretch the total delay to 14 months. Once again, though, a lender would be wise to seek confirmation of the time from the FHA.

Figure 4.3 Sample Payment Plan: Short Term Payment Plan

Mortgagor(s)_____

Case No. _____

Street Address _____

City, State, Zip Code _____

In return for the Department of Housing and Urban Development (HUD) not foreclosing on my mortgage, which is still in default under the original note, I agree to the following terms and conditions:

1. *Lump sum payment:* No later than _____, I will submit to HUD at the above address a check or money order in the amount of $_____. I understand that this lump sum payment will be used to repay some of the amount now past due on my mortgage.

2. *Monthly payments:* Beginning in _____ 20__, and continuing through _____ 20__ on the first day of each month, I will submit to HUD at the above address a check or money order in the amount of $_____.

3. *Property tax escrow:* I understand that the monthly payment required in paragraph 2 above will include an amount to be set aside (escrowed) by HUD to pay the taxes on my property. If these taxes increase, HUD may increase my monthly payment by an amount sufficient to meet escrow requirements. If taxes on the property decrease, my monthly payment will not decrease. Instead, HUD will use the extra money to help repay the past-due payments.

4. *Prepayment:* If all payments that are past due under the terms of my original note or mortgage are repaid before the end of this Payment Plan, this Payment Plan will terminate and the monthly payments required by the original note and mortgage will begin again. The amount of the original payments, however, may be increased to cover higher property taxes.

5. *Termination conditions:* HUD may terminate this Payment Plan if:
   a. I permanently leave the property;
   b. I sell or give ownership or interest in the property, note, or mortgage;
   c. The facts or circumstances that caused HUD to enter into this agreement change substantially; or
   d. I fail to meet any of the terms of this agreement or the original note and mortgage.

6. *Termination outcome:* If termination results from any of the above conditions, HUD can require that I either
   a. Enter into a new Payment Plan; or
   b. Return to the terms of the original note and mortgage. If payments are still past due at that time, this could result in foreclosure.

7. *Original note and mortgage:* I understand that all the rights and obligations of the original note and mortgage, except as changed by this Payment Plan, remain in full force and that, when this Payment Plan expires, the monthly mortgage payments due under the note and mortgage will begin again, unless HUD agrees to renew, amend, or extend the Payment Plan.

Approved:

Department of Housing and Urban Development By:		Mortgagor(s) By:
_____	_____	_____
Deputy Director, Housing Management Division	Date	Date

Since each payment made on an FHA loan must be applied to the oldest overdue amount outstanding, any payment moves the date of default forward to the next missed payment. In this way, it may be possible to continue in default status for a long time, even past a year, by making occasional payments. This type of relief is intended for small delinquencies that the lender is reasonably certain will be cured at a future time by payment of a lump sum or installments in addition to regular payments.

The lender may or may not extend informal forbearance, at its discretion. The lender may hesitate to do so because it may not be reimbursed for the loss through FHA insurance. Although this insurance covers losses on the loan, it does not cover lost interest during the period of informal forbearance.

Special Forbearance

Special forbearance permits the borrower to make either no payments or reduced payments for a limited time. This can be done without HUD approval for up to 18 months or with HUD approval for 18 to 36 months. All forms of special forbearance on HUD loans are subject to two restrictions:

1. The borrower must not own other properties with HUD-insured loans.

2. The default must be due to circumstances beyond the borrower's control, such a job loss or unpaid medical bills. Special forbearance is for borrowers who really need help, not those who just want to save money.

The agreement for special forbearance must meet all of the following conditions:

- The borrower must resume regular loan payments at the end of the forbearance period.

- The borrower must repay all sums not collected during the reduced-payment period before the end of loan term, plus 18 months.

- The plan must specify repayment dates and amounts for the missing loan payments.

It should also meet the criteria listed below for Type I or II special forbearance. A lender will need HUD approval for a special forbearance agreement beyond the short term. The agreement should be put into writing. The sample form in Figure 4.3 calls for a lump sum payment up front combined with payments over time. However, other plans could be drawn up without lump sums or with different payment amounts over time. However, a more special set of circumstances is required to go into special forbearance.

HUD has produced a basic checklist of requirements for FHA loan borrowers in default to be eligible for special forbearance, shown in figure 4.4.

Figure 4.4 FHA Special Forbearance Eligibility Checklist

1. Has the borrower experienced a loss of income or increase in living expenses?

2. Is the borrower an owner occupant?

3. Did a search of CAIVRS HUD's central computer to track mortgages determine that the borrower has no other HUD-insured loans or prior loans on which a claim has been paid in the past three years?

4. Did the borrower receive the "How to Avoid Foreclosure Brochure"?

5. Will the loan be more than three months and less than one year delinquent on the effective date of the agreement?

6. Did the surplus income analysis to determine the borrower's ability to repay the debt include the following:
   A financial statement provided by the borrower?
   A credit report?
   Income/expense verifications?
   Evidence the borrower can support the payment schedule?

7. The borrower's surplus income percentage is _____?

8. Has an inspection determined that the property has no adverse conditions affecting continued occupancy?

9. Does the written agreement executed by the borrower do the following:
   Clearly define the terms and frequency of repayment?
   Offer relief not available through a normal repayment plan?
   State that failure to comply may result in a foreclosure?
   Limit the total default to 12 months or less?

10. If the special forbearance agreement culminates in a partial claim or modification, does it show the proposed date of that action?

Type I Special Forbearance

Type I special forbearance by HUD involves negotiating and signing an agreement to repay delinquent sums. It is a stand-alone repayment plan. It does not include other types of relief, such as partial payment or loan modification. When those types of relief are combined with a repayment plan, then we have Type II special forbearance. Type I special forbearance agreements must cover the following:

- The agreement must identify the specific months for which the account is delinquent and note the total arrearage that accrued prior to the beginning of the agreement.

- The agreement, if the payments are kept up, must fully reinstate the original FHA loan.

- The agreement must ensure that the repayment installments required under its terms are based on the borrower's ability to pay. The lender must have done at least the following:

  - The lender must retain evidence in the claim review file that the lender analyzed the borrower's financial condition according to FHA guidelines.

  - The agreement's repayment schedule is supported by the financial analysis. For example, a special forbearance plan cannot include a balloon payment (big lump sum payment at the loan's end) unless the financial analysis shows how the borrower will realistically get a sum of money in the future to handle it, such as a pending work bonus.

- The agreement may include repayment of "reasonable" foreclosure costs and late fees that were owed before the plan. However, the principal, interest, and escrow advances must be paid first under the agreement. The loan cannot be considered delinquent solely because the borrower has not paid late fees or foreclosure costs.

- The special forbearance agreement must show how it provides relief an ordinary informal forbearance plan couldn't provide, such as (a) a suspension or reduction of payments for a period sufficient to allow the borrower to recover from the cause of default (such as recover from a medical operation or condition); (b) a period during which the borrower only has to make the regular mortgage payment before beginning to pay anything on the arrearage (the borrower's income may not be high enough to handle any more than that for a period of time); (c) provide for longer relief, such as six months, than an informal (or formal) forbearance plan.

- The plan must last a minimum of four months; there is no maximum.

- The agreement must not pay old late fees while the borrower performs under the special forbearance plan, nor can the underlying loan be considered delinquent while the special forbearance agreement is complied with.

- The plan must not allow an arrearage of greater than 12 months of missed principal, interest, taxes, and insurance.

- The plan must allow the borrower to prepay the delinquency at any time.

- The lender must maintain a copy of the forbearance agreement that is signed and dated by at least one borrower and an authorized agent of the lender.

If the borrower gets a fantastic new job during the period of the special forbearance agreement, the lender will check on that and renegotiate the terms of the agreement as the borrower's status changes. However, no plan can offer forbearance on a total of more than 12 missed payments.

Type II Special Forbearance: The Combo

Type II special forbearance is like a Type I plan but adds additional strong mortgage relief medicine, such as a partial claim (a low-interest loan from HUD), or modifies the underlying mortgage terms (called "recasting"). A Type II plan will contain all of the elements of a Type I plan, plus it must further do the following:

- Identify the loss mitigation initiative, such as loan modification or partial claim that will be used to cure the default.

- Require a minimum of three monthly payments before the completion of the modification or partial claim.

A HUD office should develop a payment plan that will enable the borrower to pay back the missed payments as soon as possible (given the financial ability of the borrower) and pay off the loan in full. In general, the HUD office will aim for a reduced monthly payment that does not exceed 35 percent of the borrower's net income (after subtracting W-4 withholding taxes and Social Security payments). The length of time to repay the loan can be extended to as much as ten years after the normal maturity date. This way, the extra payments made beyond the normal loan term will compensate for the extra principal and interest that will have to be paid because the borrower failed to make full payments during a period of forbearance. These payments would be at a reduced level.

Forbearance for Service People

Should someone who is dodging missiles, artillery fire, and tanks to defend our country suffer foreclosure at home by a zealous lender? Under the Soldier and Sailor's Relief Act of 1940, amended as the Servicemen's Relief Act, servicepeople who are called to active duty may stop loan payments until three months after they return from service. The period of service is excluded from any calculation of the length of time the loan has been in default.

The wars in Afghanistan and Iraq have put urgency into the FHA's programs to provide forbearance for servicepeople. Reservists who were called to active duty in the Middle East may very well be eligible for military forbearance. However, merely being in the service or being called to active duty does not entitle one to military forbearance.

First, the serviceperson must request forbearance through an application form obtained from the lender. The form should indicate that the serviceperson has suffered a material loss of income as a result of being called into military service. Second, the property must be the serviceperson's primary residence.

Upon approval of the military forbearance application, the interest rate will be limited during the time of active duty. The lender cannot foreclose during this period without court approval. Note, however, that a court may approve a foreclosure unless the serviceperson shows a material loss of income on the order of at least $100 to $200 per month.

Military forbearance is designed for those whose sudden and unexpected military service requirements interfere with the ability to make mortgage payments. Hence, an officer who was already in the military and suffered a divorce or other loss of income unrelated to military service could be denied military forbearance. If it is granted, the lender should inspect the property, check over the income reported by the serviceperson, and put the forbearance agreement to writing.

A big disadvantage of military forbearance comes from the law's provision that the mortgage should be brought current within three months of discharge from military service. This is not enough time, realistically. However, income problems caused by military service would be an excellent justification for additional relief by the lender beyond the strict requirements of the Soldier and Sailor's Relief Act of 1940. During the Persian Gulf War, some lenders actually went so far as to abandon efforts to collect money from servicepeople who were called to active duty in Saudi Arabia, Kuwait, and Iraq. It didn't cost that much, and it made for excellent public relations.

Loan Modification (Recasting)

One workout method, loan modification, involves restructuring the loan, which means altering its terms. Loan modification, sometimes called "recasting," may reduce the interest rate or extend the time over which one repays the loan. Loan modification is not very common. The lender must refuse loan modification or recasting if the borrower has other houses that HUD insures or holds loans on. Recasting requires that the borrower show that the loan default was due to circumstances beyond her control. Some forms of recasting require HUD approval, while others do not.

The borrower must work through the lender to recast the loan. The lender can obtain FHA approval by sending two copies of the loan modification agreement and a letter explaining the reasons for default and the need for an extension of the loan's term if an extension is requested. The lender is responsible for the legal paperwork.

Recasting can be done by either altering the original note and then having the changes initialed by all parties or through a separate loan modification agreement (the better approach). The FHA will not allow the loan's interest rate to be increased. The costs of recasting may not be included in the new loan balance but may be collected separately. Unpaid escrow for taxes and insurance must be handled separately, as well, rather than incorporated into the recast loan.

Besides processing approval, HUD will want a copy of the signed recasting agreement or amended note in case a default on the recast mortgage causes a claim for HUD insurance after the foreclosure. An example of a modified loan agreement is shown in figure 4.6.

Figure 4.5 shows a loan modification checklist.

Figure 4.5 Loan Modification Checklist

_____ Has the borrower experienced a verifiable loss of income or increase in living expenses?

_____ Does the borrower have a commitment to continue to occupy the property as his primary residence?

_____ Did a search of CAIVRS determine that the borrower has no other HUD-insured loans or prior loans on which a claim has been paid in the last three years?

_____ Did the borrower receive the "How to Avoid Foreclosure Brochure"?

_____ Will the loan be more than three months delinquent on the date of execution and funding? (Show number of days.)

_____ If this loan had a prior modification or partial claim within the past three years, can you justify the decision to modify it now?

_____ Did the surplus income analysis to determine the borrower's ability to repay the debt include the following:
    _____ A financial statement provided by the borrower?
    _____ A credit report?
    _____ Income/expense verifications?
    _____ Evidence of the borrower's ability to pay for at least three months?

_____ The borrower's surplus income percentage is _____?

_____ The default cannot be cured through special forbearance because _____?

_____ Has a title search established first lien status of the modified loan?
    _____ Will release of junior liens be required?
    _____ Will title endorsements be required?

_____ Has an inspection determined that the property has no adverse conditions affecting continued occupancy?

_____ Does the written modification agreement executed by the borrower do the following:
    _____ Include all advances necessary to reinstate the principal, interest, taxes, and insurance?
    _____ Exclude all legal and administrative costs?

Figure 4.6   Sample Format for Modification (Recasting Agreement)

FHA CASE NO. _____   Date   _____

This agreement is between the Secretary of Housing and Urban Development (HUD) and
_____, the Borrowers. When used below, the words *I* or *We* refer to the borrower(s)
who signed this Agreement.

A. *Present Situation*
 I understand that:

1. I have signed a mortgage and note, now owned and held by HUD, that pledges my house as security
 for the loan. The mortgage (or Deed of Trust) is recorded in the office for the recording of deeds in
 _____ County, in the State of _____, in book _____ of mortgages, page_____.

2. Because I have failed to make the monthly payments required by my mortgage and note, I now owe
 HUD $_____ in past due interest, taxes, assessments, and service charges.

3. $ _____ of my original loan or principal amount is still outstanding and must be paid to HUD in
 monthly installments.

B. *New Mortgage Payment Requirements*
 Both the Borrower(s) and HUD agree to change the payments required by the present mortgage and note.
 Subject to the conditions in Section C below, I agree to:

1. Pay HUD a "new principal or loan amount" of $_____ plus interest at the rate of percent, the rate
 specified in my original note.

2. I will pay the new principal amount in monthly installments of _____ dollars ($_____). Each
 payment will be due on the first of the month beginning on the first day of _____, 20__, and the final
 payment will be due on 20__, if not sooner paid.

C. *Security*
 I understand and agree that:

1. My mortgage will continue to give HUD a first lien (or claim) upon the property described in the
 mortgage or Deed of Trust referred to in Part A.

2. Except for the changes in Part B, all rights, obligations, and terms of the original mortgage and note will
 remain in full force and are not changed by this agreement.

D. *Signature*
 By signing below, the Borrower(s) and HUD agree to all of the above terms and conditions:

_____   _____
Secretary of HUD   (Date)   Borrower   (Date)

_____   _____
By Director   (Date)   Borrower   (Date)

DEEDS OF TRUST

NOTE: If the security instrument is a Deed of Trust and it is necessary that the Trustee execute recasting
agreements, the following acknowledgment shall be signed by the Trustee:

  The Trustee has executed this instrument to acknowledge his or her (or its) assent thereto and agrees to
continue to act in such capacity under the terms as modified herein.

TRUSTEE: _____

Partial Claim

Under the partial claim procedure, the lender will advance enough money to the borrower to reinstate
a delinquent loan, but only if there are no more than 12 months of missed payments. The borrower
will be asked to sign a note and a subordinate mortgage payable to HUD. Currently, these partial
claim notes do not require interest and do not have to be paid until the borrower pays off the first
mortgage, sells, or otherwise no longer owns the property. After reinstatement, the lender will file a
claim with HUD for reimbursement of the sums advanced and any appropriate incentive fees. The

recorded documents should be sent on to HUD. HUD has a contractor to service the partial claim notes. (Make sure they're paid.)

To do partial claims, the borrower must show long-term financial stability that can pay the regular loan payments, and the borrower can't repay the arrearage through special forbearance or loan modification. To be eligible, the borrower must be at least four payments behind but not more than 12. The loan cannot be in foreclosure when the note is signed, but a lender may remove the loan from foreclosure if the borrower's finances justify using a partial claim procedure. Here's is HUD's checklist of requirements for a partial claim:

_____ Has the borrower experienced a verifiable loss of income or increase in living expenses?

_____ Does the borrower have a commitment to continue to occupy the property as her primary residence?

_____ Did a search of CAIVRS determine that the borrower has no other HUD-insured loans or prior loans on which a claim has been paid within the past three years?

_____ Did the borrower receive the "How to Avoid Foreclosure Brochure"?

_____ Will the loan be more than four months and less than one year delinquent on the date of execution and funding?

_____ If this loan had a prior modification or partial claim within the past three years, can you justify the decision to use a partial claim now? –(You'll be limited to a 12-month total advance.)

_____ Did the surplus income analysis to determine the borrower's ability to repay the debt include:

_____ A financial statement provided by the borrower?

_____ A credit report?

_____ Income/expense verifications?

_____ Evidence of the borrower's ability to pay for at least three months?

_____ What is the borrower's surplus income percentage? (Is it greater than zero percent and less than 17 percent?)

_____ Explain why the default cannot be cured through special forbearance.

_____ Explain why the default cannot be cured through modification.

_____ Has an inspection determined that the property has no adverse conditions affecting continued occupancy?

_____ Will the written partial claim note executed by the borrower do the following:

_____ Fully reinstate the loan?

_____ Not exceed the equivalent of 12 months principal, interest, taxes, and insurance?

_____ Include only one principal, interest, and escrow advances in the note?

Here's an example adapted from a HUD example of a partial claim in action.

> It is April 6, 2000, and the borrower documents a medical emergency that increased his expenses and decreased his income. He can show verification from his employer as to when he will start getting worker's compensation payments, which will include supplemental benefits and will provide him with 90 percent of his former salary for six months during his rehabilitation. His documentation indicates he'll return to his former position, and income, at the end of this rehabilitation period. His income will then be sufficient to meet a full monthly mortgage payment, but it won't be enough to apply any additional sums to the total of the missed payments.

A partial claim is appropriate in this situation because the loan is behind for four payments and, while the borrower can now begin making regular payments, he can't offer any additional sums to apply towards the missing payment total.

CONCLUSION

FHA borrowers are among the most fortunate in terms of having workout choices. At the outset, be sure to scream for HUD counseling. Find a good counselor with whom you can work. The good ones know a lot, and better still, they're free. They can analyze your choices and figure out whether things will be better soon enough and reliably enough to try a workout option and, if so, which one is best. If a workout won't work for you, there are FHA presales and even deed in lieu procedures that can be followed, which are covered in later chapters. Don't give up until you have the answer.

Adjustable-Rate Mortgage Refinancing Programs

5

One the factor in recent downturns in the housing markets in many areas has been the presence of troublesome adjustable-rate mortgage (ARM) loans. ARMs have many advantages in an area with a flush economy, a rising home price structure, and low or falling interest rates. However, even in pretty good times, they can cause trouble, depending on how they are set up.

ARMS: AN OVERVIEW

This segment is for readers who want to gain or at least review the basics of adjustable-rate mortgages. Unlike the 1980s-era variable-rate mortgages (nicknamed "neutron bombs"because they wipe out people but leave houses standing), ARMs were supposed to protect against the old-style variable-rate mortgage (VRM) "payment shock" through sophisticated caps, indexes, margins, and other means. Unlike VRMs, ARMs were not supposed to go up or down in exact lockstep with market rates of interest. Instead, they were supposed to step up by bits or even step down, all against "life of the loan" limits. VRM interest rates could go up as fast as the market, which was sometimes so fast, the borrower couldn't afford the payments. For example, if interest rates doubled, the home payment immediately doubled.

Anytime VRMs (or ARMs) rise to a level that the luckless borrower's income can't handle the resulting payments, a quick default and foreclosure could result. For example, in late 1979 through mid-1980, the prime interest rate went from a 12 percent or so up to 23 percent. That could have doubled a house payment in months, which is too harsh for many borrowers to survive. Market mortgage interest rates have been known to go up as much as 1 percent in a single day.

Old lenders felt protected by VRMs, but they too went under when too many foreclosures occurred. ARMs were developed with protections so that the disasters of the 1980s shouldn't have reoccurred, but ARMs now have big problems. ARM defense mechanisms against payment shock aren't working and, in many cases, have outright failed to prevent payment shock.

ARM DEFENSES AGAINST PAYMENT SHOCK: STRONG AT FIRST GLANCE

ARMS have many advantages and are supposed to protect the borrower in two ways.

Caps

In theory, ARMs are supposed to buffer or limit payment changes that result when interest rates go up or down by means of two types of caps:

1. *Lifetime cap:* The highest rate the mortgage will ever go to, usually about a 5 to 6 percent total increase during the life of the loan. For example, if you start at 8 percent, the maximum you can ever go to is 8 plus 6 or 14 percent (with a 6 percent cap), even if the market goes to 20 percent or beyond.

2. *Period cap:* The highest amount the interest rate can go up in a given period, usually set at six months or one year. If you start at 8 percent, a 1 percent cap would let the rate go up to only 9 percent the first year, no matter how high the market rate went. With a 2 percent cap (which is more common), the rate could go from 8 to 10 percent the first year but no higher.

Indexes

Furthermore, ARMs are supposed to protect borrowers by designating a published, well-known interest rate as the "index" rate; for example, a one-year treasury security interest rate or a federal six-month cost-of-funds (COFI) interest rate. The index rate is usually lower than the market interest for mortgages, so ARMs often employ a margin, which is a set percentage (like 2 percent) that is added to the index rate to get the rate the ARM is actually adjusted by. There may be some variation in calculations, but a weighted-average method of evaluating the interest rate over a six-month or one-year period is commonly used.

ERODING ARM DEFENSES: TEASER RATES, RESET RATES, AND THE ARM MESS

In recent years, lenders have been tinkering with the ARM format in a couple of particulars:

1. The initial interest or "teaser" rate is set very low to aid in the loan qualification process by causing much lower payments

2. The loans reset to a market rate the very first year that may be quite a bit higher than the teaser rate.

Teaser Rate

This is the interest rate used to qualify the borrower. Although the normal market rate might be 6.25 percent, the teaser rate is deliberately set well below the market rate at, say, 4.75 percent to give the borrower a big incentive to take out an ARM. It allows the borrower to buy a much bigger house than her income could otherwise have afforded. In some areas, it was hard to buy a house without an ARM, because homes were priced so high. In theory, the borrower's income was supposed to have a capacity to rise; in practice, this criterion tended to be much neglected.

Let's look at an example:

> For a $210,000 house, our borrower puts $10,000 down and takes out a $200,000 loan. On a $200,000 fixed-rate loan, at a 4.75 percent interest rate (the teaser rate), for 30 years, the monthly principal and interest (P&I) payment is $1,039/month. Adding 2 percent in property taxes and $1,800 a year in home insurance, the monthly P&I + tax ($350) + insurance ($150) = $1,539.00 a month. At a conservative 29 percent of income, we need an income of $5,306 a month to buy this house.

Reset Rate

Suppose the market rate of interest for this particular buyer, given his rather spotty credit history, goes up from the date of the original loan to 8 percent. The borrower's interest is now reset after the first year from 4.75 percent to the full, regular market interest rate for a person of that credit rating of 8 percent.

> Recompute: On our $200,000 loan at 8 percent interest for 30 years, the monthly principal and interest (P&I) payment is $1,458. Now adding in 2 percent taxes and $1,800 a year for insurance, the monthly P&I + tax ($350) + insurance ($150) = $1,939.00 a month. At a conservative 29 percent of income, we need $6,758 a month to buy this house with a $200,000 loan and $10,000 down. That's $1,452 more a month in income needed to afford this home.

DEFAULT AND FORECLOSURE DUE TO THE INITIAL ARM RESET

The problem on many ARMs is that resetting the rate from the initial teaser rate used to qualify the borrower to a full-fledged market rate at the borrower's marginal credit rating is likely to overwhelm the borrower financially and directly cause a foreclosure. If payments skyrocket from $5,300 a month to nearly $6,800 a month, many borrowers just won't have the extra income to pay them. This is particularly so if the borrower engaged in a pattern of credit card shopping for home furnishings and improvements right after the main purchase of the house.

FIXED-RATE LOANS AS REPLACEMENTS FOR ARMS

The solution many borrowers seek to solve the problem of the ARM reset is to refinance, thereby replacing the skyrocketing ARM loan with a fixed-interest-rate, fixed-payment loan. The problem with this strategy is that the ARM was obtained when market rates of interest were a little lower. The borrower's credit may have declined a little due to factors other than the ARM payments in the meantime. As such, refinancing at a current market interest rate for a fixed-rate loan for the borrower's credit rating may not work all that well, because the payments will not be much better than what the ARM will reset to. Even if there was a step or cap built in to buffer the shock from, say, an interest rate shift from 4.75 to 8 percent, any new refinance loan would still be at current market rates for the borrower's current credit rating.

FACTORS INCREASING THE VALUE OF REFINANCING TO DEAL WITH AN ARM RESET

A few factors might increase the desirability of refinancing an ARM as a fixed-rate mortgage:

1. Was the ARM set up with any negative amortization? That is, did the lender set up the loan to increase its balance due to the insufficiency of the teaser rate? If so, then refinancing to a fixed-rate loan may prevent the negative ARM from getting any bigger, at some cost in refinancing closing charges.

2. Has the home's value gone up significantly since the initial ARM loan? If so, then a quick refinance may be advisable, because the equity the increased value has put into the property may offset the borrower's credit rating, which could result in a lower interest rate for the borrower. Of course, if the ARM is set up to rerate the borrower's credit and, therefore, the interest rate at the time of the reset, there wouldn't be as much advantage to this approach.

3. Does the borrower anticipate that interest rates will increase in the future, causing the ARM's rate to increase more? If so, then refinancing to preserve today's market rate is advisable.

Convert Feature

Some ARMs have a convert feature built in. Be sure to check for it, and if you can, exercise it. Using the convert feature means far less cost and trouble than going through a refinancing process in today's steadily worsening credit market.

Regular Refinancing Obstacles

Many ARM borrowers would gladly refinance, but they can't because (1) their credit was adversely affected by being unable to keep up with their ARM's reset and, therefore, much higher house payments and (2) in a tightening credit market, it's often difficult to obtain ARM refinancing into fixed-rate loans, at least through normal refinancing procedures.

WILL THE LENDER FOLLOW NORMAL REFINANCING PROCEDURES?

Lenders in a declining market may give ground on some of the issues that would normally stop or at least eliminate much of the advantage the borrower is trying to achieve through refinancing an ARM. If the lender doesn't give ground, the ARM could not only go into default but wind up in foreclosure, giving the lender yet another bad loan on record. Even if the mortgage servicer is not very sensitive to the borrower's plight, the loan owner and insurer probably are. They may provide the requisite authority behind the scenes to help the borrower by doing the following:

- Allowing a short payoff and/or a second lien to replace the shortfall
- Judging the borrower's credit in the light of the hardship of the ARM reset

On a regular loan, such concessions may or may not be forthcoming, but on an FHASecure, exactly these sorts of concessions can be made. Here's the program in detail.

THE FHASECURE ARM REFINANCE LOAN FOR NON-FHA LOANS

In late summer 2007, the FHA came out with its FHASecure refinance loan. This loan is not intended to refinance existing FHA loans but rather to refinance non-FHA ARM loans into fixed-rate loans. According to some estimates, more than 80,000 of some 1.9 million borrowers affected by ARM resets may be helped by FHASecure. In addition, one suspects that more help will be on the way soon. If borrowers can hang on long enough, a program may yet turn up that can aid them. FHASecure loan limits may be raised to nearly $700,000 shortly. Stay tuned.

FHASecure Requirements

The borrower's declining credit rating must have been directly caused by the higher payments after the first reset of an ARM. Therefore, the first reset must have occurred, and the borrower must otherwise have good credit.

The FHA has issued a "mortgagee letter" that details the qualification guidelines of the FHASecure loan program. The guidelines are reprinted here, and their impact is analyzed in comments after each section.

Here is what the FHA guidelines say concerning FHASecure:

Quote 1:
The Federal Housing Administration is pleased to announce an initiative that will enable homeowners to refinance various types of adjustable rate mortgages (ARMs) that have recently "reset." This mortgagee letter describes how lenders and homeowners may refinance mortgages that, due to the increased mortgage payment following the reset, have become delinquent. The mortgagee letter also reiterates guidance to lenders about making objective decisions regarding the underlying collateral in declining markets. The FHASecure initiative, which is a temporary program designed to provide refinancing opportunities to homeowners and to increase liquidity in the mortgage market, requires that the loan application be signed no later than December 31, 2008. This may be extended.

Comments:
- *Reset:* The borrower's ARM loan must have "recently" reset—that is, gone up from the initial teaser rate. *Recently* is not defined.
- *Reset caused delinquency:* The increased payment after the reset caused the borrower to become delinquent in making monthly mortgage payments.
- *Objective appraisal needed:* The FHA warns lenders to be objective regarding the appraised value of the home for the FHASecure program.
- *Deadline to apply:* The loan application for an FHA Secure loan must be signed no later than December 31, 2008.

Quote 2:
Refinancing Non-FHA Adjustable Rate Mortgages Following Resets:
FHA is currently doing a significant business in refinancing non-FHA mortgages for borrowers who are current under their existing mortgage. This mortgagee letter extends eligibility to borrowers who became delinquent under their current mortgage following the reset of the interest rate.

Comments: The FHA is clearly willing to extend refinancing credit to borrowers who have become delinquent after a reset. This would not be so under normal refinancing procedures with most lenders. They would look at the regular history.

Quote 3:
FHA recognizes that many lenders are engaged in a variety of loss mitigation activities to keep borrowers in their homes, and it applauds these efforts. This mortgagee letter explains credit policies for refinance transactions involving non-FHA adjustable rate mortgages where the homeowner's mortgage payment history during the six months prior to the reset showed no instances of making mortgage payments outside the month due.

Comments:
- *FHASecure is only for non-FHA loans:* Even though the FHASecure loan program is run by the FHA, it deals only and explicitly with non-FHA adjustable-rate mortgages.
- *Six months of no late payments:* Ouch! The borrower must have a perfect monthly payment record on the loan for six months prior to the ARM reset.

Quote 4:
These instructions are designed to permit homeowners, who, previous to their reset, demonstrated an ability to meet their mortgage obligations, an opportunity to refinance into a prime-rate FHA-insured mortgage. In many cases homeowners may be permitted to include mortgage payment arrearages into the new loan amount, subject to existing geographical mortgage limits and the loan-to-value limit shown below.

Comments:

- *Prime-rate FHA loan:* There is a large potential benefit here in that a borrower whose credit would not, under normal loan guidelines, justify a prime-rate loan, can nevertheless bootstrap into a prime-rate loan by having made six months of on-time loan payments before the ARM reset. This means the borrower might be looking at a 6 to 7 percent interest prime-rate loan rather than what the borrower's credit would otherwise have qualified him for. This could actually lower the loan payment significantly.

Quote 5:
Eligibility Highlights of the FHASecure Initiative:

The mortgage being refinanced must be a non-FHA ARM that has reset.

The mortgagor's payment history on the non-FHA ARM must show that, prior to the reset of the mortgage, the mortgagor was current in making the monthly mortgage payments; i.e., the homeowner's mortgage payment history during the six months prior to the reset showed no instances of making mortgage payments outside the month due.

If there is sufficient equity in the home, under additional eligibility instructions provided below, FHA will insure mortgages that include missed mortgage payments.

Comments: FHASecure allows the loan balance against the house to increase to include missed mortgage payments, *if* the new loan balance is still a little below the current appraised value by prudent appraisal standards.

Quote 6:
Under certain conditions explained below, FHA will insure first mortgages where (1) the existing note holder writes off the amount of indebtedness that cannot be refinanced into the FHA-insured mortgage; or (2) either the FHA-approved lender making the new mortgage or the existing note holder may take back a second lien that includes closing costs, arrearages, or previous secondary financing if the indebtedness exceeds FHA-prescribed LTV and maximum mortgage amount limits.

Comments: This is big, really big. It's a combination of short payoff plus refinance. This is potentially a very powerful tool. If the borrower's income isn't quite large enough and the value of the house isn't quite high enough, even with a new prime-rate FHA-insured loan, to make the payments on the ARM loan balance after the big initial reset, then by pruning off the excess dollars and cutting the loan down to a size the borrower's income can handle, refinancing with an FHASecure will really give borrowers an advantage.

However, under (2) above, the FHA-approved lender that made the original ARM loan can "take back a second lien" that includes closing costs, arrearages, or previous secondary (extra loan) financing if the total loan amount that results is beyond the limit of the loan size the FHA can insure for at the new interest rate and for the borrower's income under the FHA's regular maximum loan to value (LTV) ratios (See page 58) and maximum mortgage amount limits (these vary by location and must be checked on the FHA's website, *www.fha.gov*). An unanswered question here is whether the second lien that is "taken back" would or could be FHA insured to the original ARM lender if the borrower defaulted on the FHASecure loan. One suspects not, since no program seems to cover this for non-FHA loans.

Quote 7:

Mortgagees must determine, as part of the underwriting process, that the reset of the non-FHA ARM monthly payments caused the mortgagor's inability to make the monthly payments and that the mortgagor has sufficient income and resources to make the monthly payments under the new FHA-insured refinancing mortgage.

Comments:

- *ARM reset caused default:* The lender undertaking an FHASecure loan to refinance an ARM must determine if the reset of the ARM caused the borrower to default on the monthly payments. In many cases, such as a tantalizing 4.75 percent teaser rate morphing into an 8 percent budget-busting rate in the first year, the causation is pretty easy to see. However, causation is not well defined. The presence of substantial additional credit card or other debt could be a very significant factor to the underwriter here. A borrower is well advised to shop carefully for an FHASecure lender.

- *Borrowers need enough income to pay the new loan:* The FHASecure loan requires the borrower to have sufficient income and resources to make the monthly payments under the new loan. However, that might not be as bad as it sounds. Here's why: (1) if the borrower got a better interest rate, that would chop down the payment size; and (2) if the borrower, in a pinch, got the loan "cut down to size" through a short payoff, the new FHASecure loan may well be affordable—much more so than the old payment and more so than a more normal ARM refinance. The FHA will use its regular income and percentage guidelines to determine if the borrower has the ability to repay.

- FHASecure benefits versus reset ARM rate: Instead of a 4.75 percent teaser rate going to an 8 percent market rate in 1 year (8% – 4.75% = 3.25% difference), FHASecure cuts it to, say, a 6.75 percent prime rate (6.75% – 4.75% = 2.0% difference). The reduction of 1.25 percent below the looming 8 percent rate means that the monthly loan payment drops 40 percent.

- FHASecure benefits due to short payoff: If the loan balance is $100,000 upon reset and the short payoff amount is $15,000, the result will be a reduction of 15 percent in the monthly loan payment (P&I).

- Benefits of a carry-back second lien: This is analyzed in detail further on.

Quote 8:

Loan to Value is the percentage the loan is of the home's value. For example: A $90,000 loan on a $100,000 value home creates a 90% Loan-to-Value Ratio.

Maximum FHA loan-to-value ratios: The maximum loan-to-value limits are shown below and are applied to the appraiser's estimate of value, exclusive of any upfront mortgage insurance premium.

MAXIMUM LOAN TO VALUE RATIOS

States with average closing costs at or below 2.1 percent of sales price:
- 98.75 percent: For properties with appraised values equal to or less than $50,000
- 97.65 percent: For properties with appraised values in excess of $50,000 up to $125,000
- 97.15 percent: For properties with appraised values in excess of $125,000

States with average closings costs above 2.1 percent of sales price:
- 98.75 percent: For properties with appraised values equal to or less than $50,000
- 97.75 percent: For properties with appraised values in excess of $50,000

RECENT LAW 2008– These Ratios May Go To 100%
Size Limits Are Raised to $729,750 in high cost areas

Quote 9:

Calculating the Maximum FHA Mortgage Amount:

The amount of the FHASecure mortgage may not exceed either the geographical maximum mortgage limits or the loan-to-value ratios shown above. FHA will permit the inclusion of the existing first lien, any purchase money second mortgage, closing costs, prepaid expenses, discount points, prepayment penalties, and late charges. FHA will also permit arrearages (principal, interest, taxes, and insurance) to be added into the new loan amount provided the arrearages arose after the reset.

Comments:

- *FHA loans aren't big enough:* The FHASecure program's biggest weakness may be that FHA loans just aren't big enough to refinance many non-FHA ARM loans that are in desperate need of refinancing. The FHA has mortgage loan limits that vary depending on what part of the United States the property is in. These limits may be viewed on the FHA's website (*www.fha.gov*). These loan limits are based on an area's median income. Unfortunately, no small part of the mortgage market meltdown is in the very areas where home prices are very high—often well above what the average borrower can afford and, therefore, above the FHA limits. In fact, it was to buy these expensive homes that many borrowers entered into shaky ARM arrangements.

- *A fix may be in the works:* Efforts are underway to raise the ceiling on loans for the FHASecure program. Congress is authorizing changes.

- *Everything but the kitchen sink:* The FHASecure program allows the existing first lien, any second that was part of the home's purchase—as opposed to an equity loan for cash—along with the costs of the refinance program and even post-ARM reset missed payment amounts to be added into the new FHASecure refinance loan.

Quote 10:

Subordinate Financing Under the FHASecure Initiative

If the new maximum FHA loan is not enough to pay off the existing first lien, closing costs, and arrearages, the lender may execute a second lien at closing to pay the difference. The combined amount of the FHASecure first mortgage and any subordinate non-FHA insured lien may exceed the applicable FHA loan-to-value ratio and geographical maximum mortgage amount. If payments on the second are required, they must be included in qualifying the borrower. If payments are deferred, they must be so for no less than 36 months to not be considered in the qualifying ratios. Borrowers need not yet have missed any mortgage payments to be eligible for this type of subordinate financing.

Comments:

- The second mortgage plus expenses and arrearages can exceed the FHA maximum loan amount: This feature is powerful. A sizable second loan could take significant chunks of the principal balance on a floundering ARM loan and add them to the maximum loan amount FHA allows for the geographical area, without breaking the upper total loan amount limit. This is highly useful in high price areas.

- Postponing the inevitable by 36 months? It would no doubt very much help borrowers under an FHASecure loan to be able to defer payments on a second loan for over 36 months to avoid their inclusion in the borrower's debt-qualifying ratios. A big second mortgage, if lifted out of the payment qualification ratios, would help many borrowers qualify for FHASecure refinancing. However, what will happen in 36 months when the second loan's payments start coming due in addition to the first loan's? Unless the borrower's income rises enough in the three-year interim to handle the increased home payments, an FHASecure loan may only postpone the inevitable default and foreclosure. No doubt underwriters will look for indications that the borrower's income will rise in the next three years if a 36-month deferred second loan is used.

Quote 11:

Underwriting the Mortgage/Qualifying the Borrower:

FHA encourages all approved lenders to use FHA's TOTAL Mortgage Scorecard to obtain risk classifications on each mortgage originated under the FHASecure initiative. If TOTAL renders an "accept/approve," the mortgagee's underwriter need not perform a personal review of the borrower's credit history and capacity to repay. However, in the more likely event that the risk class is a "refer," the underwriter must:

- Determine that the homeowner has the capacity to make future mortgage payments as well as pay all other obligations. The payment-to-income ratio and debt-to-income ratios remain 31 percent and 43 percent, respectively. Compensating factors are to be provided by the underwriter when the ratios are exceeded.

- Analyze the homeowner's overall credit history, especially payments on the existing mortgage. The underwriter must determine that the homeowner's mortgage payment history during the six months prior to the reset showed no instances of making mortgage payments outside the month due and that other recurring obligations were paid on time. If the borrower was offered partial forbearance after interest rate reset, the underwriter must determine that he or she has made payments under the forbearance agreement in a timely manner.

- Provide comments in the "remarks" section of the mortgage credit analysis worksheet that he or she has determined that the cause of the borrower's inability to make payments was directly related to the increased payment attributable to the reset and not due to a disregard for obligations.

Comments:

The guidelines are above are fairly clear as written.

- *The 31 percent ratio:* This is the "front-end" ratio, meaning the new FHASecure loan's total monthly payment, composed of principal, interest, taxes and insurance (PITI), cannot exceed 31 percent of the borrower's gross monthly income (not take-home pay but pre-tax and deduction pay). The 43 percent "back-end ratio" refers to the total of all fixed debt payments, including the PITI on the FHASecure loan. The usual FHA details for determining what counts as a fixed debt payment, such as a car payment, insurance payments, personal loan payments and so on, all count.

- *Compensating factors:* A borrower who is self-employed may have many deductions against income that lower it for tax purposes. Some of these deductions may not be cash items, and this may serve as a compensating factor. A strong income growth pattern also may be a compensating factor, as might be one-time medical expenses.

- *Payment history:* Perfect payment history in the six months before the ARM reset is required. This may be a tough requirement for some borrowers to meet.

- *Disregard for the obligation:* Borrowers should always try to show a history of making payments, establishing that the reset mortgage broke the borrower's back and caused missed payments. Lender's dislike evidence of "disregard for the obligation."

Quote 13:
FHA recognizes that there may be tax consequences resulting from debt relief. However, since FHA does not provide tax guidance, it recommends borrowers—and mortgage lenders—in such situations seek competent tax advice.

Comments: This is addressed elsewhere in the book. Unless the borrower is discharged in a short payoff, most likely, there will be no tax consequences. Again, see the later chapter of the book on the consequences of foreclosure.

Quote 14:
The FHASecure initiative for refinancing borrowers harmed by non-FHA ARMs that have recently reset is not to be used to solicit homeowners to cease making timely mortgage payments; FHA reserves the right to reject for insurance those mortgage applications where it appears that a loan officer or other mortgagee employee suggested that the homeowners could stop making their payments, refinance into a FHA-insured mortgage, and keep, as cash, the amount of payments not made on time.

Comments:
- FHA does not want lenders to induce missed payments to hustle more business under the FHASecure program.

- It may not be easy to stop making payments and keep the missed payments in cash. In the past, FHA lenders have routinely surveyed bank accounts. If the borrower has regular income, the underwriter will no doubt see the bank statements. If the borrower suddenly quit using income to make payments and obviously increased other expenditures to use up the cash that otherwise normally went to the mortgage, this activity would stand out like a red flag—evidence that the borrower, and perhaps the loan officer, are up to no good and unnecessarily defaulting. If so, the loan will be denied.

GNMA WILL BUY THE LOANS

The FHASecure program will generate new fixed-interest, fixed-payment loans, but with some interesting features connected to them, such as borrowers who don't meet conventional guidelines for qualification. Ordinarily, when such loans are sold on the secondary market, the secondary market loan buyer would use them as the security for a "mortgage-backed security," which would be sold to investors. If the loans backing such mortgage-backed securities are suspect, the securities won't sell. No matter though, for the FHA. The Government National Mortgage Association (GNMA, or Ginnie Mae) has agreed to buy the loans. It can affix a powerful government-backed guarantee to the mortgage-backed securities it issues and this results in a lower interest rate, which can be passed back to the borrower as a lower interest rate on the loan. Further, the mortgage-backed security, despite its drawbacks, will sell. The problem: If the government starts to guarantee loan pools, particularly the securities are offered with the full faith and credit of the U.S. government behind them, then these guarantees will affect the overall U.S. debt, which can generate some additional problems—costs—for the U.S. government's own financing.

FIXED-RATE LOANS VERSUS ARMS

The typical borrower dislikes the ARM concept. The typical borrower wants a fixed-interest, fixed-payment mortgage for which the principal and interest payment (excluding taxes and insurance) will never change for the life of the loan, which may be as many as 30 years.

On the other hand, lenders love ARMs because these mortgages give them a wider margin of error when they estimate future interest rates. Lenders will therefore give lower rates of interest for ARM loans than for fixed interest, fixed payment loans, because if the interest is set too low to begin with and needs to be more in the future, the ARM mechanism will allow for an increase.

Historically, ARMs have done well. For the last two decades, interest rates have stayed remarkably stable and have even fallen, making an ARM a good bet. Lenders typically qualify a borrower at the lower rate of interest, which means that for a given income, a family can get a larger loan, and a larger house, with an ARM than it could with a fixed-rate loan. And so the potential for trouble begins....

On the other hand, borrowers with a short time frame, such as a corporate-relocated person who knew he would stay in a house only three years, might use an ARM teaser rate to knock down the first year's payment well below what it would have been, then use period caps to limit the rise by, say, 1 percent a year for the next two years. In this scenario, the borrower might have an interest rate well below market the first year, at market the second, and only 1 percent above the third year. Then the homeowner would refinance or sell. This approach was profitable and easy.

Likewise, the author can recall the story of a borrower who started at 13 percent on an ARM and was unhappy, because a "lucky" friend had gotten a 14 percent fixed-rate loan. The interest then went down to 8 percent on the ARM, the borrower used a convert feature to turn it into a fixed-rate, fixed-payment loan, and the 14 percent fixed-rate borrower couldn't handle the payments and was foreclosed on.

Mortgage Meltdown

ARMs are in trouble in part because of the very high home prices in some areas and the unfortunate use of ARMs to buy houses that are arguably beyond the means of the borrower. Some say lenders were just greedy. Massachusetts has passed a law against making loans that a lender should know payment is not realistic. (Presumably few lenders will think they violated it.) In any event, in the recent past, the profit in lending was in making the loan and selling it (with lots of fees and premium points), and no one seemed to care if it didn't work—the loan was sold to someone else.

Sometimes, borrowers contend they didn't know the whole story or were sweet-talked, but one thinks many were probably a little too willing to participate. Perhaps they assumed their incomes would rise or the home would go up and could be resold at a big profit to use as a down payment on a more reasonable house. Or perhaps they planned to refinance at a lower-interest–rate, fixed-rate mortgage (particularly if their credit rating improved). Whatever the reasoning (or lack thereof), a lot of ARM borrowers are now facing default and foreclosure, and FHASecure is one of the best cards in the deck to play right now.

Hope How Initiative

Under the "Hope Now" private initiative, nearly 65% of all loan servers and 85% of the sub prime market lenders will take measures to fight a potential tsunami of 1.8 million foreclosures that might otherwise occur in 2008 and 2009 due to ARM loan resets. Lenders plan to contact borrowers 120 days before ARM interest rates reset to identify potential foreclosure problems early on and take preventive measures before the loans even default. Since traditional case by case handling of loan defaults could be overwhelmed by the vast number of ARM cases that will occur, "fast track" procedures will be used instead. Probably sophisticated computer programs will analyze each borrowers' data, such as credit history, loan payment record, home value, market conditions and then propose a plan to deal with the situation one of three ways: (1) refinance the loan by regular means; (2) use the FHA Secure program, or possibly (3) freeze the initial interest rate for five years. Up to 1.2 million borrowers will be helped. One only hopes that lenders will be reluctant to pigeonhole cases as hopeless and foreclose, but there appear to be no real guarantees at this point. FHA Secure is still one of the best shots.

VA Workouts and Compromise Sales

6

This chapter is designed to give the veteran who is having trouble making payments on a home an overview of the many programs offered by the Department of Veteran Affairs (VA) to help distressed veteran borrowers. First, remember that VA loans are a benefit program designed to repay veterans for their service to the country. As a practical matter, however, the VA was created and is supported by veterans, not lenders.

Private lenders who make VA-guaranteed loans must follow the VA's administrative rules. The veteran should make every reasonable effort to deal with the private lender when a problem prevents making payments on a VA loan. Still, he should not hesitate to contact the VA directly for better treatment. A trip to the nearest VA office can reap direct, face-to-face assistance. If the VA office is not helping to make a lender more cooperative, the veteran should call her congressional representative and senators. Sometimes they can get the VA moving to help deal with the lender when nothing else works. Direct VA help is called "supplemental servicing." The VA is trying to decrease the emphasis on this approach, but it's still there. This arm of the government is set up to benefit veterans.

The VA has many procedures to assist distressed veterans who have trouble paying on a loan it guarantees. Under the proper circumstances, veterans may ask for lender forbearance, in which the lender accepts less than the full monthly house payment for a limited period. In addition, the veteran may ask for the modification of a loan, including refinancing at a lower rate of interest. With VA approval, a veteran may be able to arrange a compromise sale agreement in which the VA may subsidize part of the loss when the veteran must sell a house for less than the balance due on the loan.

Lenders must service VA loans according to certain procedures. Although the lender's failure to comply with these procedures won't invalidate a foreclosure, the veteran can benefit from bringing the lender's nonconformance to the attention of the VA before foreclosure.

VA loans are governed by the regulations of the Department of Veterans Affairs. Those regulations restrict a lender's power to foreclose on a home for nonpayment. A lender that ignores the VA's restrictions may not be able to collect on the VA's guarantee. Technically, of course, if the lender is willing to lose out on the VA's guarantee, it can ignore the VA's restrictions. Understandably, few lenders do so. Besides having procedures for when the borrower misses payments, the VA regulates the types of special relief that lenders, or the VA itself, may offer to distressed borrowers.

DEFAULT

If a VA loan falls into default, the private lender must report this fact to the VA on its form 26-6850a, called a "Notice of Default (NOD)." The VA must receive this form within 105 days of the first uncured default. Failure to report the default within that time could lead to a reduction in loss coverage by the VA if the loan goes into foreclosure. Therefore, the borrower should expect significant lender activity near the 105-day mark. Some borrowers are lulled by the relative inactivity of the lender after they've missed a payment, but an alert lender will not wait long before contacting the borrower. The borrower can contact the VA for help at any time after missing payments. A lender has an obligation to keep the VA up-to-date through the use of several reporting forms.

Supplemental Servicing

If the borrower meets resistance from the lender, she should ask for supplemental servicing, which means the VA will try to work with the borrower directly. The nearest VA regional office will perform supplemental servicing to make sure that each veteran borrower has the maximum opportunity to continue as a homeowner during tough times. Besides helping borrowers keep their houses, this effort minimizes the VA's loss from foreclosure. The VA is now trying to improve its computer capabilities substantially. Better loan service and claims programming will help expedite the VA's monitoring of loan defaults. Once it receives the Notice of Default, the VA will review the notice and assign a loan service representative (LSR) to determine if added servicing can help. As part of this effort, the VA will intervene with the lender, if necessary.

A VA loan service representative reviews the Notice of Default in detail. If early payment of the default appears improbable, the LSR tries to contact the borrower to provide the maximum assistance possible. The LSR asks the borrower for pertinent information, such as the reason for default and the probability of a cure in light of his domestic and financial status. The LSR tells the borrower about the various relief measures that are available and asks her to contact the lender to work out a solution to cure the default.

The borrower should try to work with the VA as much as possible. The VA can effectively force the lender to stop or delay a foreclosure as a condition of honoring its guarantee of the loan. If the borrower can document any lender violations of VA guidelines, he should report the fact to the VA, since this may serve as an excuse to delay foreclosure. The borrower should keep a record of what the lender does and doesn't do, at all times.

When the VA determines that the borrower can cure the default but cannot reach an agreement with the lender, the loan service representative will contact the lender to discuss the appropriateness of the borrower's proposal. The VA often views borrowers' proposals leniently. To protect itself, the lender may ask the VA for a written commitment that failure to adhere to the terms of the borrower's proposal will constitute grounds for an automatic foreclosure. Without this assurance, the lender may fear that the pattern will repeat itself.

VA SERVICING REQUIREMENTS

Most of this chapter applies to veterans who are having problems making payments on their house loans. Once a veteran borrower misses a payment, the lender that services the loan must make a preliminary effort to contact the borrower and analyze the situation before attempting to foreclose.

VA servicing guidelines call on lenders to try to communicate with the borrower in at least four ways before any foreclosure:

1. Letters
2. Phone calls

3. Face-to-face financial counseling

4. Field visits

The VA particularly likes phone calls. The veteran borrower should make a note of the date, time, caller's name, and substance of every phone conversation. At a later date, an issue may arise as to whether or not the lender was able to call and talk to the borrower. The veteran is better off to take the phone calls and discuss the problem than to avoid talking to the lender.

Know Your Rights

The worst thing to do after default is to give up hope. The VA is very supportive of the veteran borrower. If a lender simply starts a foreclosure without making a determined effort to contact and work with the veteran borrower, it is not servicing the loan as required by the VA. The veteran should read the remainder of this chapter to see which, if any, of the VA's many programs and procedures could apply in her situation.

VA Time Schedule

The veteran who misses a payment should expect communication from the lender according to the schedule in figure 6.1.

The borrower should answer every letter and phone call and absolutely insist on a face-to-face meeting before foreclosure. This allows the veteran to explore the full extent of any options to foreclosure that may remain.

If a reduced payment schedule or lower interest rate will not solve the problem, the veteran should try to sell the house. Even if the house is worth less than what is owed against it, the VA's compromise sale plan may be able to subsidize some of the loss and permit a sale. Anything is better than nothing, and the borrower must communicate to get results.

Figure 6.1 VA Loan Foreclosure Schedule

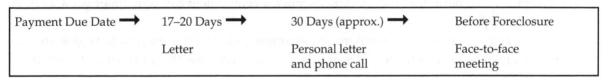

Payment Due Date ➡	17–20 Days ➡	30 Days (approx.) ➡	Before Foreclosure
	Letter	Personal letter and phone call	Face-to-face meeting

Letters

The veteran borrower who misses a payment on a VA loan should expect the lender to drop a letter in the mail within 20 days after the payment is missed. The letter should contain one or more of the following notices: (1) a notice of delinquency and request for payment; (2) a request for a personal interview between the lender's representative and the borrower; (3) a return of any checks sent by the borrower in the later stages of default (later we will review the circumstances under which the lender can return the borrower's checks uncashed); (4) an attempt to make a deal with the borrower (this can be confirmed later over the phone or by written agreement); (5) a reminder emphasizing the need to keep up the loan payments.

The VA wants letters to be worded to meet the particular circumstances of the borrower's loan. The letter should be prepared manually or by word processor. The borrower should be sure to keep a copy of any standard, computer-generated form letter and complain to the VA if the lender forecloses in a mechanical fashion without really trying to resolve the veteran's problems. The veteran should expect the lender to send a personal letter by the thirtieth day after a payment is missed.

Phone Calls

The VA wants its lenders to call borrowers about missed payments. It regards phone calls as the first and best method of communication when a borrower misses payments. The VA emphasizes proper telephone technique and thorough preparation before calling. The caller should have all pertinent information ready, as should the borrower. Sometimes the lender doesn't have all the facts straight, and the borrower should be prepared to correct any obvious errors. Once again, borrowers should keep logs of their conversations with any lender representatives. Never let the lender's representatives say they attempted to call unsuccessfully.

VA callers must let the phone ring at least eight times before giving up on a call. According to the VA's manuals, callers should speak slowly and distinctly. A borrower should ask any fast talkers to slow down and explain matters carefully. If the caller won't slow down, make a note of the date, time, and caller. The VA's callers should be able to deal with borrowers who, according to the VA, "think slowly." Don't let any lender push you to go any faster than you can or want to. The call should be a conversation, not a lecture. The caller should be willing to consider your responses.

Lenders' callers are supposed to be positive and persuasive. The veteran borrower should not accept the word of a caller who insists that nothing can be done about a foreclosure. This is not true. A homeowner should make sure the caller explains the VA's programs to avoid foreclosure.

Some lender representatives will try to railroad the borrower into a foreclosure so the lender can recover its losses from the VA without concern for the borrower. A borrower should never accept such an attitude.

The VA manuals recommend that the person calling for the lender "maintain control" over the conversation. The veteran borrower should resist this effort unless the call is meeting his needs. Never be discourteous but do be assertive. If the lender's caller is discourteous or rude, make a note of the caller's attitude in your log with the caller's name, of course, and be prepared to complain about this treatment to the VA. If a particular caller is easier to talk to or seems to be more cooperative, get that caller's name and phone number and try to deal with him as much as possible. Even better, write the caller a complimentary letter and send copies to his boss and the VA; be sure to note that you sent copies at the bottom of the letter. Remember, a compliment can sometimes get a lot more results than a complaint.

If you can catch a lender's caller making any errors or giving advice she shouldn't give, such as, "Give up—it's hopeless," then make a note of it. Later on, you can use the information to embarrass the lender when you deal directly with the VA.

Face-to-Face Financial Counseling

VA policy states that the borrower should have a face-to-face meeting with a lender representative. The purpose of the meeting is to discover the reason for the default, the borrower's intentions, and what can be done about the situation. The borrower should be prepared with information similar to that used to obtain the loan in the first place, including summaries of income and job prospects. The borrower should present information with a view to developing a workable plan of action, either to catch up payments or to arrange a sale with the VA's assistance. The borrower should be ready to discuss several kinds of information.

- **Net monthly income**: The borrower's current income from regular, steady sources or recurring overtime is important. This determines her basic ability to make payments.
- **Monthly expenditures:** The borrower should keep track of expenses, such as child support, car payments, or any other fixed loan payments. The borrower should have a budget to show what happens to the rest of the money. A good lender representative should try to detail expenses, both as they are and as they might be, showing possible reductions in expenses

on clothing, furniture, utilities, gas, entertainment, and spending money. The borrower should go through this exercise with the lender, both for self-review and to be sure the lender understands the borrower's situation. Options for forbearance (reduced payments) or help selling the house critically depend on the borrower's capacity to make payments.

- **Debts:** List all debts, including loans, department store charge accounts, credit cards, installment contracts, and insurance premiums. Fixed expenditures are particularly deadly to workout arrangements. For credit card balances, the minimum due each month should be considered. If the borrower pays off these balances every month, the payments aren't really a fixed expense.

   A lender will also consider lines of credit on cards that are not currently being used. The potential for future debt will concern the lender. The borrower may want to cut up and return cards that he doesn't need or plan to use as a demonstration of a serious desire to improve the situation. It doesn't make much real difference, but a little psychological warfare can help the cause. Sometimes lenders demand that borrowers cut up cards and return them—why not play the game in reverse?

- **Repairs:** List needed repairs and estimate their cost. Deferred maintenance, or needed repairs that haven't been made, have an unpredictable impact on the lender. Clearly a house that's in poor shape will be hard to resell if the lender forecloses. On the other hand, the lender knows that a borrower who can't make critically needed repairs may be forced to abandon the property. Perhaps the key is to assure the lender that the borrower will not likely move out due to the lack of repairs and that he will make repairs that can prevent further damage. However, there's no need to put the property in condition to be easily shown and sold unless that is the borrower's intention.

- **Assets:** The borrower should list all available assets. One problem when preparing a list of assets for a lender, particularly when the lender requests it, is that we don't know what the lender will use it for. It could be used constructively, to judge whether assets could help to buy time to get either a new job or a good sale. On the other hand, some lenders may want the list solely to aid their collection of funds due after foreclosure or as part of their foreclosure process. A borrower should try to size up the lender's sincerity and willingness to help. If the lender is hostile and uncooperative and no help appears to be forthcoming from the VA, the borrower is at risk. Certainly by this time, if not before, the borrower should seek the services of an attorney.

   With those warnings in mind, the borrower should consider the lender's request to list assets. An easily resold boat or other asset could generate cash to tide the borrower over between jobs or to help reduce the loss from a regular sale of the house to avoid a foreclosure. The key question about assets is, can they be turned into cash? Cars to which the buyer has clear title, land, bank accounts, and retirement funds are all worth consideration. Remember, too, that life insurance may have a cash value.

Once all the information is gathered and analyzed, it will help the borrower and the lender, make decisions about what must be done. If it looks as though things will get better, the borrower should sell assets and seek a reduction in payments. If not, then the assets might be sold to raise cash to help sell a house in a down market. If the house can be sold for enough to pay off the loan, that may be the best answer.

Field Visits

If the lender and the borrower can develop good working relations by mail or phone, then a face-to-face visit may not be necessary. However, such a visit is sometimes the best and most economical way to sort through the papers and other materials that may have to be analyzed in order to figure out what steps to take. According to the VA, when efforts to reach the borrower by mail or phone fail, the lender should try a field visit. A total lack of contact combined with abandonment of the house may lead to a very rapid foreclosure. A borrower who leaves the house for any reason should be sure to tell the lender how to reach her.

A good lender will be willing to send a representative to meet with the borrower in the evening if the borrower (or the borrower's spouse) works by day. One way to encourage a field visit is to suggest that someone take a look at the condition of the property. If it has certain problems, such as a need for major foundation work, the lender should be made aware of the situation. Actually, such serious repairs that are not the borrower's fault may motivate a lender to work a little more willingly with the borrower. The field visit also gives the borrower an opportunity to display willingness to work to solve the problem. It's a lot harder to foreclose on someone with whom you've met and had coffee than on someone to whom you've merely sent a routine letter. Lenders instruct their field representatives to prepare field reports like the one shown in figure 6.2.

Figure 6.2 Contents of a Field Report

Basic information
- Date of report
- Names of the individuals interviewed and their phone numbers
- Financial information
- Name and address of employer, length of employment, and type of work
- Monthly income and source
- Number and age of dependents (are they boys or girls?)
- Monthly expenses, including entertainment and spending money
- Assets and liabilities, including other property, vehicles, retirement funds, bank accounts and even trusts
- Property information
- Address of property
- Type of property
- Condition of property
- Occupancy (if rental, give basic rental information)

Remarks and recommendations
- Interviewer's impression of borrower's attitude
- Interviewer's suggestions about what should be done to assist borrower

Signatures
- The report writer's signature
- The borrower's signature to confirm the information

A Good Report Versus a Bad Report

Obviously, the borrower should work toward obtaining the most favorable field report possible as the basis for any type of relief requiring the lender's approval or assistance. The worst impression a borrower could give would be uncaring belligerence. One must show a reason for not paying besides a lack of desire. Otherwise, a quick foreclosure is likely.

A borrower who wants to play the game by the lender's rules should be sure to provide the information needed to approve a particular course of action, such as a period of reduced payments or a VA-assisted sale of the house. On the other hand, a borrower who plans to fight the foreclosure by legal means, including bankruptcy, may have little incentive to give the lender much help. The borrower should review the options with an attorney before deciding on this course of action.

The borrower should always keep a careful record of any contact with the lender. This may be useful when talking to the VA or in court—even bankruptcy court. Also, good records help to keep the lender from ignoring procedures. The lender may not realize it has missed a step without evidence in the borrower's records. Figure 6.3 shows a sample log.

Figure 6.3 Foreclosure Notice Log

Date on Letter	Date Recceived	Who Sent Letter	Subject of Letter*
Date of Call	Time of Call	Caller's Name	Person Who Took Call
Date of Meeting	Place of Meeting	Persons Present	Matters Discussed During Meeting
*Computer-generated form, ignores your past communications, based on incorrect information, etc.			

VA PROCEDURES FOR WORKING WITH BORROWERS

If the borrower's trouble stems from a truly good cause, the VA's official policy is to help as much as possible. On the other hand, if the borrower is simply unwilling to pay, the VA's official policy is to force the borrower to pay, foreclosing if necessary. A borrower should, therefore, try to show good reasons for failure to make payments.

The VA wants its lenders to do a number of things when the borrower begins having trouble making the payments on the loan. First, the lender should inquire why the borrower isn't making the payments. It will review the borrower's domestic and employment situations and overall finances carefully. The VA lender is expected to place the borrower into one of several categories, such as distressed delinquent or chronic delinquent. As discussed in detail in a later section, distressed delinquents are eligible for the VA's foreclosure avoidance measures. The VA lender is instructed to foreclose on the borrower who is perceived to be a chronic delinquent. Obviously, the borrower will want to be classified as a distressed delinquent, not a chronic delinquent.

Reasons for Nonpayment

After a borrower has worked with the lender over the phone and by letter, or at a field visit, he should try to get the lender to send out a VA-approved loan counselor. In addition to reviewing the lender's files, the loan counselor will either make the original field report or obtain further information directly from the borrower. A good loan counselor will work with the borrower to try to find a solution to the problem. After some preliminary fact-finding, the counselor will make a series of recommendations and, the borrower hopes, implement some worthwhile relief measures.

To begin, a good loan counselor will try to discover why the borrower isn't paying. The borrower should expect a VA loan counselor to ask:

Q: What caused you to be late in your payments?

Q: When can you make your payments?

As simple as these questions are, the answers are not always easy. Actually, of the several major reasons for foreclosure, employment problems, marital problems, and health problems are three of the most important.

Employment Problems

Perhaps as many as 30 to 40 percent of all foreclosures stem directly from employment problems. Either the borrower has lost a job, or commissions or other income have fallen. All too often, these events lead to foreclosure. The loan counselor will try to determine the employer's name and address, if any, and the length of employment and the type of work. Of course, the counselor will want to know when an unemployed borrower lost her job.

The counselor will also try to evaluate the borrower's prospects for future employment. Obviously, this is a key consideration. If the borrower with no other skills has been laid off in an industry that is not hiring, things look grim. If the general economy in an area is weak, the prospects for securing employment there may be grim.

A good counselor will evaluate the employment situation carefully, and so should the borrower. Obviously, if things aren't likely to get better soon and the borrower lacks the resources to make payments, it's probably best to sell the house to avoid further problems. On the other hand, if a short-term or temporary bout with unemployment (or underemployment) will likely end shortly, then some type of short-term relief, such as reduced payments, would be appropriate.

Domestic Situation

The loan counselor will want to understand the borrower's domestic situation as well, because a primary cause of foreclosure is marital discord. Upwards of one out of five foreclosures may be due directly to divorce. Loan counselors must inquire about the borrower's marital situation tactfully, looking for mutual separation, legal separation, pending divorce, or even final divorce. In any of these situations, the VA counselor will try to determine who has the ability to pay, when payments can be made, who occupies the property, and the names of any attorneys. If both the husband and wife signed the loan, then the counselor must contact both.

BORROWER MOTIVATION

If the borrower appears able to recover from a problem and make payments, then the VA will work to avoid foreclosure. If the borrower has little chance of making payments, the VA will not want to postpone the inevitable foreclosure. A borrower who simply won't make payments will suffer foreclosure. A good counselor will try to distinguish between excuses and reasons for nonpayment. The counselor will fit the borrower into one of two categories: distressed delinquent or chronic delinquent.

Distressed Delinquents

Most delinquent borrowers are distressed delinquents. Basically, these are people who have clear and reasonable causes for their failure to make payments. Some acceptable reasons include the following:

- Unemployment
- Extended illness
- An accident causing income loss
- Natural disasters such as flood, fire, and wind storms
- Marital problems
- Death

The counselor should counsel the borrower on how to cope with or eliminate such problems.

The VA wants lenders to seriously consider assisting distressed borrowers who have defaulted through no fault of their own when the problem can be overcome in a reasonable time. One experienced loan servicer reports that the VA's attitude is to do whatever is necessary to keep the borrower in the property.

Chronic Delinquents

On the other hand, if the lender judges the borrower to be a chronic delinquent, the lender should foreclose rather than offer the full set of options for relief. Borrowers should fight to maintain the image that they seriously want to pay their obligations.

The chronic delinquent borrower differs radically from the distressed borrower. Chronic delinquents are habitually late and not for reasons beyond their control. Chronic delinquents feel little incentive to make timely payments. From the lender's viewpoint, the chronic delinquent simply refuses to pay the mortgage, even though she could do so.

To avoid this damaging label, the borrower should present reasons for not paying that have some semblance of legitimacy. To develop this image, the borrower should look carefully at his payment pattern, as the lender certainly will. Chronic delinquents habitually make payments late, often despite having the same jobs as when they got their loans or even better ones. This situation is a substantial indicator for classification as a chronic delinquent. The borrower who has kept the same job should be able to show unavoidable new expenses that have prevented him from making payments on a timely basis.

If the loan counselor thinks the borrower may be a chronic delinquent, VA instructions call for asking probing, persistent questions about the borrower's spending habits. If the borrower seems uneasy at such questions, the loan counselor may suspect her good intentions. To avoid this appearance, the borrower should try to answer in a manner that does not indicate discomfort with the question. It is better to give the impression that she would really like to explain why she can't easily pay anymore.

The VA guidelines characterize a chronic delinquent as a procrastinator who will give all sorts of vague excuses for not paying on a timely basis. A borrower is well advised to anticipate questions a loan counselor might ask. It might not be a bad idea to practice responding to likely questions before talking to a loan counselor. Besides thinking through all the obvious questions, it may help to present the basic information rapidly so that the loan counselor will have less time to think up questions.

The borrower should try to determine whether the loan counselor has classed him as a chronic delinquent. It may even be worthwhile to ask the loan counselor this question directly and to ask for reasons for the classification. A loan counselor may give several clues that the borrower has been classified as a chronic delinquent, such as taking a tough attitude that absolutely no late payments are acceptable. The loan counselor may follow up constantly and demand to know why the borrower isn't making payments. The loan counselor may schedule face-to-face meetings that seem intended to pressure the borrower to pay rather than to search for a solution. You can't judge simply by the frequency of follow-up contacts; the loan counselor's attitude in dealing with the borrower is the best clue about the counselor's true thinking.

The borrower should be sure to try to counteract any appearance of being a chronic delinquent in the mind of the lender. Be sure to state a logical, legitimate reason for nonpayment. If you don't really have one, then be frank about it and give the assurance you will make payments in the future. Lenders often view a partial payment as better than nothing.

PARTIAL PAYMENTS

Many borrowers run their finances into such tight spots that they can't make full payments. Such a borrower who tries to make a partial payment will confront a number of VA policies.

First, the borrower has the right to make partial payments on a VA loan. The lender must ordinarily accept late payments equal to one month's payment or $100, whichever is less. The $100 option is almost never used. Any late payment must be credited to the oldest unpaid payment outstanding at the time. This makes it harder to go into default for nonpayment on a VA loan than on other types of loans. A hard-pressed VA borrower can stave off foreclosure by making some kind of payment.

Under some conditions, however, a lender may return late payments with a letter of explanation within ten calendar days from the date of receipt. These conditions include the following:

- When the borrower has leased the property to someone else and rent is not being applied to the payments

- When the payment is less than the lesser of one month's payment (including late charges and escrow amounts) or $100

- When the payment is less than 50 percent of the total amount of all missed payments

- When the payment is less than an agreed amount in a revised repayment plan

- When payment is made by personal check instead of cash or a certified check, when requested by the lender

- When any part of any payment is more than six months overdue

- When foreclosure has commenced, when the lender takes the first action for foreclosure under state law

- When the lender's lien position would be jeopardized by partial payments

- When the VA has given the lender permission to return partial payments from the borrower

Most VA lenders will not process partial payments in a routine manner. The borrower should expect a call or a letter from the lender asking when the default will be cured and why it occurred. Arrangements should be made to pay the balance due.

If the borrower fails to make full payment for three months, the lender may give the VA notice of intention to foreclose. The VA must receive this notice from the lender at least 30 days before the lender commences foreclosure. At the end of that time, the lender may commence the ordinary foreclosure process as defined by state law.

SPECIAL RELIEF WITHOUT VA INVOLVEMENT

The borrower should recognize that the VA does not have to approve all types of special relief. The lender can act on its own to provide certain kinds of special relief. These measures include accepting partial payments (as previously described), forbearance, and loan modification.

Forbearance

Forbearance means the lender refrains from rigidly enforcing the terms of the loan. Instead, it permits a worthy borrower to pay less than agreed or for a longer period of time than agreed. VA officials in cities with distressed economies have held seminars to inform personnel from lending institutions about the VA's procedures for dealing with troubled loans. VA guidelines state that it is the policy of VA to encourage holders to extend reasonable forbearance in the event a worthy borrower is unable to begin an immediate plan to liquidate the delinquency. VA officials are evangelists for the gospel of forbearance. Such thinking can be badly needed medicine for tough conditions.

Forbearance is granted by allowing payments to remain delinquent for a reasonable time, with a limit of 12 months before further review of the circumstances. The delinquency can then be cured by the payment of a lump sum, a schedule of increased payments, or sale of the property. Forbearance may be granted even without a liquidating plan. However, a well-organized liquidating plan stating how much money the borrower will pay and when is an excellent idea.

Figure 6.4 VA Reporting and De Facto Forbearance

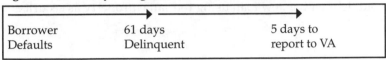

Borrower	61 days	5 days to
Defaults	Delinquent	report to VA

Forbearance is built into the VA's default reporting because the default may not be reported until after 61 days after the first report default. The VA lender servicer's foreclosure must not start before 30 days after the VA gets a notice of intention to foreclose.

At any time in the servicing process, especially after filing a Notice of Default with the VA, a written forbearance plan should be undertaken that lasts beyond the VA reporting requirements (66 days). Figure 6.4 shows the VA reporting and forbearance time line.

At any time in the servicing process, especially after filing a Notice of Default with the VA, a written forbearance should be undertaken. Lenders should keep the VA up-to-date—a new computer system is being set up to help with just that—about both the forbearance and the reasons for it. VA may even contribute supplemental servicing in this situation.

Another form of forbearance concerns the VA's foreclosure instructions. Without following the instructions, a lender who forecloses risks selling at a price the VA will not fully pay a claim on. Therefore, lenders usually won't proceed with a VA foreclosure without securing VA approval of price and terms. The price must stay fixed through foreclosure.

The VA's policy of forbearance does not apply to those borrowers who have the ability, but not the willingness, to pay. In addition, forbearance is unlikely if the borrower has no reasonable prospects of coming up with the money in the near future. A strong job holder who is going through a divorce is a good candidate for forbearance, as is a person with strong credentials who will probably be able to replace a lost job. Individuals who do not know what to do or where to go are not as likely to be granted forbearance, nor would they really benefit from it.

Borrowers should contact the VA if they cannot get help from their lenders. Many lenders complain loudly that the veterans who go to the VA for help normally induce it to advise lenders to forbear. Lenders are not merely urged but are expected to forbear. One experienced loan servicer for a lender states flatly that any borrower who can tell a good story can probably obtain forbearance. He also contends that forbearance agreements may treat the lender quite unreasonably. Not all borrowers are so lucky, though.

Modification

The VA expects lenders to proceed through forbearance first, before reaching modification. Modification involves changing the provisions of the original loan. Modification can be used when the borrower's income becomes inadequate to make the payments, but it is particularly appropriate when the borrower's reduced income is insufficient to make up delinquent or deferred payments. Payments may be reduced in at least three ways:

1. Interest rate reduction
2. Extension of the loan term (usually past 30 years)
3. Reamortization

Although it is available, modification is uncommon in practice.

Interest Rate Reduction

Reducing the interest rate by a percentage point or two and then recalculating the monthly loan payments reduces those payments. This may involve some costs, such as a new appraisal or processing fees. The borrower can try to have the interest rate reduced even when the market value of the property is below the amount owed on the loan. If the borrower has adequate equity, the VA would prefer that the loan be refinanced. Refinancing is distinguished from reducing the interest rate in that the borrower repays the old debt with a new loan using the same property as security.

Extending the Loan Term

Extending the loan term spreads payments over additional years. This reduces the amount of principal repaid with each payment and, therefore, the overall monthly loan payment. This would be most effective for an older loan. When a 30-year loan passes its 15th year, substantial portions of each month's payment cover principal. Unfortunately, most loans that go into default do so early in their terms, usually within the first five years or so. During this time, little of the monthly payment is dedicated to repaying the principal. Most of the payment, almost 95 percent during the first year, goes to pay interest.

Reamortizing the Loan

In an amortized loan, a regular payment amount is calculated to pay off the loan balance over a set period of time based on the loan's term, interest rate, and principal amount. One modification method, reamortizing the loan, allows the borrower to pick up excess payments from earlier periods and reapply them to cancel out delinquent payments. The loan would return to its original amortization schedule, rather than the faster one the borrower's earlier extra payments were aimed at achieving. When an interest rate is reduced, the accrued unpaid interest might then be added to the principal balance in a reamortization plan. A deficit in the tax or insurance escrow account might be similarly included in the loan principal to be extended and reamortized, bringing the account up to a proper level. On the other hand, any excess escrow could be used to cover missed payments.

VA Requirements for Modification

First, the agreement should be written out and signed by the parties. Also, VA strongly suggests that borrowers make the new payment for a six-month trial period before a modification agreement is formally signed and executed to show whether the modification will succeed in helping the borrower keep the payments current. Finally, the lender should send the VA a copy of the recorded modification agreement. The borrower should be aware that the VA will know what is going on with the loan modification. It will keep a permanent record.

SPECIAL RELIEF

The VA can approve special relief measures that extend the private lender's efforts enormously. Formerly, VA approval was required, but now the lender can handle the routine special relief transactions without approval. The cooperation of the private lender will nevertheless be necessary to implement the VA-approved measure. The VA does not view these strong measures as substitutes for proper loan servicing. The VA's three exceptional relief measures are these:

1. Compromise sale agreements
2. Deed in lieu of foreclosure agreementsR
3. Refunding

In a compromise sale agreement, the property is sold for less than the value of the loan, but the VA covers part of the loss, as discussed later.

In a deed in lieu of foreclosure procedure, the borrower simply hands over deed to the property to the lender in full satisfaction of the debt. This procedure is seldom used in states with strong out-of-court foreclosure laws, especially certain deed of trust states. In fact, VA loans are among the few residential loans for which this technique is used at all.

In a refunding, the VA purchases the loan from the private lender and collects the payments. Refunding has not been that common, and it is getting less common still. Congress has from time to time pressured the VA to use it. For example, Congress held field hearings in one economically troubled city that amounted to a grandstand show for the press and the public in which VA officials were pilloried for not doing more to help veteran borrowers. At one memorable moment, a certain VA official was asked, "How many refundings did you do at your VA office?" The answer, seven, did not impress the congressional inquisitors. Nontheless, refunding is still likely to be rare in the future.

Compromise Sale Agreements

A borrower who has no equity and cannot cure a default by any other type of relief may ask to be allowed to sell the home at the market price to avoid foreclosure. The VA will pick up the loss temporarily, although it will require the borrower to agree to remain liable to repay its loss. The VA will generally not consider any such arrangement in which it must pay more than its guarantee for the loan, which can be as much as $46,000, depending on the circumstances. (It may be less; generally older loans have smaller guarantees.) Again, remember that the borrower will remain liable for everything the VA pays to the lender, along with any other losses.

Early counseling about private sales can help avoid the actual foreclosure and reduce or prevent losses to all interested parties, including the borrower, the lender, and the VA. Still, a distressed borrower selling a home in a down market should inquire about compromise sale agreements. If a purchase offer is not sufficient to pay off the full amount of the existing balance on a VA loan, a compromise sale agreement will allow the deal to go through, with the VA paying the difference between the sales proceeds and the mortgage balance.

A compromise sale agreement may be particularly useful when delinquent interest increases the loan balance above the fair market value of the property. Before a compromise sale agreement can be effected, however, the borrower must find a buyer who is willing to purchase the property for its fair market value as determined by the VA. Obviously, the VA will not subsidize a fire sale.

Compromise Sale Agreements and Assumptions

Most VA loans are assumable; that is, the purchaser can take on the existing mortgage and continue payments. A compromise sale agreement can allow the buyer to assume less than the remaining balance on a VA loan. However, any purchaser who assumes less than the full balance on the original loan must be an acceptable credit risk to VA. A low interest rate on the existing loan gives considerable help in qualifying a buyer.

In any case in which a compromise sale agreement appears possible, the lender should notify VA immediately and submit the following information:

- Copy of the sales contract
- Statement of the loan account on the estimated closing date (usually not more than 60 days from the date of submission to the VA)
- Estimates of all costs anticipated to be incurred with the transaction assigned to parties that will be responsible for payment. (Details about who pays the sales commission, legal

document preparation costs, recording costs, and so on allow determination of the net proceeds of the sale.)

- Property appraisal
- Release of liability package, if the loan is to be assumed
- Veteran's statement and agreement of liability to the VA (see figure 6.5)

The VA will notify the lender when a compromise sale offer is approved and provide instructions when further action is required.

Refunding

The Department of Veteran's Affairs has the authority to refund a loan or purchase it from the lender. Normally, a lender makes a VA loan and services it, while the VA guarantees it. However, the VA can buy the loan from the lender when it has a reasonable chance of being saved from foreclosure. That's called refunding.

Borrowers do not have any right to refunding, and the VA prefers to avoid this option. Unlike FHA lenders, VA lenders are not supposed to use refunding simply to drop the burden of servicing a troubled loan characterized by late or missed payments.

VA sees refunding as a last chance to avoid foreclosure when the default may be cured but the loan owner determines that business prudence prevents it from granting such relief. In that event, VA can buy the loan and solve the problem. Because of the cost and difficulty involved, the VA will normally refund only when the solution to the problems with the loan appears fairly clear.

Figure 6.5 Statement and Agreement of Liability to the Department of Veterans Affairs on Compromise Sale Agreement

We, Dwight Borrower and Mamie Borrower, hereby acknowledge and state that we are unable to continue to pay the Deed of Trust Note monthly payments to Memorial Service Mortgage on our VA-guaranteed loan secured by the real property located at 1944 Normandy, and furthermore acknowledge that there is or will be a total amount owing on the loan of approximately $68,191 as of January 25, 2009. We have had the property listed for sale for a period of time and have accepted an offer to purchase from John Q. Saviour, in the amount of $63,000. We are desirous of selling the property, but the purchase offer is insufficient to pay our loan and all costs associated with selling the property.

Therefore, we request the Department of Veterans Affairs to pay the holder of the loan note the difference between the sales price and the amount owing on the loan. The amount to be paid by the VA is estimated to be approximately $4,500. We request the VA to pay this amount so that the sale of the property can be consummated, thereby reducing the deficit we would owe if there was a foreclosure sale. We will pay the additional sums necessary to pay off the total balance stated above, together with all costs of the closing.

In consideration of the Department of Veteran's Affairs paying the difference between the sales price and the amount owing on the loan, we agree and promise to indemnify the Department of Veteran's Affairs the amount so paid.

REMEMBER, YOU'RE ENTITLED!

The VA offers the borrower many options when he has difficulty making the payments on a loan. VA has valuable programs to reduce payments under its forbearance or refinancing plans or to subsidize a loss on a house that is sold to avoid a foreclosure.

Better still, VA staffers can assist the borrower. The borrower should remember, however, that the staff of both the lender and VA is frequently overloaded.

Conventional Loan Workouts

If a loan is not FHA-insured or VA-guaranteed, it is referred to as a "conventional loan." Troubled borrowers with conventional loans still have plenty of options. Major private lenders usually offer a variety of special relief plans, including temporary reductions in mortgage payments, refinancing, and various plans for selling houses, with or without PMI-company subsidies. The government pushes FHA and VA lenders to provide borrowers relief for which they qualify. Private lenders are more selective, but they often work more quickly and more efficiently.

RELIEF FROM THE PRIVATE LENDER

The type of special relief a lender will give often depends on what type of loan the borrower has. If the loan meets FNMA, FHLMC, or other secondary market standards, the lender will ordinarily be able to offer a variety of special workout arrangements. Generally, FNMA and FHLMC procedures are highly developed. Major private mortgage insurers also can be very helpful.

Often the borrower learns with surprise that the regular lender with whom he deals on a day-to-day basis doesn't seem to care about the loan. All too often, the lender does not have the financial incentive to worry about the loan that the borrower expects. Many loans are owned by one company but administered, or serviced, by another for a fee. The servicer may care less about whether the loan is foreclosed at a loss than whether the company has followed all the rules. In addition, any loss may be covered by insurance, protecting the lender from suffering much, if any, loss due to a foreclosure.

Borrowers should consider these facts when they deal with lenders. Since the lender will not lose anything by foreclosing on a house that is worth less than what is owed on it, threats of financial loss or appeals to financial common sense may fail. The best way for the borrower to obtain relief or special workout measures, such as reduced payments for a period of time, is to work closely and patiently with the lender.

SEEKING SPECIAL RELIEF

Some general recommendations follow for seeking special relief.

Don't Wait Until the Last Minute

To their own detriment, many people put off dealing with impending foreclosure problems. People rarely get a lender's cooperation for special relief after the property has been posted for sale a few days before the foreclosure. This is particularly tragic when the borrower would have had an excellent case for special relief—if only she had acted sooner!

Communicate with the Lender Early and Often

Lenders need to know what is going on. If you have lost a job and found a new one, for instance, inform the lender as soon as possible. Whatever your situation, talk to the lender. It is a lot easier to foreclose on a faceless and uncommunicative borrower than on one who calls regularly and seeks the lender's advice and cooperation. If you can become a person the lender's representatives know, your odds of obtaining a workout are much better.

Do Not Take a Belligerent Attitude Toward the Lender

The people who work for the lender are doing their job. Even if someone seems to be enjoying giving you a hard time, keep your cool. Remember, lenders do not always assign their friendliest people to their collection departments. Be extremely positive, if at all possible, for the best results. Do not threaten or become abusive. Think before you speak.

Do Not Make Promises You Can't Keep

Lenders note any promises you make in their records. If you fail to keep them, this will help them justify undertaking foreclosure. Tell them what you realistically can and cannot do. If you break a clear promise, the lender often becomes angry, and a foreclosure may become unavoidable. Some lenders take it almost personally if they feel you have lied to them.

Get Your Facts Straight

Be prepared when you talk to the lender. Keep records of when you make payments. Keep copies of letters you send or receive from the lender. Make notes of phone calls, including dates, times, and names of callers. The lender certainly keeps such records! It's an excellent idea to send a letter to confirm what was said in a phone conversation.

The Owner of the Loan

Sometimes borrowers have better luck in restructuring their loans if they can reach the true owners or insurers of their loans. As mentioned, often the company the borrower deals with on a day-to-day basis does not own the loan but merely services it under contract. The servicer collects payments, deals with default, and arranges foreclosures, if necessary. This company may feel little financial pain from a foreclosure that will certainly hurt the owner of the loan and the insurance company. If the borrower can reach the owner or insurer, sometimes that party can help.

Almost all loans made by mortgage companies are sold on the secondary market, as are many home loans made by savings and loan associations. The investor who buys a loan appoints a servicer to handle it. Usually this is the company that originated the loan.

The servicer handles all payments, escrow funds, and defaults in accordance with the wishes of the investor. Investors' policies on loans, including workouts and handling of delinquencies, vary. Many smaller loan buyers follow procedures set by two of the largest investors, FNMA and FHLMC. Loans arranged according to these procedures are called "conforming loans."

CONFORMING LOAN PROCEDURES

The largest single buyer of loans in the United States is the Federal National Mortgage Association (FNMA, or Fannie Mae). FNMA standards for originating and servicing loans fill a four-volume set of binders, one volume of which sets out FNMA's servicing standards in detail. The Federal Home Loan Mortgage Corporation (FHLMC, or Freddie Mac) has a two-volume set of procedure manuals, one of which deals with servicing. The standards of these major loan buyers are the standards of the industry, because many other loan buyers, including the major government buyer, the Government National Mortgage Association (GNMA, or Ginnie Mae), closely follow FNMA/FHLMC standards. The trend has favored standardization so that loan buyers and the buyers of securities they issue know what they are buying.

Mortgage companies that service conforming loans must follow detailed standards regarding delinquencies. When trouble strikes, conforming loan buyers want their servicers to do one of several things:

- Try various collection techniques, including assessing late charges, accepting partial payments, employing attorneys, assigning rents, or reapplying principal payments.
- Apply special relief provisions, including temporary indulgence, various types of forbearance, liquidating plans, or modification.
- Negotiate preforeclosure sales when appropriate.

The borrower should try to analyze which, if any, of the above strategies are best for his situation. If the borrower anticipates missing a few payments, collection options are likely. If the borrower will miss a lot of payments, then stronger special relief measures become appropriate. These include an agreed-upon reduction in payments for a limited time, called "forbearance," or closely related options, such as a temporary indulgence (a short period without payments falling due, the total amount to be made up later) or loan modification (reducing payments through a lower interest rate or longer loan term). Finally, if it looks as though the borrower will be unable to keep the payments current for an extended period of time, a preforeclosure sale should be arranged.

COLLECTION OF LATE OR MISSED PAYMENTS

When the borrower fails to make payments, the lender will employ a variety of collection techniques. A borrower who knows what type of long-term option suits her interest should immediately suggest that option to the lender. The borrower should ask for assistance from a loan counselor at the earliest possible date if a more ambitious plan, such as forbearance or a foreclosure presale, seems to be the best choice.

The borrower should not have to miss payments to get the lender's attention, but that may be necessary as a practical matter. Missed payments will affect the borrower's credit, but he should always negotiate for the most favorable credit report, regardless of the choice selected. The borrower can request that the lender remove negative information from the credit record, or not report it to begin with, as part of the deal to pay the loan on a reduced payment schedule or to sell the house.

The defaulting borrower should expect late notices, phone calls, letters, and face-to-face interviews in which the servicer will try to analyze the reason behind the default and to collect past due amounts. The servicer can assess late charges, accept partial payments, hire an attorney, or obtain assignment of rents. In the last case, a tenant who rents the borrower's house must make lease payments directly to the lender rather than to the owner/borrower.

Late Notices

There are two main types of late notices, which should be timed as follows: a payment reminder notice will arrive between 7 and 10 days after the due date, a late payment charge will be assessed 16 days after the due date, and a late payment notice will arrive around 17 days after the due date. Many borrowers have the mistaken belief that a payment is not late until the sixteenth of the month, when a late charge is assessed. Payments on most conforming loans are due on the first, and payments made after that date will show up on the borrower's payment history. This may adversely affect the borrower's ability to obtain future loans.

Phone Calls

Telephone calls should begin between 17 and 20 days after a payment due date, although they may begin as early as 7 to 10 days after the due date to a borrower whom the lender perceives as a chronic late payer. The borrower should expect the calls and be able to offer a good reason for paying late. If the borrower requests an alternative form of relief, the lender's representative should relay the message to the lender to seek action. In fact, a knowledgeable caller working for the lender should actually suggest relief of various kinds to the borrower. The borrower should make a regular record of all phone calls from the lender, noting the date and time, the caller's name, and the substance of the conversation. In fact, it would be best to keep track of all communications with the lender in a log like the one in figure 7.1.

Letters

A good lender will write the borrower individual letters rather than generating form letters. The borrower should save all such letters and keep them neatly organized in a file. The borrower should always respond in some form to any letter, preferably in writing. Mail all communications in a way that gives you a record, such as certified mail, return receipt requested, overnight express, or any other delivery method that will generate a receipt indicating that the lender received the communication.

Face-to-Face Interviews

A representative of the servicer should have a face-to-face interview with the borrower between 45 and 60 days after the date the unpaid payment was due. The servicer must make every reasonable effort to have at least one face-to-face interview before beginning foreclosure. However, a servicer cannot send a representative if the borrower states that the visit would constitute a trespass.

Generally, however, refusing an interview is not the best approach for the borrower to take. A better approach is to meet with the lender's representative as soon as possible to try to work out a solution to the problem. If the borrower wins over the representative, she recruits an inside advocate for her position. The borrower could also make an enemy, however, particularly if the representative is not reasonable or well intentioned. The borrower should consider complaining to the loan's owner or insurer, if possible, about any such sloppy servicing. However, the borrower should be careful about taking this approach without first giving the servicer an adequate chance to work things out in a reasonable way.

Figure 7.1 Foreclosure Notice Log

Letters	Date on Letter	Date Received	Who Sent Letter	Subject of Letter	Problems with Letter*
Phone Calls	Date of Call	Time of Call	Caller's Name	Person Who Took Call	Matters Discussed During Calls
Personal Interview	Date of Meeting	Place of Meeting	Persons Present	Matters Discussed During Meeting	

*Sample Problems: Computer-generated form, ignores your past communications, based on incorrect information, etc.

Communicating the Reason for Late Payments

In all of its collection efforts, one of the lender's key goals is to find out why the borrower isn't making payments. The lender wants to know whether the buyer is a chronic delinquent or someone who would like to make payments but cannot due to bad circumstances. The borrower should be ready for such questions. The borrower should always try to convince the lender that he seriously intends to pay or to deal with the default in another way that fits within the lender's guidelines.

The reason for default may suggest an appropriate remedy. For example, the borrower may have become overextended by injudicious use of credit. Credit counseling may help such a person. The servicer should also try to determine whether the reason for nonpayment is temporary or permanent. Default due to divorce may be resolved quickly, or it may drag out and render a borrower unable to pay for a long time. A job loss might look temporary or longer term, depending on the nature of the borrower's work and the prevailing job market in the area.

If the borrower cannot hope to make payments, the lender may try some type of special relief. Otherwise, collection efforts may continue prior to foreclosure.

Assorted Collection Techniques

A lender may accept partial payments if the borrower displays a good attitude toward paying the loan and has not been habitually delinquent or written checks that were returned for insufficient funds. The lender will expect the borrower to pay the balance of the payment within 30 days.

The company administering a loan may hire an attorney to try to collect past due payments. This may cause legal problems for the borrower, such as threats of a lawsuit or damage to the borrower's credit rating. Many state laws permit this technique, but the lender may hesitate to pay the attorney before it can collect the fees from the borrower. This approach may aggravate the problem rather than solving it. If the borrower has rented the property but is not paying the loan payments with the rental income, the servicer may try to obtain an assignment of rents to make the loan payments.

In a final method, the lender may reapply any extra principal payments that the borrower paid in the past. If, in better times, the borrower made extra payments to reduce the loan's principal, the servicer may, upon written request, reapply those extra payments to cure the current delinquency. The borrower must agree to pay extra funds, if needed, to make up all past due payments. Reapplication can be used together with special relief provisions.

SPECIAL RELIEF PROVISIONS

Major loan buyers, including FNMA, provide several types of relief to help deserving borrowers cure delinquencies. These provisions are administered by the loan servicer, not by the loan owner directly. FNMA wants the lender to use relief whenever appropriate; it does not want to foreclose on the mortgage if there is any chance of saving it. The borrower should not expect special relief, however, unless she can show a plan to bring the mortgage current and keep it that way. The borrower must convince the lender of her intent to pay and capacity to pay immediately or in the near future. The borrower may seek special relief of many types, although most require lender approval:

- Temporary indulgence
- Special forbearance
- Liquidating plan
- Military indulgence

If it looks as though none of these measures will work and even stronger measures are needed, FNMA will consider loss mitigation procedures, one of which is loan modification. The other three involve the loss of the borrower's property: presales, deed in lieu, and assumptions, all of which are discussed in later chapters.

Prerequisites to Special Relief

In general, the servicer will want to verify the legitimacy of the borrower's reasons for not making payments. A job loss, a divorce, or a period of illness would all be solid explanations for failure to make payments. On the other hand, a solvent investor who wanted to dump a bad investment or reduce a loss but who could otherwise make the payments would probably not be approved for special relief. If the borrower's problems appear to be legitimate, the lender will consider implementing some appropriate type of special relief that has a chance of succeeding.

The servicer may grant special relief in a process that is reminiscent of qualifying the borrower for the initial loan. The servicer may want to verify income and its stability. If the borrower's delinquency resulted from a job loss but he has since found a new job, he is probably a good candidate for special relief.

The servicer may also look for assets, just as a regular loan underwriter would. If the borrower could easily sell assets to produce money, the servicer may push for this.

The servicer may want to know all about any readily available liquid assets. This puts the borrower in a difficult position, because merely applying for special relief does not mean it will be granted. In applying, however, the borrower will have to reveal the amount and location of any assets, information that would be helpful to the lender if it suddenly decided to reject special relief, foreclose, and sue for the balance owed. Still, the servicer may insist that the borrower pay a substantial amount of money up front before granting special relief of any kind.

The borrower should expect that the lender will want to go through a process similar to an initial loan application and approval as a precondition for special relief.

Besides the borrower's capacity to pay in terms of income and assets, the servicer will also evaluate the borrower's willingness to pay. This is true of almost any loan. This can create a problem since it all takes time, and the lender may not be willing to slow down the foreclosure procedures in the meantime. Moreover, the borrower's credit history is likely to have suffered damage by whatever forces are causing the default on the house loan. Generally, the house payment is the last payment a person will quit paying; the financial situation is usually very bad by the time someone starts skipping house payments. If the lender focuses on the borrower's credit history as an important consideration in the decision to grant special relief, independent of the borrower's circumstances, the whole effort to secure special relief may be futile.

Another factor that affects the lender's decision whether or not to grant special relief is the borrower's responsiveness to phone calls, letters, and interviews. Therefore, the borrower should always return the lender's calls, respond to letters, and participate openly in any interview.

If the borrower appears to be a good risk, all things considered, special relief may be appropriate. Special relief deals are often made to work, since they are usually in both the borrower's and the lender's best interest.

TYPES OF SPECIAL RELIEF

Temporary Indulgence

Temporary indulgence means the lender simply allows the borrower not to pay for a limited period of time on the condition that the borrower will make up the missed payments within a short period. Temporary indulgence may be granted when the lender determines that the borrower will be able to bring the account current within 30 days. This may appear likely under one of the following circumstances:

- Sale or rental of the property is pending.
- An insurance settlement is being negotiated.
- Social agency assistance is pending.
- Additional time is needed to finalize a repayment plan under other relief provisions.
- Mortgage payments have been lost in transit.
- Time is needed to reapply principal payments.

Special Forbearance

Under special forbearance, the lender can reduce or suspend the borrower's monthly payments for a longer, specified period of time. Afterward, the borrower must resume the regular payments and catch up the overdue payments. This type of relief is justified by the death or illness of either the borrower or a person whose income contributed a significant portion of the payments or by a natural disaster for which the borrower lacked insurance. An unavoidable drop in the borrower's income would also justify special forbearance, as might other unusual circumstances, if they can be adequately documented. An example might be a borrower who depended on rental income from a tenant who, as a National Guard member, has been called into active service and cannot maintain rental payments. The borrower/landlord isn't allowed to evict under such circumstances, so there's an unavoidable drop in income that would justify special forbearance.

A special forbearance agreement must always be in writing. It should set out the period of reduced or suspended payments and the schedule for making additional payments when regular monthly payments are resumed. The agreement should specify the date forbearance will end, which should be within 18 months from the date of the first reduced or suspended payment, except in unusual situations.

Repayment Plan

Under a repayment plan, a borrower must immediately begin making payments on top of regular monthly payments to cure a past delinquency. This plan is appropriate for a borrower who missed payments because of some temporary hardship that has passed. When the borrower has missed fewer than three monthly payments, the repayment plan may be an oral agreement, but formal written agreements are required when the delinquency has lasted more than three months. The agreement must set out a schedule of payments and the date by which the delinquency will be cured. A repayment plan may require extra monthly payments on top of the regular payment, either every month until the overdue balance is paid or during alternating months. It may require payments more often than once a month, or it may specify whatever timing and payment amounts will cure the delinquency in the shortest possible time.

Figure 7.2 shows a sample plan that would be suitable for a private lender. However, this is not an official FNMA or FHLMC form.

Military Indulgence

In 1940, Congress passed the Soldier and Sailor's Relief Act of 1944, which has been updated as the Servicemember's Civil Relief Act. This law was originally designed to prevent people who were drafted for duty in World War II from losing their homes, since lawmakers didn't want a borrower who was out defending the country on the battlefield to suffer the loss of his home through foreclosure. This law directs FNMA to grant a special military indulgence to a borrower who cannot make payments due to military service. It requires, however, that any delinquency should be cured within three months of the borrower's discharge from the military. If this is not possible, the servicer may consider another form of special relief, such as a repayment plan or modification. In the meantime, the Servicemember's Relief Act requires a reduction in the borrower's interest rate to 6 percent, regardless of the loan's status or the military borrower's credit.

Loss Mitigation

If the borrower's circumstances rule out any of the four forms of special relief, the FNMA may consider a stronger form of relief in the form of loan modification. Modification is particularly appropriate in down market conditions when the property is upside-down, meaning that its value is less than what's still owed on the loan. Combined with a substantial involuntary reduction in income, that circumstance may justify loan modification.

MODIFICATION

Sometimes a deserving borrower can avoid foreclosure only through changes in the terms of the mortgage. Only dramatic circumstances, such as when a military borrower cannot bring a loan current within three months of discharge, a family has been permanently affected by an accident, illness, or death of the prime wage earner, or a borrower's income has declined to a level that is too low to keep the loan current and will remain too low, justify such a shift. In some other situations, altering the loan terms might cure the loan delinquency and avoid foreclosure. The loan owner typically must approve any special relief that modifies the terms of the mortgage.

When borrowers ask specific lenders for special relief, it is hard to say exactly what their answers will be. They may grant it, or they may deny it. It depends on the circumstances and is hard to predict.

Modification is obviously among the strongest forms of special relief, but it is one of the strongest. It may be the only chance a borrower has of reducing payments.

If the value of the house has declined since the origination of the loan, loan modification may work. Conventional refinancing won't work in such circumstances, because lenders generally require 10 percent positive equity before refinancing. Modification does not have such rigid requirements.

Although modification may reduce the interest rate, extend the term, or otherwise change the terms of the loan, many borrowers are somewhat disappointed because it may not produce the tremendous reduction in payments they had anticipated. In fact, it may reduce payments as little as 5 or 10 percent, which may not solve a borrower's problem. However, for some borrowers, the reduction may mean the difference between keeping the house and losing it.

ARM Modification

FNMA allows its ARM loans to be modified into fixed payment loans. It will also allow ARM plans to be modified into ARMs whose payment terms the borrower can credibly keep up with. The interest rate may be lowered to market or below market, or delinquent interest and escrow items may be capitalized into the remaining balance on the loan.

FNMA has a Form 3161, Loan Modification Agreement (Adjustable Interest Rate), to help facilitate changes in ARM loans. The loans may retain their adjustable rate nature but with less ferocious terms. In particular, a step interest rate may be used to increase interest rates more gradually and help reduce or avoid payment shock. FNMA now has a special Form 3162, Loan Modification Agreement (Step Interest Rate), to facilitate altering troublesome ARM loans. An even stronger new ARM modification is Form 3179. This is targeted at the growing problem of ARM defaults.

Nuts and Bolts of Modification

- *Qualification:* Initially, borrowers seeking modification will be run through FNMA's "Home Saver Solutions network," which is essentially a software program that is loaded with data on the borrower's financial situation, such as income, fixed payment obligations, and a property market value analysis. The program digests the information and generates recommendations as to which procedures for dealing with the default would be most effective and what the parameters of the solutions might be.

- *$500 administrative processing fee:* As of 2007, the borrower should expect to pay $500 for administrative processing fees. If the borrower can credibly show she doesn't have even that sum, then FNMA may cover it or capitalize it into the loan balance under certain circumstances (such as pool mortgage loans).

- *$10,000 increase in mortgage balance:* If the loan modification plan results in an increased loan balance (through inclusion of missed payments) of more than $10,000, then FNMA requires its lenders to obtain from any junior or subordinate lender (if there is one) an agreement for the junior or subordinate lender to stay in second place and inferior to FNMA's loan. FNMA wants to be able to wipe out the junior lienholder in foreclosure, which it may do, or threaten to do, if the agreement can't be obtained. If a subordination agreement is obtained from a junior lienholder, FNMA expects a title company to update the title.

To obtain loan modification, a borrower may have to go through an extensive approval process to satisfy both the servicer and the loan owner. He may have to pay extra fees to cover some out-of-pocket costs as well. In addition, the borrower must abide by certain new restrictions on the new loan. Finally, non-FNMA investors may handle loan modification by significantly different methods than FNMA employs. The checklist in figure 7.3 details considerations that affect loan modification.

Figure 7.2 Repayment Plan: Repays (Liquidates) Missed Payments Over Time

RE: Loan Number _____

Your request for a temporary repayment program to help you save your home has been approved.

Your loan is delinquent for the month(s) of <u>November 2008</u> through <u>January 2009</u>. The total amount necessary to reinstate your loan is <u>$2,448</u>. During the course of this agreement, the payment(s) for the month(s) of <u>February, March, April, May, June, and July</u> will also become due. The loan will be brought current by <u>July 1, 2009</u>. Therefore, the total amount to reinstate your loan will be <u>$7,328</u>. The payment schedule under our agreement involves paying each full month's payment plus 50 percent of a month's payment to make up unpaid sums, as follows:

Amount	For the Month(s) of:	Due Date
$1,221.33	November and 50% of December	February 1
$1,221.33	January and 50% of December	March 1
$1,221.33	February and 50% of March	April 1
$1,221.33	April and 50% of March	May 1
$1,221.33	May and 50% of June	June 1
$1,221.33	July and 50% of June	July 1

The payments under this agreement must be paid by cashier's check or money order, and we must receive them no later than the dates specified. Each payment must be placed in one of the special envelopes enclosed.

If you fail to pay any payment as promised, this agreement will be canceled, and if appropriate, foreclosure proceedings will start.

Please sign this agreement and return it immediately. If you have any questions, please call the Loan Counseling Department at 713-555-5555.

Accepted and Agreed:

_____   _____
Freddie Mac Mortgagor   or   Fannie Mae Mortgagor

S&LS AND THE FHLMC

S&Ls are still free to make loans as they see fit and are subject only to banking laws and regulations. There is no single set of published standards for the specifics of a loan that all S&Ls must follow. S&Ls also sell loans. In fact, they sometimes sell part of a loan instead of an entire loan. A given loan or some part of it may be sold under a participation agreement under which different lenders buy the interest. A group of S&Ls or a combination of FHLMC and S&Ls may buy full or partial loans. Usually a lead bank (or an S&L) sets the procedures for handling the loan. Of course, the full and complete loan can be routinely sold to FHLMC.

FHLMC was set up by the U. S. government to buy loans from savings and loan associations. Like FNMA, FHLMC has certain standards for originating and servicing its loans, and many other loan buyers either follow FHLMC's standards or closely parallel them. FHLMC has detailed standards regarding delinquent loans. When trouble strikes, FHLMC wants its servicers to do one of several things:

1. Try various collection techniques, including assessing late charges, accepting partial payments, employing an attorney, assigning rents, or reapplying principal payments.

2. Use special relief provisions, including temporary indulgences, various types of forbearance, liquidating plans, or modification

3. Negotiate a preforeclosure sale when appropriate.

In short, FHLMC procedures resemble FNMA's procedures.

Figure 7.3 Loan Modification Checklist

(Yes or No) Can the borrower bring the loan current?

$_____ Sum, if any, that will be paid back over time as part of the workout. This is the amount to be capitalized.

$_____ Sum, if any, that the mortgage insurance company can advance to help make the loan modification work.

Describe the loan's current status:

Describe the reason(s) for the loan's delinquency:

Give the loan type (fixed-rate/fixed-payment, adjustable rate mortgage, etc.) *before* modification:

after modification:

Interest rate _____ percent

$_____ Unpaid balance on the loan

Loan-to-value ratios (LTVs)

    before modification_____ percent

    after modification _____ percent

Extend the loan's term (Yes or No)

    If yes, number of months to extend loan term: _____

Describe how late payments are to be handled:

Vacant/occupied occupancy status?

Describe the type of house:

New Borrowers

S&Ls or their major loan buyers are particularly concerned about new borrowers. Nationwide, loans are most likely to go into default during the first five years; older, seasoned loans go into default less often. FHLMC therefore follows a well-founded policy of paying special attention to new borrowers.

In particular, new borrowers may be delinquent because they do not understand payment requirements. Servicers must make personal contact with new borrowers within 15 days after delinquency to determine the cause of late payment. New borrowers must understand the importance of paying on or before their due dates.

Abandonment

The S&L borrower should be particularly careful to avoid abandoning the property until it is absolutely necessary. As mentioned in previous chapters, once the property is abandoned, the lender is much more likely to start a foreclosure or complete one once it has started. The lender is far less willing to undertake special relief measures if the property is abandoned.

If the borrower needs to spend time in another location, the property should be secured in the borrower's absence so that the lender doesn't decide the property has been abandoned. FHLMC requires that lenders watch for abandonment and attempt to locate the borrower to find out why she left. If the property is abandoned, the lender must report that fact promptly to FHLMC.

FHLMC will secure an abandoned property against vandalism or damage. Therefore, the borrower who moves out may be kept out when the lender changes all the locks and secures the property against entry. FHLMC asks the servicer to recommend action in case of abandonment, and foreclosure is a very likely recommendation.

Buydown Funds

Since savings and loan associations hold deposits, they can make and sell to FHLMC special loans that do not appear on FNMA books. Under certain types of FHLMC-approved loans, a borrower deposits a substantial sum of money into a buy-down account with an S&L. Funds are then pulled out of the account in a prearranged amount to pay part of each monthly loan payment. Obviously, such deposits may be seized by the lender when the borrower misses payments. However, borrowers should note that FHLMC disapproves of this practice if there is a reasonable prospect that the borrower will be able to keep up the loan payments once the buy-down funds are spent. If the borrower can make payments or show that he will be able to make payments, then the lender should not seize the account.

Second Mortgages

Unlike many other loan owners, FHLMC buys second mortgages. If a property on which it owns a second mortgage is abandoned, the FHLMC demands that servicers immediately contact primary (first-lien) mortgage holders to discover the status of payments on the first loan and the primary lender's intentions. If FHLMC owns both first and second mortgages on a property, delinquency is easy to handle. Otherwise, FHLMC is at particular risk if the first lienholder forecloses, since this will destroy the second lien on the property. FHLMC's servicer would have no way to foreclose or otherwise recover the amount of the second loan other than to bid at the foreclosure sale if the property has sufficient equity. If the property value dropped after origination of the loan, FHLMC's position would probably be wiped out when the first lien foreclosed. This gives the borrower a little bit of leverage in dealing with the second lienholder if she can pay the first lienholder.

Special FHLMC Relief Provisions

FHLMC gives its loan servicers broad discretion to extend appropriate relief to cooperative but financially troubled borrowers who have due regard for their obligations. In general, it wants the lender to recommend relief rather than foreclosing. Before granting relief, the lender must establish the reason for the default and certify that the borrower's attitude and circumstances justify help. No relief should be granted unless there is a reasonable expectation that it will allow the borrower to bring the mortgage current and keep it that way. The lender may grant any of several forms of relief, including temporary indulgence, a repayment plan, special forbearance, and military indulgence. For the most part, FHLMC's requirements and procedures for relief are similar to those practiced by FNMA. A borrower who wants special forbearance should be prepared to go through an application process like that required to first obtain the loan. Figure 7.4 outlines the relief options for FHLMC loans.

FHLMC Special Relief

FHLMC distinguishes between merely bringing the loan current, as in a reinstatement, and heavier "special relief" remedies, such repayment plans and short-term forbearance. Reinstatement can be done anytime. Special relief, on the other hand, has some up-front prerequisites. FHLMC needs to see:

- involuntary income reductions, such as job loss, divorce, death of a borrower; and/or
- unavoidable expense increases, such as medical disability, natural disasters, or unexpected large house repairs.

Property condition is an issue for the FHLMC, and an inspection is needed to determine this. In particular, FHLMC is concerned about any presence of toxic matter on the property. FHLMC may also condition relief on a plan for the borrower to reduce expenditures. If it can be done in a year, it's still special relief; longer than that, it's a workout with different measures. FHLMC will look for a broker price opinion (BPO) through its special system, BPODIRECT. A form 1126 on the borrower's finances will be needed. The results may justify any of the following measures.

- **Repayment plans:** The missing payments are chopped up and added as extra amounts to the regular payment the borrower is making. This agreement must be in writing, specifying beginning and ending dates and the exact amount extra to add to the regular payment. It will fully repay the missed sums.

- **Short-term forbearance:** Payments are suspended up to three months and/or payments are reduced for up to six months. The end of the plan will be a full reinstatement, but the borrower will have to go into a further repayment plan (regular payment plus extra) or a workout plan to repay the missing sums.

- **Long-term forbearance:** Payments are suspended or reduced for up to 4 to 12 months, to be followed by a repayment plan to bring the loan current.

- **Loan modification:** This may involve reducing the interest rate on the loan, reducing the monthly payment, extending the maturity date, increasing the unpaid principal balance (UPB) at the end of the loan, or changing the product type of loan (no more ARM, for example). Loan modifications may include all modification expenses, delinquent interest, escrow shortages, advances, and expenses incurred so far. The missed payments, plus the extras, will then all be "capitalized" and turned into a balance to add to the loan. FHLMC may want to see some cash up front if it can get it. The modification has to be closed, much like a regular loan.

Short Payoff Preforeclosure Sale

FHLMC will also go into a preforeclosure sale arrangement with a "short payoff" if the sale price is less than the loan payoff. This has to be done when the borrower has no prospect to maintain ownership. The borrower must have the following characteristics:

- Be experiencing an involuntary inability to pay
- Be delinquent on payments or in imminent danger of default
- Be cooperative, completing form 1126 (revealing financial information) and allowing access for a price opinion
- Be unable to sell after listing the property at a price for an "as is" sale for 90 days
- Be making the maximum possible contribution toward any sale deficiency in cash or by a promissory note (IOU)
- Be acting on his own and not have deeded the property to a third-party "rescue" service
- Be willing to waive reimbursement of escrow, buy-down funds, or prepaids and assign any insurance proceeds to the lender

Even if there's *no* involuntary ability to pay, FHLMC will consider a sale under any of the following circumstances:

- There is a risk to the lender in property ownership (It has toxic waste on it.)
- Litigation is pending against the borrower that could jeopardize the foreclosure sale.
- The mortgage is secured by a manufactured home, and the borrower has a buyer for the property.
- The borrower has a voluntary job relocation 20 miles from the current job site but cannot afford to pay both housing expenses. The lender will get 100 percent of the "as is" value with

a 90-day marketing time, and the borrower is willing to participate in a loss to the limit of the borrower's ability. This scenario might happen if the borrower optimistically thought he could sell the old house after taking on the new job and buying a new house near the new job. When unable to sell the first house, the borrower then ends up with two payments and can't keep up with both of them.

Make-Whole Preforeclosure Sale

Of course, a make-whole preforeclosure sale will readily be approved by FHLMC for borrowers who have no prospects to maintain payments and want to sell.

Deed in Lieu

The borrower must exhaust all the previously outlined FHLMC forms of relief (see chapter 6) before a deed in lieu will be considered. This measure would be particularly appropriate when a "lengthy" judicial sale procedure must be used in the borrower's state. The following additional requirements also apply.

- The borrower must list the property for sale for 90 days in the multiple-listing service (MLS).
- The borrower must be delinquent on payments.
- The borrower must demonstrate an involuntary inability to keep up payments.
- The property must be in reasonable physical condition.

Additional factors would be if the property was over 90 days delinquent or if a deficiency judgment is not practical in the borrower's state. Also, if the debt has reached 115 percent of the probable "as is" sales price for a 90-day exposure on the market, then that's a strong indicator that deed in lieu is an appropriate procedure.

OTHER LOAN BUYERS

Local investors who own troubled loans are far easier to work with in a down market than the owners of loans that back nationally issued mortgage-backed securities. The local investors are simply more familiar with the dreadful conditions in a troubled area, and they may be able to give quick yes or no decisions on loan modification deals, if the borrower can reach them. Generally, mortgage servicers are reluctant to let borrowers reach loan investors directly. The borrower's best chance to reach the investor to discuss loan modification is through the lender.

Borrowers with loans held by national investors may not be so lucky, especially if the mortgage that needs modification serves as collateral for mortgage-backed security that promises the investor a fixed, flat return. In such a case, there may be little chance of reducing the loan payment. Imagine it from this perspective: How would a saver feel if, after buying a certificate of deposit with a fixed rate of interest at a bank, the bank said, "We've screwed up by giving loans to people who can't pay them. Would you mind accepting a lower interest rate on your CD than we guaranteed to you?" Many investors would flatly refuse. The same thing can happen with a mortgage-backed security. In fact, trying to give the investor a lower interest rate than the investor is legally entitled to receive may even be a securities law violation.

Even if the investor approves a loan modification, other problems remain.

Extra Fees for Loan Modification

Most loan modification deals require borrowers to pay extra fees. One fee will cover an updated title policy, which will allow the lender to check for new liens—in particular IRS liens. Attorney's fees will also be necessary to draw up a modification agreement. In addition, the lender may charge a qualifying or processing fee to handle the paperwork. Still more fees may be needed to pay for the two appraisals and the broker price opinion that are customary for loan modification. Finally, there may be charges on top of all of this for points to sweeten the deal for the investor and entice approval. In short, you have to be rich to prove you're poor and deserving of modification. Many loan modification attempts have foundered due to the borrowers' inability to pay the extra costs needed to make them work.

More Restrictions

Loan modification may impose added restrictions on the borrower that the original loan did not. For example, the loan may become nonassumable. Also, the borrower may have tax problems due to the forgiveness of debt. If the modification discharges some of the debt due from the borrower under the original loan plan, the borrower may realize taxable income. Tacking the missed payments onto the end of the loan may eliminate this possibility. If the borrower ends up with a balloon (a larger, lump-sum payment) due at the end of the loan, this may make the property harder to resell. Loan modification has its problems.

Figure 7.4 Freddie Mac Relief Options

	FHLMC Approval Needed?	Maximum Time to Cure Delinquency
Temporary indulgence	No	3 months
Repayment plan	No	12 months
Special forbearance	No	18 months
Military forbearance	No	Soon after discharge

Special Relief Other Than Modification

With all its faults, loan modification is still one of the best options available to prevent foreclosure, since similar requirements restrict other forms of special relief. However, other options have some advantages. For example, neither a temporary indulgence nor a liquidating plan lasting less than three months requires a signed agreement or special approval, though their details must be well documented in the lender's files. Some servicers will seek approval from investors even if it is not strictly required.

CONCLUSION

There are so many private lenders, it's hard to determine what types of relief any given lender may offer to a borrower. However, major loan buyers, such as FNMA and FHLMC, have procedures that are so standardized enough that some types of relief are sure to be available. Private mortgage insurance companies insist that lenders offer relief when it can reduce losses. Sometimes this relief is the best and most creative available. Sometimes it is the worst.

Foreclosure Presales and Short Payoffs

8

FORECLOSURE PRESALES: WHAT THEY ARE

Suppose a borrower's situation will not get better. The divorce has cut income in half. A high-salary job has been lost and it's not possible to find a replacement in the current job market, or the borrower needs to move to a different city to find new work. Perhaps a medical condition limits work hours. Under these circumstances, a foreclosure presale would probably be the best bet.

In a foreclosure presale, the lender works with the borrower to get the house sold. The lender hopes to recover the full balance due on the loan, including missed payments and expenses. If the house can be sold at a profit, the borrower may not even need the lender to do more than delay foreclosure for a short while. If the probably sale price is closer to breakeven but nevertheless will make the lender whole sale (a make-whole sale), the lender may want to work very closely with the case to make sure this happens. If the lender will accept a loss on the sale by not recovering the full loan balance (a short-payoff sale), the short payoff may be reimbursed in whole or in part by private mortgage insurance, covered in more detail later.

Down Markets and Presales

Foreclosures often occur in a down market in which a whole city or region is afflicted with failing economic conditions and falling home prices. The fall in prices can be more of a deadly contributor to foreclosure than the job loss. If home prices are still high or rising, a borrower who loses a job and can't find another can simply sell the house, pay off the loan, and downsize his lifestyle or move to a different city. It's the combination of a drop in income with a down market that triggers foreclosure. The borrower can neither fish nor cut bait—that is, the borrower can't keep up the payments and can't sell the place. Foreclosure then becomes almost an inevitability.

Enter the foreclosure presale. The astute lender realizes that the borrower must sell. The game is then on to get the house sold for the most money and, preferably from the lender's standpoint, the least amount of time. The alternative to a well-planned, well-organized foreclosure presale is a foreclosure, and neither smart borrowers nor smart lenders want to go there.

The Legal Foreclosure Sale Is a Formality

In down market conditions, foreclosures are not good for anyone, including the lender. Once the lender forecloses, much of the time, there's no cash buyer at the foreclosure sale. More than 98 percent of the houses that are foreclosed in a down market are purchased by the lender at the foreclosure sale. In most states, the foreclosure bidder must bid cash at the legal sale, and although such buyers can be found, they are looking for bargains at a real estate flea market. They don't want to buy a house for a fair price; they want steal a house at a very low price. What they really value is high equity, which they buy cheap. Houses with high equity, though, can either be sold by the original borrower through normal means or certainly through a foreclosure presale. High-equity homes shouldn't end up at a foreclosure sale unless the either the lender's or the borrower's judgment is somehow impaired (often sheer stubbornness or denial). A lender might decide to foreclose regardless—a big mistake.

REAL ESTATE OWNED (BY LENDERS), OR WHAT'S LIFE LIKE FOR THE LENDER AFTER FORECLOSURE?

What happens after the lender acquires title at foreclosure? The lender needs to sell the house. In a down market, a foreclosure sale stigmatizes a house as a "foreclosure." Bad things can happen soon afterward. Even though a well-organized lender will get an area management broker or someone else to secure the house and manage it, it's often a losing battle.

The angry borrowers who are losing their homes may not take it kindly, and although they moved out, they know how to get back in. The author recalls one use of a tire iron to smash sheetrock throughout the house. Then there was the Nazi graffiti. How about flushing down quick-set cement to ruin the plumbing—that was a good one. The really foul-minded dump toxic waste out back.

Things disappear. The neighbors? Those poor rose bushes will die for lack of water or care— better move them into my yard. Whole gardens disappear or die. The HVAC (Heating Ventilation Air Conditioning) servicepeople? They drive a van, wear uniforms, and know how to remove a compressor in a hurry. It's low-cost inventory in a tough market. They have the perfect disguise, too; they really are HVAC servicepeople. Sometimes real burglars take things from a dark, vacant, trashed-out house.

The home may have new occupants, like raccoons, rodents, and roaches. But not to worry—the local crack users and dealers don't mind the company. Or we could be lucky; it's just a harmless psychotic bum. Ants, snakes, and wasps may visit, too. Lack of air-conditioning may cause the ceiling to curl and everything to mildew. Black mold, anyone? Cold freezes the pipes. Gas may leak. If the gas company takes the meter, just try getting it back to show the house—just try.

No foreclosed home case is complete without a ransacking raid from the notorious copper bandits. They can not only educate us about how copper can be found in the most out-of-the way places, from wires, motors, and compressors to the plumbing, but they demonstrate how to obliterate any obstacles to such involuntary recycling.

By the way, the foreclosed home's price typically falls during this process. Brokers who show such houses to buyers wear combat boots, heavy jeans, and pack at least a four-battery flashlight. (It's really dark in there!) If your novice lender needs further convincing about the advisability of a presale, just photocopy these pages and send them.

Don't wait too long: the city might raze the place for violating building codes and send a bill for the demolition. That assumes it gets there before the FBI, to condemn the crack house. Or perhaps the EPA will show up in the form of workers in space suits to clean up the backyard's toxic waste, followed by a "super lien" for an out-of-this-world bill. I can't imagine who might call such people and complain.

Presale is the way to go, not foreclosure.

Some foreclosure reformers even argue that it is pointless to continue the old legal foreclosure sales at courthouses, which were perhaps more appropriate in a rural nineteenth-century setting. If there are no title troubles and the lender doesn't want to bother to sue a near-bankrupt borrower, presale is best. Today, sophisticated brokers, or, at a minimum, a well-organized commercial auction, should be used instead. For Sale by Owner (FSBO, pronounced "fizzbo") sales efforts are worse than worthless in a down market; they waste valuable time. Unlike up markets, where order takers will do, in a down market, real brokers are a must.

Given competent people, presales work by either making the lender whole, or if there is a loss, which the lender must swallow as a short payoff, the presale keeps it to a minimum. Short payoffs were once largely forgotten in the lender's manuals, but today, they are recognized as a highly useful, even critical, part of the lender's antiforeclosure toolbox to keep losses down. Private mortgage insurance may step in and help cover the loss. They may require the presale or a reasonable effort, or else they may deny payoff of the mortgage insurance claim to the lender. All the major secondary market loan-buying companies have presale programs and criteria requiring a presale for their loans. FNMA has some of the best-developed and most extensive presale procedures in its servicing manual.

ENCOURAGING PRESALES

In March 1989, FNMA decided to begin emphasizing foreclosure presales as a technique to stop foreclosures. FNMA now encourages lenders that service its loans to set up foreclosure presales. FNMA has even set specific goals for some servicers, stating the numbers of presales they should complete. All servicers should participate in this effort when possible. FNMA's new presale program calls upon lenders who service FNMA loans to do the following:

- Identify foreclosure presale candidates.
- Contact borrowers to explain the presale program.
- Determine the market values of affected properties.
- Discuss pursuing specific sales with mortgage insurers.
- Authorize presales that will reduce or eliminate losses to FNMA from foreclosures.
- Account for and report on completed presales.

General Considerations

FNMA expects its servicers to contact borrowers within 90 days after their loans have become delinquent to discuss the various options that are available. (Other sections of this book on workouts detail these options.) A number of constraints on FNMA's presale program need to be considered carefully.

- FNMA will not consider a presale if the borrower appears to be able to pay the mortgage. The presale option is an alternative to foreclosure, not merely a financial convenience for the borrower.
- FNMA wants all other workout options, such as temporary forbearance or loan modification, to be considered before a presale. A presale is a last resort.
- FNMA will not delay the foreclosure for the presale. If the borrower cannot pay the loan as agreed and no successful workout is in the cards, then FNMA demands foreclosure, whether a presale is pending or not. If the presale can be completed before the ax falls, then FNMA will not foreclose. This adds some spice, or perhaps terror, to the presale process.
- The FNMA presale program is targeted at borrowers who are experiencing difficulty in selling their homes because the homes' values are less than the amounts owed on the mortgages.
- FNMA reserves presales for borrowers who are experiencing financial hardship, such as job losses, that prevent them from making their mortgage payments.

Financial Hardship Standards

In general, the presale program defines financial hardship as either a drop in income that is beyond the borrower's control (such as being fired or laid off) or an uncontrollable increase in expenditures (such as uninsured medical bills). Here are some situations that meet FNMA's requirements:

- An involuntary reduction in income due to job loss, long-term job layoff, mandatory pay reduction, death of a principal wage earner, or decline in a self-employed person's earnings
- An involuntary increase in expenditures from medical or disability expenses

Not every reduction in income qualifies the borrower for the presale program. In general, if the borrower could control the reduction or the expenses, then he is not qualified as a financial hardship case for the presale program. Following are some situations that do not meet FNMA's requirements:

- A drop in income due to normal seasonal layoffs
- Voluntarily quitting a job
- Voluntarily reducing hours worked
- Reducing income by returning to school

Conditions that fall outside these guidelines may bar borrowers from presale arrangements, because FNMA wants borrowers to pay their mortgages if they possibly can. Presale programs are directed at those persons who need help to avoid foreclosure, not those for whom it might be advantageous. It's worth a try, even if one falls outside the guidelines, but it's unwise to get one's hopes up.

PROCEDURE FOR A PRESALE

The borrower must agree to try to sell a house by means of a presale. Usually the loan servicer will require a letter confirming the borrower's request to try a foreclosure presale. The borrower will have to document financial hardship and agree to execute all documents that are necessary to sell real estate, such as a listing contract, an earnest money contract, and closing documents. The documents will call for the sales proceeds to be paid to the lender. The borrower will be expected to maintain the property until it is sold and closed. To complete a presale, the borrower can expect to do a number of things.

1. Request a Presale

Write a formal letter requesting FNMA to consider the borrower's request for a preforeclosure sale.

2. Document Financial Hardship

The borrower should document the nature and extent of financial hardship by providing recent paycheck stubs and bank statements. A self-employed borrower should be willing to submit income tax returns for the previous two years. FNMA will input the borrower's financial information and property value information into FNMA's Home Saver Solutions Network program, which should generate a yes for the presale course of action.

3. Select a Listing Broker

The borrower should select a broker. FNMA maintains a list of approved brokers, and the loan servicer may also recommend a broker. Still, the borrower may select the broker to handle the sale. The loan servicer should be given the broker's name and address so that communication can be maintained. FNMA and the mortgage insurer must approve a prospective buyer's purchase offer.

The borrower wants a broker who has some experience with presales or at least a strong interest in doing a presale. Presales involve much more negotiation than ordinary sales. The home deal must be arranged in the regular manner; then, the presale involves additional bargaining over contributions from the seller, whom the broker represents, and from the mortgage insurance company. Lender contributions may also be negotiated.

Some brokers hesitate to undertake presales due to the large amount of work involved and the difficulty of securing an adequate commission. In general, it will be more difficult to convince a broker to handle a presale on a smaller home, in the $20,000 to $50,000 range, than on a larger home. Unfortunately, as part of the rough bargaining that characterizes the presale, the broker may be asked to give up some of the commission. Fear of this possibility discourages brokers from getting involved in presales. Finding a broker can be tough.

4. Obtain an Appraisal

FNMA determines the current market value of the property by means of an appraisal. In the past, this was done with a broker price opinion (BPO).

5. Discussion With the Mortgage Insurer

Once the loan servicer has obtained the appraisal, it continues the presale process by contacting the mortgage insurer (if the loan is insured) to discuss the deal. FNMA requires the PMI company to agree in writing to waive its property acquisition rights before a claim for insurance is filed and to stand ready to pay up to the policy limits to subsidize the presale. If the mortgage insurer won't help on the presale, it is pointless to try to put one together. FNMA may be able to help secure the cooperation of an uncooperative PMI company, as explained in a later section in this chapter.

6. Sign a Listing Contract

The presale continues as the borrower signs a listing agreement with the selected broker. The agreement will set a price on the property below what is owed on the loan. If the borrower insists, a servicer may seek FNMA's approval for a presale before the property is listed and the listing agreement is signed. FNMA may then set a minimum price, but it will provide written assurance that it will regard the entire loan as paid and satisfied in full, even though the sale will generate less than the original loan amount. The written assurance can be attached as an addendum to the listing contract.

As mentioned, FNMA adds spice to the process by refusing to stop a foreclosure until a presale is complete. Also, it requires the listing contract to include a statement that the listing will be terminated and no commission will be paid if the foreclosure occurs before the presale is complete.

If the property has already been listed when the borrower attempts a presale, the loan servicer will need the broker's name, address, and phone number so it can explain the requirements for a presale to the broker.

7. Obtain a Sales Contract

This is easier said than done in many instances. However, the skill with which prices are estimated in FNMA presales should lead to a fairly rapid sale. Any house will sell at some price; a mansion priced at $1 will sell tomorrow. There is a market for every house. The sales contract, also called the "earnest money contract," for an FNMA presale must contain the following language:

> The seller's obligation to perform on this contract is subject to the rights of the mortgage insurer (if any) and the mortgage holder to the conveyance of the property.

This means that the house is subject to foreclosure despite any sales contract. Either the loan owner or the mortgage insurer can demand that the foreclosure proceed, denying the buyer the opportunity to buy. It is entirely possible, however, that the house will subsequently be sold after foreclosure to the same prospective buyer. This is no consolation to the seller, whose credit record now lists a foreclosure.

8. Obtain FNMA Approval for the Sale

When the sale eliminates any loss to FNMA, approval is automatic. If the presale generates enough money from the buyer's purchase price and the mortgage insurer's and seller's contributions (if any) to pay off all sums owed to FNMA on the loan, then no formal FNMA approval is required.

When the sale will result in a loss to FNMA, it must approve the sales contract. In this case-by-case approval process, two things are critical. First, time is of the essence. FNMA's presale announcement states:

> Since the decision to accept a purchase offer [that will involve a loss to Fannie Mae] should generally be made within 24 hours of the offer, the servicer needs to provide Fannie Mae with as much information as soon as possible.

As soon as a purchase offer is received, FNMA wants its required documents by overnight mail. The mortgage insurer must be notified simultaneously, as well.

Another important rule for case-by-case FNMA approval of a presale is to submit the required documentation. The loan servicer must submit the following documentation with a foreclosure presale application:

- Completed Preforeclosure Sale Worksheet (FNMA Form 572)
- Copy of the mortgage insurance certificate
- Copy of the sales contract
- Copies of two (or three) broker price opinions (BPOs)
- Letter from the lender requesting the presale
- Documentation of the borrower's financial hardship
- Copies of the borrower's most recent paycheck stub and bank statement (or the past two years' tax returns for a self-employed borrower)

The FNMA loss prevention specialist or the regional office will decide very quickly whether to accept or reject the presale offer. The notification is made by phone, followed by a letter for confirmation.

9. Obtain PMI Company Approval for the Sale

The mortgage insurer must also approve any presale contract. The procedure for obtaining this approval is described in detail later in this chapter.

10. Obtain Special Financing, If Needed

FNMA expects most presale buyers to obtain financing without any special FNMA assistance. Often, the lender that made the loan now in default will provide financing for the presale.

FNMA will consider special financing on a case-by-case basis when the buyer cannot obtain regular financing elsewhere. Past FNMA plans treated borrowers very generously to promote successful foreclosure presales. FNMA's terms are subject to change with little or no advance notice, though. The terms presented here are an example only. Only FNMA or selected representatives can give up-to-date information on FNMA's special financing terms. In the past, however, FNMA's special financing plans shared several characteristics. Buyers have not been charged any discount points. Buyers have paid all customary loan fees and closing costs (other than discount points) unless otherwise agreed. Finally, FNMA has designated the lenders. Past FNMA special financing plans have included conditionally approved presale (CAPS) plans, which have offered very low down payments similar to those for FHA loans.

11. Closing the Presale

FNMA presales are closed through title insurance companies, just like regular sales. The title insurance company must, however, sidestep the issue of FNMA's release of lien. Mortgage insurers can disburse funds at the closing table, but they may require time after closing to make sure that insurance claims are proper. They will check for fraud in obtaining the loans and that the policies are valid. Once they fund the deal, it is usually done. FNMA will require a standard HUD-1 closing statement. It will also reimburse the lender for all expenses related to the foreclosure presale, including the processing fee on non pool loans.

Presale closings differ from regular closings in one important respect. The closing documents will direct payments to FNMA rather than the seller, and the seller must agree to this arrangement. The buyer's loan proceeds and the mortgage insurance check both go to FNMA. The seller will probably have to pay for some part of the closing rather than receiving money from it. Once the deal is done, however, the seller will be released from liability. He will not suffer foreclosure or further harassment for money owed under the loan, either by deficiency lawsuit or collection methods. The presale leaves the seller's credit record in much better shape than a foreclosure would.

FNMA sets the standards for the mortgage industry. Although other loan owners' policies differ in details from FNMA's, their policies are often quite similar. Rather than reviewing each company's policies one by one, one can take the FNMA and its policies as the best single guide to arranging a presale. Note, however, that other loan owners are not as large and well established. Functions that might involve specialized personnel in FNMA may be combined and assigned to one person by a non-FNMA mortgage owner.

SHORT PAYOFFS AND PREFORECLOSURE SALES (FNMA)

If all of the lender's other efforts to prevent or cure the delinquency will not be successful, if the use of special relief has not been or will not be successful, and if all measures short of foreclosure have been exhausted, then FNMA considers a foreclosure presale to be appropriate. The key is this: If "the borrower *cannot* sell his or her property for the full amount" of the unpaid loan balance, FNMA will consider accepting a payoff of less than the total amount of owed on the mortgage if it will reduce the loss FNMA would incur if FNMA foreclosed and acquired the property. Given the time and expense to foreclose legally, take title, and manage both the vacant, stigmatized house after foreclosure and the falling price it will net later, a presale is the way to go unless the sale price is far below market. (It won't be.) The servicer should inform the borrower that if sales proceeds won't pay off the loan, the lender may require the borrower to contribute his own funds to reduce the loss. This might include any unused escrow funds that were set aside for taxes and insurance but are not needed now. Alternatively, FNMA may demand that the borrower sign a promissory note for the amount of his expected contribution to help cover the loss in this situation. FNMA lenders should advise borrowers that there may be adverse tax consequences from outright forgiveness of debt. (Note: Check the later chapter on this, but the tax problem is much overrated.)

FHA PREFORECLOSURE SALES

FHA regards preforeclosure sales as a loss mitigation measure to be used whenever appropriate by FHA servicers (lenders). FHA lenders normally designate loss mitigation specialists who specialize in preforeclosure sales and related techniques. FHA lenders will work with borrowers on a preforeclosure sale if needed. FHA's studies have confirmed the beneficial nature of the preforeclosure sale option for distressed homeowners, their lenders, and for FHA as an insurer with HUD. FHA is aggressively promoting preforeclosure sales procedures nationwide.

What an FHA Preforeclosure Sale Is

According to FHA,

> A preforeclosure sale is a sale of property, at fair market value, in which the lender agrees to accept the proceeds of the sale in satisfaction of a defaulted mortgage—even though this is less than the amount owed on the mortgage—to avoid foreclosure.

A preforeclosure sale is just that: an outright sale. It's not a workout. It is not an assumption or a deed in lieu of foreclosure procedure. It's a sale to a regular buyer, usually found by a broker.

How an FHA Preforeclosure Sale Works

Recall that the FHA only insures repayment of loans to lenders. Most "FHA" loans are made by a private lender with FHA mortgage insurance. If there is a default and foreclosure and the house sells for not enough to pay back the loan, then the FHA will have to cover some or all of that loss under its insurance agreement with the lender. A preforeclosure sale could, if done well, limit the FHA's loss by allowing a sale immediately and skipping the intermediate, painful, and troublesome legal foreclosure steps. If the lender follows the proper preforeclosure sales procedures, then the lender can submit a claim to FHA and be compensated for the difference between the proceeds received from the sale and the amount owed on the mortgage and certain reimbursable costs. Even if the FHA preforeclosure sale results in a loss to FHA on its insurance, the borrower who was eligible and did the sale will *not* be pursued for the missing sums through a deficiency judgment lawsuit or claim.

Why an FHA Preforeclosure Sale Is Needed

Aside from reducing FHA's own insurance losses, the preforeclosure sale program benefits those borrowers who clearly prefer to end their mortgage obligation but are prevented from doing so by stagnant or declining property values (negative equity or upside-down houses). FHA has other measures to help borrowers who want to do everything they can to keep the house, but preforeclosure sales are for those whose loss of income, increase of expenses, and changed circumstances make it impossible to pay enough to keep the house.

Eligible Borrowers

A borrower with a title II FHA-insured loan must be an owner-occupant in a single-family house. However, borrowers with only one FHA insured loan who do not occupy the house—such as a former owner-occupant who is renting out the property (perhaps to stave off foreclosure)—can be considered for a preforeclosure sale procedure.

FHA states: "Under no circumstances shall 'walkaways' who have abandoned their mortgage obligations despite their continued ability to pay" be given the opportunity to pursue a preforeclosure sale.

When to Use the FHA Preforeclosure Sale

The FHA preforeclosure sale program is targeted at borrowers faced with the tough challenge of selling their homes in a down market. It's used when the house is upside-down—that is, more is owed on the loan than the house can be sold for. The borrower must show a "verified need to vacate the mortgaged property." This could be due to job loss, divorce, death, reduced income, or an explosion of expenses, such as for a medical problem that was uninsured or underinsured. The most common cause for middle-class bankruptcy, traditionally, has been unpaid medical bills; while many have insurance, it almost never fully covers a disastrous medical situation. The gap between what can be got from the property and the loan must be significant. By FHA standards, a mere $1,000 or less won't cut it for FHA to allow a preforeclosure sale.

Steps Leading to Participation in a Preforeclosure Sale

- *Information sheet:* FHA requires lenders to start the preforeclosure sale process by giving the borrower an "Information Sheet," a standard FHA form advising borrowers about preforeclosure sales. This should be part of a HUD pamphlet on avoiding foreclosure. Once three payments are missed, the borrower must be sent a "Request for Financial Information." A collect call number is also made available. Borrowers get to consult housing counselors before the preforeclosure sale will be undertaken.

- *Counseling:* The borrower must express an interest in the preforeclosure sale procedure. An "Application for a Preforeclosure Sale," another FHA form, should be completed by the borrower and sent in. At this point, though, FHA wants lenders to make sure that borrowers understand the difference between keeping the house and selling it.

- *Certification:* A certification form from FHA must be signed by the borrower to document that she has received information about foreclosure alternatives. FHA wants to enable the homeowner to make an informed decision.

- *Application:* FHA wants both an application form and a form for financial information to be submitted for a preforeclosure sale authorization. The lender may ask for additional information.

- *Timing:* FHA believes that "time is of the essence" and that the early preforeclosure sale is the better choice. However, it may take some counseling and exploring before a borrower comes to that conclusion.

- *Bankruptcy:* If chosen by the borrower, bankruptcy will render the borrower unfit for a preforeclosure sale, even after emerging from bankruptcy.

- *Tax issues:* Discharging any part of a borrower's debts could constitute taxable income, but under current IRS rules, it may not be such a problem. (Consult the later portions of this book for more information about potential tax liability.)

- *Appraisal:* Once these preliminary steps are completed, the lender will order a property valuation—an appraisal. This must be from an appraiser who meets FHA standards. Promptness is best. FHA wants both "as is" and "as repaired" appraisal figures. There is a procedure to reimburse the costs.

- *70%–The Minimum ratio:* To approve a preforclosure sale, a minimum ratio must exist. On an "as is" appraisal, FHA looks for the home's worth to be at least 70 percent of the homeowner's present unpaid balance. FHA will take a hit, but it won't be a catastrophe.

- *Approval to participate:* The lender must notify the borrower of the steps it is taking. When the borrower's application for a preforeclosure is accepted, the lender must send the borrower another form, the "Approval to Participate" form, which includes permission to try the preforeclosure sale, the length of time the lender will delay foreclosure for the sale, and other information.

- *Hiring a Broker:* FHA expects the borrower to retain a real estate broker or agent within seven days after the approval form is dated and sent for a preforeclosure sale application. A broker or salesperson must market the home in an FHA preforeclosure sale. For sale by owner efforts are not allowed; the FHA does not want to risk a nonprofessional effort to sell the home.

Figure 8.1 Delaying Foreclosure to Pursue a Preforeclosure Sale

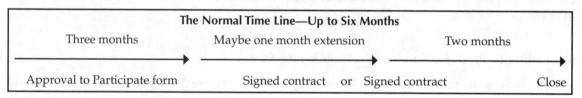

Nine months to start: The preforeclosure's six-month maximum block must begin nine months after the borrower's original default.

Frozen appraisal: The original appraisal done with the application is good for six months, which could be invaluable in a falling real estate market.

Early Termination of the Preforeclosure Sale

FHA expects its lenders to review the borrower's preforeclosure sale progress continually. The borrower will be contacted monthly and the broker within 90 days to report on the likelihood of sale. If a sale obviously isn't working, it must be terminated.

Assuming the borrower makes a good faith effort, the preforeclosure sale may need to be terminated early because, in the opinion of the broker, the house doesn't have good sales prospects or, secondly, the number of potential buyers coming to look at the house is obviously too small to work.

The lender who terminates a preforeclosure sale early must send a notice with reasons for the termination. Good reasons might include the following:

- Junior liens that cannot be discharged or released

- The borrower's refusal to work with a professional broker

Borrowers can also withdraw from a preforeclosure sale, although this would not seem to be in their best interests.

Maintaining the Property, Sales Efforts, and Ethics

Homeowners are responsible for maintaining the home during the preforeclosure sale, such keeping the grass cut. The "Approval to Participate" form contains more specifics.

In addition to signing a listing with a broker within seven days, borrowers are expected to execute needed documents and maintain an aggressive sales campaign seeking an approvable preforeclosure sale. Borrowers should get help from lenders, agents, counselors, and so on. FHA gives borrowers fact sheets with helpful advice. The listing agreement between the broker and the borrower (seller), in which the borrower hires the broker, must allow the borrower to fire the broker very readily, in case the broker does not appear to be performing according to the borrower's standards. The listing must include the following language:

> Seller may cancel this agreement prior to the ending date of the listing period without advance notice to the broker and without payment of a commission or any other consideration if the property is conveyed to the mortgage insurer or the mortgage holder.

The FHA expects an arm's-length transaction where there are no secret side deals or special understandings between the buyer, seller, appraiser, broker, closer, or lender. FHA wants a price that would prevail in the open market. Brokers should not share business interests with the lender, nor should they get into conflicts of interest or engage in self-dealings. The broker should not attempt to get a commission by selling his own property or a family member's. Brokers and agents should avoid even the appearance of impropriety.

Steps Leading to Lender's Approval of a Proposed Preforeclosure Sale

A title search must be done; its cost will be reimbursed by the FHA. Liens must be discharged or released. Any liens may be released by the use of excess from the sale proceeds, if that may be enough. The FHA can monitor such efforts to be sure they're appropriate and can be paid for.

The owner is expected to make repairs. However, if significant repairs are required for lending purposes, that fact should be in the sales contract. Funds for the repairs can be escrowed, but repairs may not commence until after the sale is closed. The cost can be deducted from the price as an expense, but the net proceeds from selling the house altogether must be at least 87 percent of the "as is" appraised value.

Standards for the Sale

The FHA has minimum standards for the "net to HUD" or "net proceeds" to FHA that it must realize to approve a preforeclosure sale.

Net proceeds are calculated as follows:

- Sales price
- Minus the broker's commission
- Minus consideration paid to borrower for selling ($750 + $250, if earned)
- Minus any amount to discharge junior liens under $1,000
- Minus local state transfer taxes and customary seller's closing costs

To approve the sale, the FHA requires *both* of the following conditions:

- Net proceeds must be 87 percent of the property's appraised value.
- Appraised value must be 70 percent of the outstanding loan balance.

If the form "Request for Variance" is filed, the FHA may approve a sale that doesn't meet its standards, but good reasons must be specified.

Otherwise, if the FHA's standards are not met, there's no preforeclosure sale. The FHA may try a deed in lieu instead, for example. FHA will get the property. It probably needs fixing up, or it may take time to sell in a very down market. Most likely, the FHA will offer it at very reduced market prices through its own sales efforts or offer it with a fix-up escrow. Unlike FNMA and private lenders, the FHA probably won't repair it.

Closing the Preforeclosure Sale

FHA requires preparation of a closing worksheet, which lists the seller's consideration all other amounts payable out of sales proceeds. The seller's consideration is $750 for successfully marketing and selling the house and $250 extra if the closing occurs within three months of the date of the approval to participate in the preforeclosure sale. This goes down as "additional settlement charges" on the HUD-1 closing statement (used in all residential sales by everyone). The closing worksheet will also list sums needed (up to $1,000) to release junior liens, a sales commission, taxes, customary seller's closing costs, and any funds FHA approved for repairs. The closer must compute the net proceeds to the FHA and furnish a HUD-1 closing statement.

Congratulations to the successful borrower!

If the Preforeclosure Sale Fails—Deed in Lieu

If a preforeclosure sale fails, then the transaction would be turned into a deed in lieu of foreclosure (deed property to lender) transaction rather than a sale. The FHA will *not* penalize the borrower in such event as a reward for at least having tried to complete a preforeclosure sale.

VA PRESALES

VA presales are called "compromise sales." They are covered in chapter 6 about the Department of Veterans Affairs.

OTHER TYPES OF PRESALES

Most loan owners can offer some type of presale arrangement, which will generally be modeled along the lines of the FHA of the FHLMC.

CONCLUSION

If a borrower has to lose a home because none of the workout solutions works, a presale or preforeclosure sale is generally the best way to go. It will get the best price for the house in the shortest time, and it will usually eliminate the borrower's deficiency judgment risk, either by reducing the size of the amount owed or because the lender agrees not to pursue a deficiency in a preforeclosure sale context. It will do much less long-term damage to a borrower's credit than either a bankruptcy or a foreclosure would. It leaves the house in the best condition and allows someone who is a regular homebuyer to have a better chance of owning it, as opposed to an investor. Presales are often the best way to resolve the foreclosure situation. Some reformers even think it ought to be required in place of true legal foreclosure or bankruptcy sales. The courthouse sales were more appropriate in the rural, 19th-century environment than in today's era of presales.

The Mortgage Insurer's Role in Foreclosure

9

LOAN INSURERS

If a borrower with a conventional loan (one made by a regular lender with no government insurance or guarantee) makes less than a 20 percent down payment, the loan will probably be covered by private mortgage insurance (PMI). Should the borrower fail to repay the loan, the private mortgage insurer will pay the lender a sum of money up to the limit on its coverage. Loan insurers play a critical role in the administration of loans that get into trouble.

A loan insurer stands to lose even more than a loan owner when a house goes into foreclosure. The loan insurer will have to pay hard cash to cover some or all of the losses from a foreclosure. A loan insurer's guiding principle is its bottom line. The loan insurer has the biggest incentive of any player in the mortgage arrangement to do something to prevent the foreclosure or minimize the loss. Loan insurers can also pressure the other players, such as loan owners and servicers, to take certain actions or not to take them.

If a loan gets into trouble, the loan insurer must be notified. The loan owner will be expected to take prompt action to minimize the loss; otherwise, the loan insurer may refuse to pay a subsequent claim for losses sustained as a result of foreclosure. If the lender forecloses, the loan insurer must approve the bid or it can refuse to cover a loss. After foreclosure or sale by the borrower, the loan insurer may try to control the terms of the subsequent resale or at least approve them; otherwise, again, it may have grounds to refuse to pay a claim for foreclosure losses. In many ways, the loan insurer is almost a shadow lender. It will want to play a key role in determining how to respond to a default and also a key role in almost every major aspect of a potential foreclosure, including determining the nature of default, approving and assisting in workouts for curable defaults, approving and assisting in early sales for incurable defaults, and minimizing and recovering foreclosure losses. The insurer's primary goal is to minimize losses through workouts, presales. or other measures.

Loan insurers classify default by cause, including default through special circumstances, such as assumptions and bankruptcies, or default by nonpayment.

DEFAULT BY SPECIAL CIRCUMSTANCES

A loan insurer will take an active interest in at least two default circumstances: bankruptcy and unauthorized assumption sales. Chapter 13 bankruptcy may be regarded as a curable default. If so, the private mortgage insurer will recommend that the lender work with the borrower. Most lenders hate Chapter 13 plans, but they get more money out of them than the alternative, Chapter 7 liquidation/bankruptcy. A borrower who files a Chapter 7 may try to discharge other debts as a means of saving enough income to make the mortgage payment. Many, if not most, states define houses as exempt property items that can be kept after bankruptcy if payments on the mortgage are kept current. If the payments are not kept up, the loan insurer usually requires the lender to file a motion to lift stay to pull the house out of the bankruptcy and allow foreclosure.

PMI companies regard unauthorized assumption sales as incurable defaults. However, they may sometimes authorize an assumption, provided a creditworthy buyer has sufficient income to pay the payments, as a vehicle for avoiding foreclosure. Mortgage insurers may also approve sales to second lienholders. Generally, however, unauthorized assumption sales lead to quick foreclosures at the command of loan insurers.

CURABLE DEFAULTS

A curable default may result from a short-term layoff; an injury that reduces income while increasing medical costs; or unusual, nonrecurring expenses. The mortgage insurer will try to mitigate losses for a curable default in any of several ways.

Credit Counseling

A mortgage insurance counselor will help the borrower prepare a family budget to reduce expenditures.

Modification

The counselor may recommend and approve modification of loan payment schedules. This may involve waiver of payments for several months in exchange for extension of the loan term. PMI companies almost always maintain strict rights to approve such plans as prerequisites to continued insurance coverage.

Forbearance Plans

The PMI company may encourage the lender to accept reduced payments or allow nonpayment for a short period. Such plans call for eventual repayment of past-due amounts by higher charges when the borrower's finances improve. PMI companies usually want to approve forbearance plans.

Subsidized Mortgage Payments

Although private mortgage insurers may not say much about it, they will sometimes supplement the borrower's monthly payments. The PMI company may, however, arrange to deduct some of these payments from the loss it will ultimately pay to the lender.

INCURABLE DEFAULTS

A default is often incurable if it results from death of the borrower, a business failure, serious marital difficulties, a job transfer in a difficult resale market, or too many loans. The PMI company may try to reduce losses from incurable defaults in any of several ways. It may encourage the borrower to sell the house to avoid foreclosure. It may allow a PMI-assisted presale, in which it compensates the lender in full when the property sells for less than the amount owed on the loan. (A later chapter covers PMI-assisted presales in detail.)

Early Sales

When requesting an early sale of the property, the PMI company will push the borrower and the lender to be realistic about setting a sales price that works. Sometimes the lender will have to take a loss, too, even after the PMI company pays out to the maximum limit of its coverage. (Most private mortgage insurers only insure a portion of the loan ranging from about 12 to 30 percent.) The PMI company requires the lender to notify it when the property is listed. The PMI company will also have to approve any sale.

When the insurance renewal date comes up (usually at the beginning of the year) while the loan is in default, the PMI company may require the lender to pay the borrower's premium to maintain coverage. Also, it usually insists on prompt notification if a borrower's default has been cured. Figure 9.1 summarizes how loan insurers deal with loans in default.

Deficiency Judgments

Many people discover to their horror that even after foreclosure, private mortgage insurance companies can pursue deficiency judgments. A later chapter deals with deficiency judgments in detail. This seems strange because most insurers do not sue to recover costs of paying claims. Still, law firms around the United States file literally thousands of suits against former homeowners to recover some or all of the losses to private mortgage insurance companies as a result of foreclosures.

The lender needn't bother to sue for a deficiency because the private mortgage insurer will. The lender simply collects from the private mortgage insurer. (In some states, earnings from diligent resale of foreclosed properties combined with payouts by PMI companies can allow lenders to recover more in foreclosure than they loaned the borrower!) Mortgage insurers who pay claims to lenders for foreclosure losses expect those lenders to take care to maintain rights to sue for any deficiency.

The bottom line: If the borrower can show the lender how it will benefit in hard dollars from a presale or modification, it is much more likely to approve that approach. Threats and complaints accomplish little, but S&Ls, mortgage companies, and PMI companies all have their bottom lines. The hardest lender to deal with is one that seems to care less about the final financial outcome than about holding a little bit of power over someone during foreclosure. Even in such a case, however, the borrower should stay cool but assertive; it works better.

Figure 9.1 How PMI Companies Deal With Default

Borrower Solves Problem Without Help	Borrower Solves Problem With Help	Borrower Doesn't Solve Problem	Lender Solves Problem	Loan Insurer Solves Problem
• Borrower brings loan current. • Borrower sells house at a profit or at no loss.	• Loan insurer approves presale and pays shortfall. • Loan insurer approves presale and allows assumption of loan	• Lender forecloses.	• Lender sells home at a profit or at no loss. • Lender sells home at a loss with loan insurer approval; PMI pays shortfall.	• Loan insurer pays lender claim and lender keeps house. • Loan insurer pays lender claim and takes title to house; insurer holds it or sells it.

Short Payoff: The Lender Accepts a Loss

One arrangement is not regularly available from loan owners or insurers but may be approved by a private lender: the short payoff. The short payoff is an arrangement in which a lender accepts less than the unpaid balance on a loan when the house is sold. For example, if the unpaid balance on a loan was $70,000 but the house could be sold for only $63,000, the lender might accept a $7,000 loss as a short payoff. This has an advantage for the lender of getting the property sold as quickly as possible.

The house would still be occupied by the borrower while being marketed to prospective buyers. The borrower is motivated to get the highest price for the house as quickly as possible to obtain the lender's consent to a short payoff. The higher price helps the lender reduce its loss and that of any private mortgage insurance company.

If the lender chose to foreclose instead of accepting a quick sale with a short payoff, the house couldn't be sold until after foreclosure proceedings. In a down market, houses sell slowly unless prices are cut severely, further dragging out the process. Also, an unoccupied house is favorite target for vandals or, even worse, professional thieves. Professionals may steal the appliances, sinks, toilets and even the entire heating and air-conditioning system.

Thieves also like to strip out copper wiring and plumbing. Even bricks have been stolen in rough areas of town. Neighbors often take landscaping plants that would die otherwise. Sometimes the borrowers take these things with them when they go if they are in a bad mood. Some people do random, senseless damage to their houses before leaving. Expensive vacancy insurance may cover only part of these losses.

The house will not sell for much in a trashed out condition, and repairs slow down the sale. Still worse, the house could be trashed again and again before finally selling. At some point, the insurance company might refuse to pay for more repairs. In a down market, brokers have plenty of houses to show buyers, and they may not bother with a trashed house unless the price is severely reduced.

All these considerations may make a short payoff look good to a lender. It's better to accept a small loss now than a big one later. Although procedures for short payoffs may not be found in lenders' manuals, they may offer the option in down markets. If the lenders can reduce losses by accepting short payoffs, they often do so.

Selling in a Down Market: Upside-Down Homes Stall Sales

One of the biggest problems in a down market is that property values fall below what homeowners owe on their mortgages. When the homeowner tries to sell such an upside-down house, the sales price cannot pay off the existing loan. Typically, the lender will not release the mortgage lien until the old loan is fully paid, and without the release, the seller cannot deliver clear title. The title insurance company will not insure such a title, and the buyer's lender will refuse to make a loan until title is clear. The poor homeowner wants to sell but can't. Foreclosure is often the bitter result.

PMI COMPANIES ASSIST PRESALES

Foreclosure presale offers a method of selling the home even if its value has fallen below what is owed on the mortgage. In a foreclosure presale, the homeowner shares some of the loss from the sale with other entities. In particular, private mortgage insurance may cover some of this loss under selected circumstances.

Recall that mortgage insurance pays money to a lender to cover a loss after it forecloses on a home but cannot recover the full balance due on the mortgage loan by selling the house. Normally, the lender files a claim for insurance after the foreclosure, and the mortgage insurer pays the cost of the smashed up mortgage just as a car insurance company would pay a driver for a smashed up auto.

Incidentally, the borrower still owes the unpaid balance on the loan at the time of foreclosure, less the amount received by reselling the property. The borrower receives no credit for the insurance money the lender collects, even though he paid for the mortgage insurance! This is true not only for private insurers, but for FHA and VA as well.

In an insurance-assisted foreclosure presale, the insurer of a mortgage offers to contribute cash to help pay off the seller's mortgage so that a buyer can buy the house at its market value free and clear of the seller's existing loan. Foreclosure is avoided because the old loan is paid off. Better still, the seller may be released from liability on the old loan.

To set up the deal, some problems must be overcome. The seller may have to make some sacrifices, a buyer must be found, and a mortgage insurer must be willing to assist. On the positive side, the foreclosure presale procedure gets around a critical problem: a fall in the home value below what is owed on the loan. Under ordinary circumstances, such a situation precludes a sale because a buyer cannot get clear title free of the seller's old loan. Normally, that makes foreclosure almost inevitable. However, a foreclosure presale deal can solve the problem without a foreclosure.

In the event of foreclosure on this house, the lender will suffer a substantial loss, because the value of the property is less than the loan balance. The mortgage insurer or guarantor is liable for some, if not all, of the loss.

Ordinarily, a buyer would not consider a house under these circumstances. Few lenders would consent to a sale at market value. The lender would foreclose in an effort to recover the full amount of the loan to which it has a legal right. However, a foreclosure presale plan may allow the lender to consent to a sale at market value.

Bridging the Gap

The plan must come up with enough extra money to pay off the lender. Few distressed sellers can hand over $20,000 on their own, assuming they would want to do so, to save their credit and prevent foreclosure. However, the mortgage insurer stands to lose the full amount of the gap. It may, therefore, authorize a contribution, provided that someone else contributes something to reduce its loss. There are several ways this might be done.

The seller can contribute by any of the following means:

- Pay cash from savings to reduce the loss.
- Sign a promissory note agreeing to pay back part of the loss over time to either the mortgage company or the mortgage insurance company.
- Arrange to sell off personal property, such as a car, camper, or boat.
- Arrange a loan with personal property as collateral.
- Borrow from friends, family, or an employer.

The mortgage lender can contribute by any of the following means:

- Accept a small loss from the presale to avoid a larger loss on the foreclosure. (Actually, the loan owner, such as FNMA, agrees to accept the loss.)
- Help arrange financing for the new buyer on advantageous terms.

The mortgage insurance company can contribute by any of the following means:

- Contribute cash to avoid paying a larger amount of cash in the event of foreclosure.
- Pressure the lender to back off from the foreclosure and accept some of the loss.

A plan should be put together to pay off the seller's loan based on some combination of contributions from the seller, the lender, and the PMI company. If the gap can be bridged and the deal can be made to work, everyone benefits. The lender is paid off. The seller escapes foreclosure and saves her credit. The mortgage insurer probably loses less than if it had to pay off the full amount of the gap.

Here is an example:

Seller contribution:	$ 5,000
Mortgage insurance contribution:	$ 15,000
Amount of bridge:	$ 20,000

A Buyer Is Essential

The deal won't work unless someone can be found who will buy the property at its fair market value ($50,000 in the example). Recall that it takes $70,000 to pay off the lender. Without a buyer, there is no way to pay off the part of the mortgage ($50,000) that is owed beyond the seller's $5,000 contribution and the mortgage insurer's $15,000 contribution. A buyer must be found! A good broker is obviously an essential element in the scheme, unless a buyer has previously appeared who is willing to buy at $50,000 and to accept the extra work and effort that may be required to put the deal together.

The Deal Can Be Wild

The first foreclosure presale closing the author attended was a bit on the wild side. As they say in the real estate business, there was blood on the closing table! But it did not have to be that way. A cantankerous seller's attorney on one side faced an irate set of homebuyers (represented by the author). The sellers were missing altogether. It set the stage for a bad afternoon.

To begin with, the buyers demanded to know if they would get clear title at the closing. The response was no, not until a release of lien could be obtained from the lender. The lender would not give such a release until the mortgage insurance company funded its part of the bargain, and its "commitment" letter to fund its part of the bargain read like Swiss cheese from a legal standpoint. Full of *ifs, buts, ands,* and *maybes,* it was at best a "definite maybe." The buyers asked if anyone could guarantee that the mortgage insurer would come through with the cash. When no one could, the buyers lost much of their enthusiasm. Even when the closer volunteered the observation that the commitment letter from the mortgage insurer was about the strongest she'd ever seen, the buyers remained unimpressed. Ultimately, the title company offered to insure the title, despite the problems, including concern for the insurance code, which forbids "insuring around" an active, unpaid lien on the property. The seller's attorney blew up at that, shouting, "You want to tell the title company THAT!" The deal failed to materialize that afternoon, but it did close later in the week.

PMI-assisted presales may not be for the fainthearted.

Criteria for Mortgage Insurer Help

Unfortunately, almost every insurer denies that it has any uniformly applied formula. Every deal is different. It is, therefore, almost impossible to put figures on paper and say when a deal can be done. The best thing to do is to contact the mortgage servicer (or lender) and see what can be done. In the meantime, it may not be a bad idea to look around for a potential buyer.

The author's experience suggests that most foreclosure presales meet at least two requirements:

1. Neither the lender nor the mortgage insurance company wants to put together a presale deal unless the seller is distressed and can't pay the mortgage payment.

2. The deal must save the mortgage insurance company some money by making a sale at a good price early on and/or by obtaining the seller's cash assistance.

PROBLEMS WITH ORGANIZING A FORECLOSURE PRESALE

Not Every Loan Insurer Will Help

Of the three primary types of mortgage insurer/guarantors—the VA, the FHA, and PMI companies—only the VA and the PMI companies offer some type of foreclosure presale procedure. The larger private mortgage insurers commonly undertake such presales. Unfortunately, the FHA does not offer mortgage insurance assistance for presales.

Primary Lender Resistance

Many borrowers assume that lenders will work with them on presales or delays in foreclosures because otherwise the lenders will have more houses on their hands in neighborhoods that are full of foreclosures. Surely they won't want that, borrowers believe. However, if the lender's potential loss on the loan is fully insured or if someone else owns the loan, the lender may care little about the foreclosure. Many hapless borrowers have dealt with power-minded lender representatives who enjoy controlling people. These borrowers' frantic begging for help has often drawn no more than Rhett Butler's familiar comment. (Of course, not all lenders are that bad.)

Problems With Mortgage Companies

Many "lenders" only service loans. This is particularly common with mortgage companies. Most mortgage companies sell the loans they make on the secondary market to such buyers as FNMA or FHLMC. The loan buyer usually appoints the mortgage company that originated the loan to service it. The loan servicer is the company that collects the borrower's payment checks, which it merely passes on to the true loan owner.

As a result, the actual loss from foreclosure may be suffered by someone other than the lender with which the borrower deals. If the loan servicer can convince the true loan owner that it complied with the proper procedures for default, then it doesn't need to care any more about foreclosure. The author has seen even more chilling situations in which loan servicers seemed intent on manufacturing documentation to show that they had actively communicated with borrowers and worked with them, when in fact they had offered no such help. Such servicers were not fulfilling their obligations to their loan owners, or to the borrowers, in good faith. Many servicers do the minimum required by the loan owners and don't really bother to try to help the borrower.

Problems With Savings and Loans

Savings and loan associations may not be willing to give troubled borrowers any more help than mortgage companies do. A savings and loan association may own all or part of the loan that is facing foreclosure. Getting a low-interest loan off its books may appeal to the savings and loan, especially if it can recover the losses from the resale of the property and mortgage insurance. Many S&Ls are desperate to generate cash to stay afloat financially or to meet government regulations. Obtaining immediate cash from a resale and from loan insurance may appeal to the savings and loan more than helping a borrower. Also, personnel who really know how to handle foreclosure presales or who can make the necessary decisions may be in short supply at an S&L. As long as it complies with government regulations, the S&L may need to have little concern for the borrower.

The Parties at Risk May Know Nothing

All too often, the mortgage insurers and mortgage owners who will suffer losses in a foreclosure are very much in the dark during the foreclosure process. The loan servicer (usually the mortgage company) cannot be relied upon to help. In fact, depending on the circumstances, the lender may resist a foreclosure presale, believing that it is undesirable to maintain a loan with a weak payment record or one that pays a low rate of interest. In fact, some lenders can even profit when they combine the proceeds from reselling properties with mortgage insurance payments.

Foreclosures usually result in a loss to someone, though. Typically, the real losers in the foreclosure, besides the borrower, are the mortgage insurer, the loan owner, and the lender's government insurer (FDIC) or regulator, if it is an S&L.

FINDING THE LOAN OWNER

All too often, neither the loan insurer nor the loan owner knows very much about a particular foreclosure. Although forms are filed that could alert them to an impending foreclosure, they may know little about the seller's ability to contribute to a presale, the chances of finding a buyer, or the attitude of the loan servicer. A critical problem is reaching these decision makers who can make the presale happen. If the loan insurer and loan owner know enough about what's happening, they can pressure the primary lender to cooperate with the presale.

The borrower needs to contact the loan owners and insurers directly or have someone else do it. The first problem here is that the borrower may have little idea who these parties are. The primary lender may not be willing to divulge their names, knowing that the borrower may try to contact them; the lender wants to be the only one to contact the loan owners or insurers. Unfortunately, no law requires the loan servicer to reveal the identities of the loan owner or insurer. Eleven states now require borrowers to be notified who the servicer is, but none requires the loan owner's name to be revealed.

The borrower may be able to guess who the loan owner is. One clue is found in the original loan papers. If these are FNMA/FHLMC forms, then FNMA or FHLMC may be the owner. This is not always true, however, since many other loan owners require the use of FNMA or FHLMC forms. FHA or VA loans are mostly sold to GNMA. Also, the FHA or VA can locate a loan owner, if needed.

Smaller, secondary market loan owners may be hard to find. One method would be to have a friend at a title company locate a notice of assignment for a mortgage in the deed records. These public records reveal any sale of the loan to a new owner and the name of the new owner. Another method would be to talk someone within the mortgage company into revealing the information. There is no violation of the federal privacy laws if lenders give out this information to the borrower or his agent. An attorney could be employed to force the lender to reveal the information, but this approach would probably take some time and money.

A good bet is to use an outside expert who has the time, the patience, and the contacts to run down the loan owner and insurer. Certain brokers, consultants, and even mortgage companies specialize in doing this. A good broker or mortgage company may know the phone numbers of key officials inside FNMA, FHLMC, or the private mortgage insurer. The brokers and mortgage companies know how to get needed information from lenders. The author strongly recommends this approach.

Once the loan owner or insurer is found, the battle is not over by any means. Not every loan owner is interested in working on a presale. Some will refuse to allow one altogether. This makes a foreclosure almost inevitable. However, owners often allow presales.

For analysis, this discussion will divide presales into two groups by loan types:

1. Conforming loans are owned by an entity that follows FNMA servicing standards.

2. Nonconforming loans operate by different rules than those set by FNMA.

Remember, the term "loan owner" is used loosely. Loan owners raise money by selling mortgage-backed securities. How the money to buy the loan was raised may affect whether the loan owner can or will approve a particular presale arrangement. Loan owners also have standards to determine when they will or will not authorize presales. The first group of standards to be considered here are FNMA's.

PRIVATE MORTGAGE INSURERS AND FORECLOSURE PRESALES

Private mortgage insurers are the key to many, if not most, foreclosure presales. When the home is worth less than what is owed against it, the owner cannot sell without assistance. PMI companies can provide that assistance by providing cash to pay off part of the old loan. The PMI company will provide the assistance needed for a presale if doing so will reduce its overall loss on the loan. A presale can save the private mortgage insurer money by speeding up the sale, avoiding property depreciation and vandalism, and securing contributions from the seller. A PMI company is in business to make money; if a presale will reduce its loss, it will seriously consider the deal. There are two keys to determining what the PMI company will be willing to do: its total loss exposure and the effect of the prospective presale deal on its loss.

PMI COMPANY'S TOTAL LOSS EXPOSURE

Private mortgage insurance is usually sold through a few major national companies. Normally, private mortgage insurance pays the lender for losses it suffers when a borrower defaults. In a presale, the private mortgage insurer will normally pay the loan owner but release the borrower from liability, at least to a significant degree. Although private mortgage insurers normally pursue deficiency suits, they agree not to in presale deals.

However, like any insurance company, private mortgage insurers are concerned about fraudulent claims. They will investigate each foreclosure situation, including presales, to make sure that the original private mortgage insurance policy was properly obtained. It will check for compliance with all of its rules when the loan was insured and for proper procedures upon default. Failure to implement proper policies and procedures may cause the PMI company to refuse to pay a claim at all.

Not all claims merit presale assistance, even if no fraud is involved. For example, a rich investor who owns property might have difficulty obtaining PMI presale assistance if she could maintain the payments from other income. PMI insures against genuine defaults for reasons beyond the borrower's control; it is not intended to insure an investor against losses from an unwise investment. The PMI company will want to make sure that the reasons for the loss are sufficient to justify presale assistance. Otherwise, it will demand foreclosure and it might sue for a deficiency judgment. PMI companies work to prevent their insurance from being abused to cover losses on ill-conceived loans or to give a windfall to borrowers who could pay their debts but just don't want to.

Assuming that a claim is to be paid, the next question is how much will have to be paid. It is important to note that private mortgage insurers do not insure the full amount of most loans. Instead, loan insurance covers only the top 12 to 30 percent of the loan. To be more specific, private mortgage insurance insures against a loss on a mortgage calculated as follows.

Estimate the Gross Loss

Unpaid principal plus delinquent interest (the cumulative interest portion of all missed payments) plus reasonable foreclosure costs and expenses equals the gross loss. To minimize the loss, the private mortgage insurer will expect a lender to begin foreclosure within four months of default.

Costs during extra months before foreclosure will probably not be covered. Interest will be covered from the time of default, plus four months, plus the time for the foreclosure. Therefore, the lender will normally want to initiate a foreclosure just after the fourth month, unless there is good reason to start earlier.

The private mortgage insurer will generally be notified after the second month of nonpayment. It may advise the lender to foreclose earlier if it sees no hope of arriving at a presale or other solution to the delinquency. This is particularly likely to occur if the borrower/owner is uncooperative.

The private mortgage insurer will also cover certain foreclosure expenses. These usually include attorney's fees, property taxes, hazard insurance premiums, property preservation costs, and a few extra foreclosure-related costs. (The next section gives more details.)

Calculate the Rough Insurance Payoff

Under standard coverage, the insurance payoff equals the gross loss multiplied by the coverage percentage. The typical coverage levels are 12 percent, 17 percent, 20 percent, 22 percent, 25 percent, and 30 percent of the loss. For example, with a gross loss of $80,000 and 30 percent coverage, the payoff is $80,000 × 30 percent = $24,000.

Under adjustor 75 coverage (used mostly on adjustable-rate mortgages), the insurance payoff equals the gross loss minus 75 percent of the home's fair market value when the loan was made. On a house worth $100,000 at loan origination with a gross loss of $80,000, the payoff is $80,000 – $75,000 ($100,000 × 75 percent) = $5,000

Adjustor coverage is usually set up so that the insurance payoff is the greater of the adjustor figure or the standard coverage figure calculated with 20 percent or 25 percent coverage. The deeper the coverage, the more likely the mortgage insurer is to cooperate in a presale, because its loss exposure is greater.

Recoverable Foreclosure Expenses

Generally, the private mortgage insurer will cover the basic expenses resulting from a foreclosure, and these increase the PMI company's potential loss. Under regular circumstances, without a presale, these expenses include the following items:

- Lender's attorney's fees: These are usually limited to 3 percent, and mortgage insurers may not reimburse fees in excess of what is reasonable. The fees are paid to outside counsel to obtain title and physical possession of the property by foreclosure. Fees paid to inside counsel who work directly for the lender do not qualify, nor do costs for other employees of the mortgage company.

- Foreclosure costs: These are the costs, other than outside attorney's fees, incurred to obtain title and physical possession of the property by foreclosure. These would include court filing fees, constable's fees, and recording fees.

- Real estate taxes paid: To be reimbursed, these taxes must be paid by the lender. They do not include late payment penalties and interest or prorated unpaid taxes. (However, these prorated amounts may be claimed as closing costs during a presale.) Special assessments for the current year that the lender has paid may be included as real estate taxes.

- Insurance premiums: Paid hazard insurance premiums, but not mortgage life insurance premiums, may be reimbursed. Costs for preservation of the property costs of securing and maintaining the property may be reimbursed, including yard care, winterizing, rekeying locks, and minimal utility bills. Repair fees may also be paid, but in sales other than presales, they are usually limited to about $750, unless more is approved in writing. Repairs would include such things as cleaning, painting, and drywall spackling. Preservation of the property does not include restoration fees, such as repair of damage caused by vandalism, theft, flood, fire, or major structural failure.

- Miscellaneous expenses: Insurance covers any expenses for things requested by the mortgage insurance company, such as appraisals.

- Presale expenses: In a foreclosure presale, a private mortgage insurer will usually give cash reimbursements for expenses in excess of those outlined above. In particular, the PMI company will probably fund attorney's fees in excess of 3 percent of the sale price, all repair expenses, and interest to the closing date.

Presale's Effect on PMI Company's Loss

If a foreclosure presale will save the private mortgage insurance company money, then it will consider approving and funding the deal. After analyzing its potential loss exposure, as described above, the PMI company needs to analyze the sale itself. The key ingredient in a successful presale is obviously the sales price. A good sales price will tend to minimize the PMI company's exposure. However, seller and lender contributions may also play roles. The PMI company may even initiate the foreclosure presale process as part of its mortgage default control program. Otherwise, the loan owner (such as FNMA), the loan servicer (usually a mortgage company), or the homeowner may initiate the foreclosure presale by calling and asking the PMI company for approval.

PMI COMPANIES' MORTGAGE DEFAULT CONTROL PROGRAMS

Most private mortgage insurance companies maintain mortgage default control programs of some kind, usually centralized in a national or large regional office. Other companies set up field offices in the areas that suffer most from foreclosure. One problem with such field offices is that they may be temporary, open only until the foreclosure problem in a given city or region subsides. A borrower lucky enough to live in an area served by a local office may find a presale easier to arrange. In a smaller office, one person may serve several functions, but such a person is often familiar with local conditions. In contrast, national or regional offices usually have specialized persons who perform specific tasks.

The large office employs several types of people who make direct contact with the troubled borrower. A claims representative or account analyst spots and tracks loan defaults that might be suitable for presales. A telephone counselor communicates with the defaulting borrower to explore options, including financial counseling, loan workouts (modifications, forbearance, etc. as described in other parts of this book), or a foreclosure presale. A loan counselor visits the borrower and discusses the options for dealing with mortgage default, including presales. A real estate specialist, either a broker or someone who knows preapproved brokers who regularly deal with the PMI company, explores the options for selling the house, including a presale.

One key task is be to determine the amount the PMI company can afford to contribute to a presale deal. This will require verifications of the seller's assets and income, like those supplied in a loan qualification process. The seller must show he has contributed everything possible to the presale. The PMI company will then take up the slack. Once the property is on the market, purchase offers should be received at the price the PMI company projected. All offers must be presented to the PMI company for approval or disapproval. Since the PMI company will have calculated its potential exposure, and since the seller will have been squeezed for everything he can contribute, the PMI company will know whether a specific sale will save money or not. If it will, it will likely be approved.

Some of the larger PMI companies have people who do nothing but analyze deals, approving or disapproving sales offers and specific presale deals. MGIC, one of the largest mortgage insurers, keeps about 40 such people at its main office in Milwaukee, Wisconsin. Once a specific sale proposal comes in, it is approved or disapproved quickly. Upon approval, a conditional letter will be written to indicate the amount the company will contribute to the sale and the terms and conditions under which the money may be disbursed. In many states, a set of instructions will be delivered to the closer to outline the terms and conditions under which the closing may take place.

The real estate specialist and/or an independent broker from the area, working with the mortgage insurer, is usually a key person in the foreclosure presale process. First, this person must evaluate the condition of the property and identify any repairs needed to market it. Second, she will prepare an estimate of value and look over any BPOs that have been prepared. Third, she will create and obtain the borrower's commitment to a marketing plan; the borrower who is about to lose the home must cooperate for the presale to succeed. Fourth, the real estate specialist will obtain approval from the PMI company management for a foreclosure presale. Fifth, this person will work with the broker to sell the house. A certain amount of bargaining may take place before an offer is approved. Remember, the PMI company's objective is to minimize its losses.

When the borrower, the buyer, the PMI company, the loan owner (such as FNMA), and the loan servicer (typically a mortgage company) finally reach agreement concerning a specific sale, it will be conditionally approved and the closing will proceed. The funding from the PMI company may not come until after the sale. Since no delay is generally allowed in the foreclosure, a smart borrower will move quickly to work out a presale. Wait too long, and it will be too late.

PROBLEMS WITH POOL MORTGAGES

In the modern world, the lender that loaned the borrower money may not own the mortgage any longer. Most mortgage companies sell the mortgages they make. Once sold, the mortgage is put together with other mortgages in a pool, which includes hundreds or even thousands of mortgages. Investors buy shares in the pool or debt instruments that are backed by the pool. Such investment shares, almost regardless of the type, are referred to as "mortgage-backed securities." Owning a part of a pool is a lot safer for the investor than owning an individual mortgage. If the one mortgage goes into default, the investor could suffer a large loss. In a pool, on the other hand, losses can be averaged over hundreds of mortgages. Throughout the United States, fewer than 1 percent of all mortgages ever go into foreclosure, and playing the law of averages gives safety in numbers. Pools can be assembled from mortgages drawn from all parts of the country, so trouble in one area, like Texas, can be offset by steady performance elsewhere. Geographic dispersion increases safety. Different kinds of mortgages from different kinds of borrowers can be put into a single pool as well.

Ownership shares in mortgage pools can be structured in several ways. The investor can own a part of the actual mortgages in the pool in a straight pass-through arrangement. All earnings and all losses from a straight pass-through pass through directly to the investor. If borrowers don't pay, investors do not get paid. In a modified pass-through, a large issuer of mortgage-backed securities, such as FNMA, could guarantee the payment of the interest, at least, to an investor who buys into the pool, but the investor would still own a chunk of the mortgages in the pool. If the issuer of the mortgage-backed securities owns the mortgages, based on which it sells a security or debt instrument, then it creates a true security. Issuers commonly guarantee the interest and principal payments on such securities.

Pools have a strong impact on presales and other workout devices. Workouts and presales are more difficult on a mortgage in a pool that backs securities with guaranteed, fixed repayments of principal and interest. The issuer of the securities will simply refuse to consider a lower interest rate or forbearance, since tampering with the mortgage could land the issuer of the mortgage-backed security in court for securities fraud. If interest is guaranteed to the investor, it must be paid or else. A modification to a mortgage that could reduce interest payments on a mortgage-backed security would be no more acceptable to investors, and no more legal, than a bank's paying its depositors lower interest rates on their CDs because it made too many bad loans. Such problems make foreclosure much more likely.

On the other hand, mortgages that underlie straight pass-through securities issued to local investors might allow easy workouts and modifications, including presales. For good cause shown, such investors might be willing to accept temporarily lower returns to avoid greater losses later on from foreclosures.

Pools affect the way loan owners behave. In particular, pools alter the servicing of mortgages. In FNMA's regular servicing arrangement, the servicer must absorb losses from foreclosure presales. In FNMA's special servicing arrangement, FNMA will pay the costs of the presale, which have included a processing fee and up to three broker price opinions.

Pools have an important impact on mortgage insurance as well. Mortgage insurers may insure not only individual mortgages but pools of mortgages. If a mortgage is in a pool, it is worthwhile to consider whether the loan insurer for the mortgage is also insuring the pool. Generally, this additional coverage helps presales, because the double coverage of the mortgage and the pool increases the PMI company's loss exposure. Generally, pools can apply for insurance after a primary claim for a loss due to a foreclosure has already occurred. The second claim is called a "supplemental claim for insurance." It must ordinarily credit the receipts of the primary claim and any subsequent resale money against what is payable on the pool insurance policy. However, there may be useful extra coverage under such circumstances. It's worth asking about when setting up a presale.

Deed in Lieu of Foreclosure

10

The theory behind a deed in lieu of foreclosure is simple. The borrower knows that he cannot make the payments, so to avoid the expense and trouble of foreclosure, why not just give the lender the deed? The borrower says, "Don't bother to foreclose. I'll save you the trouble. Here's the deed." This way he avoids the appearance of a foreclosure on a credit record and other adverse consequences. There are several problems with this theory: (1) the lender must accept any deed in lieu offer; (2) the lender often refuses to accept a deed in lieu for many good reasons; and (3) negotiating a successful deed in lieu arrangement is complex, even if the lender is willing to accept it.

The borrower has no right to give a deed in lieu of foreclosure. At a bar seminar, an unfortunate attorney rose to ask the speaker if a certain transaction was valid. He said that a borrower had not only mailed his client a deed in lieu but had recorded it as well! The speaker said the transaction was not a valid conveyance. No deed in lieu is valid without a lender's consent. Some have argued that a lender has accepted a deed in lieu if the lender does anything that implies acceptance. Some claim that leaving a deed in lieu with a secretary, perhaps obtaining a signed receipt, constitutes acceptance. It does not. The acceptance must be knowing, which requires an offer and an acceptance on both sides sufficient to meet traditional contract tests for offer and acceptance.

Generally, a lender will accept a deed in lieu in a state where foreclosure is difficult and time consuming and deficiency judgments are difficult or impossible to obtain. On the other hand, in states where foreclosures are conducted out of court and deficiency judgments are easy to obtain, the deed in lieu is less common. In such states, lenders prefer straight foreclosures.

In a state with nonjudicial foreclosure, the lender will generally refuse to accept a deed in lieu for at least three good reasons:

1. The lender might lose the right to sue the borrower for a deficiency judgment. The lender may want to sue the borrower for a deficiency judgment to recover any money the borrower still owes after resale of the property. The lender may be mad and seek the largest deficiency judgment it can get against the borrower. In accepting a deed in lieu of foreclosure, the lender usually waives its right to sue for a deficiency. In some states, acceptance of a deed in lieu bars further action against the borrower by the lender.

2. Junior lienholders and intervening purchasers may not lose their claims on the property without a foreclosure sale, leaving title unclear for a subsequent resale. These parties may retain claims in the absence of a foreclosure, forcing the original lender to contend with these parties' demands to be paid. To make sure this doesn't happen, the lender and the borrower may have to invest time and effort to verify that no such claims exist. This may require

obtaining an updated title policy and negotiating to resolve any claims. It is often easier to foreclose.

3. The lender may lose the benefits of title insurance or mortgage insurance policies. For example, the lender's title policy may become invalid if it discharges the borrower from the obligation to repay. Moreover, mortgage insurance companies may refuse to pay if the lender discharges the borrower. If the lender accepts a property that is worth less than the loan balance, it may incur a substantial loss, which may not be covered by mortgage insurance if it arbitrarily discharges the borrower from the obligation to pay.

MAKING THE DEED IN LIEU OF FORECLOSURE WORK

A deed in lieu of foreclosure is most likely to work when the property is worth more than the borrower owes against it. Under such circumstances, the lender may actually benefit by the deed in lieu of foreclosure. The lender that wants to accept a deed in lieu of foreclosure should do at least the following:

- Check with any mortgage insurers or title insurers to determine the impact on insurance coverage and any requirements they will impose.

- Have the borrower represent that there have been no new encumbrances (such as home improvement liens) or grants of title to anyone since the loan was originated.

- Run a title policy update to make sure no title problems have developed. Make sure that title insurance will be in full force with no unwanted exceptions after the deed in lieu is delivered.

- Obtain an appraisal to state that the primary lender's loan balance equals all of the home's value. Since such circumstances leave nothing for junior lienholders, this renders their claims valueless.

- Obtain any needed approvals from secondary market investors who own the mortgage.

A deed in lieu can work, but it is not a simple procedure. Lender cooperation is essential. Borrowers with FHA loans have the best chance of success with this tactic. The remainder of the chapter summarizes HUD, VA, and FNMA guidelines and procedures.

DEED IN LIEU OF FORECLOSURE FOR FHA LOANS

Although many lenders refuse deeds in lieu of foreclosure for ordinary loan defaults, HUD officially encourages the technique for its FHA loans. Normally, two requirements must be met before the deed in lieu of foreclosure is accepted. The default on the loan must be caused by hardship beyond the borrower's control. The deed in lieu should not be used when sound, persistent servicing might save the loan. Also, the deed in lieu is appropriate only when it is unlikely that the borrower will be able to make up the missed payments and keep the loan current.

If the above criteria are met, HUD lenders should accept deeds in lieu. Although a voluntary conveyance (i.e., deed in lieu) to avoid foreclosure can become a permanent part of the borrower's credit record, the stigma is less than that attached to foreclosure. This makes the deed in lieu attractive to borrowers.

Deed in Lieu for Other Than Owner/Occupants

HUD need not approve a deed in lieu when the borrower is an owner/occupant. Prior HUD approval is not required if the mortgage is default when the deed is executed and delivered and when the other requirements and procedures for a deed in lieu are followed. HUD approval is needed, however, for a corporate borrower or a borrower who owns other properties that are subject to HUD loans. HUD approval is needed, as well, for a loan held by the secretary.

A request for authority to accept a deed in lieu must be submitted to the director of the HUD area or insuring office that has jurisdiction in the area where the property is located. According to the HUD manual, this request should include the following:

- A statement of the reasons for default
- A statement of assets owned by the mortgagors (borrowers) other than the mortgaged properties
- Details of the disposition of income from such assets
- Any other information that might help in the proper consideration of the request

HUD Procedures

HUD wants the lender to resolve title problems first. The lender should check for second or junior liens or for other impediments to the clear conveyance of title. Any such problems will have to be cleared up, presumably at the borrower's expense, for the deed in lieu procedure to be used. If junior liens cannot be cleared, then HUD does not want the deed. Sometimes negotiation with lienholders will allow clear title to be granted. An alternative might be to obtain an appraisal that shows junior liens to be valueless, as described earlier, to clear the liens, if the lender and the HUD office will agree to it. At the very least, lenders are expected to contact secondary lienholders in an effort to clear title to the property.

HUD Rules

Several HUD rules govern use of the deed in lieu:

- Lenders should attempt to obtain the deed in lieu of foreclosure prior to taking any other action to foreclose.
- HUD authorizes lenders to pay borrowers necessary consideration to obtain a deed in lieu of foreclosure. This maximum should not be construed to be the customary amount.
- The lender should obtain the borrower's agreement to convey title.
- Once the borrower agrees to convey title, the deed should be created so that it delivers title directly from the borrower to the secretary of HUD. (Descriptions of two alternatives follow, though.)
- The lender can file a claim for HUD insurance to cover its losses from accepting a deed in lieu, just as if it had foreclosed instead.
- The lender can claim part of the cost of setting up the deed in lieu of foreclosure, plus any incentive fees, depending on the lender's status with HUD.
- The normal forms and procedures for filing a claim should be used with the deed in lieu.

Convey Title to an Agent

Another alternative would be to convey title to an agent for the lender, which could then foreclose on the agent and convey title to the secretary of HUD. The agent might be a corporation or other business entity. The lender will probably not want to go to so much trouble on behalf of a defaulting borrower, but it might be worth a try. This approach has an advantage in that it would clear any junior liens or intervening title claims, which HUD demands. The local HUD office should be consulted before this procedure is attempted.

Warranty Cases

HUD guarantees that the condition of the properties it sells will be good when an insured mortgage is involved. If any such property is defective and repairs are too expensive, the local HUD area or insuring office may elect to buy the house and convey it to the secretary. This obviously gives the local HUD office rather sweeping authority to repurchase properties with HUD loans. Two cautions are important: (1) the local office may not approve the repurchase if repair seems economically feasible; and (2) this procedure has obvious potential for abuse, and HUD is under pressure to watch for mischief and improper dealings with borrowers due to the recent scandals that have rocked the agency.

Convey Title to the Lender

The lender always has the option of taking title to the property and forgoing a claim against HUD for insurance. Obviously the lender will do that only if the value of the property exceeds the balance owed on the loan. The difference would probably have to be substantial to cover the lender's costs of holding and reselling the property.

If the difference between the outstanding mortgage balance and the market value of the property is high enough, the deal may be quite profitable for the lender, especially if there is a good hazard insurance policy on the property. The lender presumably would elect to keep the profit on the subsequent resale of the property. Note, however, that any borrower in this position should have arranged to sell the property by means of a broker rather than giving it up to the lender by means of a deed in lieu of foreclosure.

Time Limits

Any deed in lieu of foreclosure must be completed within one year of the date of default. Recall that the date of default is normally 30 days after the due date of the earliest unpaid monthly loan payment, if the default consisted of a failure to make payments. The HUD area or insuring office directors may, upon request, grant extensions of this limit. However, the HUD manual directs that extensions should be rare. Problems that might require an extension to solve are seldom present when the borrower has agreed to convey title voluntarily.

VA DEED IN LIEU OF FORECLOSURE POLICIES

The VA will consider accepting a deed in lieu of foreclosure under the proper circumstances, but it must approve any deed in lieu. The VA does not necessarily encourage deeds in lieu of foreclosure because of the potential loss to it or to the lender. The circumstances that VA considers to justify a deed in lieu include the following:

- The borrower's financial condition has deteriorated too far to allow her to continue to make loan payments.
- The borrower has been unable to sell the property after reasonable exposure to the market.
- The value of the property is not substantially in excess of the unpaid balance on the loan.
- The title is acceptable with no intervening claimants or secondary liens.

- The borrower is willing to remain liable for any monetary loss the VA may suffer from termination of the loan, or the borrower demonstrates clearly that he cannot make any future repayment to the VA.

A lender that is willing to consider accepting a deed in lieu of foreclosure should begin by ordering a liquidation appraisal. It must furnish the VA with Notice of Default (NOD) and a Notice of Intent to Foreclose. In addition, the lender should submit the following:

- Financial statements showing the borrower's assets and liabilities (a balance sheet) and income and expenses (an income statement)

- The borrower's written request for acceptance of a deed in lieu of foreclosure with details about why it is necessary to give up the house and what efforts were made to sell the house

- An agreement from the borrower to give up possession of the house immediately upon notification

- A copy of the preliminary title report

- Details about the status of the loan account, describing foreclosure or other liquidation actions

The lender must notify the borrower in writing that VA must approve a deed in lieu. If it approves, VA will notify the lender of the approval and provide further instructions. If it disapproves, VA will instruct the lender to proceed with the foreclosure. Upon approval, the lender must process a voluntary conveyance as fast as it can. It must send a variety of forms and documentation to the VA Loan Service and Claims department.

FNMA DEED IN LIEU OF FORECLOSURE POLICIES

FNMA will permit the use of a deed in lieu of foreclosure, but its policies are very restrictive. FNMA wants the deed in lieu only when the lender determines that the pursuit of a deficiency judgment is not practical or is likely to encounter legal obstacles. Otherwise, FNMA expects foreclosure or some other resolution of the default situation.

In all cases, FNMA must approve acceptance of the deed in lieu. Remember, failure to accept means that title does not transfer. The lender may recommend this option, but FNMA must approve it. The lender should recommend acceptance only in limited circumstances:

- The borrower acknowledges in writing that the deed in lieu is being offered to resolve the default problem. (This is an accommodation.)

- The mortgage insurer or guarantor agrees to the acceptance of a deed in lieu. (Recall that the PMI company has rights to sue for a deficiency as a precondition to payment of its insurance benefits. This allows the PMI company to sue borrowers who flippantly default.)

- The borrower is not paid to deed the property over to certain major, secondary market loan buyers. (This contrasts with the FHA policy allowing lenders to pay small sums to promote deeds in lieu.)

- The borrower can convey an acceptable, marketable title. (A title insurance policy will be required to back up this condition.)

- The property is vacant, unless the loan insurer or guarantor agrees to accept an occupied property.

- The property is not subject to junior liens, judgments, or attachments.
- The borrower agrees to assign rents, and the lender agrees to collect them.

If substantial property rehabilitation work is needed, title should be conveyed directly to FNMA or to the mortgage pool that owns the mortgage. If the deed can be recorded promptly, the title could be conveyed directly to the VA, HUD, or the private insurer if that party would accept it.

Loan Assumptions and Foreclosure

11

In an assumption, the buyer takes over the payments on the seller's loan. A true assumption is distinguishable from a lease-purchase or contract for deed arrangement. In the lease-purchase and contract for deed, the seller remains the owner while the buyer occupies the house and makes payments. In the true assumption, the buyer owns the house but makes payments on the seller's existing loan.

This has many advantages. In a simple assumption, the parties need not obtain a lender's approval. This makes it much easier to find a buyer for the house and make a sale. In a full assumption, a buyer must meet with a lender's approval, but the lender need not approve the status of the property by means of appraisals and inspections, as it would in an ordinary sale. Both simple and full assumptions can be set up more quickly and with fewer closing costs than an ordinary sale. Adjustable rate mortgages are assumable, and the rates shift, but not because of the assumption.

A person faced with a foreclosure can use loan assumptions in at least two ways to avoid or reduce the impact of foreclosure. First, a borrower may be able to sell a home easily by means of an assumption, even if it's near foreclosure. The new buyer can make up the back payments as part of the deal and keep up the payments on the old loan, preventing foreclosure. FNMA may allow an assumption to stop a foreclosure, but only if it approves the buyer's credit and income.

Assumption can help in a second way. A borrower who loses a house in foreclosure must find a new place to live. Since certain assumptions require no approval of the buyer, someone who just had a foreclosure may nevertheless be able to assume a house without sufficient credit to justify a new loan. Note, however, that most loans are not assumable at all and many now have added restrictions on assumptions. Let's consider these problems in more detail.

FHA AND VA ASSUMPTIONS

Both FHA-insured loans and VA-guaranteed loans are assumable in at least two different ways: the full assumption and the simple or "subject to" assumption. In either a full or a simple assumption, the seller moves out and the buyer moves in and begins making payments on the loan. In either kind of assumption, the buyer receives a deed and becomes the owner of the property. However, there are very important differences between the full and the simple assumptions. In essence, in a full assumption, the lender approves the buyer as an acceptable substitute for the old borrower, and the seller may be released from the responsibility to pay the loan. In a simple assumption, the lender does not approve the buyer as an acceptable substitute, so the old borrower remains liable to repay the loan. In either a full or a simple assumption, the buyer gets a deed and becomes the owner of the property. Figure 11.1 lists the characteristics of the two types of assumptions.

Many people have trouble understanding why lender approval is necessary in any type of assumption. The reason is the rule against assignments. A person cannot borrow money and then decline to be responsible for paying it back. Even if the person finds someone else who will agree to pay it, the original borrower remains liable. If not, everyone would assign all of their loan obligations to the nearest deadbeat!

Figure 11.1 Simple Versus Full Assumption

	Simple Assumption	Full Assumption
Who makes the payments?	Buyer	Buyer
Who has the deed?	Buyer	Buyer
Who is the owner?	Buyer	Buyer
Is lender approval required?	No	Yes
Who is liable to repay the loan?*	Seller	Buyer
Is there a deed of trust to secure the assumption?	Yes	No

*Look at the consideration section of the deed that transfers title from seller to buyer. Normally it has the phrase "for ten dollars and other good and valuable consideration," but if it also states that the buyer "assumes and agrees to pay," then the buyer is liable. If it states that the buyer takes title "subject to" the existing indebtedness, the seller remains liable.

FULL ASSUMPTION

VA and FHA have three basic requirements for a full assumption. The payments on the loan being assumed must be current, the buyer must agree to assume liability for the payments, and the buyer must be creditworthy. Under normal circumstances, the lender must approve the buyer's creditworthiness to complete a full assumption. This means the buyer will have to go through a qualification procedure that is very similar to that for new loans. In fact, a lender will apply the same standards to qualify a borrower for a full assumption as it applies to new borrowers. It will analyze both the buyer's ability to pay the loan, as determined by his income and assets, and the buyer's willingness to pay the loan, as indicated by his credit report. Under new laws, however, the lender must permit the buyer to fully assume the loan and release the seller from liability, if the buyer meets the normal standards for FHA and VA loans.

SIMPLE ASSUMPTIONS

Advantages

The simple assumption brings many advantages for both the seller and the buyer. Foremost among them, the buyer need not be creditworthy. Also, the property need not be qualified in terms of appraisals or inspections.

Bad credit currently prevents a lot of sales. As people suffer job loss, divorce, bankruptcy, or foreclosure, their credit often suffers, too. Then when they find new jobs or things improve in other ways, they find their credit does not recover as quickly. In a high-foreclosure environment, plenty of prospective buyers have credit problems or past histories of unstable employment that prevent them from qualifying for new loans. Simple assumptions can put such people in houses. Unlike a contract for deed arrangement, the buyer in a simple assumption obtains a deed on the first day of the sale. The buyer will lose ownership only by failure to pay on the loan. It's a dream come true for many buyers.

Disadvantages

By now, it should be apparent that a simple assumption differs dramatically from a full assumption. In a simple assumption, the seller is often not told what is happening. Believing that the house has been sold and unaware of potential problems, the seller may develop a false sense of security, even though she is still responsible to pay the loan.

The seller signs a deed and gives it to the buyer and often attends a closing. At closing, a title company makes it look like a final sale, and it is, but the seller is still liable on the loan. Brokers frequently say nothing about this liability, and it has been argued that they should say nothing because to do so would constitute practice of law without a license. (It doesn't, however.) The seller doesn't really understand the paperwork or consult an attorney. As a result, the seller just doesn't understand the liability on a simple assumption sale.

Beware of the Easy Sale

Everyone, including any broker, finds it easier to get a simple assumption sale together when the seller doesn't know what's happening. Unknown to the seller, the buyer may be quite uncreditworthy. Such buyers are easy to find. The seller is easily set up, and no one will know—unless the buyer defaults.

Unfortunately, simple assumptions all too often wind up in default and foreclosure without the seller knowing what happened until it's too late. Countless sellers have sold their houses by assumption, often moving to distant cities. When they try to buy homes in their new cities, to their horror, they discover foreclosures on their credit records. When the buyers failed to make the payments, the houses went into foreclosure, and the information was placed on the sellers' credit records. Such a foreclosure blocks the borrower from receiving a new FHA loan, because the FHA computer will not give a new loan application number to anyone who has a foreclosure, or even a pending foreclosure, on record. The same is true of other types of lenders.

Assumption Scams

In the 1980s, down markets in certain cities threw a spotlight on certain types of scams. For example, suppose an investor is having trouble making payments on an FHA loan on a rental house because declining rent payments no longer cover the mortgage payment. The investor sees salvation in an ad offering to buy such houses! The naive owner deeds the house to a buyer who offers to take over the payments on the existing FHA loan in a simple assumption. Unfortunately, this leaves the seller fully liable to the FHA lender if the buyer ever defaults. The buyer collects the rent checks but makes no mortgage payments. The investor owner discovers what's happening and tries to complain, but the buyer ignores him. The FHA lender has no choice but to foreclose, leaving the hapless investor with a foreclosure on his credit record and a possible deficiency suit to cover the FHA's loss.

This practice is called "rent skimming." To stop it, current FHA regulations require investors who assume existing FHA loans to pay down the loan balance to the point where rents will cover mortgage payments or until equity reaches 25 percent, whichever is less.

Partly in response to the many and varied scams that have popped up throughout the United States, the federal government has sought to restrict simple assumption in other ways. Figure 11.2 shows some of the new FHA and VA restrictions. The new rules will have the ultimate effect of eliminating simple assumptions on VA loans after 30 years or so, because all the pre-1988 loans will have been retired.

WRAPAROUND ARRANGEMENTS

In a wraparound, the buyer not only assumes an existing loan but creates a second loan as well. This is necessary to bridge the gap between the balance on the existing assumed loan and the value of the property. Here's an example:

Fair market value of house:	$ 50,000
Balance on old loan:	$ 20,000
Gap:	$ 30,000

There are several ways to bridge this gap. The buyer can come up with extra cash. The seller can accept payments over time for all or part of the gap, plus interest. (This is called "seller financing.") The buyer can arrange a loan from a commercial lender.

If the seller or another lender makes a loan to bridge the gap, the second loan will probably be set up as a wrap loan. Properly speaking, a wrap loan is a second- or later-lien loan that includes an obligation to pay the earlier loan(s). The second- or later-lien loan wraps around the earlier loan(s). If a buyer defaults in paying an earlier loan, the later loan can be foreclosed. The wrap loan documentation operates much the same way as a deed of trust to secure an assumption, but all that is needed is a second deed of trust. Full and simple assumptions both require second deeds of trust to set up wrap loans, because a foreclosure of any earlier loan, whether fully assumed or not, will destroy the later lienholder's position.

Foreclosure Risk for Wraparound Lender

A later lien involves a serious risk of destruction by the foreclosure of an earlier lien. Sometimes the existence of a later lien virtually forces a foreclosure. For example, let's suppose we have a first-lien loan at $55,000. A purchase adds a $25,000 second lien, which is set up as a wraparound loan. The total owed is therefore $80,000.

If the property value declines over time to $65,000, then the house may be impossible to sell. No broker could obtain a price sufficient to pay off the first and second liens. If the owner of the house can't keep up the payments on the first loan, the lender will foreclose. If the borrower can neither sell the property nor make the payments, the inevitable foreclosure will wipe out the later-lien loan. Such sad situations are common in divorces and with homes purchased as investments. A divorcing spouse often receives a note from the other spouse for all or part of the equity in a house, together with a deed of trust that can support foreclosure on the house if payments are not made. Investment situations can have the same unhappy ending.

Figure 11.2 Assumption Characteristics of FHA/VA Loans

		Permissible Assumptions
VA	Loans originated before March 1, 1988	Simple or Full
	Loans originated after March 1, 1988	Full only
FHA	Loans originated before December 1, 1986	Simple or Full
	Loans originated between December 1, 1986 and December 15, 1989	Simple* or Full
	Loans originated after December 15, 1989	Full only

*The simple assumption on loans made between 1986 and 1989 converts to a full assumption five years after the sale, assuming one buyer pays on the house during that time.

MULTIPLE ASSUMPTIONS

Another problem area for foreclosures concerns multiple assumptions. A chain of assumptions may develop when the first owner sells to the second owner, who assumes the original loan; the second owner sells to the third, who also assumes the original loan; as does the fourth owner who buys the property from the third; and so on. If one of these parties fails to pay on the original loan, foreclosure will wipe out the ownership for all subsequent claimants and set each of them up for a lawsuit for a deficiency, assuming the value of the property has gone down. In the early 1970s in Houston, whole chains of assumptions collapsed.

Since the seller is not released from liability on the assumed loan, she asks for a deed of trust to secure assumption. The buyer's failure to keep up payments on the old loan constitutes default on this deed of trust, and the seller can foreclose. If the seller fails to foreclose, the lender who is not receiving payments from the assumption buyer will foreclose on the original deed of trust, which is still valid.

Figure 11.3 Assumption Sale Pattern

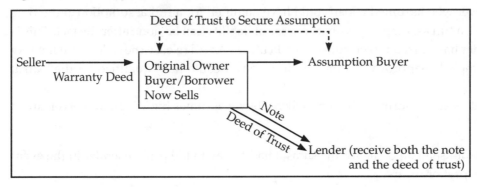

The assumption sale pattern outlined in figure 11.3 can be repeated again and again. With each passage of title, each seller receives a lien by means of a deed of trust to secure assumption. The original lender (usually a mortgage company for an FHA or VA loan) still holds the deed of trust it received from the original borrower, which remains active until the loan it secures if repaid in full. Without any release of the seller's obligation to repay the original loan, he receives a deed of trust to secure assumption to make sure the buyer pays both the payments on the assumed loan and any additional payments on seller-financed amounts. If the seller does finance part of the purchase, he should ask the assumption buyer for a real estate lien note to define the obligation for the additional payments.

ASSUMPTION HORROR STORIES

It is very important to set up arrangements on a simple assumption by which to deliver the buyer's payments reliably. Failure to do this can bring terrible consequences, which may be the fault of either the buyer or the seller. The buyer can suffer if she makes payments to the seller, who deposits each check and then should write a check to the lender. The danger is that the seller will deposit the checks but forget (or purposely neglect) to pay the lender. Although the buyer has paid steadily, she still faces foreclosure. In fact, if the foreclosure notices are forwarded to the seller, the buyer's first news of the foreclosure may be a three-day eviction notice.

The seller can also be the victim of assumption horrors. Time and again, naive sellers have failed to set up systems to ensure that buyers make payments on assumed loans. The buyer may have arranged to make the payments directly to the bank. The seller may move away thinking all will be well, only to find out too late that the buyer failed to make the payments and the lender foreclosed. Countless sellers believe they have sold houses and face no further obligation. Even the seller who understands the liability under a simple assumption may not have thought about how to make sure the buyer makes every payment. Without calling the lender constantly, the seller might never know about a buyer's failure to make payments.

Even if the buyer makes direct payments, they might not be on time, much to the seller's annoyance. The lack of timely payments will damage the seller's credit record, making it more difficult to obtain loans in the future.

SPECIAL REMEDIES FOR ASSUMPTION PROBLEMS

Since most assumptions involve VA-guaranteed or FHA-insured loans, it is worth considering options if the assumed loan goes into default. VA and FHA have special procedures for dealing with liability after a default on an assumed loan. Should the assumption buyer fail to pay the loan payments, the lender or mortgage insurer may foreclose and pursue a deficiency judgment against the original borrower. This borrower may block further liability through a retroactive release from liability. In general, retroactive release from liability is possible only with FHA or VA loans. The theory is that, if a buyer who assumed a loan could have qualified for a full assumption at the time the loan was assumed, a full assumption with its release of liability can be done after the fact. This is true whether the lender has started foreclosure or not. FHA or VA will release the seller from liability at any time after a simple, no-approval assumption if the buyer could have qualified for the loan at the time of the sale.

A veteran faces at least two forms of liability when a buyer assumes his VA-guaranteed loan on a no-approval basis:

1. The government itself could sue for the sums it had to pay to the private lender in the event of foreclosure, past or future.

2. The private lender could sue for any losses that exceeded the VA loss coverage limits.

Only the first type of liability can be eliminated by retroactive release from liability procedures. (See figure 11.4.)

Future Access to VA Loans

The question of restoring the entitlement is a separate issue from liability altogether. The government may give a release of liability but at the same time choose not to permit the veteran to obtain another VA loan. This is not a form of liability.

Three Criteria for Retroactive Release from Liability

VA or FHA will consider a retroactive release of liability if the deal meets three criteria:

1. At the time of the sale, the first 12 months of payments must have been paid, and the loan must not have been in default on the monthly payments.

2. At the time of the sale, the buyer must have agreed to assume liability on the seller's loan by signing a deed with an "assumes and agrees to pay" clause or by signing a separate document accepting liability.

3. The buyer's credit and income must have been sufficient to justify a lender's approval of a full assumption at the time of the sale.

Buyer Qualification for Lender Approval

The VA and FHA may release liability if the buyer who assumed the loan could have qualified according to the lender's ordinary criteria for a full assumption with release of liability at the time of the assumption sale. The VA or FHA needs adequate evidence of income and creditworthiness, such as tax returns, paycheck stubs, historical credit reports, or other evidence. If the credit bureau can't provide a report on the buyer's credit from the time of the assumption, then other factors may be examined to decide whether the buyer's credit was sufficient. Doubtful cases for VA loans should be resolved in favor of the vet.

Special VA Procedures: Divorce

A VA loan may be assumed by one spouse alone during the course of a divorce. Should the spouse who assumed the loan default on it, the spouse who moved out may have a liability to the government. VA may relieve such a veteran from liability if five criteria are met:

1. The divorce is final.
2. Ownership of the house is vested in the spouse who remained in the house and not the other spouse
3. The loan is current.
4. The VA's income and credit requirements can be met by the remaining spouse.
5. No property settlement makes the veteran liable to the other party for the loan.

Figure 11.4 Effects of Retroactive Release From Liability

Foreclosure Problem	Effect of Retroactive Release
Liability to government	Can be eliminated
Liability to private lender in excess of government payments	Cannot be eliminated
Restoration of entitlement	Cannot be restored

Unknown Foreclosure

The seller may argue successfully that he or she never received notice of a default. All too often the seller fails to understand that she remains liable. A former owner who can show that she received no notice of a loan default on a simple assumption may induce the VA to refuse to reimburse the lender for the loss on the foreclosure. The courts may find that the veteran seller has no liability unless the lender gave notice of the foreclosure in advance.

The Ultimate Weapon: Section 3102(b) Release

If all else fails, there is at least one route a desperate veteran might take to avoid liability for a default on an assumption: Title 38, Section 3102(b) in the U.S. Code. This section provides that a veteran may be released from liability if the VA determines that its efforts to recover money that it paid to a lender on a defaulted loan from the veteran would be "against equity and good conscience." However, the VA may not by law grant such a release if it finds indications of fraud, misrepresentation, material fault, or lack of good faith on the part of the persons seeking release from liability. The veteran should seek the section 3102(b) release within 180 days from the date the VA notifies him of indebtedness to the lender or such other and additional period as VA determines is reasonable in the case at hand.

ASSUMPTIONS: PLUSES AND MINUSES

Assumptions cause many foreclosure problems. Many buyers seek assumptions because they lack sufficient credit. This is bound to lead to a higher default rate. Also, the buyer may put little money down, which is another cause of a higher default rate. Assumptions are often wrapped with second-lien loans, making risky stacks of loans that absorb too much of the value of the properties that secure them. This, again, is bound to lead to a higher default rate. In short, assumptions are made for trouble.

However, special remedies exist for two of the most commonly assumed types of loans, FHA and VA loans. A seller may secure retroactive release of liability in some instances. There are other ways to deal with the consequences of a failed assumption deal.

On the positive side, the availability of an assumable loan is often a powerful tool to help a distressed homeowner sell a house before it's too late and the lender forecloses. For the very reasons that assumptions cause so much trouble, they can help tremendously in getting a house sold in a down market. For old VA and FHA loans, the buyer doesn't need good credit. In a down market, there are plenty of buyers without good credit who will buy readily if a house has a no-approval assumption loan. Even without the no-approval feature, a lender may approve an assumption in a down market to prevent a foreclosure. FNMA lists assumptions as a possible workout tool to avoid foreclosures.

Going to Court

12

Various states' laws define foreclosure procedures that take place either in court or out of court. If a foreclosure is due to take place out of court under a power of sale clause in a deed of trust, then it may be possible to stop or delay the foreclosure by filing a lawsuit. Obviously, if the foreclosure is filed as a lawsuit (in a judicial foreclosure), going to court won't help at all. All the borrower can do is raise defenses and point out procedural errors in the lender's acceleration or paperwork to try to deny or delay a foreclosure. The borrower can try to stop or delay a nonjudicial (out-of-court) foreclosure by means of temporary orders, injunctions, or threats of wrongful foreclosure actions. Even after a judicial or a nonjudicial foreclosure, many states give the borrower a right to redeem the property by paying up the past due balance on the loan. Persons in the military can take advantage of the Soldier and Sailor's Relief Act of 1940. Here are a few possibilities for delaying a foreclosure by court action.

TEMPORARY RESTRAINING ORDERS AND INJUNCTIONS

Depending on state law, it may be possible to stop an impending nonjudicial foreclosure by means of a temporary restraining order (TRO) or an injunction. A court may grant a TRO very quickly, sometimes within hours of the initial request, and without a formal, adversarial hearing. A TRO will stop the process for several days or weeks.

A temporary injunction usually stops the foreclosure until a trial, but it will almost certainly require an adversarial hearing before the judge. It may turn into a miniature trial on short notice. As a result, it may take longer to obtain a temporary injunction than a TRO. Unfortunately, both tactics are likely to cost a small fortune in legal fees and are best used when the foreclosure is truly being undertaken in bad faith or without reasonable cause.

Obtaining a TRO or a temporary injunction involves many problems. Neither may be granted under the law unless at least three requirements are met:

1. The borrower must show a probable right to win on the merits of the case.
2. The borrower must face probable harm if the injunction or TRO is not granted.
3. There must not be an adequate alternative remedy, such as an award of money damages. This means that only a court command can solve the problem and money damages after the fact won't help.

In a foreclosure situation, the first test, a probability of prevailing on the merits of the case, is particularly hard to meet. The sad fact is that if the lender does not receive the house payment each month, few things can interfere with its legal right to foreclose. The borrower who has missed many payments has very little basis to challenge a foreclosure, however good the reasons for missing the payments. Personal problems such as illness, divorce, or job loss generally are not relevant to the legal question of whether the lender can foreclose or not. The objective fact that payments have been missed is all that is likely to concern the court.

If, however, the lender has somehow caused or contributed to the borrower's inability to make payments, then the borrower has a case. For example, if a seller-finance lender took six checks from the borrower for monthly payments, threw them in the trash, and denied ever receiving them, then the borrower would have good cause for an injunction. If the lender refused to accept offered payments, the borrower might prevail as well. Remember, however, that the lender does not normally have to accept isolated late payments after two or more missed payments. Only if the lender flatly refuses to accept any payments does the homeowner likely have a case.

To get a TRO, the homeowner almost has to hope that the judge will treat the requirement for a likelihood to prevail rather lightly. Some jurisdictions and some judges seem willing to grant a TRO even when the probability of prevailing on the merits is questionable. However, most TRO and temporary injunction requests are denied.

It is usually easy to meet the second requirement for a TRO or injunction by showing the probable harm to the homeowner without it. A person's home is unique, and there is no real substitute. The loss of a home is unquestionably harmful.

The third test, the lack of an adequate remedy at law, is also easy to show. Money damages will not make up for the loss of one's unique home. Only that home has the familiar neighbors and view, the fine oak tree in front, and so on. Money just isn't adequate to make up for the loss.

Even after meeting the three-part test, the homeowner still has important legal hurdles to overcome to obtain either a TRO or a temporary injunction. The person seeking an injunction must ordinarily post a bond and then serve the TRO or injunction. The bond may be waived in certain cases.

Finally, to take effect, the TRO or the temporary injunction must be physically delivered to the trustee who is foreclosing on the house. Such orders must be served. This is usually done by a constable, who chases the trustee down and slaps the order into his hand. This stops the foreclosure. If the trustee continues anyway, the judge will rule the foreclosure to be invalid and hold the lender in contempt of court.

Drawbacks to TRO and Temporary Injunctions

Don't imagine that these orders are swift, simple, cheap papers that can be filed with a judge to stop a foreclosure. It's just not so. TROs and temporary injunctions are risky and potentially expensive for the homeowner. It is not totally impossible to obtain a TRO, but the homeowner must have legal cause. Inability to pay a mortgage is not, by itself, proper cause. Some judges will give TROs rather freely, but don't count on it. A person with a good case and some money has the best chance to obtain one. A person who can't pay the mortgage because of financial hardship may have a tough time finding a lawyer who will take the case and then meeting any bond requirements. This person will still have to make up the back payments to avoid continued problems.

Bond Requirement

The judge will set a bond to cover any loss that would occur if the injunction or TRO were later found to have been improperly granted. Since the order requires the judge to shoot from the hip in ruling on the request before considering all the witnesses and evidence, the person seeking the temporary order will have to pay for a possible mistake. That person must post a sum sufficient to cover the cost of the mistake as a bond. A bonding company can put up the bond, much like a bail bond for release from jail, but this is not cheap. The person seeking the bond must also pledge property that the bonding company could seize and sell if it had to pay on the bond. In short, a large bond requirement would kill the whole idea of the TRO or temporary injunction, unless the person seeking the injunction were rich and did not mind the risk.

WRONGFUL FORECLOSURE

After a foreclosure sale, a borrower may try to attack it as a wrongful foreclosure to recover ownership or obtain money damages. Most borrowers try to win money damages rather than recover title. The borrower may also present a wrongful foreclosure defense if the lender sues for any deficiency that remained after the proceeds of the foreclosure sale.

OTHER FORMS OF LENDER LIABILITY

Federal Debt Collection Law

A trustee performing a foreclosure must comply with the Federal Debt Collection Practices Act. Under this law, a trustee is a debt collector who must give the debtor the same notice as required when collecting most types of consumer debt. A 1984 amendment defines *debt collector* to include not only collection agencies but attorneys as well. However, the lender itself is excluded.

When an attorney, acting as a foreclosure trustee, makes initial contact with the debtor, she should give the Federal Debt Collection Practices Act notice as part of the demand letter that is sent to the mortgage debtor before foreclosing. The notice should inform the debtor that, if the debt was incurred for personal, household, or family purposes, certain steps will be taken upon the debtor's request. A typical Federal Debt Collection Practices Act notice may contain provisions such as the following:

- Unless the borrower disputes within 30 days, the debt collector will regard the debt as valid.
- If the debtor notifies the debt collector in writing that the debt is disputed, the debt collector will obtain and mail to the debtor verification of the debt or any portion of it.
- The debt collector will provide the name and address of the original creditor.
- The notice should include the amount of the debt and the name of the current creditor.

A law firm handling the foreclosure may commence legal action, including posting the property for foreclosure, before the 30-day dispute period ends, even if the consumer disputes the debt. However, ordinary collection practices, such as phone calls and dunning letters other than those required by law and the foreclosure notice, must stop during the 30-day period. The Federal Trade Commission has indicated that the attorney may publish the foreclosure notice.

A violation of this law may lead to enforcement by the Federal Trade Commission and/or recovery of $1,000 plus attorney's fees by a civil lawsuit.

Right of Rescission Under the Truth-in-Lending Act

If foreclosure is due to default on a mortgage loan that was used to buy the house, the lien is not subject to rescission under the federal Truth-in-Lending Act. However, the same law states that any second-lien loan, even one that provided part of the purchase money for the home, is subject to the borrower's right of rescission—the right to back out of a contract. The right of rescission would extend to any mechanic's lien loans for repairs or home improvements.

The right of rescission lasts for three days following a consumer's initial entry into a contract or until all the material disclosures required by Regulation Z of the federal Truth-in-Lending Act have been provided to the borrower. If the holder of the mechanic's lien loan for repairs or improvements failed to give the required Regulation Z notices, then the foreclosure can be stopped by invoking a rescission of the entire mechanic's lien loan contract. Regulation Z requires that any loan contract disclose the annual percentage rate (APR), the amount financed, the total finance charge, and the total for all payments. It also requires disclosure of the monthly payments, the interest to be paid, and the time schedule for payments. Failure to provide the disclosures on Regulation Z forms gives the borrower a right to rescind.

Service Member's Civil Relief Act (SCRA)

No discussion of lender liability would be complete without a discussion of the Sevicemembers' Civil Relief Act. At the beginning of World War II, Congress feared that men would be drafted into the military and sent overseas to fight and risk death protecting the nation, only to return to foreclosed homes. To prevent this, Congress passed the Soldier and Sailor's Relief Act, which forbade foreclosure on the home of a serviceperson who could not pay on a mortgage due to military service. The law was revised December 19, 2005.

Note, however, that the law doesn't allow anyone in any kind of military service to avoid foreclosure at all times. To stop a foreclosure, the act requires that the problem with paying the mortgage arise from the borrower's military service and that the mortgage obligation predate the commencement of the borrower's military service.

Someone who borrows money to buy a house while already in the military is not necesarily protected by the act. Military service must have a material adverse effect on the borrower's ability to pay the mortgage (i.e. order to Iraq). If a lender and a borrower dispute about whether or not military service has caused a problem with paying on a loan, the question can be taken to court. If the court finds that the serviceperson's case has no validity, it can order foreclosure. The burden of proof is on the creditor.

The act protects not only the serviceperson but also the serviceperson's spouse and dependents who live in the same house. It also applies to purchases of houses through contracts for deed or installment arrangements. Presumably, it covers assumptions as well. The act also restricts, but does not necessarily stop, the termination of leases and foreclosure of mortgages on personal property. A related law stops all court action if a serviceperson's military duties prevent him from mounting an effective case in court.

These laws don't give the military borrower permanent relief from paying the mortgage. The debt is still owed. The protection extends only so long as the borrower is in military service and for a three-month period after discharge.

A serviceperson can file court action to vacate any foreclosure that takes place within the period of military service or three months afterward. She should bring such an action promptly upon discharge from military duty. Such a foreclosure sale would probably be regarded as void, and any lender who knowingly violates the act is guilty of a misdemeanor. A letter and a copy of orders or a commanding officer's letter that military service prevents a court appearance, sent to a court, will cause a judge to stop proceedings for at least 90 days.

LENDER DEFENSES AGAINST WRONGFUL FORECLOSURE CLAIMS

Some borrowers may regard the best defense against foreclosure to be a good offense. Instead of waiting for the lender's ax to fall, the borrower may sue the lender. Even if the lender fires the first shot and sues the borrower, either to foreclose or for a deficiency after foreclosure, the borrower may file counterclaims against the lender alleging wrongful foreclosure. This action may do at least two things: (1) challenge the foreclosure sale itself, showing it was void or voidable; and (2) raise affirmative defenses, such as fraud and misrepresentation by the bank in inducing the borrower to sign the loan documents. This may arise if a bank misrepresented its services to the borrower by stating that future loans and loan modifications would be readily available and then withholding approval.

Unfortunately for the borrower, the lender may have some significant defenses against allegations of wrongful foreclosure. This is particularly true in the case of litigation against a bank that has been taken over by the federal government. Important lender defenses against wrongful foreclosure claims include the following:

- The D'Oench, Duhme doctrine, which may invalidate counterclaims by the borrower against the lender
- Removal of the action to federal court, with its additional burdens and complications
- Claims that the lender is in receivership with no assets to declare, making claims against it moot

Awesome Lender Defense: The D'Oench, Duhme Doctrine

Lending institution may come under government control, which is conservatorship, or liquidation, which is receivership. A borrower who is being sued by such a lending institution for a deficiency judgment may tell a heartbreaking tale of broken promises, deceit, fraud, and general skullduggery by the lender. Ordinarily, such conduct would provide the borrower with numerous defenses against the lender's lawsuit to collect on the loan.

Unfortunately, all of these claims may collapse at the feet of the D'Oench, Duhme doctrine. (The word *D'Oench* is a mystery, but the last word is often pronounced "doom"!) The D'Oench, Duhme doctrine sharply limits a borrower's legal rights against a lending institution that is taken over by the federal government. Actually, it annihilates those claims.

The D'Oench, Duhme doctrine is a federal law doctrine derived from two sources. The first is the decision of the U. S. Supreme Court in the case of D'Oench, Duhme & Co., Inc. *v.* Federal Deposit Insurance Corp. [315 U.S. 447, 62 S.Ct. 676, 86 L.Ed 956 (1942)]. The D'Oench, Duhme case prevents borrowers from defending against the enforcement of a lender's rights under a loan document, such as a note, by claiming that the lender made "secret agreements" or oral representations that it would not enforce the note.

The second source of the D'Oench, Duhme doctrine is found in the U.S. Code, as amended by the Financial Institutions Reform, Recovery and Enforcement Act (FIRREA), which was signed into law August 9, 1989. Under FIRREA, an agreement by a lending institution not to enforce a note, or otherwise to diminish its rights or powers to enforce a note, is unenforceable unless the agreement meets the following four tests:

1. It must be in writing.
2. It must be executed by both the bank and the borrower when the loan is made.
3. It must be approved by the board of directors of the bank or its loan committee, and this approval must be reflected in the official minutes of the institution.
4. It must be kept continuously as an official record of the bank from the time it was signed.

Although this four-part test had existed for some time, FIRREA clearly applied the D'Oench, Duhme doctrine to S&Ls, regular banks, and other depository institutions subject to federal regulation. A lending institution that has been taken over by the FDIC may pursue a deficiency judgment against a borrower, simply disallowing the borrower's counterclaims and defenses, including breach of contract, common-law fraud, breach of fiduciary duty, promissory estoppels, and agency contract, by using the D'Oench, Duhme doctrine.

Removal to Federal Court

One of the most significant consequences of a federal takeover of a lending institution is that any pending state court litigation against the institution by borrowers can be removed, or rather, dragged kicking and screaming, into federal court. This is true not only of deficiency suits, but of landlord-tenant matters and just about any other litigation against the government officials who take over a savings and loan association. In federal court, the D'Oench, Duhme doctrine is almost unassailable. Further, many lawyers are not admitted to practice in federal court. Also, the higher expense of litigation in federal court may wipe out a borrower who has limited means to hire an attorney to defend a deficiency suit filed by a federal-entity lender.

Under FIRREA the government can sue to collect on loans or other debts owed to the lender for up to six years after the cause of action or date of receivership instead of the more normal four years. However, no cause of action that expired prior to receivership is revived by the receivership.

The powers of the federal government in bank receiverships are awesome. It is essentially bankruptcy for banks. During the terror of the 1930s and the shock of the 1980s, the federal government acquired great power in dealing with insolvent financial institutions. Once a lender is taken over, the federal government will classify the various claims against its dwindling assets. It assigns priorities, just as in an ordinary bankruptcy. Insured depositors and secured creditors get top priority.

Even if an institution doesn't get past conservatorship, a creditor is faced with removal to federal court and an unsympathetic set of laws. The federal government may claim it is a holder in due course of loans obtained from the old bank and deny borrowers any defenses to the enforcement of the loan documents. Even if the bank forced a borrower to sign the loan documents at gunpoint and never dispensed any funds, the government could still hold the borrower liable to repay the sums owed under the loan documents. The FDIC can be sued only for their own mistakes, not the old bank's mistakes.

CONCLUSION

When the federal government takes over an S&L, the institution first goes through conservatorship. FDIC officials and federal Marshalls walk through the S&L's doors, fire the board of directors and top executives, and march them off the premises under security escort. Desks and offices are locked up. Such a takeover usually occurs on a Thursday or Friday, and employees might be asked to work the weekend.

They may stay employed under conservatorship a little longer. A defunct S&L may stay in conservatorship for up to a year while the government figures out how to sell all, or much of it. If the effort to sell the S&L fails, the government breaks up the institution and sells its assets, one of which may be a mortgage or a foreclosed house. These assets are assigned to management companies under contract to the RTC and sold as quickly as possible. The borrower must now deal with a new lender.

A borrower's rights are determined under a different set of laws when an S&L is taken over. For example, a borrower is unlikely to find relief in the courts unless he declares bankruptcy or specific state laws provide statutory procedures to stop or delay a foreclosure. Moreover, lawyers cost a lot of money. The borrower who lacks the funds to pay the mortgage payment will probably come up short on the route to court, as well. Lawyers are seldom willing to sue lenders for minor irregularities in an otherwise valid foreclosure on a contingency fee basis. If the borrower can't pay the mortgage payments, the sad truth is that, sooner or later, the lender will hammer home a foreclosure.

However, a visit to a lawyer for some general legal advice on foreclosure is a good idea in any state. Lenders do make truly serious errors in procedure. Bankruptcy can often get results, and there may be special state statutes that can help the borrower. The borrower should regard going to court as one option but should not clutch at litigation as a cure-all for a foreclosure.

Bankruptcy and Foreclosures

13

One possible way to deal with an impending or potential foreclosure is through bankruptcy. Bankruptcy is a possibility when a debtor lacks sufficient assets to meet current obligations. The bankruptcy begins when a petition in bankruptcy is filed, either voluntarily by the debtor or, involuntarily, by the creditors.

OVERVIEW OF BANKRUPTCY

The following simple example may help the reader to understand the complex bankruptcy process. Imagine that you are transported backward in time to an Old West town. A mob of angry townspeople are chasing someone who owes them money but cannot pay. The debtor runs to the sheriff's office. The sheriff comes out, fires his gun into the air to quiet the angry crowd, and then tells them that they will all clear up the problem, right then. The sheriff asks the crowd for a list of the names of people to whom the debtor owes money. Then the debtor lists all his assets. The sheriff then distributes the assets, whatever they may be, in a fair and orderly manner to pay off the creditors.

Now travel forward in time to the modern day. Bankruptcy has similarities to the Old West scene, but the bankruptcy judge replaces the sheriff. Instead of running to the sheriff, the debtor files a petition in bankruptcy, after which the bankruptcy judge issues an automatic stay (a freeze order to creditors) under the bankruptcy law.

The Automatic Stay

The automatic stay works much like firing the gun into the air. Once the automatic stay is issued, all efforts by creditors to seize the debtor's property must stop. Lawsuits in state court to collect money may be stopped. The repo man, who is backing up to a car with a "gator hook" for a quick tow, must stop if the truck's radio announces an automatic stay. A foreclosure trustee who even hears about a possibility of a bankruptcy must stop. Angry creditors may not even call the debtor to demand the money they are owed. All actions to collect debts must stop, and everyone must come to the bankruptcy court.

The Bankruptcy Court

The bankruptcy court acts as a central clearinghouse for all debt collections, rather than allowing each creditor separately to rip and tear assets away from the debtor like so many sharks. If that were allowed, then the swiftest and most avaricious creditor would win the most assets, while the friendlier creditors would lose out. Nice guys would finish last. That's why bankruptcy began as a creditor protection system! In bankruptcy, the court rounds up and inventories all the assets, then distributes them among the creditors fairly in accordance with the rules and priorities accorded by law. Assembling full and complete lists of assets and creditors absorbs much of the time in a bankruptcy.

Discharge

When all the debtor's usable assets have been distributed, the remaining debts are discharged. The creditors need not bother to pursue the debtor further, since she has nothing left to give them.

Stretch Payments

Alternatively, creditors can be repaid over a longer time than the original debts allowed. Longer terms reduce monthly payments to an amount the debtor can pay. The bankruptcy court can simply order the debts to be stretched. Even payments to the IRS can be stretched out over time. Typically, the court will stretch payoff of loans, taxes, and other debts over three to five years. However, certain debts, such as child support, cannot be stretched, and as of early 2008, home payments cannot be stretched, either.

2005 BANKRUPTCY LAW: BANKRUPTCY MADE MORE DIFFICULT

Congress revised the bankruptcy laws, effective October 18, 2005, to correct perceived abuses of the bankruptcy system. The new bankruptcy law tilted the balance to favor creditors and lenders. Abuses and their corrections in the new law that are relevant to bankruptcy in the home foreclosure context include the following:

- Protecting large assets in expensive exempt homesteads, resulting in limits on homestead exemptions

- Deliberately binge living beyond one's means to wipe out one's assets, resulting in "means testing" for bankruptcy

- Repeat, self-filed, or hastily filed bankruptcies, resulting in barriers to all but skillfully drafted filings

Asset protection limits

A famous Hollywood Movie Star (whom we shall not name) owed millions. He also had millions in assets. He decided to move to Florida. He put his assets into cash and used it to buy a huge, multimillion-dollar mansion, which he declared to be his homestead under Florida law. The old bankruptcy law allowed state definitions of homestead exemptions to be used in bankruptcy, no matter how high the home's value was. The actor then decided he could no longer pay his creditors; he owed more than he had in assets on the balance sheet (excluding the mansion, which was exempt). After blasting his creditors to zero in bankruptcy, he decided sometime later (after the time limit to pull matters back into bankruptcy expired) that he didn't really want to live in Florida after all. So he sold the mansion, recovered his millions, and lived happily ever after. Lenders and creditors railed against this abuse, and now the exemption rules have been changed in bankruptcy to give homesteads less protection.

Binge Living Beyond One's Means

Some high-income people used to break out the plastic and run up huge bills. ("I always wanted to visit Tahiti! Nice mink!") Even though they had good incomes, they couldn't budget. They ran up bills they couldn't pay and then declared bankruptcy. Congress decided that persons seeking bankruptcy protection must now undergo stiff "means testing" to see if they have over $50,000 (or so) in income, and if so, then they must go on a budget and pay quite a bit of their income to creditors on a forced five-year plan.

Filing Abuses

Under the old law, many people self-filed bankruptcy petitions without an attorney. Faced with foreclosure, some filed early and often. Every time the lender neared the foreclosure day, the debtor self-filed a bankruptcy petition, derailed the foreclosure, then withdrew the bankruptcy or forgot about it until the next time the lender got almost to the day of foreclosure. Then they filed again— and again. Congress passed new provisions that make repeat filings, self-filings, or for that matter hasty attorney filings a much more dangerous proposition that won't work well anymore.

TYPES OF BANKRUPTCY

There are several distinct types of bankruptcy, which are identified and distinguished by their chapter numbers in the federal bankruptcy code. (Bankruptcy law is part of federal law, because the Constitution gave that power to Congress out of fear that state courts would favor their own creditors over those in another state.) Congress made major revisions in the Bankruptcy Code in 1978, giving its chapters odd rather than even numbers. New chapters, however, have even numbers. The more common types of bankruptcy include these:

- *Chapter 7:* Liquidation
- *Chapter 9:* Municipal government plan (almost never used)
- *Chapter 11:* Business reorganization
- *Chapter 12:* Family farmer plan (recently added)
- *Chapter 13:* Wage earner plan
- *Chapters 1, 3, and 5* apply to all bankruptcies.

This chapter will focus on Chapters 7 and 13.

CHOICE OF CHAPTER AND THE NEW MEANS TESTING

Under the new federal law, standards are provided to measure income and expenses. Extensive worksheets must be completed to determine if the bankrupt filer passes the means test or fails it. One survey indicated that only about 11 percent of Chapter 7 filers would pass, but it enormously complicates bankruptcy filings. Here's a rough example (you must go through several multipage IRS-like worksheets to get the true answer). An income of $50,000 is used here, but the means test threshold varies around the country based on trustee's charts.

If income ≥ $50,000	If income < $50,000
Means testing: yes	Means testing: no

Debtors can't declare a Chapter 7 if they bust the limit. Instead, they must look up their income on a set of charts provided by the U.S. Trustee's office, on the internet, which sets forth expenditure limits literally down to each county in the United States. The national standard gives such figures as these (again, this is a very rough example, and more expenses may be included):

Monthly income up to $4,166 ⟶ limits:	
Food:	$175
Housekeeping Supplies:	$18
Apparel and Services:	$47
Personal Care:	$17
Miscellaneous:	$110

Much of the rest goes to creditors. The new budget will no doubt be a shock to some who are used to living a little bit more "high on the hog." Those are the new rules, however. It's beer living on a champagne income. If you can't live with it for five years, don't file bankruptcy.

CHAPTER 7 AND THE MORTGAGE

In Chapter 7 liquidation bankruptcy, a court rounds up a debtor's assets and distributes them to pay off creditors. This leaves no continuing obligation to make any payments, except for nondischargeable debts like child support, unpaid taxes for three years prior to the bankruptcy, or U.S. government–guaranteed student loans. Chapter 7 typically takes about 90 days if the debtor owns no material assets other than exempted items. Unsecured debt, such as credit cards and medical bills, will be discharged at the end of the bankruptcy. (By the way, unpaid medical debts are the largest cause of middle-class bankruptcy.) Chapter 7 may be filed by either a person or a business.

In bankruptcy, the mortgage lender is a secured creditor. The lender who loaned the money to buy the house is the "creditor," and the house is the "security" for the repayment of the loan. Secured creditors have a lot of strength in the bankruptcy. The house lender is entitled to one of two things: (1) recovery of the asset behind the loan (lender gets title to the house) or (2) continuation of payments on the loan that was used to purchase the home. The debtor may be permitted to keep a house that is a "homestead" (primary residence) so long as the debtor can continue to make the payments on the house.

Exempt Property

The bankrupt (the person who files bankruptcy) may emerge from the bankruptcy with exempt property. Exempt property can be defined in two ways: (1) by the list in federal law or (2) by the list in state law, which includes the state-defined homesteads. Since homestead laws in some states are more generous than federal laws, debtors often prefer them, particularly if they own houses or substantial personal property. On the other hand, someone with no homestead assets might choose the federal exemptions to protect something from the bankruptcy, such as some cash in a bank account.

Exemption Limits

Under the new bankruptcy laws, exemptions have been revised. A person must live in a state for two years to claim a state's exemption. Even worse for debtors: state homestead exemption limits apply only if you've owned the house for at least 910 days (40 months, or 3⅓ years). The devilish aspect of this rule is that most foreclosures happen in the first few years of a mortgage loan. A lot of people will be affected. If the home was owned for less time than stipulated, the federal exemption limit of $136,875 on the equity in the homestead (how much the house is worth above what you owe) is all you can keep after declaring bankruptcy, regardless of the size of a state's homestead exemption. If the house has more equity than that, it will be seized and sold through the bankruptcy to pay the excess (over $36,865) to the creditors in bankruptcy. There are some tricks to roll equity from long-owned homes in the state to go higher. However, new residents of the state are not allowed these additional protections. If your house will put you over the limit, be careful about filing bankruptcy; it may cause a borrower to lose the house rather than save it.

State Homestead Exemptions

Limit	State
No limit:	Washington, D.C.
Lot Size Only:	AR, FL, IA, KS, OK, SD, TX
Lot Size and Equity:	AL, HI, LA, MI, MN, MS, NB, OR
Equity Only:	AK, CA, CO, CN, GA, ID, IL, IN, KY,
	ME, MA, MO, MT, NV, NH, NM,
	NC, NY, ND, OH, RI, SC, TN, UT, VT
	VA, WA, VT, VA, WA, WV, WI, WY
No exemption:	DE, MD, NJ, PA
Tenancy by the Entirety	DE, DC,FL, HI, IL, IN, MD, MA, MI, MO, NC,
	OH, PA, RI, TN, VT, VA, WY

Tenancy by the Entirety

States with marital laws based on tenancy by the entirety have an advantage. If the house is a tenancy by the entirety and only one spouse files bankruptcy, and the other doesn't, then the entire house, regardless of its value is exempt. Handy! If both file, however, it's part of the bankruptcy.

No Restructuring of Mortgage Payments Available Currently

Some people have the mistaken impression that a bankruptcy will cancel the obligation to pay on a mortgage loan and permit the owner to keep the house debt-free. This is not true. The borrower must continue to make the payments on the mortgage to keep the house after bankruptcy. However, a bankruptcy may help a person keep a house by eliminating loans that are not related to the house, as a Chapter 7 discharge would do, or by stretching out the repayment of unsecured loans, as a Chapter 13 plan would do. That will leave more money available to make full monthly mortgage payments and keep the house.

Careless Filing

A borrower may self-file a bankruptcy, but now there are difficulties that must be overcome. The bankruptcy courts now have a checklist of items they look for in a bankruptcy filing. For example, all tax returns have to be filed within 30 days, which many people in bankruptcy can't do easily because they haven't filed returns for years. For the self-employed, it may be a nightmare to get the returns done. However, it's a checklist item: if it wasn't done or can't be timely done, the bankruptcy judge is not given discretion but must dismiss the case. Self-filers will have a tough time complying with all the checklist requirements; miss one, and the judge *must* dismiss your case promptly, within 46 days. Once thrown out, it can be difficult to reinstate—it takes quite a bit of lawyering to do so. The rules hurt not only self-filings but hasty lawyer filings as well.

A bankruptcy can delay a foreclosure, but it cannot stop it, unless the borrower is able to make the payments on the loan or loans against the house. Perhaps with nonmortgage expenses restructured, there will be enough money available to keep up the payments. The length of the delay varies and is hard to predict. The borrower is almost guaranteed a 30-day delay and will probably get 60 days.

A delay of 90 days, or more, is possible. Unless the borrower can make the house payment, however, the lender will send a lawyer to the bankruptcy court to pursue a motion to release the home from the automatic stay. The time it takes for the lender's attorney to prepare, file, and obtain a decision on a motion to lift stay determines how long the bankruptcy freeze order will delay the foreclosure. A bankruptcy can also reverse a foreclosure that has taken place, if the property was sold for less than its market value.

If the bankruptcy is dismissed, it will take an attorney a major effort to get it reinstated. You may not want to use up your bankruptcy shot until you can really use it. Self-filers run a big risk of dismissal.

Lender's Motion to Lift Stay

After a bankruptcy is filed, the automatic stay, or freeze order, prevents any collection actions outside the control of the bankruptcy court. However, secured creditors who are hurt by the freeze order may file motions to release collateral, such as the house, from the jurisdiction of the bankruptcy court and the effects of the freeze. This action takes place early in the bankruptcy, long before trial, which could take place three years or more after filing in a federal district with a large bankruptcy docket. To justify the motion to lift stay, the lender must show (1) that the house has no equity value that could be used to pay any other creditors and (2) that the continued delay in foreclosure caused by the freeze order is hurting the lender. A third requirement, to show that the house is not necessary to a reorganization plan, is important for Chapter 11 or 13 bankruptcy. The first requirement is probably the hardest to meet, but the other two are significant.

No Equity Value

A house that is worth more than the balance owed on the purchase money loan (or loans) has positive equity value. In the large majority of home foreclosures, this is not the case. In distressed areas during a market downturn, a foreclosed house usually winds up being worth less than the balance owed on its purchase money loans(s); otherwise, the owner would sell it to avoid foreclosure. Thus, in most situations, the lender can show that the house is worth nothing to the bankruptcy court. Only once in a while will a house in foreclosure will have positive equity. In this case, it may have to stay in bankruptcy because it could be sold and the profits distributed to other creditors. It may take time to arrange such a sale, so a quick motion to lift stay may be inappropriate.

Delay Harms the Lender

In bankruptcy, the lender seeking to pull collateral, such as a house, out of the bankruptcy court must show that any delay harms the lender. The lender must show a lack of adequate protection and that immediate action is needed to prevent the loss from getting bigger. If, for example, the lender can show a pattern of dropping house values in the general area and the likelihood that this pattern will continue, the lender's loss from a delay will obviously be growing. This is also true if there's not enough money to continue maintenance on the house. Also, if the home's value is already low and there is little money in the bankruptcy estate, the lender will not be able to recover either an asset or a sum of money sufficient to cover its loss.

Asset Not Necessary to Reorganization

The house should not be important or useful to any Chapter 11 or 13 plan of reorganization for the debtor. If it is, the house must remain in the bankruptcy court's jurisdiction. The freeze order will remain in effect until the reorganization plan is settled.

In sum, if the lender can justify a motion to lift stay to the satisfaction of a bankruptcy judge, then the court will lift the stay and remove the house from the bankruptcy court and back into the ordinary legal world. The bankruptcy court surrenders jurisdiction over such an asset and the lender is free to foreclose by the regular methods the state laws provide, including nonjudicial foreclosure under a deed of trust.

CHAPTER 13 AND THE MORTGAGE

Chapter 13 bankruptcy has been called the "wage earner plan." To file bankruptcy under Chapter 13, the debtor must have a source of income. The court draws up a plan to state how the person will repay loans and debts. Once complete, the plan can reduce the wage earner's monthly payments to an affordable level based on income. Instead of $500 per month, for example, the wage earner might pay only $300 per month, but over a longer period. The justification for Chapter 13 reorganization, as opposed to liquidation under Chapter 7, is that creditors receive larger total sums under Chapter 13 than under Chapter 7. However, most lenders hate Chapter 13. Even worse, such plans often fail. It is very common for someone to file a Chapter 13 bankruptcy that must, after months or years, be converted to a Chapter 7 bankruptcy. However, the net recovery is still greater with Chapter 13 plans. Many debtors like Chapter 13 because it allows them to pay off all the money they owe. Many debtors sincerely want to do that.

Who May File?

Only an individual who has a regular income may file under Chapter 13. However, not all individuals with regular incomes qualify. Individuals must also meet these requirements:

- Unsecured debts under $336,900
- Secured debts of less than $1,010,650
- Flunk the means test—income does not exceed limits
- Not a business
- Current on tax filings for past four years. The individual must provide evidence by the creditor's meeting in one month. The trustee and the judge may each give you another 120 days—maybe.
- You cannot be a securities or commodities broker, but other small business partners or sole proprietors can file (as owners, not as a business).
- Your last bankruptcy was not dismissed within 180 days due to violating a court order, a filing, being ruled a fraud, or because you tried to drop a bankruptcy after a creditor filed a motion to lift stay.
- No discharge from a Chapter 13 in the past two years or from a Chapter 7 in the last four years.

The Process

An individual filing bankruptcy under Chapter 13 must typically file the following:

- Bankruptcy petition
- A schedule listing the debtor's property
- Notice of the various bankruptcy chapters available
- The Chapter 13 statement

- The Chapter 13 plan
- Applications for attorneys' fees

Credit counseling is now required in a bankruptcy. Once filed, Chapter 13 provides for a broad automatic stay while the plan details are settled.

The Plan, the Trustee, and the Cram-Down

Unlike Chapter 11, in which creditors must approve the plan, a Chapter 13 plan needs no approval from creditors. This is a big help to the debtor. Barely 5 percent of the Chapter 11 cases filed ever wind up with approved plans. A Chapter 13 plan may be filed only by the debtor. Although the lenders and creditors can object to the plan, if they reach no agreement with the debtor, the court may simply approve the plan, despite creditors' objections. This is referred to as a "cram-down."

Three steps must be followed:

1. Compute disposable income.
2. Compare income to debts that must be paid, and if you can't pay them off in five years, go with a Chapter 7.
3. If the plan pays all required debts, any additional disposable income you have must be committed to repay other debts. If not, the judge won't confirm the plan. Also, credit counseling is required, and if their plan looks better, the judge may adopt it, not yours. The plan will ordinarily last no more than three years. Once payments under the plan are complete, the bankrupt is discharged from any further obligation to pay creditors.

Courts appoint trustees in all Chapter 13 cases. Unless otherwise directed by the court, the debtor will begin making payments to the trustee within 30 days after filing the Chapter 13 plan. The trustee will hold these payments until after the plan is confirmed. The function of a trustee is to take payments from the bankrupt and pay the money out to creditors in accordance with the plan. The trustee will not sell off property in a Chapter 13 situation, as required under Chapter 7. The trustee is normally paid a percentage of the sums of money administered. This can make the job of Chapter 13 trustee extremely lucrative. In Houston during the late 1980s, trustees could make as much as $25,000 per month.

Mortgages Under Chapter 13

Under the bankruptcy code, the payments on a loan secured by a personal residence cannot be reduced in a Chapter 13 plan. The borrower must make the payments in full. The law states that the Chapter 13 plan may modify the rights of secured claims "other than a claim secured only by a security interest in real property that is the debtor's principal residence." The courts have tended to give special treatment only to purchase money mortgage loans, namely the loan(s) used to buy a house. This excludes loans that are partially secured by real property in the house, such as loans for fixtures installed in the house. Chapter 13 can't modify purchase money loans, but it can modify other loans. However, it can reverse acceleration of the purchase money mortgage, pulling it back from foreclosure and reinstating the regular payments. Then the Chapter 13 plan can stretch any back payments over time and cure the default. The plan must cure the default within three years (or up to five years if the judge so decides), as long as this period does not go past the end of the mortgage's normal term. The lender can collect interest on back payments only if the loan agreement specifically allows it. The lender will normally ask for a reaffirmation agreement to reflect the borrower's continued obligation to make the house payments.

THE COSTS AND BENEFITS OF BANKRUPTCY

The direct benefits of a bankruptcy include eliminating the obligation to pay past-due payments. It can also eliminate a deficiency judgment. In addition, it temporarily stops the foreclosure. If monthly payments on other loans, such as credit card bills, are reduced by Chapter 13 or eliminated by Chapter 7, debtors may manage to keep home payments current.

It costs money not to have money! Bankruptcy may cost between $1,500 and $2,500, plus filing fees of upwards of $300 to have an attorney prepare the papers and file them with the bankruptcy court. Most bankruptcy attorneys charge those fees up front. An even larger long-term cost comes from damage to one's credit. The bankruptcy will appear on credit reports for at least ten years after it is filed. Although federal law requires elimination of information over seven years old from reports sent to creditors, this is not true for bankruptcy or all loans. Reports on loans over $50,000 may go back further than seven years, although a bankruptcy or loan default over seven years old is not likely to have much influence on a lender for most consumer purposes.

On the other hand, once a debtor declares bankruptcy, she cannot do so again for seven years. Some say this improves a borrower's chances with some lenders. Be that as it may, a surprising number of creditors will extend credit soon after the bankruptcy. A debtor is particularly likely to reestablish credit quickly after a bankruptcy if she can show that the bankruptcy was due to harsh financial circumstances beyond the debtor's control.

The decision to declare bankruptcy should be considered very carefully. Sometimes a careful review of one's finances and a good budget will enable matters to be put right without declaring bankruptcy.

CONCLUSIONS

Bankruptcy is still alive as an option to stop foreclosure. It's still the one sure, short stop, but it's not what it used to be. A couple of key points:

1. Be careful about filing if your home's equity goes over the $125,000 limit—you may lose the house.
2. Strongly consider hiring an attorney to help with the bankruptcy filing, and be ready to pay the attorney a substantial sum.

It is now riskier for attorneys to file bankruptcy at all. The newer proceedings are not only more complicated, but the attorney practically has to swear to the accuracy of what the borrower presents. As a result, attorneys have to make a more careful review before filing. Last-minute filings, where the homeowner goes to see the bankruptcy attorney a day before foreclosure, are to be avoided. There's a real risk the attorney will refuse to handle the case—with good reason. It may take the borrower time to get the needed financial information and documentation. Without it, the bankruptcy is at risk of being dismissed. As a result, attorneys are now charging more to handle these types of cases.

Deficiency Judgments

14

Many borrowers are shocked to discover that the lender is not limited to foreclosing on their houses, driving them out and selling their houses to new owners. The lender may also sue the borrower and further wreck his credit after, or as part of, the foreclosure process. If the foreclosure sale does not produce enough funds to pay off the balance on the loan, the lender may sue the borrower for the difference, or deficiency. Many states allow such a procedure. A deficiency judgment allows a lender to seize any property the borrower has (other than exempt property) in addition to taking the house. The deficiency judgment is one of the harshest consequences that may face a borrower who loses a house in foreclosure.

THE LENDER'S RIGHTS

A deficiency judgment has its roots in the original loan arrangement for the purchase of a house. When arranging a loan to buy real estate, the borrower generally signs both a note agreeing to repay the loan in monthly payments, including interest, and a mortgage or deed of trust, which gives the lender the power to foreclose if the borrower fails to pay on the note. When a borrower fails to pay, the lender may recover the debt in two ways: (1) by obtaining a judgment against the borrower for the sum unpaid on the note and (2) by foreclosing on the real estate and reselling it. The lender may pursue the borrower either way, or both. Some states, notably California, require the lender to bring only one action against the borrower, regardless of whether the lender pursues a claim for the unpaid balance, foreclosure, or both. Other states allow either foreclosure or a claim for the balance owed, but not both. Most states that allow lenders to pursue borrowers for both foreclosure and the balance due also require the foreclosure sale price to be credited against what the borrower owes. The lender may then pursue the borrower for the difference, or deficiency.

Deficiency judgments can be measured in different ways. If the foreclosure sale is conducted as part of judicial or court-ordered foreclosure, then the borrower will probably be liable for the difference between the price obtained at the court-ordered sale and the balance the court determined was owed on the loan. Nonjudicial, out-of-court foreclosures are often subject to much more scrutiny.

Abuses have been known to occur in states that permit the out-of-court foreclosure sale price to be used as the basis for determining a deficiency. Deficiency judgments are particularly likely to be abusive when the value of the borrower's house has dropped along with the general market prices of real estate in a city or region.

Here's how it would work. Someone borrows $150,000 to buy a house that is worth $170,000 at the time of purchase. The borrower put down $20,000 and borrowed the rest. Later on, the borrower has financial difficulties due to illness, divorce, or job loss and fails to keep up the payments on the loan. When the borrower tries to resell the house, its value has fallen to $120,000, at which point, the broker can't find a buyer who will pay enough for the house to pay off the loan. As a result, no broker wants to list the house for sale or fiddle with it at all. The borrower has no luck trying to sell the house herself in the down market. Since the payments are not being made, the lender forecloses, after which it could sue the borrower for the missing $30,000.

In states with nonjudicial, out-of-court foreclosures, the borrower's situation may be even worse. The lender may sell the house at a fire-sale price, compounding the size of the deficiency. The lack of supervision of nonjudicial foreclosure sale inevitably leads to abuse. In some states, a lender can sue for a deficiency based on the unpaid loan balance minus a ridiculously artificial foreclosure sale price of $1. Some states still permit such deficiency judgments. (In particular, Texas allows such suits, provided the foreclosure took place before April 1, 1991 or if the lender waived his rights.)

Even more outrageous deficiency suits are not unheard of but are subject to court limitation. For example, suppose a borrower who owes $55,000 finds a buyer for the property prior to the foreclosure. The parties sign a contract for $60,000. The lender then sells the property at foreclosure for $42,000 and sues the borrower for the difference between that price and the balance owed of $55,000. At the same time, the lender sells the property it bought at $42,000 for $60,000 to the buyer the borrower found. The lender would be able to add the $60,000 in sales proceeds to the $18,000 deficiency to be collected from the borrower, for a total of $78,000 in income, when all the borrower owed was $55,000! It's just not fair, but it has happened in some states.

PROTECTION AGAINST DEFICIENCY JUDGMENTS

Many states, however, have placed limits on foreclosure deficiency suits. Some major legal theories have evolved for use in limiting deficiency judgments. Some states' laws force the lender to use judicial foreclosure if it wants a deficiency judgment. These states refuse to allow the lender to use the quick, ill-supervised nonjudicial foreclosure sale as the basis for calculating a deficiency. If the lender wants a speedy, out-of-court foreclosure, it must pay the price of forgoing the right to sue the borrower for a deficiency. In such states, the lender may be forced to resort to judicial foreclosure before the state's law will allow a deficiency suit based on an inadequate foreclosure sale price.

Some states require the lender to credit the fair market value of the property against the amount due on the loan, rather than using the out-of-court foreclosure sale price. In such states, the borrower can present evidence about the market value of the property to offset the lender's claim of a deficiency.

The borrower may show that the nonjudicial foreclosure sale did not generate a price equal to the fair market value of the property. In a foreclosure sale, the property is not advertised, marketed, or sold in the same manner as a professional real estate broker would market the property. The actual foreclosure sale is a crude auction. There can be title problems and difficulties in inspecting the house or coming up with cash to buy it. Most foreclosure sales require the buyer to pay in cash. In contrast, if the lender bids at the foreclosure sale to buy the property from the trustee or sheriff (who normally takes title from the borrower at the foreclosure), the lender's bid cancels out all or part of the borrower's debt in exchange for a trustee's deed or sheriff's deed to the property.

In some states, a borrower can force the lender to choose between foreclosure and a deficiency suit. These states will not allow deficiency suits if the lender forecloses on the property.

Many states ban deficiency judgments altogether. Some ban them on a selective basis. For example, some don't allow deficiencies for foreclosure on a purchase money mortgage for a principal residence. Others don't allow deficiency suits on agricultural loans.

Some states have passed laws declaring moratoriums on foreclosures and deficiency suits. Such statutes were often passed in the 1930s. There is some question as to their constitutionality, but the general opinion in most states and in the federal courts is that such moratoriums are legal. During a moratorium, a lender may not foreclose, even if the borrower is in default. Deficiency judgments are typically banned, as well, in such moratorium situations.

States can impose complex procedural requirements. Although California does not actually ban deficiency judgments, the complexity of the California one-action rule makes it hard for a lender to obtain one. The basic concept of the one-action rule is to allow a lender to bring only one lawsuit against the borrower. The lender may seek both foreclosure and a deficiency judgment for any money the foreclosure sale does not provide, but only if the claims are consolidated in one lawsuit. If the lender fails to attend to a multitude of procedural requirements designed to be sure not to allow two actions, then the California courts will deny a deficiency judgment. The lender must not attempt to collect the loan independently from the lawsuit. Any attempt to do so is a violation of the one-action rule.

Many states set a short time limit for deficiency suits. Some have very short statutes of limitations, but in the meantime, the borrower is a sitting duck for a deficiency suit.

THE ROLE OF PRIVATE MORTGAGE INSURANCE

Deficiency judgment procedures may be complicated if the loan is covered by private mortgage insurance. If the lender collects on the loss from the PMI company, it may no longer care about pursuing a deficiency suit. Many PMI companies now seek to obtain the lender's right to sue the borrower for a deficiency in exchange for paying off the lender's unpaid loan balance. This is called "subrogation." The PMI company then turns around and sues a borrower for its loss as a result of the foreclosure. Not all PMI companies bring such suits.

This often strikes borrowers as unfair. Most types of insurance eliminate the need to sue the person who was covered. However, mortgage insurance seems to be an exception to the rule. PMI companies have begun aggressively pursuing deficiency judgments, which often offset a good portion of their losses. Moreover, the threat of deficiency suits puts pressure on borrowers to keep up payments. There's no easy out just because private mortgage insurance is in force.

Recall that a private mortgage insurance company will pay for a loss up to the amount of its coverage, which is usually no more than 33 percent of the original fair market value; most recoveries are lower still. However, if the lender wins a deficiency judgment, it must pass on any money it recovers to reimburse the private mortgage insurance company. Many private mortgage insurance companies call upon lenders to pursue deficiency judgments if at all practical.

DEFICIENCIES: WHO IS LIKELY TO SUE WHOM?

Many lenders argue that borrowers take mortgage default much too lightly. One borrower offered a sad excuse for a foreclosure: "It was too far to drive." Others have said, "I didn't like the people in the neighborhood." Such stories drive lenders and PMI companies up a wall. Lenders and loan insurers alike denounce borrowers who show a disregard for their obligations. Borrowers may talk at meetings about their foreclosures as though they have nothing to be ashamed of. Whenever the market declines in an area, foreclosures can become as common and socially acceptable as divorce.

Outraged lenders want to take action against this attitude—and now. Increasingly, this is no longer bluff and bluster. Lenders now pursue deficiencies more eagerly than ever.

Borrowers With Assets

In the past, lenders have almost always pursued any borrower they felt might have money. For this reason, a borrower who has substantial assets should certainly never disregard a mortgage and walk away from it lightly. On the loan application, the borrower probably demonstrated sufficient earnings and assets to satisfy the traditional test, which is to show the lender you don't need the money before it will let you borrow it. Many such people made large-scale real estate purchases in the boom days of the 1970s on the OPM (other people's money) plan. For a well-heeled borrower, default and foreclosure are serious matters. Unlike many foreclosures, where the destitute borrower suffers nothing except loss of title, the lender will very likely pursue the well-heeled borrower. Consider, as well, that even a borrower who is on very good terms with the executives and loan officers at a particular lending institution must worry; those friends may not be there forever. The FDIC may have them thrown out, or they could retire, and the statute of limitations for suits brought by the government is six years, even if the government acquired the cause of action from a private lender.

Borrowers Without Assets

The borrower without money has had less to fear in the past, but this is changing, too. Many borrowers have assumed that they had nothing to fear from lawsuits because their foreclosures wiped out their debts. As we have shown, this is not always so. Unless the borrower's house was worth a lot more than the outstanding balance on the loan and the lender recognized this and bid enough to cover that balance, then the borrower is probably liable for the deficiency.

Once again, the lender may buy the property from the foreclosure trustee or sheriff at most foreclosure sales in most states. In the typical foreclosure in a down market, the outstanding debt on the mortgage exceeds the value of the house. Moreover, just because the value exceeds the debt, this is no guarantee that the lender will bid enough at the foreclosure to obviate the deficiency. A low purchase price at the foreclosure sale increases the gap between what is owed and what is paid—that is, the deficiency. If the lender sues for a deficiency based on the low bid amount, the borrower will have to prove the value of the house at foreclosure by competent evidence, which he may be unable or unwilling to do. By the time the borrower has enough assets to hire a lawyer and fight the lender, the statute of limitations may have ended the borrower's rights to sue the lender. It is an excellent idea for the homeowner to obtain and save information about the prices at which comparable homes in the area were sold at about the time of the foreclosure.

Mass Litigation

In the past, private savings and loans have signed contracts with attorneys to handle deficiency suits on a large scale. Often, hundreds of lawsuits are filed against defaulting borrowers, regardless of the lack of obvious sources of wealth. The savings and loans want the deficiency judgments and are pursuing them, often in response to pressure from the FDIC.

FDIC Pursuit of Deficiencies

The FDIC can pursue deficiency suits as well. Once they take over a bank, they can acquire its loans and its rights to sue a borrower for a deficiency judgment. Even worse, they can annihilate the borrower's counterclaims under the D'Oench, Duhme doctrine. As explained in Chapter 12, under D'Oench, Duhme, a borrower loses defenses against a bank or S&L deficiency suit when the FDIC takes over. Also, any litigation pending with the former bank or S&L is usually moved to federal court.

VA Pursuit of Deficiencies

The VA has never pursued actual lawsuits against defaulting veterans very actively, although once in a while the Justice Department files such suits. However, the VA is fastidious about informing every agency in the federal government of the defaulting borrower's social security number and the fact that he owes money. This can cause no end of mischief for the defaulting borrower for years afterward. Tax refunds may be seized. Government benefits may be denied.

The worst collection story about the VA I have heard concerned a person who walked away from a house, leaving it for foreclosure, and then later rejoined the military. Most of his military paycheck was seized to pay off the VA. Direct benefits to veterans can no longer be seized, but the defaulting veteran will have much to worry about for a long time to come.

FHA Pursuit of Deficiencies

Traditionally, the FHA refused to pursue deficiencies on its loans. The FHA was a Depression-era program. During that time, the concept of a government agency pursuing hapless individuals who had already lost their houses was not politically popular. Even today, many defaulters on FHA loans are fairly safe from deficiency judgments, provided that they defaulted due to circumstances beyond their control. Currently, the FHA may pursue deficiency suits against three classes of defaulters:

1. Double defaulters, who have defaulted on two or more FHA loans
2. Investor borrowers, who don't occupy the houses they buy
3. Walkaways, who could have paid but didn't

Double defaulters are borrowers who defaulted on one FHA mortgage, managed to obtain another one, and then defaulted again. They are on the FHA's hit list along with investor borrowers, who obtained FHA loans for houses they rent out rather than occupy. FHA formerly insured loans on up to four houses. When an investor borrower defaults, the U.S. government often sues, because such borrowers tend to have more money and assets than owner–occupant borrowers. Also, they are more likely to walk away from the house even though they could have kept up the payments. This makes such people excellent targets for deficiency lawsuits.

FHA can easily identify double defaulters and investor borrowers through its own departmental records. However, the third category is more difficult. Walkaways are those who could have paid but didn't. If a person had the "apparent continued ability to pay" but failed to do so, FHA classes her as a walkaway and may pursue. It is not clear exactly how the FHA selects walkaways from its borrowers, although mortgage company information may help identify those with high incomes or assets. Apparently, FHA intends to ask mortgage companies to provide the names of likely walkaways and to communicate the details of serious abuse cases. Mortgage companies can initiate the pursuit of a deficiency by giving the local HUD office information that shows that the person should be pursued.

Conventional Lenders

Almost all major types of residential lenders are initiating programs to sue for deficiency judgments. The fact that borrowers have heard nothing for years makes little difference. In some states, a lender has as long as four years to sue for a deficiency. However, other states impose much shorter statutes of limitations for deficiency suits. In the future, many borrowers will be hit by such suits.

As recently as two or three years ago, it was fairly safe to predict that a borrower who suffered foreclosure for inability to pay was unlikely to be pursued. This just isn't so anymore. Lenders are reacting to a lot of evidence that many borrowers have defaulted for reasons other than job losses. In fact, only about 30 percent of foreclosures derive directly from job loss. About 15 percent are due to divorce. There is a lot of argument about the rest. Lenders are convinced that many of the remaining fraction simply decided it was too expensive to pay the mortgage and chose to default. Now the lenders are going after them.

DEFICIENCY SUIT TACTICS

Some attorneys have begun to refine the deficiency lawsuit to a fine art. They set it up as a letter lawsuit designed to hit the borrower with a rapid judgment. The first step is usually to locate the borrower and obtain service of process—that is, to give the borrower a copy of the suit. Often the lending institution helps a lot with this, employing skip tracers to find borrowers. Then the attorney who handles deficiencies will file a lawsuit against the borrower.

Once the borrower is served, the clock starts ticking. If the borrower fails to make a timely response, the lender's attorney will try to get the judge to sign a default judgment. Once the judge signs, the default judgment is extremely difficult to overturn.

Summary Judgments

Even if the borrower responds quickly enough to avoid a default, the lender's attorney will usually continue the pressure. A simple defendant's original answer may be enough to keep the lender from getting a default judgment, but most attorneys follow up with a motion for summary judgment.

Many borrowers simply give up based on the unfortunate assumption that, since they have no money left, there is nothing the lender can do with a judgment. That's not necessarily so!

Once a motion for summary judgment is filed by the lender (who is the plaintiff), the borrower (the defendant) must respond at least seven days prior to the date specified in the motion.

The key to defeating a summary judgment is to raise a fact issue. The theory behind a summary judgment supposes that the parties dispute no facts, so no trial is necessary since the whole purpose of a trial is to establish the facts of a case. At a trial, parties submit evidence, the judge rules upon objections, and the jury decides which of the conflicting witnesses and pieces of evidence to believe or disregard. The facts are then known. Without disputed facts, neither a jury nor a trial is needed. A judge can rule on the law of the matter one way or the other.

We know that the law entitles a lender to a deficiency judgment from a foreclosure to the extent the remaining balance on the loan exceeds the amount bid at the foreclosure. Therefore, to beat the summary judgment, the borrower must raise a fact issue. One way to do this might be to challenge the validity of the foreclosure sale due to a failure on the part of the lender to give proper notice or follow the proper procedure at the courthouse.

A favorite method of raising a fact issue at a summary judgment hearing has been to challenge the reasonableness of any attorney's fees sought by the lender. Some judges are sufficiently irritated by this approach. They require the borrower to find an expert witness, namely another attorney, who will swear out an affidavit that the fees sought by the lender's attorney are too high. Presenting such an affidavit along with an answer opposing the motion for summary judgment may induce the judge to deny the lender's motion for summary judgment and order a trial instead.

ONCE A DEFICIENCY JUDGMENT IS OBTAINED

Once the lender wins the deficiency judgment lawsuit, either by default, by summary judgment, or by a victory in a hearing or trial, then the lender may pursue collection. Many borrowers have the mistaken notion that, since they have no money, they need have no fear of the deficiency judgment. They are wrong!

Once the lender gets a judgment, it can make the borrower's life miserable, not only now but for many years. After that, it can often renew the judgment. Some lenders get deficiency judgments intending to collect later. Just because borrowers can't pay now doesn't mean they won't be able to pay several years from now. Once the borrower is back on his feet, the lender can attack the borrower's assets, credit, and peace of mind in future years, perhaps recovering many times what it cost to obtain the deficiency judgment. Once a deficiency judgment is obtained, the lender can pursue it right away or in the future by using several tools: (1) an abstract of judgment; (2) a writ of execution; (3) a writ of garnishment; and (4) a turnover order.

An abstract of judgment (AJ) is a short, one-page summary of a court judgment. The actual judgment signed by a judge may run many pages. That's too long for many purposes. The district court or county court clerk's office therefore prepares the one-page abstract with just the essentials, such as the date, the amount, the name of the plaintiff, the name of the defendant, and the court along with as little else as possible. The one-page abstract of judgment can easily be recorded. Once recorded, it creates a general lien on any property the borrower has that is not exempt. In some states, exemptions are plentiful; in other states, they are not.

A writ of garnishment is a court order directing a bank or stock brokerage firm that holds money or stocks owned by a debtor to turn over the money or the stocks to the judgment creditor. Actually, the writ is more general and may be used against any third party who holds a debtor's assets. The writ commands the third party to turn over to the creditor the debtor's assets that party holds. In some states, wages may be garnished for a foreclosure deficiency judgment. Bank accounts may be garnished in most states. As soon as a creditor finds such juicy assets, it can seize them. This makes life miserable for a debtor. Even worse, using discovery to aid in enforcing the judgment, the creditor can force the debtor to reveal money or other assets under the threat of contempt of court.

A writ of execution permits a creditor to send a sheriff or constable to seize the assets of the debtor. Armed with the writ of execution (and other armament, as well) an intrepid constable can go wherever the debtor is holding nonexempt assets and physically seize them. The sheriff or constable will conduct a sale of seized assets, giving the proceeds to the creditor to help pay off the judgment. Sometimes, the creditor will ask the constable to seize assets it knows the debtor cherishes. While watching a prized possession being seized, the debtor may crack and finally come up with the money to pay the judgment. The sheriff or constable will usually demand the immediate delivery of a cashier's check to stop the seizure. A generous one will wait 30 minutes or so.

In a turnover hearing, the creditor will list assets the debtor holds, and the judge will order the debtor to turn over the title to the asset to the creditor. The creditor should have the list ready before the hearing. If necessary, it can force the debtor by discovery (interrogatories, requests for admissions, and so on) to reveal the location and nature of the assets. Then the hearing can be set 30 days after entering the judgment, and the turnover will take place.

The creditor can make good use of the tools the law provides to collect judgments. Sooner or later, the debtor is bound to obtain some type of asset the creditor can discover and seize. The debtor may finally be driven to file bankruptcy when pressed in this manner. Alternatively, the debtor may negotiate to pay off part of the judgment all at once in return for a release of the whole judgment. The debtor winds up paying less than owed under the judgment, but the creditor gets some cash immediately.

The deficiency judgment, by its nature, is often massive and very difficult to pay off in full. This should certainly deter a borrower from abandoning a mortgage. A judgment is one of the worst potential consequences of a foreclosure. Remember, however, the lender must sue to obtain it.

HOMEOWNER OPTIONS TO MINIMIZE THE DEFICIENCY

A homeowner can do several things to minimize a potential deficiency judgment. At the time of foreclosure, a homeowner should try to verify the fair market value of the home, perhaps by contacting a real estate broker and obtaining information on comparable property sales in the area at the time of the foreclosure. Later on, this basic information could help an appraiser to establish the fair market value of a home at the time of foreclosure.

A homeowner should also be careful to save all letters and legal notices sent by the lender. The homeowner should never, never angrily throw away legal notices of any kind concerning the foreclosure. Save them all. Later, a lawyer may be able to use the notices, or lack of notice, to establish a procedural error on the part of the lender or the lender's attorney or trustee. Such an error can invalidate the lender's right to a deficiency.

Even mailing envelopes should be saved. They can provide valuable clues as to when a particular letter was actually sent. The homeowner should carefully record the dates and times of all events connected with the foreclosure. Keep a record of when payments were first missed, when letters were received (a date of receipt may be different from the date on the letter), and when any calls or other communications came from the lender. Keep a record of the date, time, and caller for each call or visit from the lender, the trustee, or the lender's attorney.

Borrowers should consider attending any foreclosure sale. Some people even videotape foreclosure sales. Once again, an error in the procedures may help later to stop a deficiency judgment. Finally, the homeowner should maintain as much communication with the lender, the loan insurer, the trustee, and any attorneys as possible. Call the lender and the trustee. Call the FHA or VA if they are involved.

Be sure to push your position at all times, but avoid being belligerent. Be assertive, not abrasive. Lenders are more likely to sue borrowers who are unfriendly or who seem not to care. A borrower who doesn't care may look like an easy target for a lawsuit, because the attorney hopes the borrower will fail to respond to the lawsuit, giving an easy win by default. Let the lender know that won't happen.

If the lender tries to obtain a deficiency judgment, the borrower should always seek advice from an attorney. Be sure to explore options other than bankruptcy. Be alert, be positive, be organized, and make it tough for a lender to win a deficiency judgment.

After Foreclosure: Credit Reports and Taxes

15

Despite the best efforts of homeowners, some foreclosures cannot be avoided. If worse comes to worst and the foreclosure goes to completion, the homeowner may breathe a sigh of relief that at least all the turmoil is in the past. Unfortunately, this is not the case. There are important consequences to consider. This chapter will look at the effect of foreclosure on future credit along with its tax consequences.

CREDIT REPORTS AND FORECLOSURE

Foreclosures affect credit reports. Prior to 1986, many foreclosures were not reported at all, and even today, many lenders do not report late payments on residential mortgage loans to credit bureaus. However, even though such delinquencies are not reported to credit bureaus, they do appear in lenders' records. When a borrower applies for a new home loan, most lenders will contact any former residential mortgage lender and obtain a full report about the borrower's payment history. In fact, FNMA requires verifying past payment history when applying for a loan that it will buy. As a result, processing of almost any loan application with a mortgage company will include a report from the former lender on payments.

Today, the regular credit bureaus list a home foreclosure under the code FCL. Almost all lenders now report foreclosure on any house to the credit bureaus. The FHA and VA require it on their loans. Many assumption buyers wrongly believe that they have no liability because the seller is still liable. However, the lender will often report the default on both the buyer's and the seller's credit record. This may surprise them both, since sellers often think that buyers have liability after taking over the house, and buyers often think that sellers retain all liability on the loan.

Credit Information Is Tough to Remove

It is virtually impossible to eliminate a foreclosure from a credit record, unless it is at least seven years old. As explained in the following section, it may even be ten years old or more. Federal law virtually immunizes credit bureaus from legal attack for libel or slander. The Fair Credit Reporting Act (FCRA) permits suits for damages based on false information in a normal credit report. However, the lender may defend its position on the grounds that it followed sound procedures to prevent the misreporting. Moreover, damages are traditionally hard to prove and limited when proved. In any event, only false information may be challenged. If the foreclosure was legal, then an attack for false information is out of the question.

False Credit Report Information

Even if the consumer discovers false information, FCRA sets a tight time frame in which to sue the credit bureau for damages. The consumer must sue a credit bureau within two years after the liability for the debt arises. However, if the credit bureau continues to issue false information in bad faith and with malicious intent, then the law measures the two years from the time the consumer discovered or reasonably could have discovered the existence of the defamatory credit report, not from the time the bureau's subscriber received the report.

When Are Credit Report Items Removed?

Under the Fair Credit Reporting Act, no consumer credit reporting agency may make any consumer credit report that contains obsolete information, which by law includes the following:

- Cases under title 11 of the United States Code [11 U.S.C. Section 101 *et sec*] or under the Bankruptcy Act that, from the date of entry of the order for relief or the date of adjudication, as the case may be, antedate the report by more than ten years
- Bankruptcies up to ten, not seven, years old (There are exceptions, though.)
- Regular court judgments up to seven years old

Under the FCRA, some court judgments are obsolete and may not be reported:

- Suits and judgments which, from date of entry, antedate the report by more than seven years, or until the governing statute of limitations has expired, whichever is the longer period.

Since a judgment is good for many years (typically ten), it may legally stay on the credit report for ten years. However, a creditor may renew a judgment in many states at the end of the ten-year period for an additional ten years, over and over again. The debtor may never be free of the judgment! This may force the debtor to declare bankruptcy to remove the judgment after the ten-year period.

The rules concerning judgments are particularly important to foreclosures because of the relative ease in some states with which a foreclosure could give rise to a deficiency judgment. Remember, a foreclosure could spawn a deficiency judgment as long as four years after the foreclosure. See Chapter 14 on deficiency judgments to understand how this is done.

The FCRA provides that most negative credit items must be taken off a report after seven years. It defines such items as these:

- Any other adverse item of information that antedates the report by more than seven years must be removed.
- Slow-pay designations and most negative items must be removed within seven years.

A credit bureau can report some things forever. In certain circumstances, adverse credit items, judgments, bankruptcies, and foreclosures may be reported even after the seven-year or ten-year period has expired. These circumstances are based on the type of loan or credit the consumer is seeking. Transactions that are exempt from the time limit include the following:

- Credit transactions involving, or that may involve, principal amounts of $50,000 or more
- Underwriting of life insurance involving, or that may reasonably be expected to involve, a face amount of $50,000 or more
- Employment of any individual at an annual salary that equals, or may reasonably be expected to equal, $20,000 or more

Many mortgage loans exceed $50,000, so look out if you're planning to buy a house. As you can see, a foreclosure may follow the consumer forever.

Repairing Damaged Credit

Unfortunately, few legal tricks for cleaning up credit work to remove a lawful foreclosure. A consumer can contact the credit bureau in writing and obtain a credit report. Anyone who is uncertain about whether or not a foreclosure still appears on his credit report should do this before applying for an important loan. If the report lists an incorrect item, the credit bureau usually has a procedure by which to challenge the item in writing. Some credit bureaus ask for sworn affidavits that items are wrong.

The credit bureau will attempt to verify the validity of the negative credit report item by contacting the creditor who reported it. If no response is received, or if the item is not confirmed within 21 to 30 days, the credit bureau will take it off the credit report. Any item the creditor confirms stays on the credit report. The person who wants to go further must attack the reporting creditor directly. The credit bureau is off the hook, unless the consumer can show that the bureau knows that the item is wrong. That's a very difficult burden of proof.

A wise debtor who has had a bad credit period, such as a business failure, a divorce, or a job loss, should attempt to restore her credit as soon as possible. As soon as the tough period is over, the person should rigorously pay bills on time. Ideally, one should show a sharp, clean break with the bad period.

If the bad period had a clearly identifiable cause, then the credit record has a less negative impact on lenders. Remember, creditors are not prohibited from lending to people with bad credit, but bad reports influence them not to do so. That negative influence can be countered by showing why credit was bad and why it is now better.

Fair and Accurate Credit Transactions ACT (FACTA) 2003

Under Section 609 of FACTA, when a consumer obtains a free annual credit report, the consumer can obtain a credit score upon request. Request it! Mortgage lenders must provide the key adverse factors that affect a consumer score as well as its source. Consumers should correct credit scores that are based on erroneous information.

Credit Cleanup Operations, Legal and Otherwise

Many business operations offer credit cleanup services. Many of these offer legitimate assistance. They can improve a credit record by spending the time and effort to do what any person is legally entitled to do, as outlined above, to clean up the credit record. However, they often charge substantial fees for their services.

Some credit cleanup operations do not operate in a legal manner. They claim to have ways to invade the credit bureau computer system and alter credit reports electronically. This is obviously illegal, and anyone who gets involved with it is committing a crime.

Credit doctors tamper with credit reports in another way. A number of these folks have operated in various troubled areas in the United States. They often operate by switching the name of one person for that of another. They literally steal a person's good name and hand it over to someone who lacks good credit. This can be ruinous for the individual whose name is stolen. Such a person may be horrified to find that someone else has applied for credit using his name, with serious problems developing when the person who stole the name runs into the same problems that ruined her credit initially. The credit doctor may be long gone by this time, leaving two people (one completely innocent, one not so innocent) to deal with the resulting mess.

A credit doctor may also build a false identity for a person with bad credit. A birth certificate, often from another state, perhaps for someone who has died, may become the foundation for a false identity. The credit doctor obtains Social Security numbers, driver's licenses, and, ultimately, credit cards based on the false identity. Bigger loans are possible as well. These practices are also illegal.

No one should patronize such credit doctor operations. They may try to masquerade as legitimate enterprises, though. A consumer should ask questions when using credit repair services, particularly those that promise too much. Real estate brokers should never take clients or customers to such operations. They may lose their licenses. Participation in such activities risks criminal penalties for obtaining loans by fraud. Beware of the credit doctor!

TAX CONSEQUENCES OF FORECLOSURE

A person who is losing a home in foreclosure may be subject to a very nasty surprise: an unexpectedly large income tax bill from the IRS. The theory behind this is that, after foreclosure, the borrower may be released, or more correctly discharged, by the lender from the obligation to pay back the loan. This generates taxable discharge of indebtedness income.

Fortunately in December 2007, a new law passed that eliminates the tax problem for 6,121 Principal Residences, up to $2 million filing jointly, and $1 million filing separately. The law will last for 3 years.

Discharge of Indebtedness Income

Whenever someone who borrows money is told by the lender that it need not be paid back (the debt is discharged), then taxable income may arise. A simple example will illustrate the process. The lender loans a $1 bill to a borrower in exchange for the borrower's IOU for $1. Did the borrowed $1 constitute income that must be reported on a Form 1040 as taxable? No. As long as the borrower has to pay back the money, it is not income.

If you borrowed $100,000 to buy a house, would you have to pay income tax on an extra $100,000 in income that year? Obviously not. Do you have to report the fact that you charged a purchase on a credit card as income? Obviously not. As long as it's a loan, it's not income.

Suppose, however, that the lender tears up the IOU and tells the borrower not to pay back the $1. Now it's income! As soon as the lender said you didn't have to pay the money back, it became income. If there were no such rule, abuses could occur. For example, an employer might "loan" an employee $20,000 or so and then tell the employee not to repay the money. To prevent such abuse, discharged debts are income. However the first 2 million (joint filing) is not taxable income.

Discharge of Indebtedness and Foreclosure

When you lose a house in foreclosure, its value may not equal the amount owed on the loan. If the lender discharges the loan obligation (i.e., tells the borrower that she need not repay the loan), this generates income. However the 1 of 2 million (joint filing) is not taxable income.

Here's an example:

Loan balance (amount the borrower still owes):	$50,000
Foreclosure bid (amount generated by sale of the house):	$14,000
Discharge income:	$36,000

The lender may generously say, "There's no hope of getting $36,000 out of a borrower who couldn't even make the monthly house loan payment" and tell the borrower not to pay back the $36,000. This discharges the borrower from the obligation to repay the $36,000, so the borrower must report an additional $36,000 in income that year and pay tax on it, just as though it were income from a job or other work.

To see the potential effect, suppose the borrower from the example made $20,000 per year. This person would have to pay tax on $56,000 for the year of the foreclosure. The taxes would take most of the taxpayer's entire income. Here is a summary of the tax bill:

Example:

Income tax on $20,000 income (1990 single rates):	$3,070
Income tax on $56,000 discharged indebtedness in income:	$13,599
Total tax bill:	$16,669

This person has lost his house and now owes more than $13,000 in extra taxes! It does give the lender a little bit of bargaining power. Maybe this borrower shouldn't have walked out on the house so soon. Again, the 2007 law stops the tax up to $2 million in income from the foreclosure sale of a principal residence.

The Relentless IRS

Unlike other bills, an income tax bill won't go away. Once assessed, unpaid taxes as far as three years back cannot be discharged by bankruptcy. The IRS can foreclose against a homestead to collect unpaid taxes, so it can take a new house, even if there is another loan against it already. IRS can also collect unpaid taxes by garnishment, forcing an employer to turn over part of a person's paycheck.

A former IRS attorney has admitted, "The IRS puts people in the collections division who like to hammer on people." That makes for a lot of trouble when you owe taxes you can't pay.

When a lender obtains a property by foreclosure or abandonment or when it sells a property to someone else, the lender must send a 1099-A form to the IRS and provide the former borrower with a copy. This form tells the IRS the following:

- The borrower's taxpayer identification number
- The date of the foreclosure sale
- The amount of the loan that remains unpaid
- The part of the loan that was paid
- The bid price the lender or other buyer paid at the foreclosure

The borrower should protest any errors on this form to the lender.

IRS calculates the taxable discharge of debt income as the difference between the fair market value of the property and the unpaid portion of the loan. It presumes that the lender's bid at the foreclosure equals the fair market value, unless clear and convincing proof shows otherwise. In many, many cases, the bid price at foreclosure for the house is not its fair market value. For one thing, the lender often appraises the property at a quick-sale value, which is its forced or liquidation value. This invariably is less than the true fair market value. Finally, the lender may arbitrarily bid very low, which means the bid at foreclosure may be much less than the market value.

The taxpayer has the right to have income calculated with the fair market value figure and nothing less. Proving the real fair market value of the house may reduce the tax on discharge of indebtedness income substantially. The taxpayer should protest both to the lender and the IRS if anything less than fair market value is used.

Proving that fair market value differs from the lender's bid price at a foreclosure sale may not be easy, because Treasury Department regulations presume otherwise:

The fair market value of the property for this purpose shall, in the absence of clear and convincing proof to the contrary, be presumed to be the amount for which it is bid in by the taxpayer. (See Treasury Reg. Section 1.166-6[b] [21].)

These rules to not apply to seller-finance transactions, however. Seller-lenders may not recognize loss.

Discharge From Liability

To generate income by discharge of indebtedness, the lender must actually discharge the taxpayer from liability. If the lender pursues the borrower for the debt, it cannot turn in a 1099-A to the IRS for the full amount of the debt. The lender cannot discharge the borrower from liability in a foreclosure unless it existed in the first place. This means the borrower against whom the 1099-A is used must have signed the note to repay the loan. Sometimes nonrecourse or nonliability loans are arranged, in which the taxpayer/borrower would not be personally liable. Still, the IRS may not respect such provisions. Sometimes the lender tries to hold the wrong person liable for the loan, especially in assumption situations, where the assuming borrower may have no personal liability to the lender.

Another possibility is a partial discharge. The lender may attempt to discharge part of the debt, declaring some of it to be uncollectible and ceasing further efforts to do so. It may still continue to pursue the borrower for the rest of what's owed. If so, the borrower will probably face both an increased tax bill and a deficiency judgment simultaneously.

Insolvency

A taxpayer who was insolvent at the time the foreclosure took place will defer the tax on income from the discharge of debt. A taxpayer is insolvent if her liabilities exceed the fair market value of her assets immediately before the discharge from paying back a foreclosed loan. The insolvency can occur outside of bankruptcy. A taxpayer may try to maneuver to appear insolvent at the time of a foreclosure. Although this does not permanently eliminate the tax, it does defer it until later, when the taxpayer returns to solvency. However, the 2007 law eliminates it up to $2,000,000 in gain.

A taxpayer faced with an inevitable foreclosure must keep careful records to show his distressed financial state. If the taxpayer can document insolvency at the time of the foreclosure, he may be able to avoid showing discharge of debt income. The taxpayer should at least be able to show balance sheet insolvency, which means showing more debts than assets. A visit to a tax consultant may be necessary to refine the taxpayer's claim to insolvency at the time of foreclosure.

Bankruptcy

Under the Bankruptcy Tax Act of 1980, the taxpayer need recognize no income by discharge of debt if the discharge occurs in a bankruptcy case and the court approves it. Prior to 1980, a hapless bankrupt could be hammered without mercy by the IRS for taxes on debts discharged out of bankruptcy that might total millions of dollars. The poor bankrupt would be subject to IRS harassment virtually forever in such situations. Fortunately, that has been stopped.

The Statute of Limitations

Years may pass after a foreclosure with a lender doing little or nothing to collect a deficiency judgment for the difference between the foreclosure bid and the amount unpaid on a loan. Often the lender knows that the borrower has no money after the foreclosure and declines to spend money to squeeze blood out of a turnip.

Perhaps the borrower has never signed a discharge from liability. In many states, however, a lawsuit may be filed up to four years after the foreclosure. Is a borrower automatically liable for the taxes on discharge of debt income? The answer appears to be yes. Arguably, a taxpayer has to report the extra income and pay tax on it in the year when the statute of limitations bars the lender from further pursuit of the deficiency. Few do, perhaps hoping that the IRS will not catch up with them. Although this is mainly a theoretical exercise at present, it may well become a very serious problem for taxpayers in the future.

Distressed Home Sales and Capital Gains

Borrowers may be surprised to learn that foreclosure sales can generate capital gains income. Suppose a borrower bought a house at $100,000. The home rises in value to $300,000. If the lender forecloses on the house and resells it for more than $100,000, then the borrower has realized capital gain income to the extent that the foreclosure sale price exceeds the borrower's original investment, or basis, in the property. The result: a big tax bill—in the past. Under the new 2007 law, up to $2 million is protected if the acquisition loan is paid off.

Home Equity Loans and Realization of Income

The excess of the value of the home over the balance on the loan it secures constitutes the borrower's equity in the home. This becomes a capital gain when a sale takes place. Many borrowers make good use of this equity by borrowing against it. In some states, it may even be possible to obtain a credit card with a $30,000 or $40,000 line of credit. The only catch is that if the borrower fails to repay the credit card loan the lender can foreclose on the borrower's home! Even so, home equity loans, in which the borrower pledges the equity in a home to obtain cash, are common throughout the United States.

Let's suppose a homeowner is trying to sell a home in a distressed market. The homeowner bought the house for $100,000, putting $20,000 down and taking out an $80,000 loan. Later, the home increased in value to $300,000, and the homeowner pledged the equity to obtain $100,000 in cash. The borrower has spent the cash and now must sell the home, which is dropping in value. Nevertheless, the homeowner finds a borrower at an outrageously low price of only $220,000. This looks to the homeowner like a huge loss compared to the peak value of $300,000. From the sale proceeds, the borrower pays off the main loan balance and the $100,000 home equity loan. The remaining $20,000 is barely enough to pay the broker's commission and the closing costs. The former homeowner has almost no cash left from the sale.

Unfortunately, the homeowner has just realized a whopping capital gain by paying off the $100,000 home equity loan. Remember, the proceeds of that loan were never taxed as income to the borrower. They were repaid entirely from the appreciated value of the property. The $100,000 with which the borrower paid back the home equity loan constitutes a capital gain from the sale, on which he must pay income tax. The $100,000 must be added to the borrower's other taxable income for the year, which will result in a large tax bill on the total income. The 2007 law applies to acquisition indebtedness, a huge shortcoming.

Some may argue that the borrower in this scenario has a loss of $80,000, since home sold for $220,000, down from a peak value of $300,000. Unfortunately, the IRS sees no loss, only a net gain from the original investment. Besides, even a true loss, in which the house sells for less than the original investment, is not deductible if the house is a personal residence. Also, the normal tax deferral rules do not apply. If a homeowner buys a new house that is worth more within two years after the sale of the old house, she can defer the income tax on the gain. The seller who pays off the home equity loan, however, is stuck with a large tax bill. The borrower must have the cash, because the IRS may not take no for an answer. Bankruptcy may be the only real option left. Tax debts for the previous three years are not dischargeable in bankruptcy, but collection can be delayed. (See the chapter on bankruptcy.) However, up to $500,000 in gain (½ that if filing separately) is not taxable if no sale has occurred in the past 2 years.

Tax Strategies for a Foreclosure Presale

A homeowner who plans to sell a home to avoid foreclosure must carefully consider the potential tax consequences, particularly if large home equity loans must be paid off when the property is sold. A visit to an accountant, an attorney, or another tax consultant is highly advisable. A homeowner should consider an installment sale, if the lenders will permit it, to spread the adverse tax effect over time. The seller should plan to purchase a new home as well, so that the gain from the sale of the old home can be rolled over into the purchase of the new home to defer paying tax on the capital gain.

Paying off home equity loans may generate large income taxes. On the other hand, the homeowner may want to realize enough cash above what is needed to pay off loans to pay the IRS bill. Careful planning is the key.

A FINAL THOUGHT ON DISCHARGE OF DEBT INCOME

The Supreme Court has distinguished tax evasion, which is illegal, from tax avoidance, which is legal. A taxpayer is not to be faulted if for arranging affairs so as to pay the least amount of taxes. When debt is discharged, taxable income arises. Suppose, however, that a loss were to offset the income in a business context. There would be no net income. Please note that losses arising in personal affairs, other than casualty losses, are generally not deductible. However, business losses are deductible against business income.

Someone might argue that a personal residence was turned into a business by renting it out, making it a business asset. The deal fared poorly, however, and the house as an asset lost value, coming to be worth less than what was owed on the loan. This generated a loss at the foreclosure sale, offsetting the income from discharge of indebtedness.

The taxpayer may need to establish real estate dealer status to escape the tax in this way. A person should seek the expert advice of a knowledgeable tax consultant before attempting such a strategy. The taxpayer should recognize that the IRS has the power to disallow deductions under circumstances that suggest the transaction is a sham to lower taxes.

THE 2007 LAW AIDS SHORT SALES AND LOAN MODIFICATION

If a short sale to avoid a foreclosure generates income from the discharge of debt, the 2007 law allows up to $2 million of it to be tax free. The same is true of loan modifications and restructuring to avoid foreclosure on a principal residence. The new law is also retroactive back to November 2007. The borrower should file an amended return if this was missed on the previous year's tax return.

Picking Up the Pieces

16

There is life after foreclosure. If you lose a house, you can recover. You may lose your home, but do not lose your head or your heart.

The first order of business is usually to find another place to live. Often, people move in with other family members, rent apartments, or even try to buy new homes, depending on the circumstances. Over the long term, credit ratings recover, and people manage to buy new homes by more regular means, through bank loans. The borrower should take the attitude that, as serious as a foreclosure may be, it, too, shall pass. On the bright side, the foreclosure may even open opportunities, either to buy a better place to live or to make a long overdue and welcome readjustment of financial priorities.

Once a foreclosure appears to be inevitable, one must choose among a number of possible new places to live. Once foreclosures heat up in an area and cause a down market, it is not as difficult to find a place to stay as one might think. Apartment rents are often low, and space tends to be available. The same is true of house rentals. Some landlords say that your job is your credit, but most want a tenant with a little more credit than employment alone. Often, they don't require much, though, especially in a down market. Security deposit requirements may be low, and a higher security deposit or first month's rent can often be traded for fewer questions about the tenant's credit.

Strangely enough, foreclosure leaves a number of possibilities for buying a house. Once again, the down market may generate some surprising opportunities. The most infamous procedure is to rent out the old house, live with parents, and then try to buy a new house. In Houston during the 1980s, the down market was severe. Homeowners grew tired of keeping up 15 percent mortgages, which they couldn't refinance once property values fell. Many people rented out their old houses and bought new ones down the street at one-third the prices of their old homes, with loans at only two-thirds the interest rates.

This virtually turned into a scam in some instances. Many borrowers moved into new houses, then ignored their old homes. As soon as tenants moved out, the buyers, safe in new homes, didn't care about foreclosure on the old ones. The homeowners could wipe out deficiency judgments with bankruptcies, if need be.

This arrangement got people who were about to lose their old homes to foreclosure into new ones at much smaller monthly payments. All it took was a little cash and a little staying power. As a result, many lenders often refuse new home loans to borrowers who will rent out existing houses to cancel out some or all of the old monthly mortgage payment. They may count only 75 percent or so of the rent as a credit against the old mortgage payment to meet income requirements. Many borrowers told their lenders that the purpose of their purchases was to buy houses in a down market at low prices, reaping gains when the market improved. To meet income qualifications, the borrower could actually show a net decrease in monthly cash payments after the transactions. The rent from the old house would cover much of the mortgage payment, resulting in a small monthly payment to make up the net loss. On the other hand, the new house would have a very low payment because of its low price and low interest rate. The combination of the subsidized loss on the old house with the low payment on the new house might actually leave the buyer paying less than the single payment on the old house. Figure 16.1 summarizes an example.

The total outflow in this arrangement is actually less than simply making the payment on the old house. The trick is to get a loan in a down market. However, that might not be so hard if the lender has an abundance of foreclosed homes that it is desperate to unload. Such sellers often provide financing and look the other way at some aspects of the buyer's credit, just to get the house sold. The arrangement works even better if the old house loan charged a higher interest rate than the new loan. Depending on the condition of the property, renters might be plentiful in a down market. People want to move out of apartments to rent houses. The key is to charge a relatively low rent.

Although renting the old house to buy the new house is feasible, it has often been done in a questionable manner. Many Texas homeowners set up such deals with the deliberate intent of walking out on their first homes. Sometimes tenants were very unstable. Anyone who sets up such an arrangement with the deliberate intent of defrauding a lender could face a suit for fraud. Some persons with plenty of income did such deals to save money on their house payments at the expense of damage to their credit when their old house fell into foreclosure.

SPECIAL FINANCIAL ARRANGEMENTS

Many unusual finance methods spring into existence in a down market. Lenders who acquire inventories of houses from foreclosure become desperate to sell. They often arrange special financing with few questions asked as a vehicle to promote the resale of these homes. As a result, a person faced with foreclosure may consider buying another, smaller property through a contract for deed, seller finance, lease that may turn into a purchase, or a simple assumption. None of these arrangements requires the buyer to have particularly strong credit.

In a contract for deed, the seller owns the property while the buyer makes the payments. According to the terms of the contract, when the payments are complete, the seller delivers a deed directly or through an intermediary to the buyer. This arrangement has many problems, not the least of which is the seller's lack of good title. Often, the buyer doesn't know whether the seller's title has problems unless the buyer is astute enough to buy title insurance at the outset. Even then, the seller may allow a lien against the property while the buyer is paying for it. The contract for deed should contain provisions that prohibit the seller from placing a lien on the property or at least define and restrict the type and purpose of such a lien.

The buyer should be sure, as well, that the contract for deed does not violate a due-on-sale clause in a previous mortgage. The buyer should never accept a contract for deed that allows the seller to cancel the buyer's right to buy for small infractions, such as paying one payment late. All in all, the contract for deed arrangement is undesirable for the buyer in most cases and should generally be avoided. However, it is better than a lease, because the contract for deed offers at least some possibility of obtaining title.

True seller-finance arrangements involve the outright sale and passage of title to the buyer, while the seller retains the right to foreclose if the payments on a note are not made as agreed by the buyer. This arrangement gives the buyer's title better protection, but the buyer should be sure to get a title insurance policy or check title before purchasing. The seller can be asked to pay the expense. Like the contract for deed, the seller-finance arrangement does not require a buyer to have good credit.

A lease, perhaps with an option to purchase, is fundamentally very similar to the contract for deed and may have many of the same problems. If the lease involves an option to purchase, it will violate due-on-sale clauses in most conventional mortgages originated after the 1980s. FHA or VA mortgages don't have these clauses, although the most recent mortgages have due-on-sale restrictions that require the buyer to qualify for the loan, regardless of whether seller wants to remain liable or not.

Finally, one of the buyer's best options is to find a house with an assumable FHA or VA loan. The buyer can take over the payments on the old loan, receiving deed to the property at the time the deal is made. Assumptions and their problems are discussed in much greater length in a previous chapter.

CREDIT DAMAGE

A foreclosure sale will adversely affect the borrower's credit for some time to come. Many lenders do not report missed mortgage payments on the borrower's credit record, but any attempt to buy a house with a new loan will lead the new lender to demand detailed information concerning the payment patterns on the old loan. This information is even more detailed and specific than a credit report. The foreclosure itself normally appears on the credit record with the designation FCL.

Figure 16.1 Strategy for Down Markets

1. Rent out the old house

Payment on old house ($80,000 loan balance)	$900.00
Less rent	–600.00
Net loss to be subsidized	$300.00

2. Buy a new house at a low price

Payment on new house ($40,000 loan balance)	$450.00
3. Total cash outflow	$750.00

Most lenders will not consider loaning to a borrower with an FCL on her record for at least three years following the foreclosure. A bankruptcy would affect the borrower for at least two years. In either case, these are minimum time periods. Shorter terms would probably violate FNMA servicing standards, depending on the circumstances.

The key limiting factor on the damage to the borrower's credit from a foreclosure is the reason for the foreclosure. If the borrower lost the house due to extraordinary circumstances beyond his control, such as unpaid medical bills, a divorce, or the loss of a job or business in a down market, then credit can be restored fairly quickly. If other factors, such as a new job, are good, and payments for the previous few years look steady, then a foreclosure three years or more old will probably not be fatal to a new loan applicant.

If the borrower failed to make payments for what lenders label "disregard for the obligation," the worst possible reason, then the borrower will not be able to obtain a new loan. Here's an example. The prospective borrower lost a house in foreclosure more than five years before an attempt to borrow money. The lender discovered that, at that time of the foreclosure, the borrower had the resources to make the payments on an investment house but chose not to because its value had declined. Instead, the borrower walked away from the house and allowed it to fall into foreclosure. The lender categorically denied the loan because the borrower lacked a good reason for failing to pay the earlier loan.

A foreclosure is often the last straw in the financial decimation of the borrower. Most people quit paying everything else before they fail to pay the mortgage. By the way, future lenders will take due note of such a pattern. If the borrower kept up all the other payments but missed the mortgage payment, the FHA sees this as a distinct negative on the borrower's credit record. It shows the first thing the borrower will leave unpaid is the mortgage, which is bad news from a mortgage lender's perspective.

To qualify for a loan, the borrower's credit report must normally show: (1) no more than two 30-day slow-pays (late payments) on revolving charge card obligations; (2) no more than one 30-day slow-pay period on any installment loan payment, such as a car loan; and (3) a perfect payment record for the previous year on the rent or the previous house payment.

In addition, the borrower should have no derogatory information, such as a bankruptcy, judgment, or foreclosure, unless the bankruptcy is over two years old and/or the foreclosure is over three years old. An active unpaid judgment, such as from a deficiency lawsuit, lasts as long as it is valid and enforceable under state law. Any bankruptcy or foreclosure should have been caused by circumstances beyond the borrower's control. If such events happened due to the borrower's poor credit management skills, then the loan should be denied. Once the borrower has credit along the lines just described, a new loan is possible; otherwise, the borrower should use alternative financing, such as leases, leases with option to purchase, contracts for deed, seller financing, or assumptions. As bad as foreclosure seems, the borrower can restore credit over time. Many persons lose homes in foreclosure in a down market, yet they actually wind up with housing that is quite adequate because a down market provides a plentiful supply of other homes.

CONCLUSION

Homeowners have many rights and options when faced with foreclosure. However, certain key points remain constant. The homeowner who cannot pay the payments on the mortgage will ultimately lose the home. The borrower can delay foreclosure by many procedures, but ultimately, the lender will be able to hammer the borrower into a foreclosure in almost any state. It's just a question of how long and how much effort the lender will have to put into the process. With enough money for attorneys, the lender will win.

On the other hand, the borrower who may be able to make payments or may be able to resume payments in the future, should act promptly as soon as he foresees trouble. The extensive relief provisions offered on VA, FHA, FNMA, FHLMC or even well-insured private mortgages of many types will prove useful only if the distressed borrower moves quickly and shows a willingness to work with the lender.

If the worst happens and foreclosure is completed, the borrower can recover someday. Depending on the circumstances, the recovery period may be short or long. A willful refusal to pay on a house when the borrower had the capability to pay is likely to take a long time to cure. On the other hand, the borrower who was caught in unfortunate circumstances may be able to recover fairly quickly. Good credit may be available in as little as three years from the date of the foreclosure.

The problem may not be so much the foreclosure as continued weak market conditions that restrict the availability of loans. However, a down market often generates plenty of properties for sale at reduced prices with easy financing terms. Sometimes in a down market, everyone seems to play a musical chairs game of switching between houses. Borrowers who lose a home in foreclosure should not lose all hope. The emotional devastation of foreclosure can balloon out of all proportion to the ultimate financial damage it causes over the long term. The financial damage can be repaired. A down market will give way to an up market. It's just a matter of time.

Appendix

SUMMARIES OF STATE FORECLOSURE LAWS

The purpose of summarizing the foreclosure laws of all 50 states is to give the reader in any given state some idea of the foreclosure laws. Foreclosure law can be complicated, and it is impossible for these brief summaries to cover all the details of the process. Advice about your state's laws and your rights under them should always be sought from a licensed attorney in that state.

Also, before reading any of the summaries below, the reader is strongly encouraged to read chapter 3 on the foreclosure process. Chapter 3 explains the terminology used in these summaries, including terms such as *posting, deficiency judgment,* and *right of redemption,* and the difference between judicial and nonjudicial foreclosure. Quick definitions of terms can be found in the glossary as well.

Remember to read your own state's summary. The foreclosure laws are often quite different from state to state.

ALABAMA

Judicial Foreclosure Available Yes

Nonjudicial Foreclosure Available Yes

Alabama allows foreclosure in one of three ways: (1) by filing a lawsuit to foreclose, (2) by a foreclosure sale conducted in accordance with the terms specified under a power of sale clause in the deed of trust or mortgage, or (3) if there is no power of sale clause, then by a public sale on the courthouse steps. Foreclosure by (1) above, filing a lawsuit seeking a court order to foreclose, is not common. The other two methods see more use.

Power of Sale Foreclosure Preliminary Notices

Advertising The sale may not take place until 30 days after advance notice of the time, place, and terms of the sale have been published once a week for four consecutive weeks in the county.

Sale Procedures

Documents May Specify Procedure If the mortgage or deed of trust contains a power of sale clause and specifies the time, place, and manner of the foreclosure sale, then that procedure must be followed.

Statutory Procedure However, *if* the mortgage or deed of trust with a power of sale clause is silent as to the place or terms of the sale or as to the type of notice of the sale, then a foreclosure sale may be made at the courthouse door of the county where the land is located, after a breach of the conditions or requirements of the mortgage or deed of trust, by selling for cash to the highest bidder. However, the title is conveyed by a foreclosure deed in the case of a sale under a mortgage or deed of trust with a power of sale clause.

Foreclosure Without a Power of Sale Clause If the mortgage or deed of trust lacks a power of sale clause and the lender chooses not to file a lawsuit to foreclose, then the lender may foreclose by selling the property for cash to the highest bidder at the courthouse door of the county where the land is located. Advance notice of the time, place, terms, and purpose of the sale must be given by publishing an ad once a week for four consecutive weeks in a newspaper in the county.

Deficiency The lender may sue to foreclose the mortgage without filing a suit to obtain a deficiency judgment. Alternatively, the lender may sue to foreclose and then sue for any resulting deficiency. It's the lender's choice.

Redemption The borrower has a right to redeem within one year after the foreclosure. Anyone who wants to redeem should obtain a statement of the price paid for the property at the foreclosure sale from whoever bought the property at the foreclosure sale. The borrower can then redeem by paying to the foreclosure buyer the foreclosure purchase price, taxes, insurance, improvements, and 10 percent interest on the price and all the legitimate charges. If necessary, the borrower can file a suit in the circuit court to redeem the property.

ALASKA

Judicial Foreclosure Available Yes

Nonjudicial Foreclosure Available Yes

Alaska offers two ways to borrow money against real estate: a true mortgage and a deed of trust. The true mortgage may be foreclosed in Superior Court, according to the rules of equity. The deed of trust names the trustee who will oversee the foreclosure sale by recording and posting a notice of sale and arranging an auction to the highest bidder. Alaska law provides a procedure to appoint a substitute trustee by recording a proper notice of the appointment.

Preferred Method of Foreclosure Nonjudicial deed of trust sale

Nonjudicial Power of Sale Foreclosure The deed of trust must be foreclosed according to its own terms, if not inconsistent with the minimum protections of Alaska's laws.

Preliminary Notices

Recording Not less than 30 days after the default and not less than three months before the sale, the trustee shall record a notice of default stating the name of the borrower and the book and page where the trust deed is recorded. It must describe the property, the borrower's default, the amount the borrower owes, and the trustee's desire to sell. It must give the date, time, and place of sale.

Mailing Within ten days after recording the notice of default, the trustee must mail a copy of the same by certified mail to the last known address of (1) the borrower, (2) any person whose claim or lien on the property appears of record or is known to the lender or trustee, and (3) any occupant. The trustee may have the notice delivered personally instead of sending it by certified mail.

Reinstatement Rights Anytime before the sale, the borrower may cure the default and stop the sale by paying a sum equal to the missed payments plus attorney's fees. The lender may not require the borrower to pay off the entire remaining principal balance of the loan to cure the default—just the missed payments and attorney's fees. However, if the lender has recorded a notice of default two times or more, then the Alaska statutes provide that the lender can refuse to accept the borrower's money for the missed payments and attorney's fees and continue with the foreclosure sale instead.

Sale Procedures

Place of Sale The front door of the courthouse for the Superior Court for the judicial district the property is in, unless the deed of trust specifies another location.

Manner of Sale The trustee can conduct the auction or bring in an auctioneer to call out the sale.

Postponement The trustee can postpone the sale by giving the person who conducts the sale a signed, written postponement request moving the foreclosure to a different time and place, which must be publicly announced at the time and place originally fixed for the sale.

Terms The trustee must sell to the highest and best bidder. The lender may bid at the auction. The trustee's deed must give the book and page where both the original deed of trust and the default notice were recorded. It must state that the notice of default was properly mailed. It must give the time, place, and manner in which the foreclosure sale was conducted and the amount paid for the property at foreclosure. After the sale, the trustee must record an affidavit that the notice of default was properly mailed.

Redemption If the lender forecloses by means of an out-of-court foreclosure sale under a deed of trust, then the borrower has no right to redeem the property. However, the borrower does have a right to redeem if the sale was the result of a lawsuit and a court order commanding the sale.

Deficiency Judgment Judicial foreclosure permits a deficiency suit. However, if the lender forecloses through an out-of-court foreclosure sale under the deed of trust, then the lender may not sue for a deficiency judgment afterward.

ARIZONA

Judicial Foreclosure Available Yes

Nonjudicial Foreclosure Available Yes

Trustees A trustee may conduct the foreclosure sale out of court under a power of sale clause if the borrower defaults on the loan. Alternatively, a trustee (or the lender) may sue to foreclose. A trustee may also sue the borrower for physical abuse to the property, waste, or other impairment of the security but only if the borrower was in possession or control of the property when the damage was done. The trustee cannot conduct a foreclosure sale under the power of sale clause until any lawsuit to foreclose is dismissed. Under Arizona law, a bank, trust company, S&L, or other institutional lender can be a trustee. Arizona-licensed attorneys, real estate brokers, and insurance agents can also be trustees. Substitute trustees may be appointed by the lender for any reason if they record a Notice of Substitution of Trustee and mail a copy to the borrower. A trustee may resign by recording a Notice of Resignation of Trustee.

Preliminary Notices

Contents The trustee shall give written notice of the time and place of sale, including a legal description of the property, by each of several methods.

Recording The trustee must record a notice of the sale in the county recorder's office in the county where the property is.

Advertising Once a week for four consecutive weeks, the notice must appear in a newspaper in the county where the property is located; the last notice must be published not less than ten days prior to the sale.

Posting (1) The trustee can post the notice, at least 20 days prior to the date of the sale, in some conspicuous place on the property to be sold, if it can be done without a breach of the peace. (2) The trustee can post the notice at the courthouse or at a specified place at the place of business of the trustee in the county in which the property to be sold is located.

Mailing The trustee or lender must mail, within five days after recording the notice of sale, by certified mail, a copy of any notice of sale to each of the persons who were parties to the trust deed except the trustee. It must be addressed to the mailing address specified in the trust deed. The notice must set forth the nature of the borrower's breach or nonperformance under the trust deed. In addition, any person will be entitled to receive a copy of the trustee's foreclosure notice if such a person records a statutory Request for Notice form.

Special Procedure For a fee up to $20, the trustee can provide information on the unpaid balance, the name and address of the owner, the date the trustee's notice was recorded, and a list of encumbrances. A trustee must honor a written request and may honor an oral request.

Sale Procedures

Time and Place The time and place of the foreclosure must be designated in the notice of sale.

Manner of Sale The trustee or the trustee's agent must conduct the sale. The sale is for cash to the highest bidder, except that the lender can make a "credit bid," which means to cancel out some part (or all) of the money the borrower owed the lender on the loan, instead of paying cash. A successful high bidder must pay the bid price by 5:00 PM of the day after the bid, other than a Saturday or a legal holiday. Every bid is an irrevocable offer until the sale is completed, which happens when the bidder pays the bid price to the trustee's satisfaction. If the high bidder fails to make payment, then the second-highest bidder has the option to buy the property. If the second-highest bidder fails to make payment by 5:00 PM the day after being notified of the option to buy, then the trustee may postpone the sale.

Postponement The trustee may postpone the sale to another time or another place by giving notice of the new date, time, and place by public declaration at the last place and time the property was offered for sale. No other notice is required. A trustee may also, by written agreement, extend the time for a buyer to come up with payment.

Postsale Matters The sales proceeds will go to the payment of the obligations secured by the trust deed that was foreclosed, then to junior lienholders in order of their priority. The successful bidder gets a trustee's deed, which constitutes conclusive evidence that the trustee conducted the foreclosure sale properly.

Deficiency An Arizona deed of trust permits the real estate that is the collateral for a loan to be sold at a foreclosure sale by a trustee. The proceeds of the sale will be paid to the lender, or the lender can take title to the property and cancel out the debt in exchange for the deed, called a "credit bid." Under Arizona law, a lender may not bring a subsequent deficiency suit against a person who lost a property of 2.5 acres or less at a foreclosure, provided the property was a single one-family or a single two-family dwelling. This is so even if the high bid at foreclosure was less than the balance due on the loan. In foreclosures against other types of property, a deficiency is limited to the difference between the balance owed and the fair market value of the property, and then only if the suit is brought within 90 days of the power of sale foreclosure.

Redemption Arizona does not recognize a subsequent right of redemption on foreclosure sales.

ARKANSAS

Judicial Foreclosure Available Yes

Nonjudicial Foreclosure Available Yes

Under Arkansas law, a residential real property mortgage held by a bank, savings and loan, or mortgage company may be foreclosed under a power of sale clause in the mortgage. Agricultural real property or construction loans operate by different rules.

Power of Sale Foreclosure Preliminary Notice

Contents of Notice The Notice of Default and Intention to Sell must name the deed of trust parties, give recording information, describe the default and the amount due on the loan, and state the trustee's or lender's intention to undertake a foreclosure sale. The notice must include in conspicuous type the following warning:

YOU MAY LOSE YOUR PROPERTY IF YOU DO NOT TAKE IMMEDIATE ACTION.

Advertising The notice of default and intention to sell must be published once a week for four consecutive weeks prior to the date of the sale in a newspaper of general circulation. The final publication must be no more than ten days before the sale.

Mailing The notice must be mailed to the borrower by certified mail to the last address the lender knows of within ten days after recording the notice. This includes any borrower of record of whom the lender has actual notice. The notice must also be mailed to anyone who records a Request for Notice that specifically describes the mortgage, including its recording information.

Recording The lender must record a copy of the Notice of Default and Intention to Sell.

Special Procedures: Reinstatement Rights The property may not be sold for 60 days after the notice is recorded. During this time, the borrower has the right to stop the foreclosure and reinstate the loan by paying all sums that may be due at that time. A notice of sale cancellation must then be recorded.

Special Procedures: Appraisement An appraisement of the property must be made before foreclosure day. The justice of the peace for the county must appoint three disinterested householders of the county where the property is located, who must take an oath that they will well and truly view and appraise the property that may be shown to them. The appraisers must then view and appraise the property, and then all or any two of them must write an appraisal report and deliver the same to the person holding the foreclosure sale. It must be made available for inspection by the person holding the sale to any interested party. The appraisers get $1 for their services, paid from the foreclosure proceeds.

In any foreclosure under a mortgage or deed of trust in Arkansas, the property must sell for not less than two-thirds of the appraised value. If it doesn't, then it may be offered for sale again within 12 months. The second sale may be to the highest bidder without reference to the appraisement.

Sale Procedures

The attorney for the mortgagee or trustee may conduct the sale and act as the auctioneer. The foreclosure sale must take place at the time, date, and place specified in the Notice of Default and Intention to Sell, but the sale must be within certain limits.

Time It must be held between 9:00 AM and 4:00 PM on a weekday and not on a Saturday, Sunday, or legal holiday.

Place It must be held either at the property being foreclosed on or the front door of the county courthouse in the county where the property is located.

Manner Any person, including the mortgagee (lender), may bid at the sale, except the trustee, who may bid on behalf of the beneficiary (lender) but not for himself in deed of trust sales. The high bidder must pay the price bid at the time of sale or within ten days. The lender may bid by canceling out what it is owed on the loan, including unpaid taxes, insurance, costs of sale, and maintenance, but for cash for any higher price. The mortgagee or trustee shall execute and deliver a trustee's deed to the high bid purchaser.

Postponement The sale may be postponed by public proclamation at the time, place, and date last appointed for sale, up to seven days past the original date; but if for a longer time, then the whole notice procedure must be performed a second time, including the 60-day wait.

Postsale Procedures The purchaser may obtain possession once the deed is recorded. The occupant of the foreclosed premises becomes a tenant at sufferance against whom the purchaser may use a writ of assistance, if necessary, to effect the eviction. The proceeds of the sale shall be applied first to pay the expenses of the sale, second to the debt owed, third to any recorded lienholders in the order of their priority, and fourth to the original borrower. Within ten days after the sale, the trustee or mortgagee shall file an affidavit stating that a sale was made in accordance with the law, including the time, place, and date of the sale and the purchase price. A copy must be mailed to all persons entitled to receive notice of the foreclosure, as described earlier.

Judicial Foreclosure In judicial foreclosure, a court decrees the amount of the indebtedness of the borrower and gives the borrower a short time to pay. If the borrower fails to pay within that time, then the clerk of the court, as commissioner, advertises the property for sale. Sales of real property under court order shall be on a credit of not less than three months nor more than six months, or on installments to not more than four months credit on the whole. To secure payment, a lien will be retained on the property for its price. The purchaser must further give a bond with surety for the purchase price. The lender may bid at the sale. The lender can bid by crediting a portion (or all) of the amount the court found was owed to the lender against the sales price of the property purchased at the foreclosure sale. If the real estate does not sell for an amount equal to what's due on the mortgage loan, then the lender may seize other property from the borrower as in an ordinary judgment.

Deficiency The lender may sue the borrower for a deficiency within 12 months of a power of sale clause foreclosure. The lender may sue for either (1) the difference between the foreclosure sale price and the balance due on the loan or (2) the balance due on the loan minus the fair market value of the property, whichever is less.

Redemption When property is sold under a chancery court order, the borrower may redeem the property up to one year from the date of sale by payment of the amount for which the property was sold, with interest. However, the mortgagor may waive the right of redemption in a mortgage or deed of trust. In the case of a deed of trust or mortgagee's sale under a power of sale clause, as described earlier, the borrower is not entitled to a right of redemption.

CALIFORNIA

Judicial Foreclosure Available Yes

Nonjudicial Foreclosure Available Yes

Nonjudicial Sale Typically a title insurance company is named as the trustee to arrange the sale of the real estate.

California is famous for its one-action rule, under which a lender must carefully elect one action to take against the borrower if the borrower defaults. If the lender forecloses the deed of trust out of court, the lender has chosen one action and may not bring a lawsuit to recover a deficiency, which would be a second action. The lender may choose to sue the borrower and obtain both a foreclosure order and, if the proceeds of the judicial sale of the real estate are not sufficient to repay the loan balance, a deficiency for the balance. Such a suit is permitted as the lender's one action. California lenders rarely elect judicial foreclosures.

Preliminary Notices: Nonjudicial

Notice of Default A notice of default must be recorded three months before the notice of sale may be given.

Notice of Sale The notice of sale must contain the name, street address, and phone number of the trustee conducting the sale and the original trustor, along with a statement warning the borrowers that their property is about to be lost at a public foreclosure sale and to contact a lawyer for an explanation.

The notice must give the street address. If no street address exists, the notice must state the address of the beneficiary from whom a set of directions to the property may be obtained, if they are requested in writing within ten days from the first publication of the foreclosure notice. The notice of sale must also contain the time and location of the foreclosure sale.

Advertising A copy of the notice of sale must be published once a week for 20 days before the sale.

Posting A copy of the notice of sale must be posted in a conspicuous place on the property to be sold at least 20 days before the sale. If access to the property is restricted by means of a central guard gate, then the notice must be posted on the guard gate. A copy of the notice also must be posted at one public place in the city where the property is to be sold (or judicial district in rural areas) at least 20 days before the sale.

Recording The notice of sale must be recorded at least 14 days before the sale.

Mailing A notice of sale must be mailed by certified mail, return receipt requested, 20 days before the foreclosure sale to the borrower, to anyone who requests notice or recorded a request and to the trustors, beneficiaries, or parties at interest.

Sale Procedures: Nonjudicial

Time All sales under a power of sale in a deed of trust shall be made between the hours of 9:00 AM and 5:00 PM on any business day, Monday through Friday, at the time specified in the notice of sale.

Place The sale shall commence at the location specified in the notice of sale.

Manner The sale must be made at public auction to the highest bidder. The trustee has the right to require every bidder to show evidence of ability to pay the full bid with cash, cashier's check, or certain bank checks. Each bid is by law an irrevocable offer to purchase. However, a higher bid cancels an earlier bid. It is unlawful and a criminal offense ($10,000 fine or up to a year in jail) to offer anyone consideration not to bid or to fix or restrain the bidding process in any manner.

Postponement Sales may be postponed by announcement at the time and location specified for the intended sale. The borrower may postpone the sale to obtain cash, provided the written request for postponement identifies the source from which the funds are to be obtained and the postponement is only for one business day. The borrower may obtain one such postponement.

Reinstatement Debtors may reinstate up to five days prior to a nonjudicial foreclosure sale.

Junior Lienholders Junior lienholders may no longer redeem, so they may try to protect themselves by (1) advancing funds to bring the senior loan payments current, then foreclosing for the sums advanced; (2) bidding at the foreclosure sale so the price will be sufficient to pay off the senior and the junior liens; or (3) acquiring the property by bidding at foreclosure. If the debtor has a right to redeem and does so, the junior lienholder who purchased the home must be reimbursed. Junior liens do not reattach if a borrower redeems a senior lien whose foreclosure extinguished the junior. This helps borrowers by encouraging junior lienholders to bid up the property to fair market value at the foreclosure sale or else lose out, giving borrowers closer to fair value at sale.

Deficiency Lenders may not seek a deficiency judgment if (1) the foreclosure is nonjudicial or if (2) the foreclosure is on a purchase money obligation. The same rules do not apply to guarantors or later lienholders. The lenders may seize alternative collateral. If the lender forecloses by filing a lawsuit, then the lender can obtain both a foreclosure sale order and a judgment against the borrower for a deficiency after the court-ordered sale, but only for the difference between the judgment and the fair value of the security.

Redemption A borrower's right to redemption is terminated when a deficiency judgment is waived or prohibited. When redemption is permitted, after judicial foreclosure, only the borrower can now redeem, and junior lienholders or "redemptionors" may not. When the lender is permitted to seek a deficiency, elects to pursue a deficiency, and forecloses judicially, the borrower may redeem 12 months after sale, but a full credit bid by lender cuts this period to 3 months.

COLORADO

Judicial Foreclosure Available Yes

Nonjudicial Foreclosure Available Yes

Public Trustee: A Colorado Concept In contrast to most states, where the trustee is usually the hired gun of the lender, Colorado has an impartial, accountable "public trustee" appointed by the governor for each county, who handles power of sale foreclosures on request and files a Notice of Election and Demand with the county clerk and recorder of the county. The public trustee may take only the compensation set by law. A private lender engages a public trustee by filing with the trustee two copies of a notice of election and demand for sale, the original note or a suitable bond, and a mailing list of persons who must receive foreclosure notices.

Preliminary Notices: Nonjudicial Foreclosure

Advertising A notice of sale giving the time and place of the foreclosure must be advertised in accordance with the terms of the deed of trust, but under Colorado law, all deeds of trust must prescribe a weekly advertising period for the notice of sale, in a newspaper of general circulation, of not less than four weeks.

Recording The public trustee must record the lender's notice of election and demand for sale.

Mailing The public trustee must mail, within ten days after the publication of the notice of election and demand for sale, a copy of the same and a notice of sale as published in the newspaper to the borrower and any owner or claimant of record at the address given in the recorded instrument. The public trustee must also mail, at least 21 days before the foreclosure sale, a notice to the borrower describing how to redeem the property.

Right-to-Cure Default If the loan default is due to nonpayment, then the borrower can give notice of an intention to cure the default at least seven days before the foreclosure sale. The trustee must then, on request, investigate and tell the borrower the sum due on the loan. If on or before noon of the day before the date of the sale, the owners, parties, or borrowers pay to the officer conducting the sale all delinquent principal and interest payments that were due as of the date of such payment, plus costs, expenses, late charges, and attorney's fees, but not future principal (since no extra debt is allowed due to acceleration), then the foreclosure must be stopped. This right may be exercised more than one time. The owner of the property may stop the foreclosure proceedings by doing two things: (1) filing an Intent to Cure with the Public Trustee's office at least 15 days prior to the foreclosure sale and then (2) paying the necessary amount to bring the loan current by noon the day before the foreclosure sale is scheduled.

Sale Procedures

Date The foreclosure sale must be held between 45 and 60 days after the recording of the election and demand for sale.

Place The public trustee may conduct the sale at any door or entrance to a courthouse, notwithstanding the deed of trust's provisions, or the trustee may conduct the sale at the location specified in the deed of trust.

Postsale Matters The trustee will pay any excess proceeds from the foreclosure sale to creditors in order of their priority and the balance to the grantor, who has five years to claim it. Title is conveyed by deed to the highest bidder, who may be the lender.

Deficiency The lender may sue for a deficiency.

Redemption The borrower has 75 days after the date of sale to redeem the premises by paying the public trustee the sum for which the property was sold, with interest. A variety of redemption periods exist for junior lienholders. Special rights exist in the case of agricultural borrowers.

CONNECTICUT

Judicial Foreclosure Available Yes

Nonjudicial Foreclosure Available No

Preferred Method: Judicial Foreclosure

Connecticut allows foreclosure by two strange judicial methods, strict foreclosure and decree of sale.

Strict Foreclosure Connecticut is one of the few states that still uses strict foreclosure. In strict foreclosure, there is no foreclosure sale at all, not even at the courthouse steps. The lender must go to court and obtain a court order showing the borrower to be in default under the terms of the mortgage. At that point, title shifts to the lender. However, the borrower has a length of time, set by the court, to redeem the property. If the borrower fails to come up with the money during that time, then the borrower is forever barred from asserting a claim to the property, and title becomes absolute in the lender. From that date, the lender has one month to record a certificate of foreclosure describing the premises, the mortgage, the foreclosure proceedings, and the date title became absolute. If the lender demands possession in the foreclosure suit, the court may issue an execution of ejectment against the person in possession of the property. Possession may also be obtained by peaceable entry, unless the mortgage says otherwise. The disadvantage to the borrower is that the lender obtains title to land that might be worth much more than what was owed on the original loan. This is a sort of windfall profit for the lender.

Decree of Sale Upon motion by any party, a court may allow a mortgage to be foreclosed by a decree of sale. In a decree of sale, the court appoints a committee to sell the property. The court also sets the time and manner of the sale. The court further appoints three appraisers. The borrower may stop the proceedings at any time by paying the balance due on the loan. If not, the committee will make the sale. Afterward, the sale will be ratified by the court, which executes a deed to the purchaser. The grantee in the deed may obtain possession of the property by court order. A supplemental judgment can direct the distribution of the proceeds of the sale. The lender need only bring those proceeds to court that exceed the balance due on the loan, including interests and costs.

Special Protections for Unemployed Borrowers

If a residential borrower has lived in a home as a principal residence for at least two years and the borrower (1) has not had a foreclosure action commenced against her in the past seven years and (2) is unemployed or underemployed as defined by law, then the borrower can claim protection from foreclosure under Connecticut statutes. Borrowers are considered underemployed or unemployed under Connecticut law if the aggregate earned income of all the homeowners of the real property during the year preceding the foreclosure was under $50,000 and less than 75 percent of the average aggregate annual income during the two years prior to the preceding year before foreclosure.

Eligibility A court may decide that borrowers are eligible for special protection after considering three criteria: (1) the likelihood the borrower will be able to make timely payments on a restructured mortgage by the time a restructuring period ends; (2) the likelihood of a substantial prejudice to a lender or a subordinate lienholder due to the restructuring of the mortgage debt; and (3) the borrower has not received an emergency mortgage assistance loan and had not applied for one for two years before applying for foreclosure protection.

Protection From Foreclosure

Under Connecticut law, borrowers can get two forms of protection: (1) foreclosure is stopped during the restructuring period, which may last up to six months, and (2) court-ordered restructuring of the mortgage so as to eliminate overdue payments.

Restructuring the Loan The ceiling for restructured debt is either (1) the amount of the original debt or (2) 90 percent of the fair market value of the property as determined by an appraiser at the time of the restructure. No additional debt may be restructured. Missed payments can be added to the balance of the loan in a Connecticut restructure. However, the borrower must pay interest on the arrearages that are added to the loan. Interest accrues on any sums added to the old mortgage debt at the end of the restructuring period, which may be fixed or variable, depending on the original note. A composite rate must be used on fixed-rate loans so that the restructured debt must pay current interest rates while the main part of the loan continues at its original rate. Such composite rates are not necessary for variable interest rate loans.

Deficiency Judgment The strict foreclosure proceeding does not include an action against the borrower for payment, but the lender can sue the borrower directly in an independent action brought prior to or during the strict foreclosure proceeding. Once the borrower's time limit to come up with the balance on the loan is past, then the lender gets title to the property; if the property is worth more than the balance owed on the loan, the lender cannot sue for a deficiency. Please note: the lender walks off with the equity without paying anything in this situation. In proceedings to foreclose by sale rather than by strict foreclosure, extra proceedings to collect debt from the borrower are stayed during the suit seeking a sale. If the proceeds of the sale exceed the appraised value of the property but are not enough to pay the lender's past-due loan balance, then a deficiency judgment may be rendered against the borrower. If at the court-ordered sale, the property is sold for less than the appraised value, then no other proceedings to collect the debt from the borrower may be undertaken until one-half the difference between the debt and the appraised value is subtracted from what the borrower owes the lender.

Redemption Redemption is determined by the court in strict foreclosure. Redemption by a junior lienholder is subject to any prior liens.

DELAWARE

Judicial Foreclosure Available Yes

Nonjudicial Foreclosure Available No

In Delaware, if a borrower defaults, the lender can take several remedies simultaneously. The lender could sue to collect on the note and foreclose the mortgage. A lender could also sue on the note first and pursue foreclosure later. However, the lender will only be permitted to recover the amount unpaid on the loan. Usually the speediest process is scire facias, a procedure that contemplates a sale of the mortgaged property for a sum that will pay the balance on the loan, or a transfer of title to the lender, after the property has been exposed at a public sale, in exchange for a credit against some part of the balance on the loan or up to the full balance owed on the loan.

Scire Facias

Scire facias is a proceeding in which the borrower must show cause that there should be no foreclosure. Usually, upon breach of the terms of the mortgage, such as through nonpayment of the note or breach of the mortgage conditions, the lender may seek a writ of scire facias from the Superior Court in the county of the mortgaged premises. The initial filing, which must be sworn to, consists of a Praecipe and Complaint. The Praecipe calls upon the Prothonotary to issue the writ of scire facias. The term *scire facias* is the name both of the writ and the proceeding it instigates. The writ is issued upon the default of the borrower in making payments or observing mortgage conditions, and it requires the borrower to show cause as to why the mortgage should not be foreclosed and the property sold.

Once the writ is issued, it will be served upon the borrower by the sheriff. If the sheriff goes out and tries to hand the borrower the writ without success after repeated effort, called "return non est," then a default liberari judgment may be obtained. (At least two separately issued, consecutive writs must be returned non est.) If the borrower is served with the writ, it will command the borrower to appear before the court to show why the mortgage premises should not be seized and sold to pay off the mortgage, with interest, or else pay off the lender's losses due to the borrower's nonperformance. If the borrower fails to appear within 20 days after being served with the writ of scire facias, then the lender will obtain a default liberari judgment. Otherwise, the borrower must prove why the foreclosure should not take place. Unless the court is satisfied with the explanation, the court will authorize the property to be seized to pay off the mortgage.

Preliminary Notices

Posting Notices of the sale must be posted publicly and at the house or property that is being foreclosed on at least ten days before the sale day.

Delivery A copy of the notice must be delivered to the borrower.

Advertising Newspaper ads must be run two weeks before the sale.

Sale Procedures

Person Conducting the Sale The sale itself will be conducted by the sheriff.

Place of Sale The place of sale must be either at the courthouse or at the site of the property being sold.

Postsale Matters The sale must be confirmed by the court. Once confirmed, no redemption is possible. A deed will be executed by the sheriff to convey title to the purchaser. Deficiency judgments are possible but only by a suit on the note in addition to the scire facias.

Unusual Procedures Since scire facias is purely a remedy at common law, equity law does not play a role in the proceedings. Although mortgages can be foreclosed by an equity suit in the Delaware Court of Chancery, this method is seldom used. Strict common law has some unusual results, however. In particular, the borrower's counterclaims will not be heard at the hearing on the scire facias, because they were not part of the original mortgage. Such counterclaims must be pursued in a separate proceeding rather than as part of the scire facias proceeding. All record owners acquiring title subject to the mortgage (terretenants) must be joined in the scire facias proceeding, however. Also, persons who have equitable or legal interests of record, such as one pursuant to a judicial sale, must be joined. These changes were made in 1986 to correct a constitutional problem with the old procedure, which, for example, could divest a person who purchased an interest in the property at a tax sale from title without notice or opportunity to be heard. The Superior Court may make the necessary rules regarding the form of the process and its manner of issuance.

Redemption Once a sale is confirmed by a court, no redemption is possible.

FLORIDA

In Florida, mortgages must be foreclosed by filing a lawsuit in court. As in any lawsuit, the borrower must be served with notice of the lawsuit and must be given an opportunity to appear and defend his rights. The lender will try to show that the borrower is in default and that foreclosure is therefore necessary under Florida equity law. Florida is unusual in that the legislature has passed very few statutes regulating foreclosures. Most of the law on the subject of foreclosures in Florida is found scattered in dozens of cases. The basic statute, Chapter 702.01, reads as follows:

> All mortgages shall be foreclosed in equity. In a mortgage foreclosure action, the court shall sever for separate trial all counterclaims against the foreclosing mortgagee. The foreclosure claim shall, if tried, be tried to the court without a jury.

Counterclaims by a borrower may be tried to a jury, but they must be tried separately from the main foreclosure lawsuit.

In Florida, because the whole lawsuit to foreclose on a borrower is a suit in equity, it is impossible to obtain an injunction to stop what is, in essence, a court-ordered sale. The other problem in Florida is that the sale may take place at a fairly low price, if ordered by the court. The fact that the price was low is no reason to set aside a sale. However, if there was an error in the procedure to foreclose, then the sale may be set aside. The court order commanding foreclosure will specify how the foreclosure is to take place, and the foreclosure must take place on those terms. If, for example, the lender's attorney gave public notice that the sale would take place at 11:00 AM and then conducted it at 2:00 PM without notifying the borrower's attorney, who had a bidder standing by, then the foreclosure sale would be invalid.

After the Florida sale takes place, the sale terms must be confirmed by the court that ordered the sale. At that time, title can be made complete in the name of the foreclosure buyer by the filing of a certificate of title, if the terms of the sale order are found to have been met. Junior lienholders can redeem the property, at the discretion of the court, up to the time of the confirmation of the sale. The equity of redemption is cut off when the sale is confirmed, but it exists prior to that time, which means the borrower can save the property from foreclosure by coming up with the money before confirmation.

Deficiency A separate action for a deficiency may be filed within four years after the foreclosure.

GEORGIA

Judicial Foreclosure Available Yes

Nonjudicial Foreclosure Available Yes

Preferred Method Nonjudicial foreclosure through the power of sale clause in a deed of trust, mortgage, or Georgia security deed is preferred.

Judicial Foreclosure

Judicial foreclosure may be done by filing a petition in Superior Court describing the case, the amount of money owed, and the property to be foreclosed. Upon the filing of the petition, a Georgia court will grant a "rule" directing that the unpaid principal, interest, and costs are to be paid to the court. The rule will be published two times per month for two months. As an alternative to publication, the notice can be served on the borrower, the borrower's agent, or the borrower's attorney at least 30 days before the money has to be paid to court.

Nonjudicial Foreclosure

Although Georgia permits nonjudicial foreclosure, such sales are in "derogation" of common law and, therefore, the lender can only foreclose if the terms and conditions of the loan documents are strictly observed.

Preliminary Notices

No sale is valid unless it is advertised and conducted at the usual time, place, and manner in which sheriff's sales are conducted in the county in which the real estate is located.

Mailing A foreclosure notice must be mailed certified mail, return receipt requested, to the debtor no later than 15 days before the date of the proposed foreclosure. The date to count the 15 days from is the date the letter is dropped in the mail, not when it is received by the debtor. The address the letter must be mailed to is the address the borrower gives to the lender by written notice. No waiver or release of the rights to notice is valid if it was signed at the same time as the original loan papers; however, a quitclaim deed conveying title voluntarily in lieu of foreclosure is effective.

Advertising Notice must be published in the newspaper in which sheriff's sales for that county are normally advertised at least once a week for four weeks preceding the foreclosure day.

Sale Procedures The sale itself must be made by public outcry on the first Tuesday of the month between 10:00 AM and 4:00 PM at the courthouse.

Deficiency Under Georgia law, a nonjudicial foreclosure cannot, by itself, serve as the basis to pursue a borrower for a deficiency. To obtain a deficiency judgment, a lender must report the sale to the

Superior Court for the county in which the land is located and seek confirmation and approval of the sale within 30 days after the sale.

Confirmation and Approval of Sale (a Prerequisite to a Deficiency) The court must hold a hearing before confirming or approving the sale. The borrower must be given further notice at least five days before the hearing. The borrower must ordinarily be served personally with the notice, although service by mail can be recognized if the borrower fails to allege nonreceipt of the notice. Before the court can issue an order confirming and approving the sale, the court will require evidence that the foreclosure sale price was at least equal to the market value of the property. If it was not, then the court may not confirm or approve the sale. Also, at the hearing, the court will pass judgment on the legality of the notice, advertisement, and "regularity" of the foreclosure sale. The court may order a new sale of the property for good cause.

HAWAII

Judicial Foreclosure Available Yes

Nonjudicial Foreclosure Available Yes

Foreclosure in Hawaii takes one of two forms: (1) judicial foreclosure by a lawsuit much like any other lawsuit or (2) sale under a power of sale clause in a mortgage.

Preferred Method Judicial. Although trust deeds are available, they are not commonly used.

Judicial Foreclosure In a judicial foreclosure, the Circuit Court may assess the amount due on a mortgage, without a jury, and render judgment for that amount and an order of foreclosure on the mortgage. The actual sale of the property will take place in the same way as normal execution sales.

Nonjudicial Foreclosure: Preliminary Notices

Advertising Out-of-court foreclosures must be advertised, in English, once per week for three consecutive weeks. The last advertisement must be run no less than 14 days before sale.

Recording An affidavit describing all the pertinent details of the sale must be recorded within 30 days after the sale.

Mailing Mortgage creditors having a mortgaged lien against the property that another mortgage creditor intends to foreclose on under a power of sale clause may, if a written request is given to the foreclosing mortgage creditor, receive notice of the lender's intent to foreclose. The foreclosing lender must mail the notice to the other mortgage creditors at least seven days prior to the date of the sale. Also, the notice must be posted on the premises not less than 21 days before the day of sale. The notice must state (1) the date, time, and place of the public sale; (2) the dates and times of the two open houses of the mortgaged property or, if there will not be any open houses, that fact; (3) the unpaid balance of the moneys owed to the mortgagee under the mortgage agreement; (4) a description of the mortgaged property, including the address or description of the location of the mortgaged property, and the tax map key number of the mortgaged property; (5) the name of the mortgagor and the borrower; (6) the name of the lender; (7) the name of any prior or junior creditors having a recorded lien on the mortgaged property before the recording of the notice of default; (8) the name, the address in the state, and the telephone number in the state of the person in the state conducting the public sale; and (9) the terms and conditions of the public sale.

Sale The highest bidder at the foreclosure sale buys the property.

Postsale Matters A buyer at the foreclosure sale holds title subject to the existing liens. Any surplus from the sale shall be paid over to the owner of the mortgaged property.

Special Procedures A notice of any foreclosure on a condominium apartment must be sent, certified or registered mail, to the owners' association for the condominium. This notice must be sent at the time the lender begins foreclosure proceedings. This provision may not be waived.

Cure Up until three days before the sale, the borrower may cure the default and stop the sale through payment of the lien debt, costs, and reasonable attorney's fees, unless the lender and the borrower have agreed otherwise.

Redemption Redemption rights have been abolished in Hawaii.

IDAHO

Preferred Method of Foreclosure Nonjudicial. Idaho permits nonjudicial foreclosure through a power of sale clause in a deed of trust. If the borrower goes into default, the property may be sold by giving the borrower the proper notice.

Preliminary Notices

Contents The foreclosure notice must describe the nature of the default and the lender's election to sell. The notice must set the date, time, place, and basis for the sale.

Recording The notice must be recorded.

Mailing The notice must be sent to anyone who requests a copy. The borrower must be given a copy at least 120 days in advance of the sale. Lessees or occupants must also be given the same notice as the borrower.

Publication The notice must be published in the newspapers in the county where the land is located at least once a week for four successive weeks. The final ad must be run not less than 30 days in advance of the foreclosure. The published notice must contain a legal description of the property, its street address, and the name and phone number of someone who can give directions.

Cure by Borrower or Other Purchasers Junior lienholders or the borrower, within 115 days in advance of the recording of the notice of default, may pay the amount due on the loan and a trustee's fee if the default is cured prior to the last newspaper publication of the sale.

Sale Procedures

The foreclosure sale must take place at the time called for in the notice, unless the sale is postponed. The sale can be postponed by the lender to a new time and place but not later than 30 days after the original date. Multiple postponements are possible. The proceeds of the sale must go first to the lender, then to any inferior recorded lienholders, then to the borrower.

Deficiency The borrower can be sued in a separate lawsuit for a deficiency within three months following the sale for whatever sum remains unpaid on the mortgage, provided the balance exceeds the fair market value (or such reasonable value as the court finds) of the property at the time of the foreclosure.

Redemption The real estate may be redeemed by the borrower up to one year after the sale if more than 20 acres are involved, or up to six months for land parcels of fewer than 20 acres.

ILLINOIS

Judicial Foreclosure Available Yes

Nonjudicial Foreclosure Available No

Preferred Method of Foreclosure Judicial. Illinois does not allow power of sale nonjudicial foreclosures; they are explicitly banned by statute. Instead, foreclosure is done by filing a lawsuit. The suit may seek either strict foreclosure or a foreclosure under the Illinois Mortgage Foreclosure Law. The latter approach is much more common than strict foreclosure. A new procedure exists for speeding up judicial foreclosure under the Illinois Mortgage Foreclosure Law called "consent foreclosure." Otherwise, the battle must go through the courts at a slow pace. The Illinois Mortgage Foreclosure Law spells out in detail what must be included in the lender's lawsuit (petition) for foreclosure. If the lender strictly observes the requirements for a proper petition, then it is quite possible for the lender to win the lawsuit by motions without having to go to trial.

Consent Foreclosure A consent foreclosure will vest all the borrower's right and title in the lender free and clear of all claims (except liens of the U.S. government), including rights of reinstatement and redemption of any junior lienholder who was properly informed and who failed to object. Upon objection, the court may hear such evidence as is required and enter an order that title vests subject to the lien, or if the junior lienholder pays the balance on the mortgage plus any additional interest within 30 days of the entry of a court order commanding the same, then the junior lienholder can redeem the property. The final judgment in a consent foreclosure must recite the lender's waiver of rights to any personal judgment for a deficiency and will bar a deficiency against not only the borrower but any coborrower or other person who is liable for the mortgage.

Parties Illinois has rather elaborate requirements about who must and who may be a party to the lawsuit. A person who must be a party is a necessary party; a person who may be a party is a permissible party. The borrower and any other person obligated on the note are necessary parties. Permissible parties include the owner of the loan note and any trustee. A few others, such as tenants or other persons in possession, guarantors, the State of Illinois, the U.S. government, a mechanic's lien claimant, an assignee, and any other mortgagee or person with any claim to title, may be joined. Any person not joined retains any lien or claim. A nonrecord claimant must come forward or lose out. Other complicated rules govern interventions, or entry of outside parties to the lawsuit.

Plaintiff's Complaint (Lender's Lawsuit)

The lender must begin the lawsuit by filing a plaintiff's complaint (also sometimes called a "petition") and having it served on the borrower. The complaint must include the following:

The nature of the instrument on which foreclosure is sought, whether it is a mortgage, a trust deed, or another instrument; the date of the mortgage; the lender's and borrower's names; the date and place of recording and the book and page number or document number; the ownership interest subject to the mortgage, such as fee simple, etc.; the amount of the original indebtedness, including subsequent advances; a legal description of the property; a description of the default, including the balance due, the date of the default, and any further information on the default; the name of the present owner; the names of persons who are joined as defendants and whose interests are sought to be terminated; the names of any persons who are to be personally liable for a deficiency; a description of the party bringing the lawsuit; any facts that justify a shorter redemption period than seven months from the service (or publication) of the summons or three months from the entry of a judgment of foreclosure (the statute suggests that a shorter period would be justified if the real estate had a value of less than 90 percent of the amount owed on the loan); a statement that the right of redemption has been waived, if it has been; facts to support attorney's fees; facts to support the appointment of a receiver, if desired by the lender; and a statement that the lender will accept title in lieu of any other action against the borrower, if the lender so desires.

The lender should conclude by asking for ("praying for") a judgment of foreclosure and sale, an order shortening the redemption period (if requested), a personal judgment for a deficiency (if requested), and an order granting possession. If these allegations are made, as described above, and supporting documents such as copies of the note and deed of trust are attached, then the lender's complaint will be deemed to include the allegations necessary for a foreclosure.

Special Matters Special matters can be put in the judgment, if requested in addition to the allegations previously described. These would include a request for a sale by sealed bid, a manner of sale other than a public auction, any fees to a broker or auctioneer, any signs to be placed on the property, the newspaper or newspapers in which the notice of sale shall be published, the formats of the ads, the requirement that title insurance be provided at the foreclosure sale, and such other matters as the court approves to ensure the most favorable commercial price for the type of real estate involved.

Regular Sale If requested and agreed to by the parties, the property can be sold to the first person who offers in writing to buy the real estate for such commercially reasonable terms as the parties may agree to, and the court shall then order the sale in such a matter, subject to its subsequent confirmation after it is closed. The advantage of this procedure is that a broker could be employed to find a buyer at a decent price, which would be better than what the property would fetch at a sheriff's auction. The only problem is that the court must confirm the sale, so a patient buyer is desirable.

Notice of Sale If the property is to be sold by a sheriff's sale, then a notice of sale must be given that includes the name, address, and phone number of a person who can be contacted regarding the purchase of the real estate. The real estate must be described in terms of its common address (other than a legal description), its legal description, and its improvements. The notice must include the times at which the property can be inspected prior to sale. The notice must include the time, place, and terms of the sale. It must include the case title, case number, and court in which the foreclosure lawsuit was filed. The notice must include any other information required by the court.

The notice must be published in the usual newspaper for legal notices in that county once a week for three consecutive calendar weeks; the first such notice must be 45 days prior to the sale and the last notice not less than 7 days prior to sale.

If the sale is postponed more than 60 days, then notice must be republished; if less than 60 days, the person conducting the sale can announce the date, time, and place for the adjourned sale.

Sale Procedures After the sale, the borrower gets a receipt that the property has been sold. Once the sale price is paid, a certificate of sale is issued to the buyer. A duplicate of the certificate must be recorded. Upon confirmation of the sale by the court, a deed may be given to the buyer at the foreclosure sale. The confirmation hearing can also provide for a deficiency.

Redemption The right to redemption may be waived by the borrower in the mortgage instrument or after the commencement of foreclosure by written consent filed with the clerk of the court, but only if the lender thereupon waives the right to a deficiency. However, waivers signed prior to July 1, 1987, may still be valid. Otherwise, the borrower has the right to redeem the property within seven months from the date the lawsuit to foreclose was filed or three months after the date the judgment was entered by the court. Other creditors have six months instead of seven to redeem. The redemption period may be extended by the court. If a bankruptcy court stays (delays) the redemption, then under Illinois law, the redemption runs to 30 days after the stay is up, or the normal period minus the period of the stay, whichever is longer. In any case, whether bankruptcy is involved or not, a notice of the intent to redeem must be filed with the court 15 days before the redemption rights are exercised.

The amount to redeem the property shall be that specified by the court in its judgment ordering foreclosure. The redemption amount shall be paid to the court clerk. If there is no objection, the clerk will give a receipt for the redemption amount, and the lender must then furnish the borrower with a release of the mortgage or satisfaction of the judgment. If there is an objection, the court will promptly hold a hearing and rule on the objection. A special right to redeem exists if the lender attempts to sell the property at foreclosure for less than the court-specified amount. The borrower can then redeem at the price for which the lender tried to sell the property.

Reinstatement The borrower has the right to reinstate the loan within the first 90 days after being served with the lawsuit.

Possession One of the most frightening features of the Illinois foreclosure law is that the lender can obtain physical possession of the premises during the foreclosure lawsuit and prior to entry of a final judgment. In fact, at an early stage in the lawsuit, upon request of the lender and for good cause shown, such as damaging the property or abandonment, the court can put the lender in possession of the property and kick the borrower out. The court must be satisfied there is a reasonable probability that the lender will prevail upon a final hearing of the case. An existing tenant cannot be kicked out, but the lender may be able to obtain the rents. A receiver may be appointed to take charge of the property and the rents. Foreclosure buyers can obtain possession within 30 days. Otherwise, a lender can obtain possession from the borrower 30 days after the confirmation of sale.

INDIANA

In Indiana, a lender can file a lawsuit to foreclose on real estate. The date the mortgage was signed determines the length of time it takes between the filing of the lawsuit and the foreclosure sale. Here are the applicable waiting periods:

Before January 1, 1958	12 months
January 1, 1958 to July 1, 1975	6 months
After July 1, 1975	3 months

If the owner files a waiver of the time limit with the court clerk, which has been signed by the lender (or judgment holder), then the foreclosure sale process may begin without the need to delay 3 to 12 months. If such a waiver is used, however, the lender loses the right to sue the borrower for a deficiency.

The foreclosure sale process involves publishing an ad once a week for three weeks. The first ad must be run 30 days before the sale. At the time the first ad is run, each owner must be served with notice of the foreclosure sale by the sheriff. The sheriff conveys title by a deed given immediately after the sale. The owner may reside in the property, rent-free, until the foreclosure sale, provided the owner is not "committing waste," which means tearing up the property.

There is no right to redemption after the foreclosure sale. The waiting precedes the sale. If the property is not a principal residence, a receiver can be appointed to take charge of it.

IOWA

Iowa law places strong restraints on foreclosures, particularly on loans for agricultural property. In Iowa, many special notices must be given to borrowers advising them of their rights. Lenders are not always permitted to foreclose; for example, a court may declare a moratorium on foreclosures due to an economic emergency. There are basically two ways to foreclose on nonagricultural property in

Iowa: (1) the alternative nonjudicial voluntary foreclosure procedure, in which the borrower deeds the property over to the lender, and (2) filing a lawsuit and obtaining judicial foreclosure under equity law.

Alternative Nonjudicial Voluntary Foreclosure

If both the lender and the borrower agree in writing, then a real estate mortgage can be foreclosed voluntarily as follows:

1. The borrower conveys title to the property to the lender.
2. The lender accepts the property and waives any rights to sue the borrower for any other claim, such as a deficiency.
3. The lender gets immediate access to the property.
4. The lender and borrower record a statement, signed by both parties, that they have elected voluntary foreclosure.
5. The lender sends, by certified mail, a notice of the voluntary foreclosure to all junior lienholders, who have 30 days to exercise any rights of redemption they may have.
6. The borrower must sign a statutory voluntary foreclosure form.

Judicial Foreclosure

Other than the voluntary foreclosure procedure described immediately above, the only way a lender can foreclose a deed of trust or a mortgage on Iowa real estate is by a lawsuit in court, governed by principles of equity law. The lender must choose either to sue on the note or sue to foreclose the mortgage, but not both. When a mortgage or deed of trust is foreclosed, the court will render judgment for the entire amount due and direct the sale of the mortgaged property, or as much as is necessary. The lender may sue a borrower for a foreclosure with or without redemption, but the latter requires the borrower to sign a waiver.

Foreclosure With Redemption The borrower retains a right to redeem the property after the sale, unless the lender has chosen to sue for foreclosure without redemption. Junior lienholders can also redeem by paying off the loan that was foreclosed.

Foreclosure Without Redemption In the event that a lender undertakes foreclosure without redemption, neither the borrower nor junior lienholders have rights to redeem. However, if the borrower bids an amount equal to the amount owed on the loan at the foreclosure sale, then the borrower gets the property regardless of the fact that junior lienholders might bid more at the sale. In foreclosure without redemption, the first page of the lender's petition to foreclose the mortgage must contain a notice, in capital letters of the same size as the type on the rest of the petition, warning the borrower that the lender has elected foreclosure without redemption. This means that the sale will occur promptly unless a written demand is filed with the court to delay the sale. If the demand is filed, the sale of a principal residence will be delayed 12 months from the entry of judgment. (Sale is delayed two months on other properties and six months on the residence if the lender's lawsuit waives recovery of a deficiency.) However, if the borrower files such a demand for delay, then the lender can sue the borrower for a deficiency. If no demand for delay is filed, the lender cannot sue for a deficiency. Either way, however, once the sale takes place, the buyer at the foreclosure sale can take possession immediately.

Right to Cure

In Iowa, a borrower has a general right to effect cure by making up missed payments prior to foreclosure. The lender must send the borrower a notice of the borrower's rights to cure as a prerequisite to foreclosure.

Notice of the Right to Cure Before filing a lawsuit or taking any action to foreclose on a borrower's one- or two-family home, any regular lender, such as a bank, S&L, or mortgage company that believes in good faith that a borrower is in default on a deed of trust or mortgage on a homestead, must give the borrower a notice of the right-to-cure default. Individuals who are lenders do not have to give the notice.

Mailing of Notice of Right to Cure Regular lenders must give the notice by direct delivery or by mail to the borrower's residence. The notice does not have to be given in nonresidential situations.

Contents of Notice of Right to Cure The notice must state (1) the name, address, and phone number of the creditor to whom payment is to be made; (2) a brief description of the obligation secured by the mortgage or deed of trust; (3) that the borrower has the right to cure the default; (4) the nature of the alleged default and the total payment, in an itemized form, of deferral charges (late fees), the amount due, and any other action needed to cure the default; and (5) the exact date by which the amount must be paid or an action must be performed.

Failure to Cure by Proper Times If the borrower fails to perform in the proper manner by the proper date, then the notice must also state that the lender can initiate foreclosure. Once notice is given, the following timetable applies:

- *30 days:* The borrower must be given no less than 30 days to cure the default by tendering (sending) either (1) a sum equal to all the missed payments due at the time of the tender or (2) the amount stated in the notice of the right to cure, whichever is less, or by tendering any other performance necessary to cure a default as described in the notice of right to cure.

- *Such extra time as the lender gives:* A lender may give more than 30 days without waiving or losing the right to commence foreclosure due to an uncured default.

- *365 days:* A borrower has a right to cure the default by bringing in the payments, unless the creditor has given the borrower a notice of the right to cure once before within the past 365 days. Curing the default restores a borrower's rights under a mortgage or a deed of trust.

Special Protection: Farm Foreclosures Due to the bad luck Iowa's farmers have sometimes experienced, the state legislature has passed many special laws regulating farm foreclosures. Iowa's legal protections for farmers against foreclosure are truly exceptional compared to those of any other state. The procedures to foreclose on agricultural property in Iowa are even more extensive than the rather extensive procedures just described. The lender must attempt mediation on land used as an individual's farm, a family farm, or a qualified farm corporation through the Farm Mediation Service. A notice and initial meeting must be held within 42 days of a request by the farmer. The farmer also has a right of first refusal when agricultural property is sold at execution. There are special deed in lieu procedures for agricultural properties. In the special deed in lieu arrangement, the lender takes title, but the farmer can lease the land back from the lender and repurchase the land within five years. The farmer may separately redeem the house and up to 40 acres from the rest of the land even after a foreclosure. Iowa's farmers should beat a path to a lawyer's office before giving up any effort to fight foreclosure. Iowa's procedures to protect against foreclosure are extensive enough that if a farmer has the will to hold on, there is often be a legal way to do so.

Regular Foreclosure After fulfilling the vast number of prerequisites required under Iowa law, as previously described, a lender may obtain a judgment against the borrower for the full amount of the balance due on the loan. The real estate may then be sold under a general execution sale. Remember, the lender may not sue both for foreclosure and to collect on the note. So if the lender sues on the note, then, if and only if the sum found to be due is sufficient, the real estate can be sold to pay off the judgment. The sales are proper sheriff's sales. Once the property is sold, it may eliminate the loan balance or reduce it. If some part of the loan balance is left unpaid, the lender can still try to collect that part

Moratorium If a borrower goes into default and is sued by the lender, the borrower may file an answer admitting a default in whole or in part and then ask for a moratorium if the default was due to such circumstances as a crop failure due to drought, flood, heat, hail, storm, or other climatic condition or due to infestation of pests. Under such circumstances, the court can extend the foreclosure date for up to one full year. The court must appoint a receiver to take care of the property in the meantime, and the original borrower is to be given preference over other choices as receiver. The receiver may apply rents and income in a statutorily defined order.

The governor of Iowa may declare a state of economic emergency applicable to various types of property, such as agricultural property, or to be applied to all types of property. The declaration makes such property eligible for a moratorium continuance, which may last as long as one year. However, a lender can apply to the court and show good-faith efforts to restructure the debt and the financial difficulties the lender is faced with if foreclosure is not granted. The lender may also show that the borrower has not paid interest on the loan. Upon weighing all these competing considerations, a court may terminate the moratorium, which would allow the foreclosure to go forward. Only one continuance can be granted per mortgage instrument under the governor's moratorium provisions.

KANSAS

Judicial Foreclosure Available Yes

Nonjudicial Foreclosure Available No

Preliminary Notices

Advertising Notice of the time and place of sale must be advertised once a week for three consecutive weeks, with the last publication no more than 14 and no less than 7 days before the foreclosure day.

Mailing Notice must be sent to the defaulting borrower within five days of the first ad.

Sale Procedures

Place The sale must be at the courthouse, although the district judge may order the sale on the premises or at another location.

Manner The sale is by public auction to the highest bidder. The sheriff will at once give the buyer at the foreclosure sale a certificate of purchase. The certificate of purchase is all the buyer gets until the borrower's redemption rights expire.

Confirmation The foreclosure sale must be confirmed by the court after the sale. The court has discretion to refuse to honor the sale and require a minimum bid or force the crediting of the market value against what was owed on the loan. Once confirmed, a sheriff's deed can be issued, and it will vest good and perfect title in the foreclosure buyer. However, the court may specify as a condition of confirmation that the redemption period, 12 months unless reduced, may run first.

Special Procedures A judgment can stay unenforced up to five years, at which point it becomes dormant but is subject to revival for another two years. Afterward, the judgment is barred from enforcement, and the court records must reflect that fact.

Deficiency A deficiency judgment may be obtained for the difference between the foreclosure sale price and the amount due on the loan. Deficiencies are common. However, the court may refuse to confirm a sale where the price is not equal to the judgment, which helps prevent abusive deficiency judgments.

Redemption The borrower can redeem any real property sold at foreclosure at any time up to 12 months from the date of sale by paying the holder of the certificate of purchase the purchase price plus costs and interest. If the judge finds the property is abandoned or not occupied in good faith, then the redemption period is six months. Lien creditors must undertake redemption within three months. The former borrower's redemption period may be reduced from one year to six months if the lien is only one-third of the original indebtedness. However, the court may conduct a hearing on market value, and if the debt is one-third of the court-perceived market value, then 12 months for redemption may be allowed before the court will confirm the sale.

KENTUCKY

Judicial Foreclosure Available Yes

Nonjudicial Foreclosure Available Effectively, no

Kentucky has a rigid rule on foreclosures: no out-of-court foreclosures are valid other than voluntary sales by the borrower. A deed of trust sale, a power of sale clause in a mortgage, or sale by a trustee will not work in Kentucky. The only forced foreclosure sale that is permitted is one pursuant to a court order. Also, common-law or strict foreclosure is forbidden in Kentucky. The lender must be prepared to engage in litigation to foreclose. Often the lender can win by default or summary judgment, but if not, the case is tried to a jury.

Possession On the other hand, if the borrower abandons the home, the lender may obtain possession of the property once the borrower goes into default. The lender may operate the property for the benefit of the borrower. Any income produced goes to the lender, not the borrower, but will be credited toward paying off what the borrower owes. If the borrower does not abandon the home, the lender may not take possession until the court confirms the foreclosure sale.

Redemption and Appraisal Prior to a foreclosure sale, the property must be appraised. If the actual foreclosure sale price is less than two-thirds of the appraised value, then for one year after the sale, the borrower has the right to redeem the property from the buyer for the buyer's purchase price plus 10 percent interest. Interestingly, the borrower's right to redeem may also be sold.

Deficiency In Kentucky, it is possible to obtain a deficiency judgment against the borrower for the difference between the amount the borrower owed on the old loan and the foreclosure sale price, but only if the borrower was personally served with the lawsuit or failed an answer to one.

LOUISIANA

Judicial Foreclosure Available Yes

Nonjudicial Foreclosure Available No

In contrast to the laws of most of the states, which are based on the English common-law system, Louisiana laws are based on the civil law system used throughout most of Europe and much of the world. Under Louisiana's system of laws, judicial foreclosure is the rule and deed of trust or power of sale foreclosures are not permitted (though Roman law itself would have allowed it).

Two Methods of Judicial Foreclosure

Louisiana's two foreclosure methods are (1) ordinary process and (2) executory process. Ordinary process operates as an ordinary lawsuit in Louisiana.

Executory Process This is an accelerated procedure of a summary nature by which the lender uses a mortgage that includes an "authentic act that imparts a confession of judgment." In practice, this means the mortgage is signed before a notary and two witnesses. The borrower declares and acknowledges the obligations under the mortgage. Later, when the lender wants to foreclose, the lender files a suit in court and attaches the original note and a certified copy of the mortgage. The court can then enter an order for the issuance of executory process.

In the past, executory process skipped citation, contradictory hearings, and judgments. The problem with such procedures in the past has been constitutional. The U.S. Supreme Court, in the famous case of Fuentes *v.* Shevin [407 U.S. 67 (1972)], held that the defendant in any lawsuit must be given notice of the suit and an opportunity to be heard in court. Louisiana's current executory process procedures barely comply with these requirements. Once executory process begins, the borrower is served with a demand for payments that are due and unpaid on the loan. The borrower has three days to come up with the money. If the borrower doesn't pay, the court will issue a writ of seizure and sale. Armed with this, the sheriff will seize the real estate. The borrower gets a notice of seizure. The property is then advertised once a week for 30 days. The sheriff will then sell the property at auction to pay down or pay off the loan. Executory process is harsh and exacting, allowing a lender to seize possession of the property prior to reselling it at a foreclosure sale.

Ordinary Process In ordinary process, the lender files a lawsuit to foreclose the mortgage. The borrower is served as a regular defendant in the lawsuit, and the procedures for an ordinary lawsuit are followed. If the borrower loses, the court will enter judgment in favor of the lender. After that, a writ of fieri facias will be issued, directing the property to be sold to pay off the loan.

Deficiency Judgments The lender must obtain a deficiency judgment by an ordinary lawsuit, either in conjunction with executory process or as a separate suit. A deficiency cannot be obtained by executory process alone. Executory process allows seizure and sale of the property, but a personal judgment does not.

Redemption Louisiana does not recognize a right of redemption.

MAINE

Judicial Foreclosure Available Yes

Nonjudicial Foreclosure Available No

Maine offers several methods of foreclosure. Most residential mortgage foreclosures are done by filing a lawsuit in the District or Superior Court. On the other hand, a foreclosure against a corporation may be done by a power of sale procedure. Otherwise, Maine still maintains the common-law strict foreclosure doctrine in which the lender owns the property and the borrower loses any rights to the property by breaking a condition in the mortgage, such as failing to make the loan payment. Although Maine is a strict foreclosure state, it nevertheless permits a lawsuit to be filed in the form of a bill in equity, which asks the court to cut off any further rights the borrower has to the property. This would be done only in special cases. Generally, foreclosures in Maine are by strict foreclosure, which, for convenience, can be divided into those circumstances in which the lender seeks possession as part of the foreclosure and those situations where the lender does not seek possession as part of the foreclosure.

Strict Foreclosure With Possession In Maine, the lender may want to take over the borrower's old property. After regaining title by legal means, the lender could sell the property at a later date, without giving the borrower the benefit of any excess the lender gets out of the sale over and above what the borrower owed on the old loan. Alternatively, the lender could simply keep the property and rent it out. In sum, strict foreclosure allows the lender to become the owner, pure and simple. To become the owner through strict foreclosure, however, the lender must follow some specialized procedures. In particular, the lender must obtain possession of the property and hold it throughout the redemption period, which is one year on pre-1975 mortgages and three months on post-1975 mortgages.

In Maine, there are three methods for the lender to regain possession as part of the strict foreclosure process:

1. A lender can obtain a writ of possession (which authorizes the sheriff to throw the borrower out) from a court by filing a lawsuit that asks for the writ as part of a conditional judgment.

2. The lender can enter the property and take possession if the borrower consented to the entry in writing.

3. The lender may enter the premises peacefully, openly, and without opposition in the presence of two witnesses.

Strict Foreclosure Without Possession In Maine, a lender can foreclose the borrower's rights to the property without regaining possession at the time of foreclosure by arranging to sell the borrower's property. Initially, the lender files a lawsuit and wins a judgment that the borrower owes the money; then the lender must wait until the end of the redemption period, as described previously. At the end of the redemption period, the lender will sell the property by a special procedure.

The procedure is to publish public notice of the impending foreclosure for three successive weeks in a newspaper of general circulation in the county where the land is located. The notice should state that the lender is claiming the property due to a breach of the mortgage conditions (such as nonpayment of the loan) and give a description of the property, the date of the mortgage, and the nature of the breach. A copy of the printed notice and the name and date of the newspaper in which it was last published must be recorded within 30 days of the last publication of the notice. Alternatively, an attested (sworn) copy of the printed notice may be served on the borrower by the sheriff, and a copy of the notice and the sheriff's return (indicating that it was served) may be recorded within 30 days after service.

The foreclosure sale must take place no less than 30 days and no more than 45 days after the initial publication of notice. The property must be sold at public sale to the highest bidder, which may be the lender or anyone else. At the end of the sale, the sales costs are deducted, and the lender must disburse the remaining money in accordance with the foreclosure judgment. Junior lienholders should already have been joined when the foreclosure suit was first filed, so they may get some part of the proceeds. Any surplus proceeds from the sale must be paid to the borrower. The borrower may contest the accounting within 30 days after the sale, but the high bidder at the foreclosure sale will still retain title.

Deficiency Any deficiency based on the foreclosure sale is limited to the difference between the fair market value of the property at the time of the foreclosure, as established by an appraisal, and the amount of money the court found the lender was still owed on the loan, as set forth in the court's final judgment.

Redemption Maine offers the borrower a fairly powerful right of redemption. There are two redemption periods:

Pre-October 1, 1975, mortgages	one year
Post-October 1, 1975, mortgages	three months

The time period begins once the lender wins a judgment in the foreclosure lawsuit. The borrower may redeem the property by paying off the loan. The Maine statutes cannot shorten the one-year period on pre-1975 mortgages, because to do so would violate the Maine state constitution by impairing the existing provisions of a contract.

Waiver Maine has a waiver procedure that can be deadly to the lender and helpful to the borrower. If the lender accepts money or anything of value on the mortgage debt after the foreclosure has begun and before the redemption period has expired, then the lender waives the foreclosure procedure. However, the lender may receive the income from the property after properly taking possession without triggering a waiver.

MARYLAND

Judicial Foreclosure Available Yes

Nonjudicial Foreclosure Available No (but assent to decree is allowed)

Maryland offers two basic methods of foreclosure: (1) power of sale foreclosure, in which the lender or another person named in the mortgage or deed of trust may sell the property, and (2) assent to decree foreclosure, in which the borrower agrees to permit the court to order foreclosure. In either case, however, the lender must file a lawsuit in court to foreclose. The same is true if the mortgage instrument lacks either a power of sale clause or an assent to decree clause, but in that event, the lawsuit will be more complicated. When the mortgage contains a power of sale or assent to decree clause, and if 25 percent of the involved lenders (as measured by the percentage of the total dollars of mortgage debt against the property) consent or make application for sale, then no service of process, answer, or hearing is required. This simplifies the lawsuit. On the other hand, if the mortgage contains neither a consent to a decree clause nor a power of sale clause or if a foreclosure sale is desired prior to the court's final decree, then there must be service of process, an answer, and a hearing. However, in the latter case, 25 percent of the lenders do not have to join in filing the initial lawsuit.

Power of Sale Foreclosure Power of sale clause foreclosures must be done under court supervision in Maryland. A person desiring foreclosure must file a lawsuit asking for foreclosure pursuant to the power of sale clause. The lender must do take the following steps:

1. Include in the lawsuit paperwork a sworn statement of the amount of the mortgage debt and a certified copy of the mortgage.
2. Post bond for the amount approved by the clerk.
3. Publish notice of the time, place, and terms of the sale once a week for three weeks prior to the sale, with at least 15 days' notice of the foreclosure sale.
4. Mail the foreclosure notice by certified mail, return receipt requested, to the borrower no less than 10 and no more than 30 days before sale. The notice must also be mailed to the present owner and holder of any junior mortgage or other lien that has been recorded who also recorded a request for notice.

Assent to Decree Foreclosure Under an assent to decree foreclosure, the lender must file a lawsuit in court to foreclose. The court will then enter a decree ordering the property to be sold and appoint the trustee to conduct the sale. The trustee must post a bond and sell the property according to the terms fixed by the court. The court will later confirm the sale. It is not necessary that a hearing be held prior to the foreclosure sale.

Deficiency In Maryland, a deficiency judgment may be obtained if the lender makes a motion for it within three years after the accounting for the foreclosure is complete.

Redemption Maryland foreclosure proceedings take place as an action under equity law. Maryland has not seen fit to establish a specific time limit on how long the borrower has to wait to redeem real estate lost in foreclosure. However, the doctrine of laches prevents this period from being unreasonably long.

MASSACHUSETTS

In Massachusetts, there are two methods by which a mortgage may be foreclosed: (1) the lender may enter and take possession of the property by several alternative means, in which case the lender's ownership can become final after three years, and (2) the lender may complete a nonjudicial sale under a power of sale clause. The first method, entry and possession, is seldom used as the primary means of foreclosure. Instead, it is used as a backup in case of a technical error in nonjudicial sale procedures. The first method is essentially a variation on the strict foreclosure theme. The second method, a foreclosure sale under a power of sale clause, is the usual procedure. The power of sale foreclosure takes place out of court. In spite of the fact that the power of sale foreclosure is conducted out of court, it is nevertheless customary to file a lawsuit before attempting such a sale to make sure that the federal Servicemember's Civil Relief Act does not apply to the borrower's situation.

Entry and Possession Procedures

A lender can foreclose in Massachusetts by lawfully taking possession of the premises and then waiting three years for title to become final in the name of the lender. Lawful recovery of possession can be done by several means: (1) file a lawsuit and obtain a court order giving the lender possession; (2) enter peaceably and take possession; or (3) obtain the borrower's proper consent to entry.

Under method (1) above, the lender's lawsuit must allege that there was a breach of a condition in the mortgage, such as failing to pay the loan. If so, the court may render a conditional judgment giving the lender possession. The court will also grant a writ of entry, which will permit eviction of the borrower. However, the borrower may recover possession within two months by paying the amount due under the mortgage or correcting any other breach of the mortgage. However, unless the borrower can come up with enough money to pay off the mortgage within three years, the lender's ownership becomes final and the borrower's right to redeem the property is cut off.

Under method (2), the lender openly and peaceably enters the mortgaged premises. Two witnesses must swear that the entry was proper. Once in possession, the lender has to wait three years for full title.

Under method (3), the borrower must sign and record a written memorandum to the mortgage deed. The recording must be done within 30 days from the signing. Once again, the lender must wait three years for full title under this method.

During the time the lender obtains possession pending foreclosure, the lender must account for rents and profits. The lender may deduct the costs of reasonable repairs and improvements.

Power of Sale

In Massachusetts, the usual method of foreclosure is through sale under a power of sale clause in the mortgage. The sale must be conducted in accordance with the requirements specified in the power of sale clause.

Notice of Sale Notice of the foreclosure must be published once a week for three weeks in a newspaper of general circulation in the town where the land is located. The first publication must be at least 21 days before sale. Notice must also be sent by registered mail to any owner whose interest was recorded as of 30 days prior to the sale. The actual date of mailing must be at least 14 days prior to the foreclosure sale.

There is an exhaustive list of potential addresses to which the lender must mail the foreclosure notice, the purpose of which is to make sure the borrower gets a copy of the notice if at all possible. Initially, the lender should mail the notice to the address found in the registered land records or, if none is found, then to the last known address appearing in the lender's records or, if none is found, then to the address on the deed or probate petition. If the address is still not found, then the notice should be mailed to the last address to which a tax bill was sent anytime within the previous three years, and if that address can't be found, then to any address shown in the deed or documentation for any other land owned by the same owner. Nevertheless, there is no requirement for the borrower to receive the notice, merely for the lender to make a diligent effort to locate the borrower. Notice should also be sent to any junior lienholders.

Sale Procedures The actual sale must be conducted at the date, time, and place specified in the notice. The sale will be made to the highest bidder. Within 30 days after the sale, the person selling the property at foreclosure must record a copy of the notice of sale and an affidavit that the foreclosure sale was properly conducted. Any lien or encumbrance on the property that was not part of the mortgage that was foreclosed on and not included in the auctioneer's bargain remains intact and can affect the title to the property after the foreclosure sale. If there is any money left from the foreclosure sale after paying off the lender, the surplus goes to the borrower. A proper sale prevents the borrower from exercising any right to reclaim the property through redemption.

If a suit in equity is filed to clear up problems that could result from the Servicemember's Civil Relief Act of 1940, service is considered sufficient if the above described notices were published 21 days before the return day and mailed 14 days before the return day for the lawsuit. The return day is the day by which the lawsuit must be answered.

Deficiency If the foreclosure sale proceeds are not enough to pay off the lender, then the borrower is liable for any deficiency. However, the statutory notice of intention to foreclose must have been sent at least 21 days before the sale. Furthermore, the affidavit that the sale was complete must be on record 30 days after the sale. Otherwise, no deficiency can be obtained. The statute of limitations on deficiency judgments is two years after the date of foreclosure or two years after the loan payments were accelerated and the loan's unpaid balance was made due entirely. If there was no foreclosure sale under a power of sale clause, and the lender attempts to sue the borrower on the theory that the value of the real estate the lender obtained at foreclosure was less than the balance due on the loan, then the borrower has a right to bring a suit for redemption within one year after recovery under such a judgment.

Redemption The basic rule in Massachusetts is that the foreclosure under a properly conducted power of sale clause cuts off the borrower's right to redeem. The sale must be conducted in good faith, and the lender must use due diligence to comply with the statutory requirements for a power of sale foreclosure, as previously outlined.

Interestingly enough, the borrower may use the right of redemption as a vehicle for slowing down a foreclosure sale, even though the lender is attempting to foreclose under a power of sale clause, which normally cuts off the right of redemption. A borrower may bring a suit to redeem the property before the first notice of sale is published. Such a suit will delay the foreclosure sale. The court must determine the amount due under the mortgage on which conditions remain unperformed such that if the amount is paid or the conditions are performed, the borrower will have a right to redeem. The court can specify a time period and manner for payment or performance, and if the borrower complies with the court's specified conditions, the borrower will have a right to discharge the mortgage and receive a decree regaining possession. If the borrower fails to perform by the time and in the manner specified by the court, the lender can proceed to mail and publish the foreclosure notices (14 days and 21 days, respectively) and then hold the foreclosure sale.

The Massachusetts Uniform Fraudulent Conveyance Act and Bankruptcy The Massachusetts bankruptcy courts have shown a particular willingness to invalidate foreclosure sales. Because of this propensity, numerous additional steps should be taken if a lender forecloses in Massachusetts. The U.S. bankruptcy courts for Massachusetts have ruled that all the statutory procedures outlined previously may be insufficient to guard against invalidation of the foreclosure sale if the borrower files bankruptcy after the foreclosure. If the sale took place for less than market value, it may be ruled to be a fraudulent conveyance under section 548 of the Bankruptcy Code, which commands that reasonably equivalent value must be obtained before the foreclosure sale will be left undisturbed by the bankruptcy court. "Reasonably equivalent value" is market value.

The invalidation of a foreclosure at less than market value can also be accomplished through the application of the Massachusetts Uniform Fraudulent Conveyance Act. Therefore, the lender should take further precautions by appraising the property at the time of foreclosure, by advertising it in the real estate section of the newspapers, by mailing a notice of the sale to anyone who expressed an interest in buying the property, and by notifying real estate brokers in the immediate vicinity that the property is for sale. All of these steps should be taken if the lender wants to be sure to avoid future trouble from the borrower's bankruptcy petition after the sale or a suit to set the sale aside under the Massachusetts Uniform Fraudulent Conveyance Act.

MICHIGAN

Michigan uses two forms of foreclosure: foreclosure by court action and foreclosure by advertisement. A mortgage may be foreclosed by filing a lawsuit in the Michigan circuit court. The court may order the property sold six months after the initial filing of the lawsuit. The property will be sold by the circuit court commissioner or any other person who is appointed by the court to conduct the sale. After the sale, the borrower has six months to redeem.

Foreclosure by Advertisement

If the mortgage contains a power of sale clause and there has been a breach of the terms of the mortgage, such as nonpayment of the loan, then the property may be foreclosed on through a nonjudicial foreclosure by advertisement, unless the mortgage is held by the Michigan state housing development authority. Nonpayment of any installment of a mortgage constitutes a separate act that justifies foreclosure.

Notices of Sale The notice of a foreclosure sale must be published once a week for four weeks in a newspaper of general circulation in the county where the land is situated. Within 15 days after the first publication, a true copy of the foreclosure notice must be posted in a conspicuous place on the premises described in the foreclosure notice. The lender or the lender's agents have a right to enter the mortgaged premises to post or deliver foreclosure notices.

Sale Procedures The sale must be a public sale, conducted between the hours of nine "in the forenoon" and four o'clock in the afternoon. The sale must be at the courthouse or place where the circuit court for the county tries lawsuits. The sale is to be conducted by the person appointed for the purpose in the mortgage or by the sheriff, undersheriff, or deputy sheriff. The sale must be made by auction to the highest bidder. The sale may be adjourned (postponed) from time to time by posting a notice of such adjournment at the time and place where the sale would otherwise have been made. Any adjournment for more than a week must also be published in the same newspaper as the original notice, within ten days from the date the sale was adjourned and again once per week for each week the sale is adjourned.

The officer or person conducting the sale will execute, acknowledge, and deliver a deed to the premises to the high bidder at the foreclosure sale. The deed must specify the last date by which the borrower can redeem the property. The deed must be recorded within 20 days after the sale. The register who records the deed shall endorse the time the deed was received. If the property is ever redeemed, the register will destroy the deed and record the word *redeemed* on the face of the special book for foreclosure deeds. The deed and the foreclosure do not wipe out liens or claims that existed prior to the date of the original mortgage.

Redemption The borrower may redeem by paying the lender the sum for which the property was sold at foreclosure, plus interest at the same rate as the mortgage. If the foreclosure buyer recorded an affidavit stating how much in taxes and insurance the foreclosure buyer paid following the foreclosure sale, then the borrower must repay that amount as part of the redemption process.

If a property is over four units or three acres and has not been abandoned, then the period for redemption is one year from the date of the foreclosure sale. If the property has been abandoned and the balance is over two-thirds of the original loan, then the redemption period is one month. If the balance is two-thirds or less of the original loan, use one year. If the property is four units or less and does not exceed three acres in size, then two different redemption periods apply.

If the mortgage was originated after 1965 and the amount that remains unpaid on the loan is more than two-thirds of the original debt, then the borrower still has six months to redeem. However, if the unpaid balance on a mortgage is less than two-thirds of the original debt, then the borrower has only three months to redeem if the property has been abandoned.

Abandonment For residential property of four units or less or three acres or less, abandonment shall be presumed in the following circumstances:

- Personal inspection: The lender has made a personal inspection of the premises and the inspection does not reveal anyone who is presently occupying or about to occupy the premises.
- Borrower fails to respond to proper notice: The lender has posted a notice at the time the personal inspection was made and mailed it by certified mail, return receipt requested, to the borrower's last known address. The notice must state that the lender considers the premises to be abandoned and that the redemption period in such event will be only 30 days. If the borrower does not respond to these notices within 15 days by mailing to the lender (via first-class mail) a letter stating the premises are not abandoned, then the premises are considered to be abandoned. Obviously, a borrower who wants to preserve her rights should get busy and write the lender to show the premises are not abandoned, or else the borrower will lose most of the benefits of the right of redemption.

Deficiency A lender is restricted to foreclosing against the property as the sole remedy, unless the lender has a separate document that obligates the borrower to pay a sum certain, such as a promissory note, or the borrower has otherwise agreed to pay a sum in a specific amount stated in the mortgage document. To recover a deficiency amount, which would be the balance due on the mortgage minus the sum collected at the foreclosure sale (or credited if the lender bids by canceling out some of the borrower's obligation), the lender must file a lawsuit. The borrower can defend by showing the foreclosure sale price was less than the true value of the property at the time and place of the sale. If the sale was for substantially less than the true value, the deficiency sum the lender can recover may be either defeated or reduced by crediting the property's fair value against the unpaid loan balance at the time of the foreclosure. However, these defenses do not apply if the lender forecloses by court action rather than by foreclosure by advertisement.

MINNESOTA

Judicial Foreclosure Available Yes

Nonjudicial Foreclosure Available Yes

Minnesota allows foreclosure in two ways: by advertisement and by court action. If court action is selected, the lender must file a lawsuit and obtain a judgment for the amount due and a court order commanding the property to be sold. Prior to attempting any foreclosure, the lender should give at least 30 days' notice of the existence of a default. For agricultural property, complex mandatory mediation procedures must be followed.

Nonjudicial Sale by Advertisement

If the mortgage contains a power of sale clause, it may be foreclosed by advertisement. However, a number of conditions must be met before sale by advertisement can be undertaken: (1) there must be a default on the mortgage; (2) no lawsuit to collect on the mortgage may be underway; (3) the mortgage itself and any assignments of the mortgage to new lenders must have been recorded; and (4) the notice must be given eight weeks before foreclosure on a homestead. If an attorney is involved in the foreclosure, the attorney's authority must be shown by a power of attorney that has been properly recorded. Attorney's fees are set by statute for foreclosure sales. Hence, the borrower cannot be billed indiscriminately for attorney's fees during the foreclosure.

Sale Procedures

Documentation Before the sale, the lender must file a verified, itemized statement with the sheriff showing the amount due. This statement must be read during the sale by the sheriff.

Place and Time The time, place, and date of the foreclosure are set forth in the foreclosure notice.

Manner In Minnesota, the actual foreclosure sale must be conducted by public auction. The sale is to the highest bidder.

Certificate of Sale After the sale, the sheriff will prepare a certificate showing the amount of the sale and the amount left unpaid on the loan.

Special Procedure: Right of First Refusal Borrowers have a complex right of first refusal when land is acquired by a state agency, a federal agency, a limited partnership, or a corporation (other than a family farm corporation). Once the agency or business acquires land by foreclosure, it will ultimately try to resell it. When it tries to resell, the old owner who lost the property in foreclosure must be offered the property in preference to any other purchaser at the price and terms an outside buyer is willing to accept for the property. The lender must make a good-faith effort to let the old owner buy it first—hence, the term *right of first refusal.* The law applies for the first five years after the property was foreclosed on. The right of first refusal may not be waived or assigned, except to family members by inheritance.

Deficiency Any deficiency is limited to the difference between the fair market value of the property, as determined by a jury, and the unpaid balance remaining on the old loan. To recover a deficiency judgment against the borrower, the lender must file a lawsuit against the borrower. If the lender already seeks foreclosure by a lawsuit, then all the lender has to do is add a claim to the existing lawsuit. However, when the foreclosure is by advertisement, then an independent lawsuit must be filed to recover a deficiency.

Redemption Redemption is unusual in Minnesota. The borrower or a junior lienholder may redeem for up to a year after the foreclosure by paying all the past due payments rather than the entire loan balance after acceleration.

Preliminary Notice The foreclosure notice must name the borrower, the original lender, any takeover lender, the original loan amount, the date of the mortgage, recording information, the amount currently due on the loan including back taxes and unpaid insurance, a property description, the time and place of the impending foreclosure sale, and the time allowed by law for the borrower to redeem the property.

MISSISSIPPI

Judicial Foreclosure Available Yes

Nonjudicial Foreclosure Available Yes

Mississippi offers two methods of foreclosure: (1) by filing a lawsuit asking for foreclosure in a Chancery Court and (2) by sale, if authorized in the mortgage and conducted in compliance with Mississippi's statutes. The borrower's right to proper conduct of the sale, after proper notice and advertisement of the sale, may not be waived in the loan documents. Any defect in the sale that would cause it to be void may not be corrected by the statute of limitations until ten years have passed from the date of the defective sale.

If the deed of trust contains an authorization for the lender to call upon a trustee to sell the real estate due to the borrower's default on the loan, such as by nonpayment, then the real estate may be sold by the trustee named in the deed of trust (or later appointed as a substitute) to try to pay off the loan. No sale by a substitute trustee is valid unless it was first recorded in the office of the chancery clerk of the county where the land is located prior to the first posting or publishing of the foreclosure sale notice. If the lender, instead of some other buyer, acquires title to the real estate at foreclosure, then the lender will give credit for the foreclosure sale price against what was due on the loan.

Preliminary Notices

Advertising To be valid, the foreclosure sale must be advertised for three consecutive weeks before the sale in a newspaper of general circulation in the county in which the land is located.

Posting A notice must be posted for the same time as the advertising at the county courthouse door. The notice must name the borrowers who will lose title.

Cure Procedure The borrower may stop the foreclosure at any time prior to the sale by coming up with the missed payments, accrued costs, and attorney's and trustee's fees. Only the amount that is actually past due needs to be paid. Even though the loan documents provided that the lender could accelerate the loan and make all future payments due, the borrower has the legal right to disregard the acceleration and stop the foreclosure by paying up the missed payments, accrued costs, and attorney's and trustee's fees. The loan is then to be treated as though it was not accelerated. The borrower may continue to own and occupy the property, and the lender may not foreclose.

Sale Procedures

Place The place of sale should be the same as the place of sale for sheriff's sales of property in the county, which is usually the courthouse.

Manner The sale must be made by public outcry in the county where the land is located or in the county where the borrower lives. The sale must be for cash to the highest bidder.

Postsale Matters After the sale, the trustee or substitute trustee must deliver a trustee's deed to the successful high bidder. The deed should give the names specified in the old deed of trust that was foreclosed on. The trustee's deed should also give information sufficient to locate the foreclosed deed of trust or mortgage in the deed records.

Special Procedures: Foreclosure and Major Disasters In Mississippi, the governor may declare that a natural disaster, an enemy attack, or a man-made technological disaster makes it imperative to impose a moratorium on foreclosures. The moratorium may last for up to two years after the governor's declaration. The borrower can go to court and file a lawsuit to enjoin a lender from foreclosing due to damage to the mortgaged premises or because of economic conditions brought about due to the enemy attack, natural disaster, or man-made technological disaster that have caused the fair market value of the property to decline by 15 percent, if refinancing is impractical under the circumstances. No bond is required on the injunction. The borrower must act, however, because otherwise a foreclosure conducted while the borrower did nothing is valid, even though the borrower could have won by exercising these rights.

Redemption A foreclosure sale under a deed of trust is final in Mississippi. There is no right of redemption.

MISSOURI

Missouri permits two types of foreclosure: judicial and nonjudicial under a power of sale clause. In judicial foreclosure, the lender may file a petition in the office of the circuit court against the borrower and the tenants or occupiers of the property. The petition states the nature of the mortgage and formally requests the court to render judgment for the amount of the debt, to foreclose the equity of redemption (prevent the borrower from recovering the property by paying up on the mortgage), and to order the property sold to satisfy the amount due. Such a lawsuit will be handled in the same manner as other civil lawsuits. The borrower may be served in person or by constructive notice through publication if personal service efforts prove to be fruitless.

Power of Sale Foreclosures Missouri permits foreclosure under a power of sale clause in a mortgage. Before proceeding with a foreclosure sale under the power of sale clause, the lender must give the borrower 20 days notice of the sale, whether the mortgage or deed of trust provides for such notice or not. The property must be advertised for sale as follows:

- In counties with more than 50,000 inhabitants, the notice of foreclosure sale must be published at least 20 times in a daily newspaper and continued to the day of sale.

- In counties with less than 50,000 inhabitants, the notice of foreclosure must be published once per week on the same day each week in a daily, triweekly, or semiweekly newspaper for four successive issues, with the last insertion to be not more than one week prior to the foreclosure sale. An affidavit of the printer or publisher may serve as evidence of publication.

Notices of Sale

Mailing The trustee who conducts the foreclosure sale must mail a notice of the foreclosure sale not less than 20 days prior to the scheduled date of the sale to the following parties:

- The borrower named in the deed of trust or mortgage at the last known address for the borrower

- The person shown by the office of the recorder's deed records to be the owner of the property as of 40 days before the foreclosure sale at the last known address as shown in the lender's records for such record owner

- Any person whose name and address is set forth in a request for notice that has been duly recorded 40 days in advance of the foreclosure sale date

Content The notice must be in the following format:

In accordance with R.S.Mo, 443.325, request is hereby made that notice of sale under the deed of trust (or mortgage) recorded the _____ day of 20_____ (as recorder's number _____ or in Book _____Page _____,) of the records of_____County, Missouri, the legal description of the property being_____

In_____ County, Missouri, executed by _____ as Grantor (or Mortgagor) in which _____ is named as beneficiary (or Mortgagee) and _____ as Trustee, be mailed to _____ (Name) at _____ (Address), _____ (City) _____ (State).

(Signature)

_____

(Acknowledgment)

_____

Receipt of Foreclosure: Notice Not Necessary The borrower does not have to receive the envelope containing the notice of foreclosure pursuant to a deed of trust or mortgage. Recording of the receipt issued by the U.S. Post Office for certified or registered mail to evidence that the envelope has been delivered by the sender to the U.S. Post Office shall constitute proof of compliance with the notice requirements.

Trustees The person named in the deed of trust or mortgage must conduct the foreclosure sale. However, if the trustee is dead, neglects this duty, or is incapacitated, a new trustee can be appointed if the lender files a motion in court requesting a new trustee and the court feels the circumstances justify an appointment, in which case the sheriff or another suitable person approved by the judge can conduct the sale. A foreign corporation may not be a trustee for foreclosure in the state of Missouri, unless a cotrustee who is a resident of Missouri is named. Certain nearby states can authorize a Missouri corporation to act in a fiduciary capacity for an outside corporation. A trustee may collect a 2 percent commission on the first $1,000, 1 percent on sums over that amount but under $5,000, and 0.5 percent on sums over that amount.

Sale Procedures The trustee must conduct the sale in a fair manner at the time and place and in the manner specified in the notice of foreclosure, the deed of trust, and the statute. The property is to be called out for sale and sold to the highest bidder. The lender may purchase at the sale, but if it does so, a right of redemption applies.

Redemption If any person other than the lender, or someone purchasing on behalf of the lender, buys the property at a fairly and properly conducted foreclosure sale, then no right of redemption exists. If, on the other hand, the lender buys at the foreclosure sale, as is so often the case, then the borrower has a right to redeem the property for one year from the date of sale.

To obtain the right of redemption, however, the borrower must meet many requirements. First, the borrower must give the trustee or other person conducting the sale advance notice, ten days prior to the sale, of the borrower's intent to redeem. Second, the borrower must arrange a bond on which there is one good surety, besides the borrower, who can stand good for a sum of money equal to the interest that would accrue throughout the year on the mortgage and on any prior lien loan, together with the foreclosure costs, taxes, and assessments and, furthermore, a sum equal to 6 percent of all the sums bid by the successful bidder at the foreclosure sale, whether they were advanced in cash or not. The bond must be sufficient to cover any waste or damages inflicted on the property by the borrower. The bond must be in place 20 days after the sale, or else the borrower has no right to redeem.

MONTANA

Real estate may be foreclosed on by filing a lawsuit or by conducting a nonjudicial private foreclosure sale in compliance with Montana law. Montana has some unusual mortgage provisions, which have been largely replaced by the Small Tract Financing Act of Montana for homesteads and small business real estate. If the tract of land is 15 acres or less, then the lender may use a trust deed that provides for a relatively quick and inexpensive foreclosure procedure. Unless the Small Tract Financing Act applies, then the lender must foreclose either by filing a lawsuit and seeking an order of sale or else by following a special foreclosure procedure.

Under Montana's special foreclosure procedures, if applicable, the lender or person conducting the foreclosure sale must publish, post, and serve a foreclosure notice at least 30 days in advance of the foreclosure sale. The notices must be advertised in a newspaper where the real estate is located, and if there is no newspaper, then by posting the notices in five conspicuous places in the county. Two other notices must be posted in conspicuous places in the township in which the land is situated, and one such notice must be in such a conspicuous place as will be most likely to give notice to all persons of the sale, and the other must be posted at the front door of the county courthouse. The notice of sale must be further served on the occupant of the property to be foreclosed on and upon every person claiming an interest in the property who may be found in the state of Montana.

Small Tract Financing Act Foreclosure Procedure If the tract of land is less than 15 acres, then the Small Tract Financing Act applies to the foreclosure under the power of sale provisions of a deed of trust. If there is a default on the loan obligation secured by the deed of trust and there is recorded a notice of sale, duly executed and acknowledged by the trustee named in the deed of trust, that sets forth the proper information, then the foreclosure may be done out of court. The contents of the foreclosure notice must include the names of the borrower, lender, and trustee; a description of the property to be foreclosed upon; a description of the default causing the foreclosure; the book and page where the trust deed is recorded; the sum owing on the defaulted loan; the trustee's or lender's intention to sell the property to pay off the debt; the date of the sale, which shall be not less than 120 days subsequent to the date the foreclosure notice is filed for record; the time of the sale, which shall be between the hours of 9:00 AM and 4:00 PM Mountain Standard Time; and the place of the sale, which shall be at the courthouse of the county in which the property is located or at the office or usual place of business of the trustee if it's within the county in which the property is located.

Mailing of Foreclosure Notices The trustee, at least 120 days before the date fixed for the foreclosure sale, must mail foreclosure notices by registered or certified mail to the following persons:

- The borrower, at the borrower's last known address
- Any person who recorded a request for notice
- Any record title owner as of the notice filing date

Posting At least 20 days before the date fixed for the trustee's sale, a copy of the recorded notice of sale must be posted in a conspicuous place on the property to be sold. The trustee may request the sheriff or constable of the county to post the notice. A copy of the notice shall be published in a newspaper of general circulation in the county in which the property is located once per week for three successive weeks. The posting and the last publication shall be made at least 20 days before the date fixed for the trustee's sale.

Recording On or before the date of the sale, the trustee must record an affidavit stating that the requirements of mailing, posting, and publication have been met.

Sale Procedures At the date, time, and place specified for foreclosure in the notice of sale, the trustee or the trustee's attorney shall sell the property at public auction to the highest bidder. The sale may be postponed up to 15 days by a proclamation made at the time the foreclosure sale would otherwise have taken place. The purchaser must pay the high-bid price in cash. In return, the purchaser will receive a trustee's deed. If the purchaser fails to pay, then the trustee can resell the property at any time to the highest bidder. The trustee may reject any further bidding by a bidder who fails to produce cash in response to winning a bid.

Redemption Although the old statutes provided for a one-year right of redemption, the Small Tract Financing Act eliminates the borrower's right to redeem after a properly conducted foreclosure sale.

Deficiency Montana does not allow a deficiency judgment unless the foreclosure was done by filing a lawsuit and the sale proceeds were insufficient to pay the judgment. Small Tract Financing Act foreclosures done out of court by advertisement do not give the lender any right to collect a deficiency from the borrower.

Possession The lender may obtain possession on the tenth day following the sale. Any person still in the house or property is to be treated as a tenant at will (a nonpaying tenant).

NEBRASKA

Foreclosures in Nebraska take place judicially, through the filing of petitions for foreclosure in the Nebraska District Court for the county where the property is located. If a prior lawsuit has been won by the lender for the amount due on a loan, it does not stop a lender from filing a subsequent lawsuit seeking a foreclosure sale of mortgaged premises. However, before the court will hear a petition for foreclosure, the lender must prove it has been unable to collect what was judged to be owed in the prior lawsuit. If a suit has been brought for satisfaction of a mortgage rather than a true petition for foreclosure, the lender can only seek the amount due and possession of the property rather than true foreclosure. Whenever a petition for foreclosure is filed, either alone or in conjunction with a petition for satisfaction of a mortgage, then the court can decree a sale of the mortgaged premises or such part as is needed to pay off the loan and the costs of suit.

While the lawsuit is pending, the borrower has the right to bring in the past-due payments, including principal and interest and costs, and the lawsuit proceedings will be suspended (stayed). Nevertheless, the court will enter a decree of foreclosure and sale. This will not be enforced unless there is a further order of the court, which will not be given unless the borrower defaults in the future payment of any installment or a portion of one.

The court may order the entire property to be sold or some part of it, based on a report by the sheriff as to what appears to be the most feasible. The order of sale may be stayed up to nine months after the judgment if the borrower files a written request for a delay (stay) with the clerk of the court within 20 days after the judgment is rendered. Otherwise, the order commanding the sale of the mortgaged property will be given 20 days after the judgment.

The sheriff or officer holding the sale must give public notice of the time and place of the sale by posting the notice on the courthouse door and at five other public locations in the county where the property is located. Two of the five locations must be in the precinct where the property is located. In addition, the sheriff must advertise the property for sale once a week for four weeks in a newspaper either printed in the county or generally circulated in the county. After making the sale, the sheriff or officer will report it back to the court, which will then confirm the sale. Once the sale is confirmed, the borrower has no right to redeem the property.

A deed shall be executed by the sheriff, and it will vest in the purchaser the same title the borrower had. The sales proceeds will be applied to discharge the lender's debt. If there is a surplus, it goes to other persons who are entitled to it, or it must stay with the court for three months before it can be paid to the borrower.

Deficiency A deficiency is only possible as a continuation of a foreclosure suit but not while the foreclosure action is pending or remains incomplete.

NEVADA

Judicial Foreclosure Available Yes

Nonjudicial Foreclosure Available Yes

The lender may use a deed of trust with a power of sale clause as the mortgage. This permits the lender to foreclose by following a statutory procedure for sale without the necessity of filing a lawsuit in court.

Preliminary Notices: Nonjudicial Foreclosure The borrower has three months from the date a notice of default and election to sell is recorded to perform and cure the default under the deed of trust. If the borrower fails to do so, then the property will be sold at foreclosure.

Recording A notice of default and election to sell must be recorded by the deed of trust's trustee.

Mailing A copy of the notice of default and election to sell must be mailed certified, return receipt requested, to the borrower and any owner of the property on the date the notice is recorded. The notice must be mailed to the last address the lender has, but if the current address of the borrower is not known, the trustee may send it to the property which is to be foreclosed on. The trustee must send the notice of default and election to sell to the borrower within ten days of recording the same to anyone who recorded a request for such a notice.

Advertising and Posting The property must be advertised and posted in the same manner as for an execution sale.

Cure The borrower has 35 days from the first day following the day on which the notice of default and election to sell was recorded to cure the default. The borrower may cure the default by performing under the loan agreement. Usually, this would mean paying the missed payments or other sums due to the lender but not the accelerated loan balance.

Sale Procedures

Time The time of sale must be specified in the foreclosure notice. It should be for a time no less than that which would be specified for an execution sale.

Place The foreclosure sale may be made at the trustee's office, even if the office is not in the same county as the property.

Manner The property should be sold in the manner required by law for the sale of real property on execution.

Special Procedures Property owners may stop foreclosure by filing an "Intent to Cure" with the Public Trustee's office at least 15 days before foreclosure by bringing the loan current by noon the day before the foreclosure sale. The court may issue an injunction to restrain waste (destruction) of the property during foreclosure.

Deficiency If the foreclosure fails to generate sufficient proceeds to pay off what remained due on the loan, then the lender may sue for a deficiency within three months after the foreclosure sale. A hearing will be held to determine the market value of the property. Notice of such hearing must be served at least 15 days before the hearing. An appraiser may be appointed by the court, on its own motion or on request, to have the foreclosed property appraised to find the market value. At the hearing, the greater of the market value or the foreclosure sale price must be credited against what remained unpaid on the loan. The court may award a deficiency judgment for the difference. The deficiency judgment must be sought within six months after the date of foreclosure. Even if multiple properties are being foreclosed on by the lender, the deficiency must be sought within two years of the initial foreclosure on the first of the multiple properties.

Redemption A deed of trust sale gives the foreclosure purchaser clear title free of any right of redemption for the old borrower. There is a one-year redemption on judicial sales.

NEW HAMPSHIRE

New Hampshire has two broad classes of mortgage foreclosures: (1) foreclosures made on mortgages without power of sale clauses and (2) foreclosures made on mortgages with power of sale clauses. Foreclosures made without power of sale clauses are done along lines that are very similar to those of strict foreclosure in which the lender must work to obtain possession of the premises. Foreclosures made with power of sale clauses revolve around giving the proper notices and conducting proper foreclosure sales.

Foreclosures Without Power of Sale Clauses

Although mortgages with power of sale clauses are much more common than those without, it is still possible to have a mortgage without a power of sale clause in New Hampshire. In this event, the foreclosure works much like strict foreclosure in other New England states. To foreclose, a lender must recover possession lawfully and hold it for a required length of time (one year in New Hampshire) before title becomes final in the name of the lender. There are three ways to recover possession:

1. *Entry under process:* The lender files a lawsuit and obtains a court order authorizing entry.

2. *Entry and subsequent publication*: The lender peaceably enters the premises and continues occupation for a year. An affidavit from the party and witnesses as to the time, manner, and purposes of the entry should be recorded. A notice stating the time at which the possession by the lender for the purpose of foreclosure was commenced should be published three weeks successively, with the first publication to be at least six months before the right to redeem would be foreclosed. The notice should give the date of the mortgage and a description of the property. A copy of the notice and a sworn affidavit as to when, where, and how it was published should also be recorded.

3. *Possession and publication:* The lender already is in possession and simply publishes a notice stating that from a certain day forward, the lender retains possession because the mortgage conditions were broken by the borrower and that the purpose of the lender's continued possession is foreclosure. The date of the mortgage and a description of the premises should also be stated. The day stated in the notice should be not later than four weeks after the initial advertisement. The notice should be published in a newspaper of general circulation in the county where the real estate is located. A copy of the notice and an affidavit stating when, where, and how it was published should be recorded.

Foreclosures With Power of Sale Clauses

It is possible to foreclosure a mortgage with a power of sale clause in New Hampshire by filing a lawsuit in court and obtaining a court decree commanding the sale of the property with a confirmation of the completed sale by the court. On the other hand, it is much more common to publish and serve notice of a foreclosure sale in the proper manner and then sell the property at the sale to the highest bidder.

A foreclosure sale without court action must be preceded by the appropriate notices. The borrower must be sent a notice at least 25 days before the sale. The notice should contain the following warning:

> You are hereby notified that you have the right to petition the Superior Court for the county in which the mortgaged premises are situated, with service upon the mortgagee (lender), and upon such bond as the court may require, to enjoin the scheduled foreclosure sale.

Unless the borrower sues prior to the foreclosure sale, the borrower may not challenge the foreclosure in court at a later date. The lender should also publish a notice of the foreclosure sale once a week for three weeks in a newspaper of general circulation in the county or town where the property is located. The first publication must not be less than 20 days before the foreclosure sale.

The actual foreclosure sale must be held at the house or on the real property that is being foreclosed, unless the mortgage specifies a different location. A report of the sale must be made in ten days. The person who sells the property at the foreclosure sale must record the deed, a copy of the notice of sale, and an affidavit describing the sales procedure within 30 days of the sale. Title passes with the recording of the deed.

NEW JERSEY

Foreclosures in New Jersey take place by filing a lawsuit. New Jersey doesn't use privately conducted mortgage foreclosure sales. A lender begins by filing a complaint in foreclosure in the Superior Court. Constructive notice can be given by recording a lis pendens with the clerk or register of the county where the land is located. A lender may file a foreclosure suit simply to collect the unpaid payments rather than the entire unpaid principal balance. If so, the lender can get a judgment for the missed payments and hold the mortgage and the note intact for the rest of loan balance. The property may be sold through a foreclosure sale with the mortgage lien and note still in place so that the buyer at the foreclosure sale holds title subject to the existing mortgage lien and note. In this type of sale, however, the lender may not collect a deficiency judgment against the borrower.

Preliminary Notices In New Jersey, once the lender wins a judgment to foreclose on the real estate, either in part, as just described, or in whole, the sale will be conducted by the sheriff or another officer by a writ of execution. The foreclosure notice must be posted in the county office of the county where the property is located and on the property to be foreclosed on. The notice must be advertised in two newspapers in the county, one of which must be located in either the county seat or the largest municipality in the county. The person seeking the foreclosure must notify the property owner and any other parties to the foreclosure lawsuit of the foreclosure at least ten days before the sale. The newspaper ad must disclose title defects at least ten days before sale, unless the court has ordered the foreclosure sale to be completed free of any liens. If the title defects were not disclosed or the sale was not ordered to be made free of liens, then the buyer at the foreclosure sale may back out of the purchase by satisfying the court that title defects exist.

Sale Procedures The sheriff may then proceed to sell the property in the manner directed by the court. The sheriff must deliver the deed unless an objection to the sale is made within ten days after the sale or the objection is made before the deed was delivered, if delivery is past ten days from the sale. Unless there are valid objections, the court will confirm the sale. Thereafter, the sheriff must file a report of the sale with the court within a reasonable time.

Deficiency Judgments Deficiency judgments are permitted in New Jersey. A lawsuit for a deficiency must be commenced within three months from the date of the foreclosure sale or confirmation of the sale, if confirmation was required. Although the deficiency suit is a separate lawsuit, it can only be brought against a person who was joined to the foreclosure lawsuit and who is personally responsible for the mortgage debt. Such a person must be served with process. On a note that is dated on or after May 1, 1980, the debtor may dispute the deficiency by introducing evidence of the fair market value of the mortgaged premises at the time of the foreclosure sale. The deficiency is limited to the difference between the fair market value of the premises and the balance due on the loan. However, a borrower should object to the foreclosure sale price prior to the confirmation of the sale. The failure to do so may set the borrower up for a larger deficiency. However, some New Jersey courts are refusing to confirm the foreclosure sale unless the lender agrees, as part of the confirmation, not to sue the borrower for a deficiency greater than the difference between the fair market value and the balance owed on the loan.

Redemption Redemption is possible during the ten days a borrower has to object after a foreclosure sale. If the borrower objected to the sale, then redemption is possible anytime until the court rules on the objections, which may be longer than ten days.

Deficiency If the lender sues the borrower for a deficiency, the effect is to reopen the foreclosure sale, which would otherwise have been final and proof against a right of redemption. A deficiency gives a borrower the right to bring an action to redeem the property within six months after the lender's deficiency judgment is rendered. However, persons who answered the deficiency suit, disputing its amount, and lost may not redeem.

NEW MEXICO

Judicial Foreclosure Available Yes

Nonjudicial Foreclosure Available Yes

A lender must file a lawsuit and undertake judicial foreclosure unless the loan is covered by the Deed of Trust Act, which allows nonjudicial foreclosure. However, the Deed of Trust Act applies only to business and commercial loans on real estate in excess of $500,000 and then only if the borrower agreed, in writing, to the deed of trust arrangement. Otherwise, in a typical foreclosure on a house, whether under a mortgage, trust deed, or deed of trust, the lender must arrange to file a lawsuit, win a judgment ordering foreclosure, and arrange a foreclosure sale in the manner required by law.

Judicial Sale Once the lender wins a judgment, it can arrange to sell the property to pay off what the borrower owes in accordance with the court judgment. A notice of sale must first be given; then a sale can take place in 30 days.

Contents The notice of sale should specify the date, time, and place of sale. It should also give a legal description of the property.

Advertising The notice of sale must be published once a week for four consecutive weeks. The last ad must be published at least three days before the foreclosure sale.

Cure The borrower may prevent the foreclosure by paying the amount of the judgment.

Time The sale may not take place until 30 days after the date the court grants a judgment in favor of the lender.

Manner The property will be sold to the highest bidder. However, if the sale fails due to lack of bidding, then the property may be reoffered for sale any time before the return date on the writ of execution issued by the court to enforce its judgment.

Redemption After the sale, the real estate may be redeemed by the former borrower or owner by paying, at any time within nine months from the date of sale, the amount of the successful foreclosure bid with interest at 10 percent a year, plus taxes and other costs. The parties may agree to a term that is shorter but not less than one month. For good cause, however, the court can increase the period to not more than nine months.

Once the borrower files the suit for redemption and serves it on the lender, the lender has 30 days to respond. Sometime after the response, or by default, the court will hold a hearing to determine the amount of money necessary for redemption. At the conclusion of the hearing, the clerk of the court will issue a certificate of redemption.

Deficiency A lender may obtain a deficiency judgment. The matter is unregulated by statute.

NEW YORK

Judicial Foreclosure Available Yes

Nonjudicial Foreclosure Available Yes

Preferred Method: Judicial Foreclosure

Most residential mortgages are foreclosed in New York by filing a lawsuit. Although nonjudicial foreclosure is available, it is seldom used. Nonjudicial foreclosure procedures are sufficiently intricate to lead to potential title disputes. Such problems might make it very difficult to evict a tenant. Junior lienholders might also dispute the title and tie the matter up in litigation. Therefore, judicial foreclosure is the safest approach.

Typically the foreclosure sale is advertised for four to six weeks. The sale is made by public auction to the highest bidder. The lender may bid, as well. The lender must distribute the proceeds according to the terms of the judgment signed by the judge. Surplus money will normally be held by a referee. Within 30 days after the sale and signing the deed to the purchaser, the court officer who conducted the sale must file a report of sale and a receipt from the lender with the court clerk. Unless the court orders otherwise, the sale can't be confirmed until three months after filing of the report of sale.

Deficiency If the mortgage contains an express covenant to pay, then the lender may seek a deficiency judgment against the borrower if the court-ordered sale does not produce sufficient funds. The lender can ask the court for a deficiency judgment for the amount left unpaid after the foreclosure sale. The motion for the deficiency judgment must be made within 90 days after the foreclosure sale. The court must determine the market value and credit the greater of the market value or the foreclosure sales price against what remains unpaid on the loan.

Redemption After the judicial foreclosure, there is no redemption period. This is true of nonjudicial foreclosure, as well.

NORTH CAROLINA

North Carolina offers two methods of foreclosure: (1) by filing a lawsuit seeking foreclosure and (2) by conducting an out-of-court foreclosure sale under the terms of a power of sale clause in a deed of trust. In the event the lender elects to foreclose by filing a lawsuit, it will try to get a default judgment. Once the lender gets a judgment, the court clerks for the Superior Court have the power of the judge to appoint commissioners to make the foreclosure sale, receive the reports on the sale, and confirm the reported sale. They may order the execution and delivery of a deed to the property. The clerk may also issue writs of assistance to evict any occupants, provided ten days' advance notice is given to such occupants.

Deed of Trust Foreclosure

In North Carolina, a deed of trust foreclosure has several unusual features. First, there must be a preliminary hearing as whether to foreclose or not. Interested parties must receive notice of the hearing. The clerk of the court, not the judge, holds the hearing. Afterward, a notice of the foreclosure sale must be given; then the sale is conducted. A deposit must be made at the sale. After the sale, however, a very unusual procedure called an "upset bid" exists. An upset bid consists of making a higher bid than the foreclosure bid within a set time, which will cause the property to go through a resale, which may happen again and again! After the final sale, the sale is reported to the court clerk.

Judicial Foreclosure

Judicial foreclosure begins when the lender files a lawsuit. The lender will sue the borrower and any person who has a claim to the ownership or a possessory interest. The lender, as plaintiff, has a summons and a complaint served on the borrower. The summons commands the borrower to come to court and answer the lender's complaint; the complaint is the lawsuit proper, which describes the lender's legal and factual basis for foreclosure. A notice of lis pendens must be filed. The lis pendens is a notice that a lawsuit is pending, the outcome of which affects title. Often, the borrower fails to answer. In that event, the court will appoint a referee to compute a figure for the foreclosure. The court may then sign a judgment of foreclosure and sale. If the borrower appears and defends against the lawsuit, the court will determine the merits of the defense. The referee will need an oral hearing. If the lender wins, a judgment of foreclosure and sale will be awarded following a statutorily prescribed procedure.

At the outset, a hearing must be held before the court clerk (not the judge) to determine whether the foreclosure should take place or not. Notice of the hearing must be served in the manner in which a lawsuit is served or by certified mail, return receipt requested. Alternatively, if no other process to give notice works after diligent effort, then the notice of the hearing can be posted in a conspicuous place on the property that will be foreclosed on.

Notice of the Foreclosure Hearing

Notice of the hearing must be sent to the borrower, anyone who owes money or could owe money on the loan, and every person who has a recorded claim or lien on the real estate that would be affected by the foreclosure. The notice must describe the real estate, give the name and address of the current lender, describe the nature of the default, state whether the loan has been accelerated, and mention any right the borrower has to pay cure the default.

The notice must state that the borrower has the right to appear before the clerk of the court at the date and time specified and show cause as to why the foreclosure should not be held. The notice must state that the borrower does not have to appear and that failure to attend does not preclude the buyer from trying to cure the default or buy at the foreclosure sale.

The notice should warn the borrower that the foreclosure buyer will be entitled to possession as soon as the foreclosure buyer accepts delivery of the deed to the property. The borrower is further advised to keep the lender informed as to the borrower's latest address to aid delivery of copies of any subsequent foreclosure notices.

The right to receive a notice of hearing may be waived but only if the debt is over $100,000 and the waiver is in writing and signed in the presence of the witness. When such written waivers are delivered to the court clerk, the clerk may skip the hearing on whether the foreclosure should take place or not.

The Hearing The clerk will hold the hearing. During the hearing, the clerk will consider evidence as to whether the debt exists, whether a default has occurred, and whether the lender has the right to foreclose. If the clerk answers those questions in the lender's favor, the clerk will authorize the foreclosure. Either side may appeal the clerk's ruling to the judge within ten days. (This is likely to be fruitless.)

Notice of Sale

Contents The notice of sale shall describe the loan instruments. It must identify the original borrowers as they are shown in the deed records within ten days prior to the posting of the foreclosure notice. If someone other than the borrower owns or claims ownership of the property in an instrument that has been recorded, then such a person must be mentioned in the notice of the foreclosure sale. The notice must give the date, hour, and place of the sale, provided such date, hour, and place are consistent with the state law regulating such sales. (More details will follow on the sale itself.) The notice must describe the property and state the terms of the sale and that the property will be sold subject to taxes, special assessments, and any other terms required by the deed of trust, which must be specifically described.

Posting and Publishing The notice of the sale of the real estate must be posted at the courthouse door for 20 days prior to the sale. In addition, it must be published once a week for two successive weeks. The two ads must be published at least eight days apart. The last ad cannot be published less than ten days before the sale. The notice of the sale must be mailed via first-class mail at least 20 days before the sale to the borrower and any other owner or record title or lien claimant at the address last known to the trustee or the lender. The notice must further be sent to anyone who has recorded a request for copy of notice in the statutory form as follows:

In accordance with the provisions of G.S. 45-21.17(5), request is hereby made that a copy of any notice of sale under the deed of trust (mortgage) recorded on 20____, in Book____, page _____ records of _____ County, North Carolina, executed by _____ as trustor (mortgagor) in which _____ is named as beneficiary (mortgagee), and _____ as trustee, to be mailed to _____ at the following address.

Signature: _____

If the sale is made to someone other than the lender or if the lender resells to a good-faith buyer and such a buyer holds the land for six months, then a person who did not receive a notice of sale loses the right to challenge the foreclosure. To challenge the sale, the party must post a bond equal to what the lender is owed on the loan against the property. The bond is irrevocable, pending the final decision of the court.

Time of Sale A sale shall begin at the time designated in the notice of sale, never on a Sunday and always between the hours of 10:00 AM and 4:00 PM. The sale may be continued or postponed. However, a postponement may only be for good cause, such as bad weather, an excessive number of competing sales, illness, or another good reason. The postponement must be announced at the time and place the regular sale would have taken place. A notice of the postponement must be posted on the courthouse door and be given orally to each party who is normally entitled to notice of a foreclosure sale. The notice has to state the hour and date to which the sale is postponed and the reason for the postponement, and it must be signed.

Place of Sale The property must be sold at the courthouse door in the county where the land is located, unless the deed of trust provides for a different location. If the deed of trust gives the trustee the authority to designate a place of sale, then the place of sale will be the place the trustee designates on the notice of sale. The deed of trust may require a cash deposit at the sale and set the amount. If the required cash deposit is not specified in the deed of trust, then the trustee holding the sale may require the highest bidder at the sale to pay a cash deposit, not to exceed 10 percent of the bid up to $1,000 and 5 percent of the amount by which the bid exceeds $1,000. If the high bidder fails to make the deposit at the sale, then the trustee may immediately reoffer the property for sale to any bidders.

Report A preliminary report of the sale must be made to the court within five days after the sale. The report must give the name of the borrower; the lender; the date, time, and place of the sale; recording information about the deed; the name of the foreclosure buyer; the price at which the property was sold; and the name of the person making the report.

Proceeds of the Sale The foreclosure sale proceeds should be used to pay off the costs of the sale, the taxes on the property, and any special assessments. Next the money goes to pay the balance due on the loan and then to creditors in order of their seniority. Anything left over goes to the borrower or the borrower's estate. A special proceeding is available to contest the distribution of the sales proceeds.

Upset Bids One of the most intriguing features of North Carolina law is the upset bid on real estate sold at foreclosure. Even after the sale, a potential buyer can come in and make an upset bid. An upset bid is an increased bid whereby a bidder offers to buy the real estate previously sold at foreclosure for an amount exceeding the reported foreclosure sale price by 10 percent of the first $1,000 and 5 percent of the amount over $1,000 of the old foreclosure bid. Such a sum, in the form of cash or a cashier's check, must be deposited with the clerk of the Superior Court within ten days after the clerk receives a report on the old foreclosure sale. The clerk may also require a bond in the amount of the upset bid price, minus the cash deposit. The clerk may then order a resale of the property.

Resales Under Upset Bids When the clerk offers the property for resale due to the deposit of an upset bid, then the notice of the resale must be posted at the courthouse door for 15 days prior to the sale. A newspaper ad must be published once a week for two successive weeks before the sale. Eight days must separate the two ads. The last ad must be run no less than seven days before sale. A notice of the resale must be mailed to each party. The sale will take place in the same manner as the original sale. Once again, a high bidder will emerge, who may well be the person who put down the upset bid deposit. The entire resale may be done again and again as often as upset bids are submitted!

Final Report A final report on the sale and the disposition of the proceeds must be given to the clerk by the person who held the foreclosure sale within 30 days after receipt of the proceeds of the sale. The final report should show what part or parts of the property were sold. The clerk must audit the report and record it. A copy of the notice of sale or resale and an affidavit of publication should also be recorded. At this point, the sale is final. Special procedures exist to validate foreclosure sales well after they took place when the proper procedures were not complied with or when the trustee was also the lender.

Injunctions It is possible to enjoin a foreclosure sale in North Carolina.

Deficiency A lender may not sue for a deficiency if the loan that went into default was for the purchase price of the real estate. However, in other cases, a lender may sue for deficiency, but the borrower has the right in a deficiency suit to prove the reasonable value of the property as a defense or offset to the lender's claims. The borrower is not restricted to forcing the lender to credit only the foreclosure bid against the property; the borrower can instead assert and prove the market value of the property as an offset to a deficiency suit by the lender.

NORTH DAKOTA

In North Dakota, a lawsuit may be brought in District Court for foreclosure or for satisfaction of a mortgage on real estate. Prior to bringing any lawsuit, the lender must give the borrower no less than 30 days' advance notice of the lender's intent to foreclose. This notice must be sent no later than

90 days before the suit is filed. The notice must contain a description of the real estate; the date and amount of the mortgage; the amount due for principal, interest, and taxes paid by the lender, stated separately; and a statement that if the amount due is not paid within 30 days from the date of mailing or service, then a lawsuit will be filed to foreclose. The notice must also state the time period for redemption, which is either one year or, for small tracts with substantial balances and the properly worded mortgages, six months.

Notice of Sale The notice must be served by registered or certified mail addressed to the owner of record at the post office address shown on the mortgage or recorded by the register of deeds. The notice may be served personally in the same manner as a lawsuit. A U.S. Post Office registry return receipt showing the envelope was delivered to the title owner is evidence the owner received it. If the borrower brings in the missing payments any time within 30 days after receipt of the notice, the loan must be reinstated.

Lawsuit Allegations North Dakota law requires the lawsuit paperwork to include several allegations that are unusual. First, North Dakota law requires the attorney bringing the suit to hold a power of attorney to act on behalf of the lender. The lawsuit itself should allege this is so. Second, the lender must also declare in the original lawsuit whether or not the lender will pursue a deficiency judgment against the borrower if the foreclosure sale does not bring in enough money to pay off the outstanding loan balance. The lender may not ask for a deficiency in the foreclosure suit if it has already brought another suit just to collect on the loan. If the borrower can bring in the missed payments plus foreclosure costs before the decree of sale is issued by the court, then the lender's lawsuit to foreclose must be dismissed.

Sale Procedure All sales must be made by the sheriff or deputy of the county where the judgment is rendered. The sale must take place in the county where the land is located. The sale will normally be at the courthouse or another place designated by the trust deed. Whenever the real estate is sold at foreclosure, the sheriff or deputy must give the buyer a certificate of sale and, at the expiration of the redemption period, a deed must be given to the buyer. The lender cannot obtain possession during the redemption period. However, the lender can obtain a court injunction barring the borrower from committing waste (destruction) against the property during the redemption period if the borrower continues to occupy the premises. Any cash surplus from the sale, beyond that needed to pay off the mortgage and the foreclosure costs, must be paid to the borrower.

Redemption The normal redemption period is one year. Within that period, if the borrower can come up with the balance due on the loan plus costs, the property can be redeemed. Property sold at foreclosure can be redeemed not only by the borrower but by a creditor who holds a lien against the property. A creditor who wants to redeem is called a "redemptioner." Interestingly, one redemptioner can redeem from another redemptioner who took title by redemption. Each redemptioner must wait 60 days after the last redemption. The amount paid to redeem must be the amount of the original purchase price with interest at the rate stated in the original loan documents or the one on which the foreclosure took place. In either case, the amount should include the foreclosure costs plus taxes and insurance.

Short-Term Redemption The short-term redemption period is six months. To claim short-term redemption, the mortgage must contain the following wording:

> The parties agree that the provisions of the short-term mortgage redemption act shall govern this mortgage.

The mortgage should also contain the words, in capital letters:

MORTGAGE—SHORT-TERM MORTGAGE REDEMPTION

The area covered must be ten acres or less. Short-term redemption is available if the amount claimed upon the mortgage at the date of the notice before foreclosure is more than 66⅔ percent of the original indebtedness secured by the mortgage.

Moratorium The North Dakota courts have the power to postpone the entry of judgment in foreclosure proceedings if the balance owed on the loan is less than the market value of the property. These provisions are applicable to persons who would be deprived of a home.

Trustee for Commercial Property Commercial property in North Dakota may be placed in the charge of a trustee pending the expiration of the period of redemption. The trustee can take possession of the premises; pay utilities, taxes, and insurance; receive rentals from tenants and remove them if they don't pay; or rent the premises if there are no tenants.

OHIO

Judicial Foreclosure Available Yes

Nonjudicial Foreclosure Available No

The Ohio standard mortgage provides for a conditional transfer of title to the lender. If the borrower pays the principal and interest; performs the obligations of the mortgage, including payment of taxes, assessments, and hazard insurance; and does not commit waste, then the borrower will obtain full title at the end of the mortgage term. Ohio mortgages must be foreclosed by court action.

Lawsuit The lender must sue the borrower in the county where the property is located. The lender must ask the court to foreclose the mortgage and order a sale of the property.

Sale Procedures

Appraisement When land is to be sold under a foreclosure order, the officer conducting the sale shall call upon three disinterested freeholders of the county to give an estimate of the value of the property. A copy of the appraised value must be left with the court clerk. The property must forthwith be offered for sale at a price of not less than two-thirds the appraisement.

Advertising The land will not be sold until the officer handling the foreclosure gives public notice of the sale by advertising the time and place of the sale at least 30 days in advance of the sale. The advertisements will be sufficient if they are published once a week for three consecutive weeks before the day of the sale, with each ad on the same day of the week.

Method of Sale The sheriff handles foreclosure sales in Ohio. The officer will sell to the highest bidder at the time and place indicated in the advertised notice. The sale must take place at the courthouse. If the bidder fails to pay the price, the court "shall punish as for contempt any purchaser of real property who fails to pay the purchase money therefore." If there is no sale for lack of bidders, then the court may order a new appraisement and order the sale for one-third in cash and the balance later.

Confirmation The sheriff returns the writ of execution indicating that a sale was made to the court, which upon examination of the sale proceedings to make sure they were in conformity with the law and with the court orders, enters into its records a confirmation of the legality of the sale and directs the officer who made the sale to create and deliver the purchaser a deed for the property.

Special Procedures If the property is in danger of being damaged, the court may appoint a receiver to take charge of it.

Deficiency A deficiency judgment may be obtained by the lender along with the order commanding a foreclosure sale. The deficiency is void two years after the foreclosure sale is confirmed. However, the enforcement may continue if the debtor signs an agreement to postpone the enforcement past two years.

Redemption The debtor can redeem by paying the amount of the judgment plus costs and interest up until the confirmation of the sale, but not afterward.

OKLAHOMA

Judicial Foreclosure Available Yes

Nonjudicial Foreclosure Available Yes

In Oklahoma, both judicial and nonjudicial foreclosures are available. The judicial sales are governed by the age-old principles of common-law equity and some statutes. The nonjudicial sales are governed by the Oklahoma Power of Sale Mortgage Foreclosure Act, which was passed in 1986. However, the lender who chooses the nonjudicial route effectively gives up the right to sue for a deficiency if the foreclosure involves homestead property. Moreover, a borrower may force the lender into judicial foreclosure if the property involved is a homestead by recording and then mailing a written notice to the lender ten days before the foreclosure sale claiming the property as homestead. At that point, only judicial foreclosure may be used. This right is not available on other types of property.

Judicial Foreclosure

Mortgages on real estate can be foreclosed by filing a lawsuit under principles of equity in the District Court of the county where the land is located. If the borrower has defaulted on the requirements of the loan, such as by not paying the payments, then the court will order a foreclosure sale. The price may be determined through a special appraisal procedure. Unless the borrower waives the right to an appraisal in the mortgage, the property must be appraised before it can be sold at foreclosure. At the foreclosure sale, the property may not be sold for less than two-thirds of the appraised value.

Advertising The impending foreclosure sale must be advertised at least 30 days in advance of the sale.

Nonjudicial Foreclosure

Mortgages that can be foreclosed out of court must include the following statement, in bold and underlined type:

> A power of sale has been granted in this mortgage. A power of sale may allow the mortgagee (lender) to take the mortgaged property and sell it without going to court in a foreclosure action upon default by the mortgagor under this mortgage.

Notice

A written notice of intention to foreclose by power of sale must be sent by certified mail to the borrower at the borrower's last known address. The notice shall describe the defaults of the borrower under the loan and give the borrower 35 days from the date the notice is sent to cure the problem. If the borrower comes up with the missed payments during the 35 days, then the foreclosure can be stopped. It cannot be accelerated. However, if there have been three defaults, then the lender need not send another notice of intent to foreclose, and if the borrower has been in default four times in the past 24 months and has been notified as above, then no further notice is required to accelerate.

Contents The notice must describe in detail the nature of the borrower's default on the loan.

Time The lender's notice informs the borrower that if the house is the borrower's homestead, then the borrower has ten days to elect judicial foreclosure or else face out-of-court foreclosure under a power of sale clause.

Advertising The notice must be published once a day for four consecutive weeks, but the first date must be not less than 30 days before sale.

Recording The notice, plus an affidavit confirming the validity of the trustee's procedures, must be recorded within 10 days after the borrower has gone through the 35-day notice period.

Service The borrower must be served with the papers advising the buyer of the default. The papers should be served in the same manner as for court. These papers should not only be served, but the wise lender will preserve proof of receipt, return of service, or an affidavit in lieu of personal service along with proof of publication. All of these affidavits and a copy of the notice must be recorded.

Sale Procedures

Time and Place The time and place of the sale must be specified in the notice of foreclosure.

Manner The property will be sold at public auction to the highest bidder. If a purchaser at a foreclosure sale other than the borrower fails to post cash or certified funds equal to 10 percent of the bid amount, then the lender may proceed with the sale and accept the next-highest bid.

Redemption Once the court confirms a foreclosure sale, there can be no redemption. There is no right of redemption on power of sale foreclosures, either, although the borrower has the right to redeem until the foreclosure sale.

Deficiency A lender may sue judicially to obtain a deficiency judgment. Under the Oklahoma Power of Sale Mortgage Foreclosure Act, any action for a deficiency must be commenced within 90 days after the date of sale. In such event, the lender shall establish that the fair market value of the property on the date of the foreclosure sale exceeded the foreclosure sale price. If it did, then the higher figure must be credited against the balance due on the loan. If the house is the borrower's homestead and the borrower elects judicial foreclosure, the borrower may be hit with a deficiency suit. On the other hand, if the borrower does nothing, then the lender cannot sue for a deficiency.

OREGON

Judicial Foreclosure Available Yes

Nonjudicial Foreclosure Available Yes

Foreclosure in Oregon may be either by court action or by advertisement and sale.

Nonjudicial Foreclosure Preliminary Notices

Recording The trustee must record a notice of default.

Contents of Notice of Sale The notice of sale should include a property description; recording information on the trust deed; a description of the default; the sum owing on the loan; the lender's election to sell; and the date, time, and place of sale.

Mailing After recording the Notice of Default and at least 120 days before the foreclosure sale, notice of the sale must be either served or mailed by both first-class and certified mail to the borrower, the state Department of Revenue, any owner of record, and any person requesting notice.

Service A copy of the notice of sale must be served on the occupant of the property 120 days before the foreclosure sale day.

Advertising A copy of the notice must be published once a week for four successive weeks. The last publication must be made at least 20 days prior to the foreclosure sale day. The trustee must prepare and record an affidavit stating that the proper notices and advertising have been given.

Cure The borrower or any junior lienholder or claimant may cure the default prior to foreclosure by paying all past-due sums plus costs. On a residential trust deed foreclosure, the borrower may be charged the lesser of the actual charges or a total of $550 for trustee's and attorney's fees. Reasonable charges may be made for other foreclosures.

Sale Procedures

Date The date shall be the date given in the notice.

Time and Place The sale must be conducted between 9:00 AM and 4:00 PM at a place designated in the notice.

Manner The sale must be at auction to the highest bidder for cash. Any person, including the lender but excluding the trustee, may bid at the foreclosure sale. The purchaser must pay the bid price at the time of the sale. The trustee must give the buyer a deed within ten days. The buyer is also entitled to possession within ten days. The sale may be postponed up to 180 days, provided 20 days' advance notice is given by mail to the same persons as the original notice. A new time and place must be specified.

Special Procedures If the foreclosure is stayed by bankruptcy, the trustee may give an amended notice of sale and sell the property with only 20 days' notice as soon as the bankruptcy stay is lifted.

Deficiency A deficiency judgment cannot be obtained through a nonjudicial deed of trust foreclosure by advertisement. On commercial property secured by a trust deed, a deficiency judgment can be obtained by filing suit, but not on property covered by a purchase money mortgage. A purchase money mortgage is any mortgage with an unpaid balance of $50,000 or more on a primary or secondary single family residence. There are no other particular limits on deficiency judgments.

Redemption A person who was entitled to receive notice of the foreclosure but did not receive it may sue to invalidate the foreclosure and redeem the property for a period of five years following the sale. On a judicial foreclosure, the borrower or a successor in interest may redeem property within 180 days after sale by paying the purchase price plus 9 percent plus the foreclosure purchaser's expenses in operating and maintaining the property. A notice of no less than 2 nor more than 30 days must be given to the sheriff to redeem. There are restrictions on redemption rights if the borrower has transferred the property.

PENNSYLVANIA

Pennsylvania's judicial foreclosure is not easy for lenders. All actions to foreclose, accelerate, or take possession are stayed until the borrower is sent an "Act 91" notice giving the borrower 30 days to meet the lender or a consumer credit agency, which are listed on the notice. Starting from the day of the first meeting, the borrower has another 30-day delay to try to resolve the problem by restructuring loan payments or otherwise, but if this approach is unsuccessful, the borrower can apply for a Homeowner's Emergency Mortgage Assistance Program Loan and gain an extra 60-day delay on foreclosure to process the application. If the borrower has had good residential credit for the past five years, is 60 days delinquent, and has reasonable prospects of resuming loan payments in full in 36 months, then the borrower should be approved. If the loan is not approved or no meetings took place after the first 30 days, the lender may foreclose.

For reimbursement under "Act 6," which applies to home loans under $60,000 and is limited to a maximum of 24 months from the date of the mortgage delinquency, the borrower must be sent a 30-day notice of the foreclosure, during which time attorney's fees are limited to $50. Also, the borrower may pay the past-due payments and stop the foreclosure up to one hour before the bidding at the sheriff's sale, and the borrower may do this up to three times in a calendar year.

The Foreclosure Lawsuit The foreclosure complaint (lawsuit) must be filed and served on the borrower. It must describe the property to be foreclosed on. It must state the names of the borrower and the lender, the itemized amounts due, the fact that the mortgage is in default, and a demand for judgment. Although the lender may state more than one reason to foreclose, the lender may not sue to collect the money owed on the loan in addition to the suit to force the sale of the property by foreclosure. The defendant may file a counterclaim against the lender. The lawsuit, however, must be tried before a judge, without a jury. If the court orders foreclosure, then at least 30 days before foreclosure, the sheriff must give notice by putting a handbill on the property, serving a copy on the borrower, and advertising the property for sale for three consecutive weeks. The sale takes place a month or two after the court's order.

Redemption There is no right of redemption after the sale.

Deficiency Under the Pennsylvania Deficiency Judgment Act, the lender may file a lawsuit to collect on the promissory note signed by the borrower within six months of foreclosure. This lawsuit must be separate from the foreclosure lawsuit. The borrower has the right to force the lender to credit the fair market value of the property sold at the foreclosure sale against what is owed on the note. The suit must be filed within six months after the foreclosure.

RHODE ISLAND

Rhode Island mortgages may contain a statutory power of sale clause, which may be incorporated by reference into the mortgage document. If the mortgage does not contain a power of sale clause, then the lender has four options: (1) file a lawsuit seeking a court-ordered sale; (2) file a lawsuit seeking ejectment (to throw the borrower out of the house); (3) peaceably enter the house in the presence of two witnesses, who must give a certificate of possession that they must acknowledge (notarize) before a notary or a justice of the peace; or (4) have the borrower voluntarily agree to give up possession before a notary public or a justice of the peace. If the lender maintains possession, then after a time, the lender gets full title. The borrower has three years to file a lawsuit to redeem the property by paying up the full sum, both principal and interest, that is due on the mortgage (but not interest for future years). Rhode Island does not bar deficiency lawsuits.

Power of Sale Foreclosure Lenders in Rhode Island generally prefer to foreclose under a power of sale clause. The lender first accelerates the loan, then conducts a foreclosure sale after giving proper notice. The lender must send a notice of the foreclosure by certified mail, return receipt requested, to the buyer 20 days before publishing the first newspaper ad. Notice of the time and place of the sale must be published once a week for three weeks in the proper newspaper. The notice must be published not only on the day before sale but on the same weekday for each of the three weeks preceding the sale. Furthermore, the power of sale statute literally spells out which city's newspaper must be used! The statute further specifies that the sale must take place at a public auction conducted on the premises or at a location specified in the deed. The lender may bid at the sale in the same manner as other bidders.

SOUTH CAROLINA

Judicial Foreclosure Available Yes

Nonjudicial Foreclosure Available No

South Carolina uses judicial foreclosure. The lender must file a lawsuit and seek either an order of sale or a judgment for the loan balance against the borrower or both.

Sale Procedures

Time The hours of sale shall be between 11:00 AM and 5:00 PM. However, no sale may be made after the sheriff declares the day's sales are closed.

Place The sale takes place at the courthouse of the county where the real estate is located.

Manner South Carolina foreclosure sales are conducted by the sheriff at public auction to the highest bidder for cash. The sheriff will prepare and deliver a deed to the high bidder.

Special Procedures: Upset Bids Bidding remains open until 30 days after the sale. During that time, an upset bidder may make a suitable deposit, which is refundable, and outbid whoever made the highest bid at the actual foreclosure sale. A 5 percent higher bid is an upset bid, although a lower figure may be acceptable to the court. However, if no deficiency judgment is sought, then the upset bid procedure will not be followed.

Deficiency The lender can sue for and the court may adjudge and direct that if any part of the mortgage debt remains unpaid after the sale of the mortgaged premises, then the lender may seek a court order directing the borrower to pay the unpaid sum or residue. The judgment may be enforced as in other cases. However, within 30 days after the sale, if a defendant was sued for a deficiency, he may apply to the court for an order of appraisal. The defendant appoints one appraiser, the judgment creditor appoints another, and the judge appoints another. If the appraised value is greater than what remains owed on the loan, after subtracting the foreclosure sale proceeds, then there is no deficiency. However if it is less, then the borrower still gets credit against the judgment for the appraised value of the property. The lender can collect only what's left.

Redemption South Carolina does not recognize a right of redemption after foreclosure.

SOUTH DAKOTA

Judicial Foreclosure Available Yes

Nonjudicial Foreclosure Available Yes

If the mortgage contains a power of sale clause, then it may be foreclosed by advertisement, provided that there is a default on the mortgage. Alternatively, the lender may sue for a judgment against the borrower for the amount of the debt due and an order of sale.

Nonjudicial Foreclosure Preliminary Notices The foreclosure notice must give the names of the borrower and lender, the mortgage date, the amount due, a description of the premises, and the time and place of sale. A foreclosure notice must be published once a week for four successive weeks in a newspaper in the county where the premises are located.

Sale Procedures

Time The time must be between 9:00 AM and 5:00 PM.

Manner The sale is made by the sheriff at public auction to the highest bidder. The lender may bid, too. The winner gets a certificate of sale. Once the redemption period runs out, the buyer gets a deed. Any surplus remains on deposit with the clerk of the court for three months for possible claimants.

Postponement The sale may be postponed.

Judicial Foreclosure A lender may foreclose by filing a lawsuit in the circuit court of the county where the property is located. Service of process may be obtained by publication if necessary. The lender may seek either or both an order of sale and a judgment for the balance due on the mortgage. Once the court finds foreclosure to be appropriate, then the sale may be made by a referee or sheriff or anyone else appointed by the court. If the lender plans to bid but the borrower submits competent evidence as to value, then the court may order the premises to be sold at their fair and reasonable value less the balance due on the loan. The borrower will receive a certificate of sale at the foreclosure. A deed will be issued once the redemption period expires.

Deficiency If the mortgage is a purchase money mortgage (a loan or loans used to buy the person's property), then a deficiency judgment is not permitted in South Dakota.

Redemption If the tract of land is 40 acres or less and the mortgage contains a special power of sale clause, then a 180-day period of redemption exists. If the property is abandoned, the period becomes only 60 days. Generally, unless the special short-term redemption mortgage provisions apply, all persons may redeem within one year of the date of sale.

TENNESSEE

Judicial Foreclosure Available Yes, but rarely used

Nonjudicial Foreclosure Available Yes

In Tennessee, foreclosures are usually done under a deed of trust accompanied by a note. Regular mortgages requiring judicial foreclosure are seldom used.

Nonjudicial Foreclosure Nonjudicial foreclosure is usually done under a deed of trust that has a power of sale provision. If the deed of trust lacks such a provision, then the borrower must file a lawsuit (bill in chancery) and undertake judicial foreclosure.

Preliminary Notices

Contents The foreclosure notice should give the names of the borrower and lender, describe the property, give its street address, and state the time and place of sale.

Advertising The notice of foreclosure sale must be first published at least 30 days before the sale. The ad must be published three different times in a newspaper in the county where the land is located, and the notice of sale must be posted in at least five public places within the county, if no newspaper is published in the county. A minimum of one of these notices must be placed at the courthouse door and one more in the neighborhood where the property is located.

Sale Procedures

Time The time of sale shall be between the hours of 10:00 AM and 4:00 PM on the day specified in the foreclosure notice.

Place The sale is made at the place specified in the foreclosure notice, which is normally the courthouse door.

Manner The sheriff of each county in the state of Tennessee may set a minimum acceptable price for the property as long as the price is equal to or greater than 50 percent of the fair market value.

Deficiency A lender may seek a deficiency judgment against persons who assume debt.

Redemption The redemption period is two years. The right of redemption can be waived in the original deed of trust.

TEXAS

Judicial Foreclosure Available Yes

Nonjudicial Foreclosure Available Yes.

Nonjudicial foreclosure using the power of sale clause in a deed of trust is the most common form of foreclosure.

Preliminary Notices

Twenty-Day Demand Letter The lender must mail a residential borrower a demand letter giving the borrower 20 days to come up with all missed payments before proceeding with a foreclosure or sending the 21-day notice.

Foreclosure Notice (21 Days) The trustee must send a foreclosure notice stating the date, place, and earliest time of foreclosure.

Method of Giving Notice

Advertising Texas does not require preliminary advertising of the foreclosure in a newspaper.

Posting Texas requires a foreclosure notice to be posted at the county courthouse door 21 days before foreclosure.

Recording/Filing Texas requires a foreclosure notice to be filed with the county clerk 21days before foreclosure.

Mailing A foreclosure notice must be mailed to the borrower at the last known address as shown in the records of the lender 21 days before foreclosure.

Sale Procedures The foreclosure sale must take place on the first Tuesday of any month, even if it is a holiday such as the Fourth of July or New Year's Day, but only after the proper preliminary notices have been given. The sale is on the courthouse steps by auction to the highest bidder for cash. Lenders, however, can bid by canceling out the balance due on the note or some part of it. There is no organization to the sales. The trustee named in the deed of trust simply shows up and calls out the property for sale. The trustee or a lender representative then bids for the lender. Investors must find the trustee in a noisy crowd to bid against the lender. The title is transferred by means of a trustee's deed.

Redemption There is no right of redemption in Texas.

Deficiency Texas now limits deficiency judgments to the difference between fair market value and the balance owed on the loan, although the borrower may have to give evidence about the market value to be sure the deficiency is kept to a minimum.

Unusual Features Texas is a very simple state in which to foreclose.

UTAH

Judicial Foreclosure Available Yes

Nonjudicial Foreclosure Available Yes

Utah recognizes judicial foreclosure. There may be but one action for recovery of the debt or any foreclosure sale. Lenders can foreclose either judicially or nonjudicially, but only one of the two can be used—not both. That's the one-action rule.

Judicial Foreclosure

Procedure The lender must file a lawsuit seeking foreclosure. If the court finds there has been a default, it may order the foreclosure sale to proceed. The court will also adjudge the amount due on the defaulted loan. The sheriff will conduct the sale under court order in the same manner as normal execution sales. The sheriff will publish notices and conduct a public sale. Any surplus from the sale will go to the person who is owed the money, by court order, or stay on deposit with the court until it decides how to distribute it.

Special Procedures The borrower may be restrained by a court injunction from injuring the real property during the foreclosure of the mortgage or during a foreclosure execution sale.

Deficiency Utah allows deficiency judgments. If the foreclosure sale proceeds are insufficient to pay off the loan balance to the lender, then execution may be issued by the court after the sale to seize property until the debt is repaid.

Redemption Utah recognizes a right of redemption after the sale in the same way as for regular judgments. However, a Utah court sitting in equity may extend the time for redemption, so there is no set length of time.

Nonjudicial Foreclosure The formal foreclosure proceedings begin when the lender instructs a trustee (usually an attorney) to record a Notice of Default with the county recorders office. From the time that the notice is recorded, the borrower has a 90-day reinstatement period. During this time, to the borrower may bring the loan current by paying all the back payments along with late charges, interest, attorney's fees, etc. After this 90-day reinstatement period, the trustee will usually record a Notice of Trustees' Sale. This starts the final right of redemption period, which lasts three weeks. During this time, notice is placed on the property and in a regularly circulating newspaper for three consecutive weeks, giving the time, date, and location of the trustees' sale. After the final right of redemption period, the property is sold at auction to the highest bidder.

VERMONT

Vermont allows foreclosure either by filing a lawsuit to obtain strict foreclosure, in which the title given to the lender by deed will be ruled to be final, or by filing a lawsuit to foreclose under a power of sale clause in a deed of trust. Both procedures are governed by the Vermont Rules of Civil Procedure. There is a statute for deed of trust foreclosure (Vt Stat. Ann tit 12, §4531a). Under Vermont's strict foreclosure procedures, the lender gets a deed to the property at the outset of the loan, but the deed also provides that the borrower can get the title back by repaying the loan. All the lender has to do is get a court declaration that the borrower has failed to meet the condition, and the title becomes final in the name of the lender after a statutory redemption period passes, during which the borrower can recover the property by paying off the rest of the loan.

Strict Foreclosure In strict foreclosure, a complaint (lawsuit) must be filed in county court. The complaint and a summons to the borrower to appear and answer the complaint must be served on the borrower. The complaint must state the borrower's and lender's names, the date of the mortgage deed, a description of the debt owed, and a claim for attorney's fees, if any are sought. It must state that the reason the lender is foreclosing is a breach in the deed's conditions. Although the lawsuit prays for the court to foreclose the borrower's right to redeem the property, the borrower nevertheless has a right to redeem under Vermont's statutes. Under Vermont statutes, the time for redemption is one year for pre-1968 mortgages and six months for post-1968 mortgages. However, the lender can request a shorter time for good cause. Once the complaint is served, the lender may move for summary judgment to avoid a trial.

Nonjudicial Foreclosure Due to Vermont's long tradition of strict foreclosure, a foreclosure sale under a power of sale clause has only recently become common in residential loans, although it has been common in commercial transactions. In Vermont, a lender must still bring a lawsuit to foreclose a deed of trust and obtain an order for a sale. However, the foreclosure may not take place until seven months have passed from the date the lawsuit was served on the borrower, unless the borrower and lender agree otherwise or the borrower is damaging the property.

Deficiency In Vermont a lender may sue the borrower to collect deficiency if the foreclosure sale under the deed of trust was not sufficient to repay the loan plus the foreclosure expenses. However, if the lender buys at the foreclosure sale, the borrower can force the lender to credit the fair market value of the property against the total amount owed, which includes the loan balance and the foreclosure expenses. If the foreclosure sale generates a surplus, junior lienholders and creditors may claim it up to the amount owed in the order of their priority.

VIRGINIA

Judicial Foreclosure Available Yes

Nonjudicial Foreclosure Available Yes

Either a judicial foreclosure in the form of a bill of equity or a sale by advertisement pursuant to a power of sale clause in a deed of trust is permitted in Virginia.

Judicial Foreclosure In Virginia, a mortgage may be foreclosed by filing a type of lawsuit known as a "bill in equity." When and if necessary, a deed of trust could also be foreclosed through court action. In either case, a court order can be issued that specifies the terms and conditions of the sale, which are controlled by the mortgage contract. Commissioners are appointed to handle such sales. The court must confirm the sale.

Nonjudicial Foreclosure The trustee under the deed of trust may accelerate the note, give the necessary preliminary notices, and arrange the foreclosure sale.

Preliminary Notices

Contents The foreclosure sale ad must include anything required by the deed of trust and may include a legal description of the property, a street address, and a tax map identification or general information about the property's location. The notice must include the time, place, and terms of sale. It must give the name of the trustee and the address and phone number of a person who will be able to respond to inquiries about the foreclosure sale.

Advertising Even if the deed of trust provides for advertising, ads should be published no less once a day for three days, which may be consecutive days. If the deed of trust does not provide for advertising, then the ad shall be run once a week for four successive weeks. However, near a city, an ad on five different days, which may be consecutive, will be sufficient.

Mailing A copy of the advertisement or a notice with the same information must be mailed to the borrower at least 14 days before the foreclosure sale.

Sale Procedures

Time of Sale The sale must be made no earlier than 8 days after the first ad and no more than 30 days after the last advertisement.

Special Procedures Written one-price bids may be made and received by the trustee for entry by announcement at the foreclosure sale. Any bidder who attends the foreclosure may inspect the written bids.

Manner The sale is to be made at auction to the highest bidder. Unless otherwise required by the deed of trust, the trustee may require a bidder to make a 10 percent cash deposit. The trustee must apply the proceeds of the sale first to expenses of the sale, including a 5 percent trustee's commission; second to unpaid taxes, assessments, and levies; third to liens in order of their priority; and the balance, if any, to the borrower. The trustee will execute and deliver a deed to the buyer.

Deficiency A lender may pursue a borrower for a deficiency judgment in Virginia. No limits are imposed.

Redemption In a court-ordered foreclosure sale, the court may give the borrower a redemption period. The borrower has 240 days from the date of the sale to redeem the property by paying the amount for which the property was sold, plus 6 percent interest. Otherwise, Virginia does not give borrowers redemption rights.

WASHINGTON

Judicial Foreclosure Available Yes

Nonjudicial Foreclosure Available Yes

Nonjudicial Foreclosure Nonjudicial foreclosure proceedings are permitted in Washington, provided there is a power of sale clause in the trust deed and the real property is not used for agricultural purposes. There can be no pending lawsuit for foreclosure at the same time as a nonjudicial procedure is attempted. Default must be defined in the trust deed.

Preliminary Notices

Advertising The trustee must publish the notice of sale as follows: once between the 32nd and 28th days before sale and once between the eleventh and seventh days before sale.

Mailing A written notice of the foreclosure sale must be mailed certified mail, return receipt requested, to the borrower at her last known address at least 30 days before recording the notice of sale (120 days before foreclosure). It may be personally served instead.

Recording At least 90 days before sale, the trustee must record a notice of the foreclosure sale and mail it to any person with a lien or claim against the property.

Posting At least 90 days before sale, the trustee must post the foreclosure notice on the premises to be foreclosed on.

Cure Until 11 days before the sale, the borrower may cure the default by paying the past-due payments plus expenses, including the trustee's and attorney's fees. Curing the default stops the foreclosure.

Sale Procedures

Time The time of sale is specified in the notice of sale, but it must be not less than 190 days from the date of default.

Postponement The trustee may postpone the sale.

Manner The sale is to the highest bidder.

Deficiency If nonjudicial foreclosure is selected by the lender, then it cannot sue for a deficiency judgment. On judicial foreclosure sales, the borrower can be sued for a deficiency, unless the property is found to be abandoned for six months before the decree of foreclosure.

WASHINGTON, D.C.

Washington, D.C., under the D.C. Code, uses nonjudicial foreclosure under a power of sale clause granted in a deed of trust.

Sales Procedures Normally, a Washington, D.C., deed of trust will fix the time periods for notice of the foreclosure sale. If it does not, then the dates may be set by any interested party by going to court and getting a court order to set them.

Preliminary Notices A notice of sale must be given to the owner of the property at his last known address and furnished to the mayor, or the mayor's agent at least 30 days before the foreclosure sale. Otherwise, the foreclosure is not valid.

Reinstatement Once in a given year, the debtor may reinstate the loan up to five days before the foreclosure sale by paying all sums that are past due on the loan, including late charges and penalties, regardless of whether the loan was accelerated or not.

Sale The sale will be made by a trustee by public bid.

Redemption There is no right of redemption after a deed of trust foreclosure sale.

Deficiency A lawsuit for a deficiency may be brought against the borrower for any amount due on the loan that was left unpaid after the foreclosure sale.

WEST VIRGINIA

Judicial Foreclosure Available Yes

Nonjudicial Foreclosure Available Yes

Although judicial foreclosure is available for vendor's lien foreclosures, West Virginia uses the deed of trust almost exclusively. Mortgages have largely disappeared. If there is a default under the deed of trust, then the trustee must send out preliminary notices and then sell the property when the lender so requests.

Preliminary Notices

Contents A notice of sale must contain the time and place of the foreclosure sale, the names of the parties to the deed, the date of the deed, recording information, a property description, and the terms of the sale.

Advertising In pre-1980 deeds of trust, the buyer may have waived the right to published notice. Later deeds of trust must publish a Class III legal advertisement countywide before the sale at least once a week for four weeks.

Posting The notice of sale must be posted at least 20 days prior to sale on the front door of the courthouse for the county in which the property to be sold is located and in three other public places, one of which must be the property to be foreclosed on.

Service Unless expressly waived in the deed of trust, the borrower must be served with a copy of the notice of foreclosure at least 20 days before the foreclosure sale.

Mailing Notice of the foreclosure sale should be mailed to the borrower and subordinate lienholders 20 days prior to sale.

Sale Procedures

Time and Place The time and place of sale are specified in the foreclosure notice.

Manner The sale is completed by public auction to the highest bidder.

Terms The deed may specify the terms of sale. Otherwise, a buyer may pay one-third in cash at the sale, one-third a year later, and one-third two years from the day of sale.

Report A report of the sale must be filed with the clerk of the county and recorded.

Deficiency A lender can maintain a deficiency action only by filing a separate lawsuit. However, if the lawsuit is filed to collect, the deed of trust foreclosure must then be delayed during the lawsuit.

Redemption There is no right to redeem after a deed of trust sale.

WISCONSIN

Judicial Foreclosure Available Yes

Nonjudicial Foreclosure Available Yes

If the mortgage contains a power of sale clause, it may be foreclosed by advertisement in Wisconsin without going through a lawsuit. On the other hand, if there is no power of sale clause, the mortgage must be foreclosed judicially by filing a lawsuit and obtaining a court-ordered sale.

Judicial Foreclosure The lender may file a lawsuit seeking a court order for foreclosure and/or a deficiency judgment for any money the sale doesn't produce. The court will set the date, time, place, and manner of sale. Usually, it is conducted by the sheriff. No sale may be made for one year from the date the judgment is entered, unless the lender waives the right to a deficiency, in which case the delay is six months, or two months if the property is abandoned. Sales by consent may be earlier.

Foreclosure by Advertisement Preliminary Notices

Contents The foreclosure notice must specify the names of the borrower and lender, the date the mortgage was recorded, the amount due at the date of the notice, a property description, and the time and place of sale.

Recording The foreclosure notice must be recorded when the foreclosure notice is first published.

Advertising A foreclosure notice with the time and place of sale must be published once a week for six consecutive weeks in a newspaper published in the county where the real estate is located.

Service Mailing is not adequate. The foreclosure notice must be served upon the borrower in the same manner that civil process in a lawsuit is served. If the borrower cannot be found, then the notice shall be posted in a conspicuous spot on the mortgaged premises and served on any occupant.

Sale Procedures

Time The sale takes place between 9:00 AM and sunset.

Place The sale occurs at the place given in the foreclosure notice.

Manner The sale shall be at public auction to the highest bidder. The person who normally calls out the sale must be either the person appointed for the task in the mortgage or the sheriff. The sale may be postponed, if necessary. The person making the sale must give the purchaser a certificate, in writing, entitling the buyer to a deed. The certificate must be filed where deeds are recorded. If the property is not redeemed, the person making the sale must execute a deed to the buyer.

Sale Confirmation Wisconsin law provides a procedure by which a foreclosure sale may be confirmed by court order after it is made.

Redemption If a sale is confirmed, then there is no right of redemption. Otherwise, there is a one-year right of redemption if the high bid at the foreclosure sale, plus interest, is paid. During such a period, the borrower may also retain possession.

Deficiency A deficiency judgment is not allowed unless the application for sales confirmation states the lender's intent to seek one. Otherwise, it is a separate portion of any existing legal action or a separate action altogether. It will not be final until on or after the sale confirmation.

WYOMING

Judicial Foreclosure Available Yes

Nonjudicial Foreclosure Available No

Foreclosure by Advertisement Wyoming permits the use of a deed of trust that allows foreclosure by advertisement. The deed of trust names a trustee who will conduct the foreclosure.

Preliminary Notices

Advertising Notice of the foreclosure must be published once a week for four consecutive weeks in the newspaper for the county in which the property is located.

Mailing Notice must be mailed or delivered to the borrower and the occupant at least ten days before the first publication of ads in the newspapers.

Time The foreclosure sale must take place at public auction between the hours of 9:00 AM and 5:00 PM.

Judicial Foreclosure In judicial foreclosure, the lender forecloses by filing a lawsuit and obtaining a court-ordered sale. There are no prescribed advertising procedures on court-ordered sales, but they are usually advertised. The sheriff usually conducts the sale. The sale takes place between the hours of 10:00 AM and 5:00 PM. The sheriff will then issue a certificate of purchase to the high bidder at public auction.

Deficiency A lender may sue for a deficiency if there is a note associated with the mortgage or deed of trust or it contains a separate covenant to pay.

Redemption Redemption is permitted.

Special Addendum

FORECLOSURE RESCUE SCHEMES ANS SCAMS

Foreclosure is a frightening situation. Many people are so embarrassed about, or frightened about, or confused about foreclosure that they must have outside help. Experts are available, but often for a price, such as attorneys. Good real estate brokers can be invaluable, but they are usually looking for a sale and a commission, and that may not be the route you want to go. Worst of all, homeowners faced with foreclosure put off confronting the situation too long, hoping against hope, that somehow, things will get better. At that point, out of time for better approaches, yet faced with a desperate foreclosure situation, unsuspecting homeowners may be scammed by "foreclosure rescue services." Although there are legitimate foreclosure help agencies and operations which can helpful, particularly some of the non—profit and governmentally sponsored programs in some states, there are those that are not. Homeowners faced with foreclosure should be aware that scam artists exploit the type of situation you may be in, to their advantage, not yours. Sadly, these hucksters are widespread. For an analysis and examples of some of the foreclosure scam buccaneers of the home piracy industry, go to the following website for a detailed, highly readable, and free 68 page report on foreclosure scams: www.consumerlaw.org/news/ForeclosureReportFinald.pdf

This report is mandatory reading for those faced with foreclosure in general and in particular, anyone who is considering using a foreclosure consulting firm. If they look like a scammer, avoid them. Look hard. Under affinity marketing methods, the scammers may target you with a someone of the same ethnicity, language, race, military service, background and so on—a "one of us" approach that is cruelly deceptive. Remember scam artists often work through someone they think you might know and trust.

At the other end of the scale—there are some unorthodox but legal tools that can be used if unusual circumstances are there. It is also worthwhile to point out that buried in some of these scams are the threads of legitimate rescue techniques which a homeowner might well use—beyond simply fighting the foreclosure in court, declaring bankruptcy, or, as is the main theme of this book, running through every option with the lender. Depending on how talented you are at dealing with your predicament, you might be surprised at what ingenuity can come up with—besides a new job or source of income—there are ways and means that can work and we'll describe some of them here. First, however, it's fun to learn how to work the levers by learning about the scams. The key to scammers is to focus on: (1) where the money might come from (we know who it goes to—the scammer); (2) what tricks to use to separate the homeowner from their money or assets; and (3) how to tell legitimate and helpful folks from illegitimate folks.

Look at Matters from a Scam Artists View—Keep Your Eye on the Money

One of the best ways to detect or analyze a scam is to keep a careful eye on the money—where is it coming from and where is it going to. It's going to the scammer, of course, but it may do so through many indirect channels. The real key is to understand where the money might be coming from—and that's the better view to start from. In a foreclosure situation, the homeowner really doesn't have much money—so how is the scam artist going to get money off of you? Here are some likely opportunities:

1. The foreclosure sufferer happens to have positive equity in the house—it's worth more than is owed, but the homeowner just can't keep up the payments. The scam artist will try to get to this equity source of wealth one way or the other. *If you have equity and are faced with foreclosure—beware—the scam artists and others of this world are looking for you—you're in just the situation they want. Be extra careful and on guard.*

2. The homeowner, faced with foreclosure, is willing to charge or otherwise pay a few dollars for supposedly helpful foreclosure services.

3. Sometimes borrowers are still able to make a few extra home payments before foreclosure, or continued payments at a reduced level. By the way, if this is so, I hope you have read the earlier chapters in this book and explored the vast number of programs and methods out there that are available from the typical lender that might be able to help you with your situation if all you can pay is reduced payments for a while, or what to do if it looks like a permanent, involuntary reduction in income or an unanticipated increase in expenses.

SOME EXAMPLES OF FRAUD SCHEMES—AMONG THE MANY

Consulting Fee Scams—"Phantom Services"

"We're experts at dealing with the lender. We know how to bargain them down. We'll get some relief for you in terms of reduced payments or a payout plan. We charge only modest fees. " In one California case (in the Consumer law report website), one such entity charged several fees totaling nearly $2,000. The report mentioned they had an estimated 1,800 clients. Now, as a hypothetical matter, consider that if a consulting service got $2,000 in fees, from 2,000 people, that's a cool four (4) million dollars. What do bogus consulting operations do for their fees? Basically, little or nothing except collect through the debit card or bank draft authorization you give them to make sure they get their fees. It's a scam.

Payment Scams:

" Just send us your payments and we'll get to work getting you out of foreclosure on the missing payments." The scam artists talk you into sending your house payment to the scam artist, who does not send it to the lender. Wham, he's gone, and so is the money. That's the sting. Many other excuses might be made—it's an "assumption" situation—deed the property to us, we'll take over your loan, send us a reduced payment as rent, and you'll be out of this jam before you know. You may not find out until the angry lender alerts you that you are yet more payments behind—now with reduced resources and foreclosure imminent. Your cash reserves, such as they were, are shot, either by making the payments, or even faster if the scam artist argued for "cash up front" to be willing to take on an "upside down" house which will take time to go up in value, or a home whose rental value won't equal the current market rate, so a "subsidy" in cash is needed.

The Equity Rip—off

There are many variations on this theme. All of them have one element in common: one way or the other, the scammer is trying to get your equity in your house away from you and pocket it. Many different schemes exist for accomplishing this.

Equity in House—Find Out How Much, If Any, You Have

Equity is the amount by which the house is worth more than what you owe. If your house will sell for a fair price of $400,000, and you owe only $250,000 on your mortgage, you've got $150,000 in equity. ($400,000=$250,000 = $150,000). If you're not sure about how much, if any equity you have, you need to find out how much it is, badly. If you know a broker who can give you a BPO (Broker Price Opinion — $50—$100) , or if you know an appraiser and are willing to pay $300—$400 (the most accurate method), or in some states, tax value from the internet may be helpful, but be very careful about assuming the tax value is the home's fair market value. In many cases, it's computed differently. What we need to know, is about how much your house should sell for in a fair sale. Then find out how much you owe, either by studying your documents from the closing from the lender (amortization table) or getting on—line and google or yahoo "mortgage calculator" and millions of "hits" we'll show a site that you can plug in your home's interest rate, loan amount, and term into and it will generate an amortization table that you can check through until you see how far along you are in dollar terms in paying off your mortgage. Subtract loan balance from the home's worth, and "presto" there's your equity.

Equity Scams

There are many types of scam that are designed to extract the equity in your house for the benefit of the foreclosure rescue service. Here are a few basic types:

Rent to Own—Sorry borrower, you're so close to foreclosure and your credit situation is so bad, there's only one thing to do—convey the title to your house to our trusty third party. At the same time, we'll make up the missed payments on the mortgage. We'll then rent the house to you for low payments at first, but later on, as you get back on your feet, they'll increase. Of course, we'll count every penny towards your purchase. If you get enough money together, fast enough, you'll succeed in buying back your house. At least this way, you won't lose it in foreclosure, and above all, you can continue to live in it.

The Drawbacks—What the scam artists do is have an attorney draw up paperwork that makes it very difficult to ever pay enough to actually get the house back. The rent may escalate. Fail to pay it and they will ruthlessly, and heartlessly evict. They will also abruptly terminate any further counting of your payments towards the purchase. They may not even tell you that's happened. Breach of any of the terms of the contract, which may become very burdensome over time, and they're right there to cut you off. They want you to fail, because then they'll get your house and all your equity—and you signed it over to them, trusting you were saving yourself. It was more like out of the frying pan and into the fire.

Lease with Option to Purchase — This is similar to rent to own. You get to stay in the property, for now. You deed the property to the rescue company to avoid foreclosure at the last minute. They pick up the back payments. (We hope). They produce paperwork for you to sign. The deal is structured so that the payments count only as rent and not towards any purchase. However, for a small extra fee, they will give you an "option" to buy back you house, which you may exercise when you get the money.

The Drawbacks: Unfortunately the price may be close to market price and you're actually buying back your house at full value, or near it, with the rescue company keeping the paid back equity as a profit. Once again, they want you to default so the option is lost by its own terms.

Move Out and Deed the Property Over the Rescue Service. If the borrower can't afford any payments at all, this works. The theory that is foisted on the borrowers is that by moving out, the house can now be rented, which provides the income stream necessary to refinance the property. The rescue service will arrange the refinance, or use their own funds to make arrangements with the principal lender who was about to foreclose.

The Drawbacks—You've not only deeded your house to someo ne else, but moved out and let them have the rent from a tenant as well. Even if you get your house back someday, it may not be like it once was — much worse for the wear. That's just the problem, the rescue service's contract will no doubt impose heavy burdens, such as sharp time limits to exercise a repurchase option, or perhaps mechanisms for skyrocketing the buyback figure. They want to make it as hard as possible for the buyer to get their home back. Few borrowers succeed in recovering their home. However, the rescue service will recover your equity and often pocket a princely sum. It was money you could have had by selling the house through a good broker for market value. Alternatively, things might have been worked out with the lender through forbearance and even loan modification.

Equity Fraudsters

Misrepresentation–Not all the equity scammers are up front about what they're doing. They may write documents that look innocent enough, or resemble documents they think you're more comfortable signing. In reality, they may have the legendary fine print or half hidden provisions that in fact deed the property to the rescue outfit. They may outright lie or misrepresent the situation to get you to sign.

Blanks to Fill In– Another variation on this theme is to get you to sign a document with blanks left to be filled in. They will fill them in for you in ways they don't tell you about—ways that will cause you to lose your home and your equity. And you signed it. I hope borrowers always remember to get a copy of whatever they sign, exactly the way they signed it, at the exact time they signed it. Never let people send it to you the next day, or come back and pick it up later. Now, period. This is true even if it's closed at a title company or a lawyer's office.

Forgers

Forgers are among the scariest people to deal with. This is outright criminal behavior. There's a rule of law you should know: in most states, a forged deed will not stand up in court. The courts will not give good, legal title from a bad, forged deed. If they did, the world would be much more full of skilled forgers. However, the goal of the outright forgers may be to pass title to a supposedly "innocent third party" who hotly denies they knew anything about the forgery and hotly protests they paid in full—sue the forger, not me for the damages, I'm innocent! However, the forgers are all too seldom found at this point, and if you can find them, I'll bet you won't find the money with them. Rescue service forgeries may revolve around the naive homeowner facing foreclosure to give up plenty of information about the status of title and then forge ahead with their purchase—and your loss.

PREDATORY LENDERS

Foreclosure rescue services sometimes come in the guise of lenders who will give you a loan no regular lender would. Your credit may be shot, your income isn't there, but you have equity, and that's the key to the mysteriously generous nature of the credit predatory lenders extend. The predatory lenders may well give you a loan, pay off the old lender, and then turn around and start charging ever increasing "adjustable rate" interest to the point you can't afford to pay. They will foreclose in a heartbeat to get your equity—one little slip on payments may be all it takes. There's the problem: they aren't out for the interest, they're out for your house and pocketing your equity.

Predatory lenders are often more likely to be caught afoul of lending regulations or consumer lending protection regulations in various states than pure investor buyers. However, the mortgage industry nationwide has been one of the last strongholds of non or low regulation for years. The predatory lending may well be done by people who were connected with legitimate lending for years and know the ropes and where to step to stay just out of trouble. Check out any foreclosure rescue lenders you deal with.

Drawbacks—These lenders intend to make you a loan they know you have no reasonable prospect of paying back given your circumstances, which they check out pretty carefully. (Credit report, appraisal, , and so on). In some states, making a loan with no reasonable prospects for repayment is illegal. Unfortunately, some of this has been done by regular lenders in the ARM and related fields, which may make it difficult to attack legally unless the state you're in has unusually stringent laws.

Sharp Dealers

Sometimes people come to buy your house when you're facing foreclosure and they do not really represent themselves as a rescue service per se, but they argue that their deal is better than foreclosure. Some of them don't even do that much, they tell the hapless borrower very little, but waive cash, literally cash, in front of funds starved homeowners about to be foreclosed on in exchange for signing papers that will give up most of your equity. If they lie or misrepresent the situation, there will be recourse. However, if they merely get you to sign away your property for a song, it may be tough to attack through the legal system.

Drawback– These deals are set up so they're not easy to reverse. Additionally, the sharp dealers are often a bottomless pit of money compared to the homeowner who has little to pay a lawyer with. Lawyers are hard to find who would ever handle such cases pro—bono or on a "contingency basis."

Borderline Dealers

Sometimes the borderline dealer is actually open and on the table about the deal. Let's say, the homeowner is one day before foreclosure and has done virtually nothing. It's usually too late at this point to go back to the lender, although you could always try. A straight sale by a broker to a regular buyer is pretty much out of the question time wise. The borderline investor buyer may simply say: if you deed the property to me, in full, now, I'll pay you several thousand in cash, which you can really use right now. That won't protect your equity, but if it's too late, if you don't sell now, you may lose much or all your equity in tomorrow's foreclosure sale—best to sell now." It may be very true in that state. Sell to them now may be the best bet from strict economics, even if it's not fair. (Go talk to a bankruptcy attorney first though—but one day may not be enough even for them). The buyer hammers the message home: Best to sell to us, now! Besides, we'll pull the loan current and it will only show as a sale , not a foreclosure, on your credit record. You'll recover much faster this way than simply letting it go to foreclosure. Unfortunately, there may be a point close enough to foreclosure that everything they say is quite true. Your choice, albeit one with harsh consequences. They'll probably have the deed ready for you to sign.

Drawbacks—once in a while the buyer does a double check, decides it really isn't such a good deal, throws the deed in the trash, and leave s the borrower to his or her fate. One thing for sure, the borrower's credit is sure to be blasted. They may not even know... Most borrowers wouldn't be quick enough to sign a contract that forced the buyer to pay off the foreclosure, it would be just assumed they would do so. Don't assume. Don't guess, get your own lawyer to look out for your interests, the borderline dealers surely won't do so.

METHODS OF AVOIDING TROUBLE

There are many things homeowners faced with foreclosure should do to avoid falling into the clutches of fraudulent foreclosure rescue services.

Act Early to Deal with Your Foreclosure– Homeowners should realize that procrastination by borrowers is one of the best and most faithful allies the foreclosure rip off artist has to work with. By starting early, the lender can analyze your situation, you might find a good workout specialist to work with, and they may get you back on your feet with a good forbearance or modification plan. Failing in that, or not even trying because you know it won't work, getting busy early allows listing the house with a competent, capable regular real estate broker who can hard market the property to get you the best price within the time frame you have. If you have less than needed, you still get as much as you could, under the circumstances.

Use the Proper Experts– Find a good workout specialist with your lender. Win them over to your side. If so, they may know all kinds of tricks to slide you through. Make them want to help you. Many do. If you sell, consider using a competent, capable, professional broker. Why not do a for sale by owner? (FSB0) You can try, but FSBO's seem to work best in a very up market where brokers function more like order takers than brokers. It's in a down market that brokers and salespersons really earn their stripes as top notch real estate agents. They know where to find the scarce buyers, they know where and how to find the scarce financing and they know how to work with lenders. In down market areas you'll see many websites for excellent brokers who market to the foreclosure side of the business. Study them carefully, ask many questions, check references and choose. Help from a trustworthy friend who is a licensed broker, such as the one who helped you buy the house, may be a great place to start. Retired brokers. Family member brokers. Fine someone who knows brokers and can give you a referral to a first class broker. Find good attorneys much the same way. Look for credentials. CRS for brokers, for example. Certification as a real estate specialist for attorneys. Check for experience and background. If you have standards, scam artists need not apply.

Act Diligently. Dig up needed documents. Make appointments. Think about your situation, even if you hate to. Diligence is the key to dealing successfully with foreclosure.

Recognize the Risks–Sometimes people miss a payment, and nothing much happens. Then another, and again, nothing much happens. Unfortunately, the day will come when things really will happen and you may wish very much you had taken prompt, earlier action to deal with the situation. If you don't take the situation seriously, you could lose your house.

Review Documents Carefully Before Signing. If at all possible, get an attorney. Please! Por favor! If there's no way, and you feel you must sign legal documents, read them very carefully. If you can't stand them, take them to an attorney. Ask questions. Get confirmations of promises in writing. E— mails can be very, very handy for this purpose—and devastating the other way—be careful what you say on the net.

Keep You Eyes Open– Don't respond to pushy people. Foreclosure rescue services who try to control you are very bad. For example, they might tell you not to talk to attorneys, not to talk to brokers, not to talk to the lender. This advice is almost always bad advice. They're trying to isolate you from people who could help you and who may care. Once you're isolated, you're far easier to manipulate and control. In general, you're better off seeking an expert than letting one find you in a mass solicitation.

CHECK LIST FOR SCAM PREVENTION

The Department of Justice's U.S. Trustee program has a good checklist—summarize:

Here are several ways to spot possible scam operations:

- They call themselves a "mortgage consultant" a "foreclosure rescue service" or something similar.

- The y market by ads and solicitations to people who are immediately faced with foreclosure, this is PARTICULARLY TRUE IF YOU HAVE EQUITY in you r home (that makes a prime target—many, many people faced with foreclosure ¹ little or no equity).

- They try to charge fees BEFORE provid¡~ ʳCAUTION: bankruptcy attorneys will get money up front!)

- Tells you to m⌐¹ company, and not your lender. THIᶜ ⌐

npany. GET AN ATTORNEY do it.

ᵖPROACHES TO

ssible, such as attorneys

Th
or ⱼ

't's not the best set of
her, a sister, or other
single person who
les and unmarried
rd and rent it out.
it people think—
k on naive, new
omplexes. Use
lsewhere and
er procedure
it's smooth
runnin
2. A "rich ⌐t of it. They
may evei ou know. Surprisingly,
even an "ε and it wasn't a bitter divorce. This
person can ɪoan, bring it current, or otherwise give a lot
of power to ᴜsure. The documents, however, should all be carefully
prepare and an attorney first, even though it's family or friends you're dealing
with, and mos. particularly because we want to make sure everyone knows what their rights
and obligations are and it will act to preserve rather than damage a valuable relationship.
They can get a secured loan back against the equity in your home. The loan can be paid as
agreed, or just save repayment until the house is later sold, or the house is refinanced.
3. Sell a car, a boat, or something of value—even jewelry. Sometimes people forget they may
own something that they would rather part with than their house. Selling the item to raise the
needed money for a workout or for some other foreclosure deal may be just the thing to make
it fly by providing a little badly needed cash. In Houston in the 1980's we were treated to the

spectacle of the "RIver Oaks" pawnshop—they sent out a limousine with tinted windows, to preserve appearances and be discrete. The limo dropped the rich (or onetime rich) passenger off at the special back entrance. Individual service followed and careful handling of the items to be pawned. It was all very, very upscale and the operation did quite a business. Crude, but just as effective in a rich neighborhood as a poor one. In these days of e-bay, things can be sold with surprising speed.

4. We must assume you've made a careful check of 401(K)'s, (retirement funds may be tapped), or of the cash value of life insurance, or loans on your life insurance. It's there, use it.

CONCLUSIONS: THINK IT THROUGH

If you get the needed information and expert advice, act early, keep your eyes open and try, your odds of surviving a foreclosure with as good a result as you might expect, and maybe better, just might save your home. Don't give up. Don't go into depression or suspend all belief in reality. Sometimes the mental battle is more than half the battle in dealing with foreclosure. Think it through —it's worth it.

Glossary

Abandonment The situation in which a homeowner leaves a house with no intention to return.

Abstract of judgment (AJ) An abstract is a summary; an abstract of judgment is a summary of a judgment, and a judgment is the end result of a lawsuit. A judgment may run many pages, while an abstract of judgment typically runs one or two pages. It shows who won the lawsuit, who lost, how much is owed, what court made the decision, the date of the judgment, and the attorney for the winner of the lawsuit. Once the abstract of judgment is recorded (filed with the county clerk or county recorder), it creates a general lien on the judgment debtor's property, including the real estate. An abstract of judgment will be discovered by a title company whenever a landowner tries to sell the land. Most title companies will demand that it be paid off as a condition of insuring the resale.

Acceleration To make the future payments on a loan due immediately so that the entire unpaid portion of the loan is due. When a borrower misses payments, the lender does not have to sue for each missed payment one by one until the end of the loan. Instead, the lender can sue the borrower for the entire amount of the principal balance that remains unpaid. However, the lender may not sue for future interest.

Adjustable rate mortgage A loan that has an interest rate that can go up or down at certain intervals, called periods, and within certain limits, called "caps." The loan is secured by a house, on which the lender will foreclose if the loan is not paid.

AJ *See* Abstract of judgment.

Amortization A method of calculating the payments on a loan such that, at a given interest rate, a loan payment of a set size will repay the loan over a certain period of time. Amortization is used to determine the amount of mortgage payments.

As is When a property is sold as is, the seller does not warrant or guarantee that the property is free of defects. The buyer accepts the property in its present condition, without modification.

Assignment A procedure in which a loan is turned over to the secretary of Housing and Urban Development. The loan, which started out as a privately owned but FHA-insured loan, becomes a HUD-owned loan.

Assignment of rents A procedure in which a borrower gives a lender the right to receive the rents collected from a tenant in a building owned by the borrower.

Assumes and agrees to pay A clause in a deed or related document under which a buyer who takes over payments on the seller's old loan also agrees to pay the old loan. The buyer will normally receive title and make the payments. The "assumes and agrees to pay" language is often found in the consideration section of the deed that transfers title from the seller to the buyer in such an assumption. The seller may or may not be released from liability, but in either case, the buyer is legally responsible to make payments on the loan.

Assumption A procedure in which a buyer takes over payments on the seller's old loan. Title is transferred from the seller to the buyer.

Auction The process of selling property at a public sale to the highest bidder. The person conducting the sale will call out the initial asking price and each price that anyone in the audience bids until no one will bid a higher price. The auctioneer then calls out, "Going once, going twice, sold to the highest bidder!"

Automatic stay A bankruptcy court order. When bankruptcy is filed, the bankruptcy court issues a court order that prevents any creditor from attempting to collect any debt from the person who declared bankruptcy. Creditors, even though they are owed money, may not undertake foreclosure, repossession, eviction, or seizure or even call or write the debtor demanding payment. Instead, they must come to the bankruptcy court and seek the money they are owed together with other creditors. Also called a "freeze order."

Balance owed on the loan The part of the loan that remains unpaid by the borrower at a given point in time.

Bankruptcy A specialized court proceeding in which a person who owes more than he has and lacks the resources to pay obligations on a current basis can either restructure loan payments or have all but a few debts discharged. The person must in turn give up all but a few exempt assets in an effort to pay creditors what they are owed.

Bill of complaint The initial paperwork filed in many states to begin a foreclosure. It is part of the process of filing a lawsuit.

Bond Money or assets that are available if needed to pay to a court or other named person upon a certain event.

BPO *See* Broker price opinion.

Broker price opinion (BPO) A real estate broker's estimate of the price for which property can reasonably be sold. The broker price opinion is often much cheaper than a professional appraisal, but it is often just as good or even more useful, because it tells the owner at what price the property can be marketed successfully.

Buydown An arrangement in which the seller of real estate pays some or all of the buyer's loan costs, usually measured by increments of 1 percent of the loan (called "points"). The seller pays enough points to the lender to permit it to offer the buyer's loan at a reduced interest rate, which reduces the monthly payment. The cost to the seller is small, but the reduction in payments to the buyer is often quite substantial. Buydown arrangements are often structured to reduce the interest rate, and therefore the monthly payments, in the early years of the loan. In a 3-2-1 buydown, for example, a seller will pay enough points to reduce the buyer's interest rate by 3 percent, such as from 10 percent to 7 percent, the first year; then by 2 percent the second year; and by 1 percent the third year. In the fourth year, the loan interest rate and the monthly payments would return to the normal market rate of interest as set when the loan was obtained.

Certificate of reasonable value (CRV) A VA appraisal.

Certificate of sale A document indicating that a property has been sold to a buyer at foreclosure, subject to a right of redemption for a set period after the foreclosure sale. The redemption period is different for different types of foreclosures; as an example, in an IRS sale, the redemption period is 180 days. Many foreclosures take place without any certificate of sale. Instead, the sale is final, or near final, and the buyer gets a deed rather than a certificate of sale.

Chapter 7 One of the chapters in the federal Bankruptcy Code, Chapter 7 is liquidation bankruptcy in which a debtor's nonexempt assets are gathered together and given up or sold for the benefit of creditors in order of their priority. Priority creditors get much of the cash, if any. If their debts are not fully repaid, they are not discharged. Secured creditors receive continued payments or the asset that served as collateral for the loan. Unsecured creditors are usually given little or nothing in a Chapter 7 bankruptcy.

Chapter 13 One of the bankruptcy chapters in the federal Bankruptcy Code. Under Chapter 13, a wage earner can reduce debt payments through a bankruptcy court order according to the terms of a plan that will allow the debtor to pay much or even all of the original amounts owed.

Clear title Ownership rights to a piece of real estate that are not diminished by liens, leases, or other types of encumbrances—that is, no other ownership claims exist.

Collateralized mortgage obligation (CMO) A type of security sold to investors to raise money to buy mortgages.

Collections An activity in which lenders or their agents employ various techniques to put pressure on borrowers to pay what they owe.

Compromise sale A sale in which the balance owed on a VA loan is greater than the house's sale price. The difference, or loss, may be partly covered by the VA.

Condominium A land ownership arrangement in which one owns an individual unit and a percentage of common areas.

Conforming loans Loans that meet FNMA standards.

Conservatorship A state of affairs in which a bank or savings and loan association has been taken over by the FDIC or RTC, federal government agencies that manage it on a caretaker basis, either directly or through hired managers. The institution will be preserved in its existing form until it can be sold complete or broken down into its major components.

Consideration Something of value exchanged between the parties to a contract. It may consist of goods, services, or promises.

Contingency fee An employment arrangement commonly used by attorneys in which the attorney is paid a percentage of whatever money damages are awarded at the final judgment in a lawsuit.

Contract for deed A sales arrangement in which the seller holds title until the buyer finishes paying for the property. The terms of the sale and the payments are set in a written contract signed by the buyer and the seller. At the end of the payment period, the buyer gets title to the real estate by means of a deed.

Conventional lender A lender that makes conventional loans.

Conventional loan A loan that is not insured or guaranteed by any agency of the federal government—that is, a private loan.

Conveyance The process of transferring title or some interest in real estate to a new owner.

Coverage The amount of money an insurance company will pay in response to a claim.

Cram-down A Chapter 13 bankruptcy arrangement in which a plan to repay lenders and creditors, which was developed by the debtor's attorney, is ordered into effect by the bankruptcy court. It is "crammed down" on the sometimes unwilling creditors.

Credit The willingness of a borrower to repay borrowed money. It is usually measured by a borrower's past record of payments on loans and debts, which is documented in a credit report.

Credit doctor An individual who specializes in stealing or otherwise fraudulently (and criminally) obtaining good credit for a noncreditworthy borrower.

CRV *See* Certificate of reasonable value.

Cured default Correction of a borrower's failure to make payments or meet the terms of a loan to the lender's satisfaction.

Damages Monetary compensation set by a court for a loss suffered by a party to a lawsuit.

Debt collector Under federal law, a person or entity, including an attorney, that regularly collects debts for others. Debt collectors must give certain notices and follow certain procedures under the Federal Debt Collection Practices Act.

Decree The final order of a court in many states.

Deed The legal document commonly used to transfer ownership of real estate from one owner to the next.

Deed in lieu of foreclosure Instead of waiting until the lender forces the sale of the house in foreclosure, usually to the lender, the borrower just deeds the property to the lender.

Deed of trust In spite of its name, this document is really neither a deed nor a trust. Instead, it is more proper to regard it as a three-party mortgage arrangement among the borrower, the lender, and a trustee. If the borrower fails to pay, the trustee is preauthorized by the borrower to sell the house and apply the sales proceeds to pay off what remains unpaid on the loan secured by the deed of trust or to give the deed to the lender in exchange for cancellation of some or all of the borrower's debt.

Default Nonperformance or breach of one's obligations as stipulated by the legal documents that control the loan arrangement.

Defeased In medieval times, ownership rights constituted a "fee." To be defeased meant to lose the fee or, today, to lose ownership.

Defendant's original answer The first responsive pleading of a defendant in a lawsuit.

Deficiency Money a borrower who has lost real estate in foreclosure still owes to the lender because the foreclosure sale failed to generate enough to pay off the loan. Frequently, lenders acquire title to real estate at foreclosure, in which case they most often give credit only for the fair market value of the property against the balance due on the loan. Any unpaid balance on the loan after all just credits are applied is the usual amount of a deficiency. Many states limit or restrict deficiencies.

Deficiency judgment A court judgment that a defaulting borrower owes a deficiency.

Delinquency The state of affairs when payments on a note or other loan obligation are past due.

Department of Veterans Affairs (VA) The arm of the federal government that guarantees loans and performs other services for veterans. This agency was formerly known as the Veterans Administration.

Depository institution A bank or savings and loan (S&L) that accepts deposits.

Discharge of indebtedness A lender tells a borrower that a loan doesn't have to be paid back. Also called "discharge of debt."

Discovery The phase of a lawsuit in which respective parties are permitted to ask each other formal written and oral questions, obtain copies of documents, and in general find out the facts related to the lawsuit.

D'Oench, Duhme doctrine A legal doctrine that holds that when the FDIC or RTC takes over a lender, it may disallow almost any counterclaims by borrowers against such fallen lenders. The name is taken from the original law case that created the doctrine.

Double whammy Some lenders refuse to permit assumptions (one blow), while at the same time insisting on a hefty prepayment penalty when the nonassumable loan is paid off early (a second blow).

Down payment The initial cash a borrower pays to the seller to purchase a property. It does not include closing costs.

Due on encumbrance A clause in a mortgage that prevents a borrower from encumbering the title to the property with liens, leases, or other encumbrances without the lender's consent.

Due on sale A clause in a mortgage that demands that the borrower pay off the loan in full if the house is sold. The lender can't prevent the sale, but it can demand payment in full on the loan balance, which often has the same practical effect. In the absence of a due-on-sale clause, the loan is assumable without the lender's consent. Older FHA and VA loans are assumable without the consent of the lender.

Early sale A borrower faced with foreclosure tries to arrange with the lender to sell the house as early as possible to minimize any losses that would result from a normal foreclosure and subsequent resale of the home.

Earnest money contract A contract in which the seller agrees to sell and the buyer agrees to buy.

Ejectment A common-law action to obtain a court order commanding the occupant of land or a house to leave.

Entitlement The amount of money the Department of Veterans Affairs will pay on behalf of a veteran defaulting on a VA loan.

Entry and possession A method of foreclosure used in some states in which the lender, who already owns the property, re-enters it and takes possession away from the borrower, either by mutual agreement or by court order.

Equity The excess of fair market value over the outstanding loan balance.

Equity of redemption *See* Redemption.

Equity skimmer A scam artist who assumes a loan and collects money up front, and possibly rents, then refuses to make the payments on the assumed loan while keeping the cash paid up front.

Escrow A deposit held ready for some use, such as to pay taxes and insurance on a mortgaged property.

Eviction The legal procedure to have a tenant forcibly removed from a dwelling.

Execution sale The sale of property by a sheriff pursuant to a court order.

Extending the loan term Giving the borrower more time to repay a loan.

Fair Credit Reporting Act (FCRA) A federal law that regulates credit bureaus and credit reports and gives persons certain rights regarding both.

Fair market value The value that a willing and knowledgeable buyer would pay and a willing and knowledgeable seller would accept in an arm's-length transaction for a property.

Fannie Mae *See* Federal National Mortgage Association.

FCL The abbreviation a lender puts on a borrower's credit record to indicate a foreclosure.

FCRA *See* Fair Credit Reporting Act.

FDIC *See* Federal Deposit Insurance Corporation.

Federal Debt Collection Practices Act A federal law that regulates the manner in which debts are collected. It requires that certain notices and opportunities to dispute debts must be given to borrowers when debt collectors attempt to collect money.

Federal Deposit Insurance Corporation (FDIC) The corporation set up by the federal government to insure deposits in banks and savings and loans (S&Ls).

Federal Home Loan Bank Board (FHLBB) A former agency of the federal government that regulated savings and loans (S&Ls).

Federal Home Loan Mortgage Corporation (FHLMC) A government-chartered but privately owned corporation that buys mortgages from savings and loans (S&Ls). Also called "Freddie Mac."

Federal Housing Administration (FHA) An agency of the federal government that regulates many aspects of the real estate industry and that insures repayment of certain home loans.

Federal National Mortgage Association (FNMA) A government-chartered but privately owned corporation that buys mortgages from mortgage companies. Also called "Fannie Mae."

Federal Savings and Loan Insurance Corporation (FSLIC) A corporation formerly run by the federal government that insured deposits in savings and loans (S&Ls); FDIC has taken over this function. FSLIC deposit insurance funds—what were left of them—were transferred to an FDIC fund called the "Savings Association Insurance Fund (SAIF)."

FHA *See* Federal Housing Administration.

FHA guidelines Rules that specify income and credit requirements for a borrower and the condition and value of a property to allow an insured loan of a particular size.

FHA insurance Federal Housing Administration insurance that compensates lenders if a borrower fails to repay an insured loan.

FHLBB *See* Federal Home Loan Bank Board.

FHLMC *See* Federal Home Loan Mortgage Corporation.

Financial counseling Advice to a borrower from an expert on how better to manage the family budget.

Financial Institutions Reform, Recovery and Enforcement Act (FIRREA) A federal law that abolished the FSLIC and FHLBB and created the Resolution Trust Corporation (RTC). This law made the most sweeping changes in U.S. banking laws since the Depression.

FIRREA *See* Financial Institutions Reform, Recovery and Enforcement Act.

First lien The initial claim against a piece of real estate that gives a lender the right to force its sale to pay a debt.

Fizzbo *See* For sale by owner (FSBO).

FNMA *See* Federal National Mortgage Association.

Forbearance A lender voluntarily accepts payments that are lower than originally agreed for a limited time to allow the borrower to recover financially. The borrower must eventually repay the missing or reduced payments, as well as all other remaining payments on the loan.

Foreclosure The forced sale of a piece of real estate to repay a debt.

For sale by owner (FSBO) A property being marketed by its owner without the help of a real estate broker. Often pronounced "fizzbo."

Fraud Intentional false statements that were believed and relied on by a person who suffered loss as a result.

Freddie Mac *See* Federal Home Loan Mortgage Corporation.

Freeze order *See* Automatic stay.

FSA A designation for Federal Savings Association.

FSBO *See* For sale by owner.

FSLIC *See* Federal Savings and Loan Insurance Corporation.

Full assumption An arrangement in which a buyer takes title to the house and takes over the payments on the seller's old loan with the full permission of the lender, which evaluates the buyer's ability to show adequate income and creditworthiness by the lender's traditional standards. The process of obtaining lender approval is called "qualifying."

Ginnie Mae *See* Government National Mortgage Association.

GNMA *See* Government National Mortgage Association.

Good repair A borrower has an obligation to maintain the condition of mortgaged property—in other words, to keep the property in good repair.

Government National Mortgage Association (GNMA) An arm of the federal government that purchases loans. Currently, GNMA buys over 90 percent of all VA loans. Also called "Ginnie Mae."

Grant A transfer of an interest in land.

Guarantee The VA guarantees repayment of a VA loan to the private lender who made it; it agrees to cover a loss up to a certain dollar figure on a loan of a given size that goes into default and foreclosure.

Hearing A proceeding before a court.

Holder in due course A legal doctrine that holds that a person or entity that obtains a note without notice of any borrower defenses to its enforcement may enforce payment of that note in a court despite any borrower defense or other reason for not paying.

Homestead Special legal protection that many states give to a person's principal residence.

Housing and Urban Development (HUD) A department of the federal government that administers housing programs. *See also* Federal Housing Authority.

HUD *See* Housing and Urban Development.

Instrument A legal document.

Intermediate theory Some states hold that the borrower owns a mortgaged property, while other states hold that the lender owns a mortgaged property. Intermediate theory states give some ownership rights to each.

Internal Revenue Service (IRS) The arm of the U.S. government that collects taxes.

IOU An obligation to pay money.

IRS *See* Internal Revenue Service.

Judgment The final decision of a court. *See also* Abstract of judgment.

Judicial foreclosure Court-ordered foreclosure. The lender obtains the right to foreclose by filing and winning a lawsuit.

Junior lienholder A holder of a right to force the sale of property that is inferior and subordinate to another lienholder's right to do the same. A junior lienholder who forces the sale of the real estate must either pay off the senior lien or make arrangements to make payments on it to prevent it from being foreclosed. The foreclosure of a first lien destroys the right of a junior lienholder to foreclose, but the foreclosure of a junior lien does not affect the right of a senior lienholder to foreclose. *See also* First lien.

Key toss The practice of mailing the house keys to a lender upon abandoning a home in advance of a foreclosure.

Late payments Payments that are made past their due dates according to the loan documents.

Lease with option to buy An arrangement in which the owner of a property rents it to a tenant and gives the tenant the right to purchase the property on agreed terms.

Lender approval A lender's agreement to allow an assumption after its review of a borrower's creditworthiness and income. Lender approval can also apply to an initial loan.

Lender liability The legal doctrine that holds lenders legally responsible to pay damages for legal misdeeds committed against borrowers in the course of making loans.

Liability The obligation to pay a debt.

Lien The right to force the sale of property to pay a debt.

Lienholder The person or institution that controls a lien.

Lien theory A legal theory followed by some states that the borrower owns a property while repaying a loan on it.

Liquidation appraisal An estimate of the value of property when it is sold quickly in a forced sale. Usually this figure is lower than the fair market value for a regularly conducted sale.

Liquidation plan A plan by which a borrower pays missed payments to the lender over time.

Lis pendens A recorded notice that tells the world that a lawsuit is in progress, the outcome of which could affect the title to a particular piece of land.

Listing agreement The agreement by which a seller hires a real estate broker to sell a house, usually for a commission.

Loan balance The amount a borrower owes on a loan.

Loan default *See* Default.

Loan modification A procedure in which a loan's terms, such as the interest rate, monthly payment, or term, are altered.

Loan officer A person who is paid commissions to find and sign up borrowers for loans.

Loan pool A group of mortgages in which investors own shares. *See also* Collateralized mortgage obligation (CMO).

Loan processor The person who gathers and prepares the paperwork used by a lender to decide whether or not a loan should be made.

Market value *See* Fair market value.

MGIC *See* Mortgage Guaranty Insurance Corporation.

MI *See* Mortgage insurance.

Misrepresentation Making false statements in the course of a business transaction.

Modification *See* Loan modification.

Mod Squad The personnel in a lending institution who arrange loan modifications.

Money damages *See* Damages.

Moot The legal doctrine that an issue has effectively been resolved or decided prior to being brought to court.

Mortgage The French words *mort* and *gage* together mean "dead pledge." This is an arrangement in which a borrower agrees to give up title to a piece of property if she fails to repay a loan as agreed. The pledge of the property ceases, or "dies," when the loan is paid off as agreed.

Mortgage company A company that makes home loans to borrowers. Most mortgage companies sell the loans they make on the secondary market to loan buyers but continue to service the loans under contracts, collecting payments from borrowers and handling any trouble with loans, such as defaults and foreclosures.

Mortgagee The lender.

Mortgagee's title policy A title insurance policy that will pay off the lender's loss if the title to the mortgaged property fails.

Mortgage Guaranty Insurance Corporation (MGIC) A major private insurer of mortgage loans in the United States.

Mortgage instrument The legal paperwork that creates a mortgage.

Mortgage insurance (MI) Insurance that will compensate a lender for a loss if an insured loan is not repaid by the borrower.

Mortgage lien The right of a mortgage lender to force the sale of the mortgaged property if the borrower fails to repay the loan as agreed.

Mortgagor The borrower.

Motion to lift stay A formal request to a bankruptcy court to dissolve an automatic stay that prevents a lender from foreclosing. Once the motion is granted, the lender may proceed to foreclose unless the borrower can keep up payments on the loan.

Negative equity A position in which a borrower owes more on a property than the property is worth.

No bid A situation in which the VA will not take title to a house that a lender has acquired through foreclosure on a VA loan, because the fair market value of the property is so low that VA could not resell it for a sum equal to the loan balance minus the amount of the guarantee. In this event, the VA will write the lender a check for the full amount of its guarantee and tell the lender to keep the house and resell it without VA assistance.

Nonjudicial foreclosure Foreclosure on a mortgage without filing a lawsuit or obtaining a court order. Generally such sales occur because the borrower has signed a document, such as a deed of trust, giving a trustee preauthorization to sell the real estate to pay off the debt.

Note The legal document that specifies the terms of the borrower's loan, such as the length of time to repay it, the interest rate, the monthly payment amounts, and provisions to deal with the borrower's failure to pay on a timely basis.

One action rule A rule of law, used heavily in California, that forces a lender to bring only one court action or proceeding against a borrower in a foreclosure. The one action rule makes it difficult for a lender to obtain a deficiency judgment against a borrower.

Original petition *See* Plaintiff's original petition.

Origination Creation of a loan.

Out-of-court foreclosure *See* Nonjudicial foreclosure.

Owner-occupied The borrower who owns the home lives in it, making it "owner-occupied."

Partial payments Payments that are less than the full payment the borrower owes on a loan.

Plaintiff's original petition The initial document filed by a person who starts a lawsuit.

PMI *See* Mortgage insurance.

PMI-assisted presale An arrangement in which a private mortgage insurance company pays for part of the loss that occurs when a house with negative equity (one worth less than the balance on the existing mortgage loan) is sold by regular means prior to a foreclosure.

Positive equity The situation in which a house has a value in excess of what is due on the mortgage.

Posting The act of placing a legal notice, such as a notice specifying the date, time, and place of a foreclosure sale, on public display in the proper place for such notices.

Power of sale clause The clause in a deed of trust or mortgage by which the borrower preauthorizes the sale of a house to pay off the balance on a loan in the event of the borrower's default. Usually a trustee conducts the sale, although in some states, the sheriff or constable does this.

Prepaids The costs of purchasing a house that the buyer must pay at the time of closing to a party other than the seller.

Presale *See* PMI-assisted presale.

Primary lender The lender that deals directly with the borrower.

Promissory estoppel A legal doctrine that holds that lenders and sellers must honor their promises and are legally prevented, or estopped, from denying the obligation to honor promises.

Promissory note *See* Note.

Property condition The physical state of the property.

Prorations The division of the ongoing yearly costs of operating a property, such as property taxes, between the seller and the buyer at closing. Each party usually pays for the portion of the year in which that party occupied the house.

Publicly post *See* Posting.

Qualifying The process a lender undertakes prior to agreeing to make a loan, which consists of evaluating a buyer's income and credit and the property's physical condition and comparing the information with the lender's guidelines. If the guidelines are met or exceeded, then the lender will approve a mortgage loan.

Real estate lien note *See* Note.

Real estate owned (REO) When a financial institution forecloses on homes or other real estate, the properties so acquired are referred to as "real estate owned."

Recasting Restructuring a loan with a new interest rate and term. It may be the same loan from the same lender, but the terms change. The FHA has a formal procedure to recast loans to assist homebuyers to stay in their houses.

Receivership After a bank is taken over by the FDIC, it may be placed in receivership to liquidate its assets. The employees are fired and the assets shipped off to be sold at auction. The real estate is turned over to the RTC or the FDIC's liquidation division. Existing contracts with the institution in receivership are voidable at the option of the FDIC.

Recording The process of filing documents with an official state agency to be held as a permanent record. Deeds and other documents that affect title must be recorded.

Redemption The right of a borrower to recover title to real estate lost in a foreclosure sale. This is done by paying up missing payments in some states or the full unpaid loan balance in other states. State statutes normally define redemption rights, specifying longer or shorter periods. IRS and most property tax foreclosure sales also have rights of redemption.

Refinancing The process of replacing an old loan with a high interest rate with a new one, usually at a lower interest rate.

Refunding A VA procedure in which it purchases a loan from a private lender. The VA then services the loan. This procedure helps borrowers who are having trouble making payments under circumstances that appear to justify giving them added time.

Release from liability The document that relieves a person who is obligated to pay a loan of any further obligation. It may be obtained when a buyer takes over the payments on a seller's old loan, provided the buyer meets the lender's standards for income and creditworthiness. If granted, the release of liability means the seller will not be responsible if the buyer fails to pay.

Relief Various types of loans, depending on their insurers (FHA, PMI companies, etc.) or their owners (FNMA, FHLMC), will offer various types of special payment plans or other assistance for borrowers who have missed payments. If it appears that the borrower can bring the loan current, the lender can allow a period of reduced payments with the difference to be made up at later . The lender could also assist with an early sale.

Removal The process of transferring a case from state court to federal court.

REO *See* Real estate owned.

Repayment plan A plan for repaying missed payments over time.

Resolution Trust Corporation (RTC) A government-chartered corporation whose primary function is to manage and liquidate the assets of savings and loans (S&Ls) that have lost too much money and been taken over and shut down by the FDIC. The Resolution Trust Corporation, created by the Financial Institutions Reform, Recovery and Enforcement Act (FIRREA), is probably the largest owner of real estate in the world.

Retroactive release from liability A VA procedure in which a borrower who sold a house on a simple assumption to a buyer who then defaulted may show that the buyer made the first 12 monthly payments, agreed to be liable for the loan, and was sufficiently creditworthy to merit lender approval. This evidence allows the seller, who would have been liable for the default, to escape the obligation to pay the loan. However, the borrower who secures a retroactive release of liability may not obtain a new VA loan until the VA's loss on the old one is repaid.

Right of redemption *See* Redemption.

Right of rescission The right to back out of a contract.

RTC *See* Resolution Trust Corporation.

Rule against assignments The legal concept that a debtor may not give away the obligation to pay on a debt without the lender's permission. Even if a buyer assumes a loan, the seller remains liable to repay the loan unless the lender approves the buyer's income and creditworthiness and releases the seller from liability.

S&L *See* Savings and Loan Association.

Sales contract *See* Earnest money contract.

Savings and loan association (S&L) A financial institution that makes loans. Savings and loans were originally set up to make home loans, but since the 1980s, deregulation has allowed them to make commercial loans as well.

Scire facias A court command to a borrower to show up at a hearing and show cause as to why a foreclosure should not be authorized.

Secondary market The market in which investors buy loans from primary lenders, who deal directly with borrowers to originate loans.

Second lien *See* Junior lienholder.

Second mortgage *See* Junior lienholder.

Servicing The process of administering a mortgage loan, including collecting payments; maintaining insurance; and undertaking special measures, such as workouts and foreclosures, when necessary

Short payoff A workout procedure in which the lender accepts less than the full balance due on the loan as part of a deal in which the borrower cooperates with the lender to obtain a quick sale. The lender skips foreclosure, which would take time; cost money; and expose the house to vandalism, further declines in market value, and marketing costs for resale.

Silent wrap An illegal assumption arrangement in which the seller moves out and the buyer moves in and makes payments in violation of a due-on-sale or due-on-encumbrance clause. This violation gives the lender a legal right to foreclose. However, the lender may not discover the arrangement for some time, if ever.

Simple assumption An assumption arrangement in which the seller conveys title to the property to the buyer and moves out, while the buyer moves in and makes payment on the old loan. The lender does not approve the buyer's credit and income, so the deal may be called a "no-approval loan." The seller remains liable on the old loan under such circumstances. Only loans without strong due-on-sale clauses are assumable without approval. This includes VA loans made before March 1, 1988, FHA loans made before December 15, 1989, and conventional loans made before 1973.

Special relief *See* Relief.

Special servicing *See* Servicing.

Statute of limitations The time limit during which a potential litigant must file a lawsuit before being barred by the passage of time. Most states have elaborate and complex statutes of limitations, many imposing short statutes of limitations for deficiency judgments or foreclosure-related claims.

Stay *See* Automatic stay.

Strict foreclosure A legal premise followed by some states that the lender owns the property and may evict the borrower for nonpayment and gain full and complete title free of the borrower's claims simply by waiting a prescribed period of time until the borrower's right to redeem ends. The lender gains the value of the land above what is owed on the loan.

"Subject to" clause A clause in a deed that transfers title from a seller to a buyer in an assumption transaction, or a clause in other paperwork for an assumption transaction, in which the borrower refuses to accept legal liability to make payments although the buyer expects to do so. The lender's remedy for nonpayment is limited to foreclosure, and neither the lender nor the seller can sue the defaulting buyer for missed payments on the loan balance.

Subrogation for mortgage insurers The right of a mortgage insurance company to file a suit to recover from the borrower sums it must pay out to a lender as a result of the borrower's default on a loan.

Summary judgment A legal procedure in which one side wins a lawsuit without a trial by showing that the case involves no material fact issues, only legal issues that can be decided by the judge. If the judge agrees, then one side wins by summary judgment.

Supplemental servicing Extra servicing that the VA will perform beyond that performed by the lender. *See also* Servicing.

Temporary injunction A court order that freezes the status quo for an extended period, typically until a full court trial on the merits of a case can be held. It often requires posting a bond, although many states' laws waive the bond requirement in cases involving the foreclosure of a home.

Temporary restraining order (TRO) A court command that freezes the status quo for a short period, until other legal relief is awarded or a settlement between the litigants can be reached.

Title Ownership.

Title insurance A specialized form of insurance that verifies that a borrower has obtained full ownership of real property, subject to a few exceptions stated in the policy.

Title report A report issued by a title insurance company that shows current ownership and nonowners' claims to a piece of real estate and the terms on which a title company would be willing to insure title.

Title theory A legal concept that holds that the lender owns real property while the borrower repays a loan used to buy it.

TRO *See* Temporary restraining order.

Trust deed A type of mortgage that gives a lender the power to foreclose and take title away from the borrower.

Trustee A person who is named in a deed of trust or other mortgage to conduct any foreclosure proceedings and sell the property to pay off the mortgage loan balance if needed.

Trustee's deed A type of deed issued to the buyer at a foreclosure by the trustee.

Truth in Lending Act A federal law that requires lenders to make certain disclosures to borrowers concerning a loan, such as the interest, the annual percentage rate, the total cost of the loan, the total of all payments, and the use of disclosure forms at the loan application and closing.

Turnover order A court command to a debtor to give title to certain assets to a creditor.

Underwriter The person who makes the final decision on whether a loan should be granted or not at most mortgage companies.

Upside-down home A house that is worth less than what is owed on the mortgage it secures.

VA *See* Department of Veterans Affairs.

VA guarantee The dollar figure the VA agrees to pay for a loss to a lender from foreclosing on a VA loan.

Verification of deposit (VOD) A form sent to a financial institution by a lender to verify that a prospective borrower has a certain sum on deposit.

Verification of employment (VOE) A form sent to an employer by a lender to verify that a prospective borrower is employed at a certain salary.

Veterans Administration *See* Department of Veterans Affairs.

VOD *See* Verification of deposit.

VOE *See* Verification of employment.

Wage earner plan A nickname for Chapter 13 bankruptcy. *See also* Chapter 13.

Walk the house The act of abandoning a house to the lender, which will foreclose on it.

Warranty deed A deed in which the seller guarantees (warrants) that good title can be traced backward in time from true owner to true owner to the time when the land was owned by a country, such as the United States. *See also* Deed.

Workout The process by which a borrower comes to a mutually acceptable financial arrangement with a lender to avoid an impending foreclosure.

Wraparound A type of mortgage in which the obligation to pay a second- or later-lien mortgage includes the obligation to pay an earlier-lien mortgage. The later mortgage "wraps around" the earlier mortgage. Default on the earlier-lien mortgage is automatically a default on the later-lien mortgage.

Writ of entry Very similar to a writ of possession.

Writ of execution A court order authorizing the holder to seize and sell a debtor's property to pay off a judgment.

Writ of garnishment A court order commanding a person who holds assets for another person, such as a banker who holds funds on deposit, an employer who holds a paycheck, or a stock broker who holds an account for an investor, to give those assets up to a creditor.

Writ of possession A court document (writ) that authorizes a constable or other officer of the law to break down a tenant's door, drag the tenant from the premises, and throw the tenant's belongings out of the house or apartment.

Wrongful foreclosure A foreclosure that was legally improper and that caused a borrower to suffer damages.

Index